JUSTICE FOR SALE

Graft, Greed, and a Crooked Federal Judge
in 1930s Gotham

GARY STEIN

Essex, Connecticut

An imprint of Globe Pequot, the trade division of
The Rowman & Littlefield Publishing Group, Inc.
4501 Forbes Blvd., Ste. 200
Lanham, MD 20706
www.rowman.com

Distributed by NATIONAL BOOK NETWORK

British Library Cataloguing in Publication Information available

Library of Congress Cataloging-in-Publication Data available
ISBN 978-1-4930-7256-9 (cloth: alk. paper)
ISBN 978-1-4930-7257-6 (electronic)

♾️™ The paper used in this publication meets the minimum requirements of American National
Standard for Information Sciences—Permanence of Paper for Printed Library Materials, ANSI/
NISO Z39.48-1992.

To my parents,

Nancy and Sol Stein

CONTENTS

PROLOGUE

On a chilly late winter morning in the midst of the Great Depression, a bald and fretful middle-aged man ascended the steps leading into a gleaming granite skyscraper in downtown Manhattan. Once a prominent banker and lawyer, John L. Lotsch had, like so many other New Yorkers, fallen on hard times. When money grew scarce, so did his scruples. He had gotten mixed up in a racket of sorts, and he needed to make a payment—a big-time payment—to ensure his protection.

This was the heyday of "the racket." The word had not entered common usage until a few years earlier. Yet now, in March 1936, racketeers held a firm grip on virtually every business, legitimate and illegitimate alike, in New York City. There was a numbers racket, a pinball racket, a horse racing racket, an abortion racket, and a dirty movie racket, to name a few of its seedier incarnations. But there was also a milk racket, a bakery racket, a real estate racket, a restaurant racket, an artichoke racket, a diamond racket, a parking garage racket, a laundry racket, and a kosher chicken racket. "There is today scarcely a business in New York which does not somehow pay its tribute to the underworld," declared Thomas E. Dewey, a newly appointed special prosecutor, in a radio address in July 1935.[1]

Rising to confront the proliferating racketeer was a new breed of law enforcement official, the racket-buster. Dewey, a brash thirty-three-year-old lawyer with a trim build and a pencil mustache, was one of them. Dewey's appointment by the governor underscored the inability and even unwillingness of the city's existing law enforcement apparatus to crack down on organized crime. The US Department of Justice had also entered the fray, convening a special federal grand jury to focus on racketeering in New York. "There is a vast field to cover," lamented the *New York Times* as the new year began. "Almost the entire racket structure in New York is so far impregnable against assault."[2]

No government agent had an eye out for illegal payoffs in the building Lotsch entered, and none were watching as Lotsch met up with three associates inside. The brand-new building, designed by one of the nation's leading architects, was meant for more noble pursuits. Built in what was formerly known as the Five Points district, a den of gang violence, moral pestilence, and Tammany Hall corruption, it climbed thirty-one stories high—as if striving to escape that ignominious past—into an uncontested slice of the Manhattan skyline, culminating in a triangular crown of terra cotta covered in gold leaf. Classical motifs harkened back to an earlier era of probity and a well-functioning polity. Roundels resembling ancient coins, and bearing the profiles of ancient lawgivers, were carved into the exterior, symbolizing the symbiotic relationship between law and commerce.

That relationship, as it happened, was also on Lotsch's mind that morning. Lotsch's associates were there to deliver him the payoff money—$10,000 in cash. This, in the vernacular of the underworld, was some "heavy sugar." Median family income at the time was only $1,160 per year, and the average new house cost around $4,000.[3] Lugging his secret hoard, Lotsch crossed the green-and-white veined marble floor to the elevators, their doors bronzed with images of dolphins, owls, and grasshoppers. He was grateful, perhaps, that he did not have to walk up: a building workers strike had shut down elevator service in many locations, forcing thousands of New Yorkers to the stairwells and prompting Mayor Fiorello La Guardia to declare a state of emergency.[4]

Emerging from the elevator on the twenty-fourth floor, Lotsch entered a well-appointed, walnut-paneled office with a panoramic view. He was ushered into the private chamber of the man he was there to meet and whose protection he needed, a man at the height of his powers, exuding confidence, authority, prestige. Framed photographs of dignitaries hung prominently on the wall, including one of President Franklin D. Roosevelt; if Lotsch had looked carefully he would have seen FDR's personal autograph, inscribing the photograph to "my very good friend."[5]

Yet the man who controlled Lotsch's fate was much like Lotsch, capsized financially by the Depression and willing to do whatever it took to keep himself afloat.

Their mutual avarice now produced an almost comical illustration of the lack of honor among thieves. Although the two men had agreed on a price of $10,000, and although Lotsch had more than that on him, Lotsch forked over only half that amount. "I was only able to get $5,000," he lied.[6]

The occupant of the office was not about to be shortchanged. "You have to get the other $5,000," he commanded, glaring at Lotsch from behind pince-nez glasses. He explained that "Thomas," his confederate, would insist on the full $10,000. Lotsch would have to come back the next morning with the balance. With that, the man took the $5,000, dialed open a safe in his office, and stuck the cash inside. Lotsch left the office.

But Lotsch did not leave the building. He had another appointment on a different floor. He was the defendant in a federal criminal case entitled *United States v. John L. Lotsch*. The trial in the case was about to begin. And it would be held in this same building—the new federal courthouse at 40 Centre Street in Foley Square. The "Thomas" who was insisting on $10,000 was Judge Edwin S. Thomas, the trial judge. And the man who had just stuck Lotsch's cash in the safe in his office was Martin T. Manton, the senior judge of the US Court of Appeals for the Second Circuit.

The month before, after Lotsch had been indicted—ironically enough, for soliciting a bribe—he went to see Judge Manton in Manton's twenty-fourth-floor chambers. For $10,000, Manton told Lotsch, he could arrange for the case to be assigned to Judge Thomas and for Thomas to get rid of it. Lotsch had good reason to believe Judge Manton would deliver on this promise. As a lawyer, Lotsch had made illicit payments to Manton on behalf of clients who had appeals pending before the Second Circuit. Those payments were followed by decisions in favor of Lotsch's clients, written by Judge Manton.

Manton did not disappoint Lotsch this time either. The following week—after Lotsch had coughed up the $5,000 balance—Judge Thomas directed the jury hearing the case to acquit Lotsch. The legal grounds were flimsy, but that was of little consequence, for the government has no right to appeal a directed verdict in a federal criminal case. Lotsch was free, and some combination of Judges Manton and Thomas were $10,000 richer.

This was how Martin T. Manton administered justice from his perch atop the Second Circuit, the most important federal court in the country other than the US Supreme Court. "One of the most monstrous plots to buy and sell justice was born and flourished within the walls of this courthouse," the US attorney who later prosecuted Manton said to the jury who convicted him. "It became, instead of a courthouse, a counting house."[7] Amid the multitude of rackets at work in the 1930s, Judge Manton was operating one of his own: a justice racket.

CHAPTER ONE

"A Person Best Left Unremembered"

A Blot on the Federal Judiciary

MARTIN T. MANTON IS LITTLE-REMEMBERED TODAY. YET FOR THE better part of 1939, as the sordid details of his abuse of office tumbled into public view, the saga of Judge Manton took center stage, simultaneously enraging and entertaining New York and much of the nation. Front-page reports cycled through the familiar phases of a high-profile scandal: revelation, resignation, investigation, indictment, trial, appeal, imprisonment. Prominent businessmen and lawyers were dragged down in Manton's wake. Others were lifted up; Manton's downfall secured a Pulitzer Prize for the reporter who broke the story, S. Burton Heath of the *New York World-Telegram*, and helped launch the political career of Manhattan District Attorney Thomas E. Dewey, the former special prosecutor who originally investigated Manton. Reverberations reached into the White House, where President Roosevelt scrambled to distance himself from the disgraced jurist he previously referred to as an "old friend."

When the judge at Manton's trial instructed the jury in June 1939, he told them that the alleged offense—a federal appellate judge conspiring "to sell justice"—was "hitherto unprecedented in the 150 years of the federal judiciary." When the jury, after only four hours of deliberations, pronounced Manton guilty, its verdict was hailed as "a triumph for decency and justice" and "one of the most important events of our times." And when the cell door locked behind Manton at Lewisburg Federal

Penitentiary in central Pennsylvania in March 1940, it put an end to "one of the great legal dramas of that era."[1]

The passage of time explains, in part, Manton's current obscurity—but only in part. The names and misdeeds of other corrupt officials of Manton's era still echo down through the decades: Tom Pendergast, the Kansas City political boss who pled guilty to tax evasion on the same day in May 1939 that Manton's trial began; Jimmy Hines, the Tammany Hall leader who openly cavorted with mobsters before his racketeering conviction in 1939; Jimmy Walker, the flamboyant New York mayor forced to resign in 1932 amid disclosures of the fortune he amassed from businessmen awarded municipal contracts; Joe Crater, the New York state court judge who mysteriously vanished one summer night in 1930, never to be heard from again, after destroying court papers and emptying his safe deposit box. If not exactly household names today, these men and their exploits retain a fair degree of notoriety. Historians, at least, continue to write books and articles about them.

By contrast, no book-length account of Manton's life has ever been written, despite the novelty and extraordinary scale of his malfeasance.[2] During a crime spree that lasted several years, Manton raked in gifts and sham "loans" from litigants in cases before him totaling some $823,000—in today's dollars, about $17 million. Nothing like this had happened before; no federal judge had ever been convicted of a crime for his official actions, let alone a judge who served for more than two decades on the most important and prestigious of the federal courts of appeals, was known as "the tenth-ranking judge in the United States" after the nine members of the Supreme Court, and came within a whisker of sitting on the Supreme Court himself.

Paradoxically Manton's position of prominence in the federal judiciary may help explain his descent into obscurity. A society's political health and stability depend on there being, in perception if not reality, a place where truth may be ascertained and justice dispensed fairly and impartially. More than any other institution, the federal courts satisfy that psychic need for Americans. Appointed for life to ensure their independence, federal judges are by design insulated from partisan politics, the press of commerce, and other earthly pursuits and entanglements.

Manton contaminated that ideal and destabilized a core faith in our system of government. If Manton's impurities have receded from our collective consciousness it is, perhaps, because we have *wanted* to forget them.

Certainly that has been the mindset of the US Court of Appeals for the Second Circuit, which has, almost literally, airbrushed Manton out of its history. In 2009, the Second Circuit had to decide what to do with a portrait of Manton, painted in 1922. The portrait had sat for decades in storage, covered with dirt, until it was salvaged in the 1980s by a crusty and irreverent district judge in the Southern District of New York, Charles L. Brieant III, who hung it in his chambers. Brieant "viewed Manton as a scoundrel," but felt it was "important to keep the story alive." When Brieant died in 2008, the chief judge of the Second Circuit, Dennis Jacobs, one of Manton's successors, asked for the painting back—not to display it, but to ensure that it was *not* displayed. The portrait "is just an old picture of a person best left unremembered," Chief Judge Jacobs wrote the chief judge of the Southern District of New York, adding, "I'm kind of hoping that Judge Manton will disappear."[3]

Judge Jacobs's wish encapsulates the Second Circuit's attitude toward Manton ever since he resigned from the court on February 7, 1939. In the words of one legal historian, Manton has been an "unspeakable embarrassment" for this most august tribunal. Second Circuit judges used to instruct their law clerks never to cite one of his opinions, whether from a case related to his crimes or not. It was all a matter of "eras[ing]" Manton's legacy from the court's history. When the Second Circuit Historical and Commemorative Events Committee—populated by sitting Second Circuit judges, lower-court judges from within the Circuit, and distinguished members of the bar—published biographical sketches of the court's prior members on the occasion of its centennial anniversary in 1991, they summed up Manton's legacy bluntly: "Martin T. Manton is known as the judge who disgraced the Second Circuit."[4]

* * *

The Second Circuit judges who served with Manton did not hold him in high regard either. When Manton took over the reins as senior circuit judge in 1927, the court's three other full-time members were Learned

3

Hand, a towering intellect, widely considered to be the greatest American judge never to have sat on the Supreme Court; his older first cousin Augustus Noble ("Gus") Hand, a formidable legal thinker in his own right; and Thomas Walter Swan, former dean of the Yale Law School.[5] All sons of lawyers, all Harvard Law School graduates and serious students of the law, all pillars of integrity and rectitude revered by the bar, the two Hands and Swan formed "the core of what for decades would be recognized as the strongest appellate court in the United States."[6] In 1929 they were joined by Harrie B. Chase, a Vermont state court judge who, while not of the same caliber or industriousness, served with distinction into the 1960s. These were the men who throughout the 1930s would, in panels of three, sit with Manton to hear oral argument, analyze the strengths and weakness of the parties' positions, and debate fine points of law, all while unaware that Manton was in the pocket of one of the litigants.

Manton had been a superb trial lawyer and was a capable judge. But no one accused him of having a brilliant legal mind. Lawyers who argued before him felt that "his air of domineering omniscience" seemed "seldom justified by his understanding of their cases."[7] Even had his tarnished reputation not rendered his opinions radioactive as precedent, Manton would not have left much of a lasting imprint on American jurisprudence. Perhaps his most widely read decision was a dissenting opinion that would have allowed the government to ban James Joyce's *Ulysses* as obscene—and it was widely read only because Manton had identified the novel's raciest passages by page number, making it a handy guide for "students of the pornographic."[8] Manton's own prose, pedestrian at best and often obscure and indecipherable, demonstrated little dedication to the judicial craft. In the harsh-but-fair verdict of Learned Hand's biographer, law professor Gerald Gunther, Manton seemed "incapable of turning out memoranda and opinions that could earn him respect from the bar or bench."[9]

Second Circuit law clerks of the era quickly realized that the other judges "didn't like Manton," who was regarded within the court as "sort of a loner," "the odd man out," "a pariah," a "second-rate judge," a "lousy judge by any standard," and a "no-good politician who shouldn't have been on the bench."[10] The Hands were particularly disdainful. A master stylist, Learned Hand labored over opinions with a fountain pen on a writing board resting on his lap, dropping completed pages one by one on the floor for his secretary to pick up. A clerk once asked Hand why he did not dictate his opinions instead. Hand, the clerk recalled, "withered me with a glance and a statement that 'Manton dictated *his* opinions.'" Gus Hand once asked one of his clerks to review an opinion Manton had drafted. The clerk reported back that he felt the opinion should rest on other grounds, and within minutes found a Second Circuit case Manton had missed. His boss explained to the fresh-out-of-law-school clerk, "Judge Manton hasn't had the training that you and I have had."[11]

Frequently Manton simply cribbed his opinions from the parties' briefs, in what was known, in those pre-computer days, as a "scissors and paste-pot" job. Noting one clumsy instance of that practice, Gus Hand felt the need to show the opinion to Manton's secretary and call her attention to the fact that "she had left out a line when copying from the [winning party's] brief." When a Manton opinion came into his chambers, Learned Hand would "eagerly" compare it to the briefs and "gleefully" shout out to his law clerk when he discovered another example of cutting-and-pasting, as he invariably did.[12]

What Manton's opinions lacked in quality, however, they made up for in volume. During his twenty and one-half years on the Second Circuit, Manton wrote approximately 1,150 opinions, for the most part opinions for the court but also concurrences and dissents. That translates into fifty-six opinions a year, or more than one a week, an extraordinary rate of production that outpaces that of any other Second Circuit judge in its history. Only Learned Hand and Swan exceeded Manton's output, by about one hundred opinions each, but they served on the court for thirty-six years and forty-nine years, respectively. Gus Hand and Chase produced many fewer opinions than Manton despite their much longer tenures (twenty-six years and forty years, respectively). The same is true of numerous other Second Circuit judges who sat on the court for more than three or four decades.

Manton's production is all the more impressive considering the many administrative responsibilities he was saddled with as senior circuit judge.

Manton decided the schedule for which circuit judges would sit at what times. He oversaw the various district courts within the Second Circuit, which then as now embraced New York, Connecticut, and Vermont. He was chiefly responsible for ruling, by himself, on bail applications and other matters that could be decided by a single judge. The senior circuit judge then had the discretion to appoint himself to sit as a district judge in particular cases. Manton exercised all these powers controversially, and, it would later emerge, corruptly.

In those days the Second Circuit was, by far, the busiest and most consequential federal circuit court in the country. In the five years preceding Manton's resignation, the Second Circuit disposed of one-fifth—19.9 percent—of all federal appeals, far more than any of the then-ten other circuit courts.[13] Its rulings in the area of commercial, patent, bankruptcy, and admiralty law commanded nationwide attention and influence. No one today would call the chief judge of the Second Circuit the nation's "tenth-ranking" judge. The explosion of public administrative law shifted power and prestige to Washington, DC, and to the DC Circuit Court of Appeals, and the Ninth Circuit Court of Appeals, covering all of California and seven other states, now handles the largest volume of appeals.[14] But in the 1930s it aptly characterized Manton's station.

Manton's full-time judicial duties occupied only part of his calendar. He also maintained a rich and varied religious, civic, and political life. A generous donor to the Catholic Church and active in a variety of Catholic organizations, Manton received the Church's highest honor for a layperson when Pope Pius XI named him a Knight of St. Gregory in 1924. He delivered keynote addresses at International Eucharistic Congresses "filled with sturdy Catholic doctrine."[15] A traditionalist on social issues, Manton warned against the loosening of parental discipline, "insufficiently clad" women parishioners, the spreading use of birth control, and, in his *Ulysses* dissent, literature "produced by men given to obscenity and lustful thoughts—men who have no Master."[16] Yet he also firmly opposed the isolationist strain in American Catholicism, championing the League of Nations and global peace efforts generally. Within weeks of Adolf Hitler's rise to power in 1933, Manton joined dozens of other prominent Christian-Americans in issuing an interfaith appeal demanding that the German government put an end to persecution and violence against Jews.[17]

Manton's politics leaned progressive. As devout a Democrat as a Catholic, he became a committed Wilsonian, and it was President Wilson who, in 1916, appointed Manton, at age thirty-six, the youngest federal judge in the country. Like Wilson, Manton believed that government should check the monopolistic and avaricious tendencies of large corporations; in private practice, he spent most of his time suing large corporations on behalf of accident victims. He supported FDR's reforms and publicly denounced the Supreme Court's conservative wing for blocking the New Deal. "[N]o ivory tower judge," Manton "believed that social and economic phenomena 'give life and substance to the law.'"[18] More unusually, almost incomprehensibly from today's standpoint, Manton did not view the federal judiciary as a monastery isolated from the world of politics. He continued to regularly meet with leading New York Democratic politicians, attend Democratic rallies and meetings, endorse Democratic candidates, and participate in the quadrennial Democratic presidential nominating conventions.

On top of all this, Judge Manton managed a small business empire. He held controlling or substantial interests in at least seventeen corporations, most of which he formed while a federal judge. Manton's business interests spanned a dizzying array of industries: apartment houses, single-family homes, and undeveloped land throughout the city; laundries in Brooklyn; a manufacturer of facial tissues and sanitary napkins near Syracuse; a carpet cleaning company, a coal company, and a milk bottling business; a hog ranch and a working farm in Long Island. Although he hired others to handle the day-to-day operations, Manton kept an active hand in the affairs of most of these companies; his longtime secretary, Marie D. Schmalz, maintained some of the corporate books and records in the judge's chambers.

Then there was Manton's other, illicit business, itself a sizeable operation. Manton, and his cohort of conduits, solicited payoffs from litigants not episodically but regularly, on literally dozens of occasions. Separately, Manton solicited dozens of loans—most of which were not repaid—from lawyers and businessmen who had no pending business before the

Second Circuit, but who had little economic reason for extending Manton credit, aside from his being a person of great influence. Combining these loans with outright payoffs raises Manton's total haul to over $2 million, or about $40 million in today's dollars, encompassing upwards of one hundred different transactions.

Imagining an appellate judge's chambers conjures up scenes of thoughtful reflection, silent composition, and leafing through musty law books. Manton's chambers were nothing like that. They were bustling with activity, more Grand Central Terminal than New York Public Library. Through his door paraded a steady stream of litigants and lenders, lawyers and lackeys, business associates and politicians, dignitaries and lowlifes and, not infrequently, underworld figures. Once inside, the visitor might have to take a seat on one of the chairs that were lined up all the way across, "like a doctor's office," waiting his turn.[19]

Presiding over it all was Manton, imperious, self-important, with a severe expression that often curdled into a scowl, yet not without charm and possessed of an astute, practical, calculating mind. White-haired, solidly built and tall for his times at 5' 11", with piercing brown eyes, Manton looked the part of a judge, or a businessman. The trouble is, he was both, and at the same time.

* * *

Manton's crimes are typically attributed to the Great Depression. The value of Manton's investments, including corporate equities and extensive real estate holdings, plummeted after the Crash of 1929, leaving him unable to repay outstanding debts. He then resorted to extorting loans and payments from litigants in order to avoid financial ruin. Manton, said the judge who sentenced him, "was possessed of a great personal fortune which . . . was seriously threatened by financial conditions existing a few years ago," leading him to "[violate] the most fundamental feature of his judicial office" in order "to bolster up his fading fortune."[20]

While not inaccurate, this conventional narrative is too simplistic, and gives Manton both more and less credit than he deserves. Manton was not an otherwise upright and honorable jurist who succumbed to the unique pressures and temptations presented by the Great Depression.

Nor was he a uniquely malignant force poisoning an otherwise pristine justice system.

The Depression had a more muted impact on Manton than it did on the vast majority of his fellow New Yorkers and countrymen. It certainly did not endanger his economic survival. Federal appellate judges then earned $12,500 per year, comparable to what they are paid today ($236,900). Because the Constitution guarantees life tenure to federal judges and prohibits a diminution of their salary while in office, Manton did not have to worry about losing his job or suffering a pay cut. As such, Manton has to be considered one of the fortunate few among the millions of New Yorkers, including previously highly compensated professionals, "all thrown together into a vast pit of misery" by the collapse of the city's and the nation's economy. In 1933, six out of seven architects, one-half of engineers, and nearly as high a percentage of doctors in New York could no longer find work. Lawyers were not immune. Many felt the practice of law had become "a dignified road to starvation," and by 1934 nearly fifteen hundred attorneys were prepared to take a pauper's oath to qualify for work relief.[21]

As the *New Republic* perceptively observed following Manton's conviction, his misdeeds said more about the 1920s than the 1930s. Manton was not just "one bad apple in a good barrel." While he may have been unique "in his brazen methods and the size of the take," the magazine wrote, "[w]hat is really important . . . is that business men and politicians in their own practice did much the same sort of thing. The idea of the twenties was that the first law is Get The Money and the second law is Don't Get Caught."[22] Where Manton went wrong was in believing, even after amassing considerable wealth in private practice, that he could continue to Get The Money after he put on the robes of a federal judge. It did not take an economic calamity for Manton to improperly mix his personal interests with his judicial duties. He was doing that from almost the moment he donned a black robe.

The roots of Manton's corruption reach back to the days before he was appointed a federal judge. Manton spent fifteen years in private practice litigating almost entirely in the New York state courts, then dominated by the Tammany Hall Democratic political machine. Tammany

Hall viewed the judiciary, as it did all agencies of government, as a source of profit and patronage. Lawyers had to fork over as much as $10,000 to Tammany leaders to obtain plum State Supreme Court judgeships. Once on the bench, they were expected to do Tammany's bidding, and they crossed the machine at their peril.[23]

In turn, state court judges looked for ways to monetize their official positions. New York Supreme Court justice Albert Cardozo—father of the future justice of the US Supreme Court—resigned in disgrace after accusations that he split fees with bankruptcy receivers he appointed and engaged in other corrupt and partisan conduct on the bench.[24] Corruption was particularly rampant in the city's magistrates' courts, which handled criminal cases. "Gangsters lavished payoffs" on magistrate judges to get cases killed, and scandals often erupted after magistrates were found to be living well beyond their apparent means.[25] As a young lawyer Manton defended a Brooklyn magistrate charged with selling judicial favors. These were the customs and mores of the judicial system that Manton grew up in. Manton cannot simply be labeled a "Tammany judge"; his relationship with the political machine was more complicated than that. But he did take with him onto the federal bench some of the unsavory practices of Tammany judges and politicians, even to the point of protecting the interests of organized crime, with which the machine enjoyed a most unholy alliance.

Importantly, the crime Manton was convicted of was *conspiracy*. He did not act alone; he had literally scores of co-conspirators. An assortment of bag men, front men, fixers, and at least one federal judge (Judge Thomas) served, in effect, as workers in Manton's racketeering enterprise. The litigants who bribed Manton to win their cases included the top executives of some of the largest and most important corporations in the country, aided and abetted by bankers, accountants, and several leading figures in the New York bar, who knowingly arranged for illicit payments or turned a blind eye to them. Four men, indicted along with Manton, pled guilty or were found guilty at trial, and a name partner at a leading Wall Street law firm was disbarred. But for death, insanity, the statute of limitations, and prosecutorial discretion, numerous other conspirators could have joined Manton in jail.

Still others, though breaking no law, contributed through their silence. Lawyers too pure to submit to Manton's shakedowns were also too afraid to blow the whistle. Manton's judicial colleagues had ample reason to suspect he was up to no good, and some did have their suspicions, but they too took no action. Even after allegations reached the top echelons of FDR's Justice Department, nothing was done to bring Manton to brook. Dark as Manton's deeds were, the fact that they nearly never came to light at all is, in a way, even more disconcerting. Manton almost Didn't Get Caught.

The Manton scandal, then, is not the story of a single rogue federal judge who temporarily lost his moral bearings amid the whirlwind of the Great Depression. It is the story of a New York City culture so suffused with corruption and greed that it did not even make an exception for the judicial system. It was a culture that simply did not prize, or enforce, the norms of judicial independence, integrity, and impartiality in the way that we now take for granted.

As Manton was the principal protagonist, the story naturally centers on, and begins with, him.

PART ONE

MANTON'S RISE

CHAPTER TWO

"New Ways of Making Money"

Becoming a Lawyer

MARTIN THOMAS MANTON WAS BORN IN BROOKLYN, ON AUGUST 2, 1880. Back then Brooklyn was still an independent city, separated from Manhattan both geographically (the Brooklyn Bridge was not completed until 1883) and politically (the two were not consolidated into the modern five-borough New York City until 1898). The divide between Brooklyn and Manhattan was something Manton would never fully bridge. Despite the considerable educational, professional, and financial success that he would attain across the East River, Manton remained fundamentally an outsider, looked down upon by the Wall Street legal establishment and by his colleagues on the federal bench. He would force his way into Manhattan's legal elite by sheer will, without ever truly being considered *of* it.

Many accounts depict Manton as rising from poverty. "Manton grew up in Brooklyn in the 1880s in a poor but striving Irish immigrant family," according to a 2016 profile in the *New York Daily News*.[1] "A poor Brooklyn youth" is how Senator Estes Kefauver summed up Manton's origins in a 1963 *New York Times* book review.[2] This rags-to-riches narrative was woven into Manton's life story even before he became notorious. When Manton was first named a federal district judge in 1916, Gus Hand, then on the same court, expressed alarm to his cousin Learned about reports of Manton's money-grubbing as a lawyer. Yet at the same time Hand wondered if he was being unfair to Manton, "a man who began [life] struggling with poverty."[3] For some, Manton's deprived upbringing contextualized and rationalized his avarice, perhaps even mitigated it.

Except that the premise is wrong. Manton did not grow up poor. Nor did he grow up in Brooklyn. When he was five years old his family moved to Sayville, New York, on the South Shore of eastern Long Island, far removed from cramped tenement life. A small village of "industrious, peaceful, contented people, for the most part well-to-do,"[4] Sayville prospered during the latter half of the nineteenth century when Manton's family arrived. Sauntering along the shoreline, young Martin—he would be "Martin" all his life, never "Marty"—would have seen oystermen returning with their hauls of Blue Points from the Great South Bay, center of the world's oyster production. With the advent of the Long Island Rail Road, Sayville turned into a popular resort destination for wealthy New Yorkers escaping the city's summer heat and smells.

Sayville may have seemed like an odd destination for Manton's parents, Michael and Catherine. Both born in County Galway in western Ireland in the early 1840s, shortly before the outbreak of the Great Famine, Michael and Catherine separately emigrated to the United States in their early 20s. Michael Manton's talents lay neither in oystering nor in catering to tourists. And the village did not even have a Catholic church. But it did house some Mantons: two uncles of Michael, one also named Michael Manton, the other John Manton. The elder Michael Manton was the town's eccentric, an unmarried and reputedly wealthy recluse, dubbed "the hermit of Sayville," who lived in solitude in a hut in the woods just north of town.[5]

While not rich like his uncle, Manton's father presided over what was considered a "well-to-do and respected family." He had run a coal business in Brooklyn, and he established a coal and wood yard in Sayville. "Dealer in the best of Red and White-Ash and all grades of Coal," read his ads in the *Suffolk County News*. The community welcomed him. "Mr. Michael Manton, our new and obliging coal dealer, has been building an extensive coal yard west of the depot, and is receiving his share of the public patronage," the newspaper noted. "We congratulate Mr. Manton, and consider him a public spirited citizen." Manton sold his coal and wood yard in 1893, and dabbled in real estate and Democratic politics.[6]

Manton's parents married in 1868 and proceeded to have eight children, two of whom died before their first birthday. The remaining six children divided equally along gender lines. Martin was the middle son. His older brother Michael would go on to be a dogcatcher, a teamster, and the postmaster of Sayville. Patrick, the youngest, became a priest, serving as a chaplain in World War I and eventually heading the Church of St. Theresa in Woodside, Queens. Manton's three sisters, Mary, Annie, and Elizabeth, all married and moved back to Brooklyn. From all appearances Manton enjoyed close relationships with his siblings into adulthood. He escorted Elizabeth, the last to marry, down the aisle after their father had passed away, donated money for a new school building at one of Patrick's pulpits, and arranged for jobs for Michael.[7]

Academically, Manton stood out from his siblings. He graduated with honors from Sayville High School and scored at the top of his class on state Regents Exams, with especially high marks in economics. Outside the classroom, he headed the school's Athletics Club and captained its football team.[8]

At his high school graduation, the seventeen-year-old delivered an oration entitled "New Ways of Making Money," which the local newspaper found "quite interesting." To a large crowd assembled in Sayville's Methodist church, Manton noted, approvingly, "the changes wrought by women" making their way into pursuits "hitherto considered suitable only for men," and enumerated "many peculiar and unusual callings which have been developed by modern conditions." In the end, Manton acknowledged, "there is 'No royal road to wealth'"; "labor holds the only key to fortune's purse."[9] For the young orator, "New Ways of Making Money" proved to be more than just a passing high school fancy.

* * *

While still in high school, Manton got to experience firsthand what a nasty, high-profile litigation looks like. In 1896, his great-uncle, "the Hermit of Sayville," died, days after bequeathing to his brother John virtually the entirety of his estate. Feeling cheated out of their rightful inheritance, Manton's father, along with other nieces and nephews, filed a lawsuit charging that John Manton had manipulated his mentally impaired ninety-two-year-old brother into cutting them out of his will during his final illness.

The case turned into a protracted slugfest and a local cause célèbre, covered extensively by the press in Suffolk County and even in Brooklyn. At a hearing in 1897, Manton's parents, brothers, and the sixteen-year-old Manton himself presented sensational testimony of Uncle Michael's unsound mind. This included that he had once lit his pipe with a $100 bill (worth over $3,500 today), and that $600 in cash (more than $20,000) was found in a pair of old overalls in a rubbish heap at his property. For his part, John Manton called witnesses who claimed that Uncle Michael feared that his nephew's family, i.e., Manton's parents, would poison him as he believed they had done to another relative from whom they inherited a large sum of money.[10]

This may have been when Manton decided to become a lawyer. In the fall of 1898 he began his studies at Columbia Law School in Morningside Heights, the university's new home. As is the norm today, most students first spent four years obtaining a liberal arts degree or other undergraduate degree, and then entered the law school. But a college education was not a prerequisite: High school graduates who passed an entrance examination could also gain admission and enter the legal profession just three years later.[11] Such was the path that Manton, young man in a hurry, chose.

For all of Manton's self-confidence, it must have been disorienting, if not deflating, for the South Shore teenager, accustomed to easy triumphs in Sayville's public schools, to find himself coexisting and competing with classmates drawn largely from America's patrician, overwhelmingly Protestant upper class, who had already spent four years at an elite college such as Columbia or Yale or Harvard, who in many cases had attended an equally elite preparatory school before college, who were *men*, several years older than Manton at a stage of life that amplifies such differences. Social relations, as Manton's classmate Louis S. Levy recalled, "were largely determined by the colleges that the men had come from; the Yale men"—of which Levy was one—"usually stuck together; the Harvard men stuck together and the Amherst men stuck together." And unlike his better-pedigreed classmates, Manton had to work his way through law school to help pay Columbia's $150 tuition. Perhaps because of these handicaps, Manton's academic record at Columbia was not especially distinguished.[12]

Over time, whether at Manton's instigation or not, his law school exploits developed embellishments. After Manton received his degree, the *Suffolk County News* reported with local pride that "Martin Manton, son of Mr. and Mrs. Michael Manton, graduated with honors from the Columbia Law School last week." Yet the commencement program does not reflect any honors awarded to Manton, and it seems unlikely Manton won any. In fact, Manton struggled in law school and frequently obtained assistance from Levy, one of the stars of the class, "to explain to him what the cases were about" and the questions asked by professors during the lectures.[13] It also has been reported that Manton was "a founder of the school's law review in 1901," but this is also untrue. The *Columbia Law Review* did indeed begin publication in 1901, Manton's final year, but he was not one of its founders or original members, all of whom had obtained college degrees before going to law school.[14]

Strangest of all, as a young lawyer making his mark, Manton apparently falsely took credit for being a star football player during his Columbia days. In a short profile published in 1907 while Manton was representing the defendant in a high-profile murder case, the *Brooklyn Daily Eagle* broke the news that Manton "turns out to be the famous 'Morley' of the Columbia football team of a few years ago." Manton adopted a pseudonym, according to the newspaper, to hide his extracurricular activity from his father, who did not want his son distracted from his studies. Later, when he discovered the truth, Manton's father, "with true Irish love of sport and joke, patted his son on the back and said: 'Go on my boy; play the game for all you're worth.'"[15] In fact, although Manton did try out for the Columbia football squad, there is no evidence he made the team. He certainly was not the same person as Bill Morley, the team captain and electrifying two-time All-America halfback, who played for the Lions and who later was inducted into the College Football Hall of Fame.[16]

Big Wall Street law firms staffed with armies of highly paid associates still lay in the future when Manton graduated Columbia in June 1901. Manton did not want, and probably could not have procured, a Wall Street position in any event. Instead, after clerking for another lawyer for just a few months, Manton set up shop in the borough of his birth, Brooklyn. He opened his own law office in the Germania Savings Bank Building at 375 Fulton Street, opposite Brooklyn City Hall. Announcing Manton's new venture, the *Suffolk County News* offered encouragement to "one of Sayville's most promising young sons." "We trust and predict," the paper wrote, "that clients a-plenty will be attracted by the hanging out of his new shingle."[17]

Manton did attract clients. He specialized in "anything I could get." He handled small civil matters in Brooklyn and Long Island state court. In one of his first cases, he sued an express company for $50 for losing his client's bicycle. He also brought suit on behalf of a housekeeper who maintained what was then euphemistically called "confidential relations" with her employer and who, after the employer died, claimed ownership of money in a bank account held in both their names. Manton lost at trial, persuaded the Appellate Division to order a new trial, won a $477.13 verdict at the retrial, and then saw the verdict set aside by the trial judge. In another case, Manton won a trial verdict for conversion of jewelry, only to be on the losing end of an Appellate Division reversal by a 3–2 vote.[18] Thus did Manton experience and absorb the ups and downs of litigation, the razor's edge on which outcomes are precariously balanced, how different judges can view the same legal issues differently, and different juries arrive at different verdicts on the same facts, how both sides can believe with equal firmness, and apparent good faith, in the rightness of their cause—insights that would prove indispensable to his future corruption.

Manton also forayed into criminal defense. He represented a man accused of ending a quarrel over fifty cents by shooting his disputant to death on a hot August night in a Queens saloon. He assisted a well-known Brooklyn lawyer and former prosecutor, William O. Miles, in defending a man accused of murdering his paramour's husband, a Brooklyn saloon owner. That trial ended badly: the client was convicted and sentenced to die in the electric chair. So did Miles's legal career: named as a central figure in a scandal involving hundreds of bogus claims for damages from purportedly flooded sewers, he was convicted of defrauding the city, sentenced to a year in prison, and disbarred.[19]

Now as a lawyer rather than a witness, Manton also lent aid to the family's "Hermit Manton" litigation, which was still going on, but not going well. In early 1901, a jury found the will to be valid. That left a separate lawsuit challenging Uncle Michael's eve-of-death conveyance of his Sayville real estate to his brother. "There now being a lawyer in the family," Manton's father sought to substitute his twenty-one-year-old son, just months out of law school, for a veteran local litigator as his counsel when the case headed for trial in 1902. But the court refused, and the case was lost. Manton came in to prosecute the appeal and also to dispute the lawyer's demand for payment of his legal bill. He failed on both counts.[20] In the end the Mantons wound up with nothing from their uncle's estate, other than the costs and aggravation of litigation.

Then a true tragedy struck the Manton family.

* * *

On the morning of December 18, 1903, Manton's mother, Catherine, set out from the family's home on Lincoln Avenue to take care of some shopping. Christmas was only a week away and Catherine Manton had six children and two granddaughters. Below-freezing temperatures greeted her as she stepped outside and headed south toward town. Bundled up against the cold, a shawl wrapped around her head, she crossed the railroad tracks on her way to Gerber's department store on North Main Street. "Never in the history of our Holiday selling have we had such an enormous variety of Christmas Gifts to choose from," boasted Francis Gerber's holiday advertisements.[21] Finding the right one, he advised, would give the giver a "happy Christmas feeling," and Catherine may have experienced that joy as she selected and paid for several items. Although Gerber's offered delivery service, she decided she would carry her acquisitions home herself.

A little after 10:00 a.m., Catherine left Gerber's, her shoes crunching the oyster shells that paved North Main Street, an accommodation to the horseless carriages now careening around the village. As she neared the train tracks, a westbound Long Island Rail Road train rounded a sharp curve just to the east, approaching the Sayville station. The train, running express from Patchogue and not scheduled to stop in Sayville, was moving fast, around forty miles per hour. The engineer blew his whistle; a small boy shouted a warning; Catherine, her head-shawl muffling the noise, did not hear at first. Finally eyeing the rapidly approaching train, "she hesitated for a moment, apparently bewildered, and then hurried on." A "large woman," burdened with her Christmas shopping and, at age sixty-one, not as sprightly as she once was, Catherine did not make it across the tracks in time. She was struck by the cow-catcher, the V-shaped device mounted on the front of the train to clear obstacles from the track, and hurled a distance of fifty feet into a ditch. Catherine Manton died instantly, a victim of her "moment of indecision" crossing the tracks.[22]

A coroner's inquest determined that the accident was unavoidable and exonerated the railroad men of all blame.[23] There is no indication the Manton family filed any litigation against the Long Island Rail Road. But after his mother's death, Manton began to represent plaintiffs in personal injury lawsuits. Finding the field relatively uncluttered by competition—the specialized personal injury bar did not yet exist—Manton amassed a string of favorable jury verdicts and built a "highly lucrative negligence practice."[24] He mainly represented clients disfigured, maimed, and injured in accidents involving one form of motorized transportation or another, or, when the accident was fatal, the victim's estate. Very often, Manton was suing a railroad, and quite frequently, it was the Long Island Rail Road. Victims killed or injured crossing railroad tracks, or thrown sixty feet after colliding with a locomotive, or struck by a trolley car crossing the street, and disputes over whether the engineer rang the bell or blew the whistle, or whether the victim's contributory negligence barred the claim—the fact patterns of these cases must have forced Manton time and again to replay in his mind the calamity that claimed his mother's life.

Manton's personal injury practice later provoked scorn from those who complain about how lawyers profit from others' misfortune (and whose interests, not coincidentally, are often aligned with the corporations who seek to limit liability for accidents). Manton was disparaged as a former "ambulance chaser" by, among others, the investigative reporter who spurred his downfall, an FBI agent summarizing Manton's life history, and Chief Justice William H. Taft, when Taft was angling to keep Manton off the Supreme Court in 1922.[25]

No doubt financial considerations played a role in attracting Manton to negligence cases; here was one of those "new ways of making money" in a "peculiar calling developed by modern conditions" that Manton spoke about at his high school graduation. Yet it is impossible to ignore the psychic satisfaction that Manton must have felt from suing, and obtaining judgments against, railroads and in particular the Long Island Rail Road on behalf of accident victims like his mother. In this instance, at least, Manton's critics did him a disservice.

Chapter Three

"Preying Manton"

A Young Lawyer's Rapid Rise

PERSONAL INJURY CASES WERE NOT THE FOCUS OF MANTON'S EARLY legal career or how he initially achieved renown. Manton clawed his way to the top of the legal profession through murder—dozens upon dozens of shootings, stabbings, slit throats, strangulations, and the occasional axe decapitation. These were not Manton's own acts, of course, but crimes allegedly, and often actually, committed by Manton's clients. Within just a few years of hanging his shingle Manton established himself as a leading criminal defense lawyer in Suffolk County, particularly for those facing society's most serious charge and ultimate penalty. Guilty or not, many of Manton's clients could literally thank him for saving their life, whether through an acquittal, a reversal on appeal, or a conviction on a lesser charge.

Manton first turned heads as the twenty-three-year-old assigned counsel for Frank Chanowski, accused of bludgeoning junk dealer Michael Bianco to death in North Bellport, Long Island. Tall and slim, with "a number of sweethearts," the nineteen-year-old Chanowski was "rather good looking." The evidence against him, however, looked rather bad. Eyewitnesses saw him working at the victim's home the day of the murder, and showing off a large roll of money the day after; police found blood-stained clothes and a heavy lead "slungshot," capable of delivering the fatal blow, in his possession.

"Lawyer Manton," as the newspapers referred to him, mounted an alibi defense and "scored a big victory" when the jury acquitted his seemingly guilty client. Shocked by the verdict, the normally mild-mannered trial judge told the jury it was "about the worst miscarriage of justice I have ever known." Equally enraged, Suffolk County District Attorney Livingston Smith sputtered that "if I had twelve monkeys on the jury I could have fared no worse, and it is possible that I might have gotten a verdict."[1]

No alibi could be offered for another early Manton client, Sandow Meringola. Walking through the fields with his brother Dominica in Huntington, Meringola suddenly knelt down, kissed Dominica's feet, said "excuse me if I do something to you," stood back up, and, in full view of Dominica's fifteen-year-old daughter, swung an axe into his brother's neck, nearly severing head from body. Continuing his rampage, Meringola ran to the home of an acquaintance, pumped three bullets into the man's wife (who survived, barely), and then, cornered, shot at police before slashing his own throat with a knife. In what was "probably one of the shortest murder trials on record," District Attorney Smith took all of one hour to prove his case. Manton "put in a strong case of insanity," calling witnesses who said that Meringola heard voices and ran away from nonexistent pursuers. Although the jury still found Manton's client guilty, they convicted him only of second-degree murder, thus sparing his life.

This partial success became a complete triumph on appeal. Citing the "cogent proof of defendant's unbalanced mind" at the time of the murder, the appellate court reversed Meringola's conviction. "Lawyer Manton has won a signal victory," the press reported. Suffolk County residents, District Attorney Smith not the least among them, "were quite surprised" by the appellate decision. Manton then sought the appointment of a commission to determine Meringola's current mental state. The commission declared Meringola sane and set him free.[2]

As Manton read the Meringola ruling in June 1906, he was preparing for trial in another case of interfamilial homicide.[3] His client, Otis Hinksman, a nineteen-year-old Black man from Speonk, stood accused of shooting his father to death after a quarrel on Thanksgiving night. Manton, who by this time had "gained quite a reputation in Suffolk in murder cases," was assigned as counsel for Hinksman. The prosecution's case was purely circumstantial, and one of their key witnesses "was subjected to a severe cross-examination by Lawyer Manton." But Hinksman himself made a poor witness and was convicted of capital murder, some jurors saying afterwards that "the prosecution had no case at all until the defense was put in."

This time, Manton had to appeal all the way to New York's highest court, the Court of Appeals, to find relief. The Court of Appeals reversed Hinksman's conviction, on evidentiary grounds, and characterized the government's case as "weak." When the case returned to the Riverhead trial court, Manton negotiated a plea to manslaughter and Hinksman was sentenced to ten to fourteen years in prison. The press chalked up another "Victory for Lawyer Manton."[4]

* * *

While Manton waited for the jury to finish its deliberations in the Hinksman case, another accused murderer was brought into the same Riverhead courtroom. Claiming indigency, the defendant told the judge who he wanted to represent him: Martin T. Manton. Dr. James W. Simpson, a tall, debonair thirty-two-year-old with dark wavy hair and eyebrows and mustache to match, did not seem like a candidate for assigned counsel. A Virginia-born dentist who "occupied expensive offices" just off Fifth Avenue in Manhattan and enjoyed "a good income," Simpson had also married well, to the daughter of a wealthy Northport merchant, Bartley T. Horner. But Simpson's "propensity for spending money far outshone his ability to make it"; he was said to have "a too great fondness" for horse races and card games and he frequently borrowed money from his mother-in-law, Nellie Horner. His mother-in-law, however, was in no mood to lend him money for a criminal defense lawyer, for the crime he was charged with was shooting her husband Bartley to death in the family home in Northport.[5]

Bartley Horner, who acted as "self-appointed censor of his son-in-law's morals," had begun talking, in Simpson's presence, about changing his will to prevent Simpson from squandering his money. Two nights before Christmas 1905 a game of pinochle ended in acrimony when the elder man threw down his cards in disgust, accusing Simpson of cheating him. A few days later Horner went to see his lawyer, prompting Simpson to fret at supper with his mother-in-law and his wife, Julia, that Horner had "gone to fix his money so we can't get one cent of it."[6]

When Horner arrived home, Simpson retrieved his shotgun and began marching around the house with it, playing soldier. Horner went into the kitchen to talk to a Polish boy in his employ; Simpson followed, carrying the gun. Minutes later, a shot rang out. Horner lay on the floor, mortally wounded. Simpson claimed his gun went off accidentally as he "broke" it apart to clean it. The district attorney did not believe him and in March 1906 Simpson was indicted for capital murder.

Simpson's fight for his life became a public spectacle in Suffolk County, with each day of the trial bringing overflow and sometimes unruly crowds to the Riverhead courthouse. It also drew considerable coverage from the major New York City dailies. Manton seized this bigger stage, turning it into a showcase for his burgeoning talents and a theater of pain for the seemingly overmatched district attorney, George H. Furman, who complained of a "severe headache" on the first day of trial. As one government witness after another failed to testify as the prosecution expected, Furman grew "white with anger" and asked questions that implicitly accused Manton of witness tampering.[7]

Manton's cross-examinations shredded the prosecution's case. With one witness, Simpson's former office cleaning lady, Manton engaged in "a battle of wits and words from which the witness emerged a poor second." From the prosecution's gun expert, who testified that Simpson's fatal shots could not have been the result of an accident, Manton extracted the signally important admission that cartridges in a gun might accidentally explode after all. Another witness, nearly blind, who testified about things he saw and heard the night of the shooting, was easily dispatched when Manton asked him if he could see Manton speaking to him ("Only indistinctly") and if he could see the other people in the courtroom ("No, it's all a haze"). "That's all," Manton said and sat down. It may well have been during the Simpson trial that Manton earned his nickname "Preying Manton," which some have assumed arose from his corrupt conduct as a judge but which actually referred to "his ability to set cunning court-room traps" as a lawyer.[8]

Manton even turned the alleged murder weapon into an inanimate witness for the defense. At one point Simpson's shotgun was passed around to the jurors—all hunters themselves—who spent a full ten minutes inspecting it, testing the hammer, pounding it on the floor and taking it apart. When Manton handled the gun, he used it to rhetorical effect, "accidentally," as he said, snapping the hammers twice, which drew a vociferous objection from District Attorney Furman and an instruction from the judge not to do it again. "Accidents will happen," Manton archly responded, thus underscoring to the jury the whole point of the defense.[9]

Most devastating of all was the "severe interrogation" and "stern cross-examination" to which Manton subjected Simpson's wife and mother-in-law, which highlighted stark contradictions in their testimony. In an age when men expected unquestioning devotion from their wives—and every member of the Simpson jury was a man—there was an even more visceral, psychological contradiction that Manton wanted to exploit: how a woman who supposedly loved her husband could simultaneously seek his annihilation. Dropping his voice several decibels for effect, Manton asked Mrs. Simpson softly, "You love your husband, don't you?" "I do," she replied, her voice scarcely audible.[10]

In his two-hour summation, "Manton's wrath was poured out on the heads of Mrs. Horner and Mrs. Simpson." He ridiculed Julia Simpson for doing "all she could do to have her husband convicted" while claiming she still loved him: "That is the way she loves him?," he sarcastically asked the jury. The newspapers reported: "There were handkerchiefs in evidence before Manton had finished and Simpson's head was low on his chest." The jury, after only an hour and a half of deliberations, found Simpson not guilty, freeing him to resume his lucrative Fifth Avenue dentist's practice.[11]

But Simpson's troubles with the Horner family and his need for Manton's services were not over. A year after his acquittal, Simpson returned to the Horner home in Northport in hopes of visiting Julia. When Simpson began banging on the door and jiggling the doorknob, Nellie Horner ran upstairs to get a .38-caliber revolver. She fired two shots at Simpson through a glass panel in the front door, striking him in the left lung and liver. Simpson hovered near death for days, and when he recovered, he retained Manton to sue his mother-in-law for damages. After two trials in State Supreme Court in Manhattan (Manton must have calculated that Simpson was not *that* popular in Suffolk County), Manton secured a $1,500 jury verdict in Simpson's favor.[12]

Thus does Dr. James Simpson lie at the intersection of Manton's two paths to fame and fortune as a lawyer: successful defendant in a murder case, and successful plaintiff in a personal injury lawsuit.

* * *

Shortly after winning the Simpson trial, Manton was hired to represent a murder defendant in Chicago, Frank J. Constantine, a New Yorker charged with slitting the throat of a young woman in the apartment where he was a boarder. This trial did not go as well; after a prosecutor's summation built on bile (he condemned Constantine as a "sly, murderous black-hearted Mephistopheles") and topped with a generous heaping of nativism ("There are many good Italians in this country, but if they have any more in New York like Constantine they had better keep them there"), Constantine was convicted. When Manton requested a new trial, the judge asked, "This is a joke, is it?"[13]

Manton had more luck as a suitor outside the courtroom in Chicago. On July 3, 1907, Manton and Marguerite Morier, known as Eva, were married in Chicago at the home of the bride's parents. A year younger and about a foot shorter than Manton, the attractive and good-natured Eva grew up in Evanston, one of five sisters. Edmond Morier, her father, was, like Manton's, in the coal business.[14] Newspapers in Brooklyn and Suffolk County applauded the nuptials for the twenty-six-year-old "graduate of great promise of the Sayville High School" who, despite his youth, was already "well-known" as "a criminal lawyer of marked ability."[15]

The new couple lived in comfort in the Flatbush section of Brooklyn. They could afford to hire a housekeeper, even though it was just the two of them, as for many years they were unable to expand the size of the household. Manton owned a car, first a one-cylinder Rambler and then the larger, faster, and more stylish four-cylinder Pope-Hartford.

Automobiles were then a luxury item (fewer than 1 percent of adult American males owned one), but for Manton, who shuttled back and forth regularly to Suffolk County, where most of his clients and cases were, it was a professional necessity. The young lawyer embraced the new technology of the age; his newspaper advertisements invited prospective clients to call on the phone ("Telephone, 1865 Main"), in contrast to the adjoining ads of older lawyers, who listed only their address.[16]

If Manton shared details of his workday with Eva before turning off the lights at night, Eva must have sometimes had a hard time falling asleep, mulling over his grisly tales of spousal homicide. In one four-month span, Manton represented a Long Island man charged with cutting his wife's throat after she became infatuated with a boarder; a Brooklyn man who strangled his second wife and buried her in the cellar, all to clear the way for him to marry her daughter (his stepdaughter); and an eighteen-year-old Brooklyn newlywed, Rosa Gratzione, who shot her husband six months into their marriage. The two men were convicted,[17] but Rosa Gratzione walked away free on the strength of Manton's spousal abuse defense, centered on testimony that Gratzione's hot-tempered husband beat her and, on the morning of the shooting, tied her up with a rope and threatened to force her into a life of prostitution. After the jury's verdict "the young woman was carried out of the court house on the shoulders of her friends."[18]

If high-profile murder cases were Manton's path to fame, his negligence practice accounted for most of his income. The sheer volume of accident cases Manton handled is impressive. No case seems to have been too small; even as a relatively accomplished and sought-after lawyer with several years under his belt, he was still filing claims against the City alleging personal injuries due to "carelessness of a driver of a City cart," "slipping on [an] icy sidewalk," and "falling on a pile of dirt."[19] Manton succeeded, according to his own reckoning, through "careful" study of "every point" in his case. He "spent days" delving into the technical aspects of malfunctioning machinery, and in cases where medical experts were necessary, "studied medical books with an enthusiasm that would bring me a diploma in a medical college."[20]

Shrewd business practices contributed at least equally to Manton's ascent. Until New York outlawed the practice in 1917, accident lawyers employed paid "runners" to locate and solicit victims who could become plaintiffs. Wily solicitors even approached victims when they were still in the hospital recovering from their injuries. Manton used a veritable army of these "runners." He kept on his payroll the "walking delegate" for the ironworkers' union, whose job it was to visit union members at different locations. As a result, "whenever an iron worker was injured or killed in an accident on the job, the delegate would bring the case to Manton."[21]

As Manton's reputation rose so did the quality of his cases. Juries throughout the metropolitan area returned substantial verdicts in favor of his clients: $7,500 for a pedestrian standing on Flatbush Avenue when a trolley car jumped the tracks and plowed into him; $8,000 for the widow of a dock builder killed when a heavy pile driver slipped its moorings and knocked him into Flushing Bay; $12,500 for the widow of a construction worker killed when building a tube for a railroad under the Hudson River; $14,000 for a Long Island Rail Road brakeman whose leg was cut off when he was thrown under the train; $20,000 for a steamship passenger who fell down a stairway and lost his vision in both eyes.[22] These were large awards in those days. (One study indicates that 75 to 80 percent of accident verdicts in 1905 were below $5,000, in death and non-death cases.)[23] Frequently appellate courts overturned, as unsupported by the evidence, jury verdicts in favor of Manton's personal injury clients.[24] This reflects, in part, the tendency of early twentieth century appellate judges to protect corporations against tort liability. But it also testifies to Manton's strengths as an advocate in persuading juries even when his case was weak.

Doctors, Manton found, were the easiest witnesses to rattle on cross-examination. Trickery was sometimes his means to that end. Cross-examining one well-known medical expert, Manton laid out three treatises by celebrated doctors at counsel table. Picking one up and inserting his finger between the leaves as if to mark a page, Manton asked the defense expert how he would react if the author of the treatise disagreed with the opinion he had just given. The witness said he was not sure that the author did disagree with him. Manton, moving toward the witness stand with the book, invited the doctor to read the relevant passage to the jury. "Well, I'll take your word for it," the doctor said. "I'll not read it." Manton did the same thing with the second treatise, with the same result, as the doctor's confidence slipped. "As a matter of fact," Manton later triumphantly related, "the two authors agreed with the witness." By the time Manton asked about the third treatise, the expert was "pretty well worked up" and acknowledged the author disagreed with him (which, in that instance, was true), snapping "but he's an ass." After the trial concluded, the doctor came over to Manton and asked to read from the first two treatises. "Why did you say those men disagreed from me?," he asked the lawyer. "I didn't say so," Manton replied. "I simply asked you to read what they said to the jury and you refused."[25]

* * *

Political connections were another way for Manton to generate professional opportunities. For a young Irish-Catholic lawyer in Brooklyn, party affiliation was not a matter of genuine debate. The vast majority of Irish Catholics in New York voted Democratic and Irish-Catholics held the levers of power in the Tammany Hall political machine. As a twenty-two-year-old barely one year out of law school, Manton spent the 1902 election season hopping from one Democratic campaign rally in Brooklyn to another, drawing attention as a "very forcible and impressive speaker."[26] Two years later he gave "one of the strongest speeches" heard in Brooklyn during the 1904 presidential campaign, denouncing President Theodore Roosevelt as a phony trust-buster and the GOP as "the party of plunder."[27] Manton joined the Flatbush Democratic Club, contributed money to Democratic campaigns, and served as a delegate to the Democratic State Convention in Albany.[28]

In 1909 Manton's efforts paid off when he was tapped to assist in the defense of Henry J. Furlong, a Brooklyn magistrate indicted for bribery. Well-connected in Democratic circles, Furlong was appointed to the bench in 1901 by Tammany-installed Mayor Robert Anderson Van Wyck.[29] Van Wyck, who had also served as a state court judge, was later routed from office by his own corruption scandal. Under his stewardship, the city allowed the American Ice Company to become its sole ice supplier, a privileged position the company exploited to double prices during the unusually scorching summer of 1900. Van Wyck and Tammany boss Richard Croker, it was revealed, had received free stock in American Ice from its appreciative owners.[30]

Furlong's involvement in Democratic politics continued after he joined the judiciary. By day he toiled away in police court on Gates Avenue in Brooklyn, processing a never-ending parade of mostly petty criminals. In fine Tammany tradition, he deployed his judicial office to dispense justice to others and cash to himself. Using a former clerk named Jacob Gottleft as a go-between, Furlong would set bail for defendants brought before him in exchange for a one-third share of the bail bond fees. Furlong's scheme collapsed when the Brooklyn Bar Association filed a complaint and Gottleft turned state's evidence. His arrest came as no surprise to knowledgeable court observers. "Stories concerning Furlong's conduct both as a man and as a Magistrate had long been in circulation in the borough," the press reported. "His court for a long while was the preferred recourse of shady lawyers and knavish and rotten transgressors."[31]

Parallels abound between the Furlong case and Manton's own case three decades later. When his own corruption scandal broke in January 1939, Judge Manton acknowledged receiving money or loans from litigants, but denied that these payments affected his rulings in any way, and maintained that unless they did he was guilty of no crime. That defense eerily echoed what Lawyer Manton said of the charge that Magistrate Furlong split bail bond fees in cases before him. Even assuming that this was so, Manton argued, "If you will look up the [bribery] statute you will see that a magistrate who divides fees is not committing a crime, unless it is proven that such a division of fees was intended to influence the magistrate's action on the bench."[32]

Manton conducted Furlong's defense together with a more senior and far more renowned lawyer, W. Bourke Cockran, a former (and future) Democratic congressman from Manhattan. The Irish-born, independent-minded Cockran maintained his own, uneasy, relationship with Tammany. Cockran had been Tammany's "Grand Sachem" until the year before, when he had a falling out with Tammany boss Charles

Murphy, just as he had previously broken with Murphy's predecessor Richard Croker. Known as one of the greatest orators of the age—Winston Churchill credited Cockran as his oratorical model and inspiration for his stirring speeches during World War II—Cockran had often moved fellow congressmen, Democratic nominating conventions, and juries with his eloquence and logic.[33]

But neither Cockran's oratory nor Manton's cunning could save Henry Furlong. While Furlong (like Judge Manton) used intermediaries and nominees to cover his tracks, he (also like Manton) left incriminating documents in his own handwriting that allowed prosecutors to pick up the trail. And (unlike Manton) Furlong variegated greed with lust; the prosecutor's cross-examination "was based almost entirely on Magistrate Furlong's alleged immorality" in seducing young women. As spectators "gasped in amazement" and reporters took "a fresh grip on their pencils," the prosecutor marched Furlong through one illicit liaison after another ("You debauched her, too, didn't you?" became the prosecutor's refrain). Several of the women were impregnated by the married magistrate, and one of them was paid hush money when she threatened to expose his adultery. The jury did not buy Furlong's denials or Cockran and Manton's argument that their client was the victim of a grand "political conspiracy" to remove him as a potential rival to the incumbent Democratic Assembly District leader. Furlong was sentenced to one to two years in Sing-Sing.[34]

On appeal, the appellate court resoundingly rejected Cockran and Manton's theory that the bribery indictment against Furlong was defective because it did not charge him with actually performing a corrupt act in any single case. The law, the court explained, "would be violated as much by an agreement for compensation from private parties to take special pains to decide, even properly, a matter coming before the officer as it would by an agreement to decide it improperly." Furlong's case was "one of great pathos," but "as he was fairly tried, after a skillful and resourceful defense by counsel of distinction and experience," there was no reason to disturb his conviction.[35]

Pathos—and irony—surely describes Manton's subsequent conviction, imprisonment, and disgrace for having succumbed to the same temptation that left his former client, Furlong, a "broken man."[36] What happened to Furlong should have served as an object lesson for Judge Manton, the appellate court's words as a warning: steer clear of even the appearance of impropriety. That Manton instead emulated Furlong's conduct, and on a much grander stage and scale, no doubt believing that he would avoid Furlong's mistakes and never get caught, or talk his way out of trouble if he did, is a testament to the obstinacy of human arrogance.

CHAPTER FOUR

"Source of Pride"

The Nation's Youngest Federal Judge

MANTON LOST THE FURLONG CASE BUT AS A BYPRODUCT GAINED A LAW partner and a place in the Manhattan legal community. In July 1911, he and his trial partner, W. Bourke Cockran, announced the formation of Cockran & Manton, located at 31 Nassau Street in the heart of the financial district. Cockran had turned fifty-seven and no doubt was thrilled to have a thirty-year-old junior partner shouldering much of the heavy burden of litigation. This freed up more time for Cockran's very vigorous public and political pursuits. He had already served six terms in Congress from two different districts in New York City and would serve a seventh term from a third before his death in 1923.

Practicing law with Cockran broadened Manton's horizons. For the first time he began handling significant commercial cases. He and Cockran brought suit on behalf of minority stockholders in the Brooklyn Union Gas Co. charging mismanagement by the company's officers and wrongful withholding of $7 million in profits. They also filed a $750,000 antitrust action against Eastman Kodak Co., contending that its monopolistic practices forced their client, a small Brooklyn camera manufacturer, out of business.[1] Between cases such as these and his personal injury practice, Manton had sharpened into quite a thorn in the side of corporate America. Unlike so many federal judges, then and now, especially in Manhattan, it does not appear that Manton handled any significant matter for a big corporation before going on the bench.

Even after setting up shop with Cockran in Manhattan, personal injury litigation and criminal defense continued to be Manton's bread and butter. His verdicts grew larger.[2] Often a trial was unnecessary, because Manton's track record incentivized companies to settle rather than fight when sued by "the celebrated damage lawyer," as the press referred to him.[3] To drive this point home, Manton printed and distributed pamphlets headed "Amounts Recovered in cases recently tried and settled by Lawyer Martin T. Manton" listing nearly 150 cases against railroads, power companies, and other corporations along with the amounts recovered in each.[4]

Murder remained a mainstay too. Acting pro bono, Manton secured an acquittal in State Supreme Court for a city clerk charged with fatally shooting a woman in her apartment when he saw her with another man; his defense was that the gun went off in a struggle when she tried to prevent him from committing suicide. The acquittal "was one of the most complete surprises the Supreme Court has known for some time." Tears streaking his face, the acquitted man embraced Manton in a stunned and soundless Brooklyn courtroom.[5]

It was the murder of a small-time gambling house proprietor named Herman Rosenthal, however, that gave rise to the most famous case of Manton's legal career.

* * *

On a sticky, steamy night in July 1912, a 1909 Packard pulled up near the Café Metropole, a popular watering hole housed in a hotel on West 43rd Street in what was known as the Tenderloin district. Out of the car stepped several armed gangsters, who were waiting as Rosenthal emerged from the hotel lobby clutching copies of that day's *New York World*. The gunmen pumped four bullets into Rosenthal's face and neck, climbed back into the Packard, and sped away. As Rosenthal bled to death on the street, the copies of the *World* slipped from his grasp, displaying a sensational front-page story that, the authorities would later allege, established the motive for his killing. Days before, Rosenthal had handed *World* reporter Herbert Bayard Swopes a giant scoop: NYPD lieutenant Charles Becker, the head of a special task force charged with eradicating gambling, was actually a secret partner in Rosenthal's gambling enterprise.[6]

Rosenthal's murder ignited a media firestorm. "Never in their history had New York newspapers found room for as relentless coverage of a story as they did for the Rosenthal murder" and the two trials of Becker that followed.[7] Gangland slayings were hardly a novelty in New York and Rosenthal, a small-potatoes gambler viewed as a nuisance and trouble-maker even within the underworld, was hardly a sympathetic victim. But the potential involvement of a corrupt cop unleashed a long-festering fury felt by many New Yorkers, particularly pro-reform city elites.

In the latter half of the nineteenth century, as New York's police department developed into a modern urban professional force, it fell under Tammany's sway the same as other city agencies. Newly hired cops had to kick back a third of their annual salary to the machine. For many the cost was more than offset by the unofficial financial benefits attainable with a police badge. A legislative committee investigating police corruption in 1895 concluded that city cops were "bound together" by their common devotion to "public plunder" and characterized the NYPD as "not only corrupt," but "oppressive and repulsive to a degree beyond endurance."[8] Nowhere was that more evident than in the Tenderloin district, saturated with gambling dens and brothels that offered plentiful opportunities for shakedowns. Which, in fact, is how the Tenderloin got its name. When Police Inspector Alexander "Clubber" Williams, notorious for his corruption and gratuitous violence, was put in charge of the area, he quipped, "I've been having chuck steak ever since I've been on the force, and now I'm going to have a bit of tenderloin."[9]

When Becker, the son of Bavarian immigrants, joined the force in the 1890s after working as a bouncer in a German beer hall, "Clubber" Williams became his mentor. Like Williams, Becker would beat up or arrest citizens for no apparent reason, or in one instance, chronicled by the young novelist Stephen Crane, because they had insulted a fellow police officer. Becker also followed in his mentor's footsteps when named to head up a special squad in charge of driving the gamblers out of the Tenderloin. Long on show and short on substance, these squads made 203 raids and 898 arrests citywide in 1913, but had only 103 convictions to show for it, and most of those resulted in suspended sentences or small fines. Becker "apparently often arranged for his men to be afflicted with almost total amnesia when the case reached court."[10]

This was the kindling lit when Rosenthal was killed right after threatening to expose police graft on a grand scale. Seizing the moment, the district attorney, Charles S. Whitman, a Republican who ran on an anti-Tammany platform, immediately identified Becker as the lead suspect and the Police Department as his adversary rather than ally in solving the crime. Whitman's mistrust of the police ran so deep that during the investigation he worked out of a large suite in the Waldorf-Astoria Hotel, deeming his office too close for comfort to police headquarters. Whitman also hired a private detective agency to perform investigative functions normally the province of the NYPD. Bankrolling these unusual expenditures was the cream of New York society, business titans and eminent lawyers such as J. Pierpont Morgan, John D. Rockefeller Jr., and US senator and former secretary of state Elihu Root.[11]

Good-government forces gathered at a raucous rally in Cooper Hall organized by "a large delegation associated with municipal righteousness." Cheers and applause "shook the storied structure" as speakers presented the battle against police graft as a fight for the city's soul. "We would be recreant to our duty," the Reverend Lyman Abbott implored, "if we did not rise in strong, vehement, hot, wrathful revolt" upon learning that "the men who are employed to protect us from crime were protecting the criminal from us." The crowd reserved its loudest and most prolonged applause for Whitman, who called the murder of Rosenthal "a challenge to our very civilization itself."[12]

Soon Whitman arrested four underworld figures seen in or around the Metropole on the night of the Rosenthal murder. Facing a potential death sentence, these men—Jacob Rosenzweig, known as "Bald Jack Rose," Bridgey Webber, Harry Vallon, and Sam Schepps—cut deals to testify for the prosecution in exchange for immunity. The turncoat gamblers' stories closely tracked one another and confirmed Whitman's theory of the case, which, critics charged, was no surprise since Whitman allowed them to all talk together while in prison. They fingered the gunmen: Frank Cirofici, aka "Dago Frank"; Harry Horowitz, aka "Gyp the

Blood"; Louis Rosenberg, aka "Lefty Louie"; and Jacob Seidenschmer, aka "Whitey Lewis." And they claimed Becker was the mastermind of the plot. After separate trials before an aggressively pro-prosecution state court judge (who, as committee counsel, had authored the 1895 legislative investigative report so disparaging of the NYPD), Becker and the four gunmen were all convicted and sentenced to die in the electric chair.

In February 1914, the Court of Appeals overturned Becker's conviction, holding that he had been denied a fair trial by virtue of the trial judge's slanted rulings and jury charge. (No such luck favored the gunmen, whose appeals were denied and who were all electrocuted the morning after Easter Sunday.) Becker's appellate lawyer, Joseph Shay, who did not have significant criminal trial experience and was feuding with Becker's brother, then withdrew from the case.[13]

Enter Manton. By this time he had defended at least eighty-eight accused murderers in New York and elsewhere.[14] Becker had heard good things about Manton from a fellow inmate, a former president of a Brooklyn bank convicted of misappropriating bank assets, and asked Manton to meet with him in prison. Manton agreed to take Becker's case just three weeks before the retrial was scheduled to begin. "Any lawyer taking up the case now will have to do almost herculean work in order to acquaint himself thoroughly with the details of the case and the witnesses," a reporter observed.[15]

Optimism nonetheless reigned in Becker's camp. "As the case is now prepared," Shay told the press, "I don't think there is a possible chance of Becker ever being convicted." Becker too was "sure I shall be acquitted." Their confidence may have been boosted by the Court of Appeals' 6–1 decision, which had expressed grave doubts about Becker's guilt. The prosecution's case, the court wrote, rested entirely on the testimony of "desperate and degenerate witnesses" who had been confined together in prison where "ample opportunities existed for collaboration on the evidence they were to give under their life-saving agreement to convict Becker."[16]

Before the second trial began in May 1914, Manton almost lost top billing to his senior partner, Bourke Cockran. Cockran, who had publicly praised Whitman after Becker's first conviction, had since come to believe in Becker's innocence. In the lead-up to the retrial, he became enraged by what he believed was a deliberate attempt by the prosecution to taint the jury pool through leaks to the press. Showing up unexpectedly on the first day of trial, Cockran beseeched the new judge, Samuel Seabury, to hold Whitman in contempt for orchestrating the leaks and to transfer venue outside of the city. When Seabury denied his motions, a purple-faced Cockran stomped out of the courtroom, never to return. "I am through with the Becker case, through with it," Cockran fumed to reporters. "This is not a trial, it is an assassination."[17]

With Cockran's abrupt exit Manton took center stage of the Becker defense, in the glare of an intense public spotlight. At stake, partisans on both sides felt, was not just one man's fate but the integrity of the criminal justice system itself. As with the first trial, the retrial—and Manton's name—were splashed across the front pages of all the major New York City dailies and newspapers nationwide. Inside the Criminal Court Building, a throng of thousands vied for a seat to watch Manton's cross-examination of Bald Jack Rose, the prosecution's chief witness. When the courtroom doors opened, a "riot" broke out in the corridor as "men and women were bowled over and trampled on or hurled down the marble staircases," many of them "severely bruised."[18]

Manton's cross-examination style differed from that of Becker's first counsel. "It is purely a psychological proposition," Manton once told an interviewer. "The madder your witness gets the better it is for you, provided you keep cool yourself."[19] Instead of going at witnesses hammer-and-tongs, Manton was quietly insistent, calm, even "suave" according to reporters. "He went at Rose smilingly, but it was a sarcastic, contemptuous smile." He began eccentrically, with a hint of anti-Semitism. Manton paused for thirty seconds, peering at Rose, then asked, "You were a Jew up to the last trial?" "I still am," Rose retorted. (Rose, Vallon, Webber, and Schepps were all Jewish, as was Rosenthal. Manton may have been placating his client, or playing on the jury's racial prejudices.) Five hours of Manton's "grilling, grinding cross-examination" exploited discrepancies between Rose's testimony at the two trials and yielded admissions that Rose had lied to the police even after he was arrested. At one point Rose lost his temper, his "yellow skin flushed to a deep orange all over his head." Yet on the whole, the press concluded, Rose's story "was unshaken in any material part. . . . The expected smashing of District Attorney Whitman's case did not arrive."[20]

Nor did Manton make much headway with Justice Seabury, an anti-Tammany crusader who, nearly two decades later, would spearhead an investigation of corruption in the municipal courts. Manton and Seabury clashed repeatedly. Seabury barred Manton from referring to the Court of Appeals' ruling after a witness changed his testimony (though not before Manton had asked, in front of the jury, whether the witness added new details because the Court of Appeals had described the prior testimony as "unlikely to be true").[21] After Seabury's charge to the jury, Manton rose angrily to "object to the entire charge made by you to the jury on the ground that it was an animated argument" for the prosecution. Visibly incensed, his face flushed with resentment, Seabury dismissed Manton's objection as "entirely unwarranted."[22]

Whether swayed by Seabury's charge or not, the jury, after only four hours of deliberation, convicted Becker of first-degree murder. Justice Seabury pronounced the death sentence. Manton filed an appeal, hoping Becker would again find salvation in the Court of Appeals. Manton raised twenty separate claims of error in an appellate brief that weighed in at an obese 540 pages. (Years later, when he was on the Second Circuit, Manton chastised lawyers for filing overlength briefs and urged them "to be brief in argument and in court. A brief should be brief, as its name implies." Lawyers and judges simply have different perspectives on this issue.) Manton claimed the brief was "the result of sixty long nights of hard work by me," for which he received "not one dollar of compensation." He even paid the printing costs out of his own pocket, because, he told a reporter, "I believe Becker is innocent."[23]

But in the year since Becker's first appeal, two members of the court had left, and a third was about to be replaced by none other than Samuel Seabury, who had been elected to the Court of Appeals in November 1914. While Seabury did not participate in the Court of Appeals' deliberations, the judges who did may not have been eager to greet their new colleague by reversing him in such a high-profile case. The court (including Benjamin Cardozo, one of the new members) unanimously upheld the result of the retrial. "Doubtless, a very strong argument can be made in favor of the defendant," the Court of Appeals wrote. Nonetheless, Becker's guilt "was a question for the jury with whose determination we are not justified in interfering."[24]

Manton had one more card to play: a request for clemency from the governor. A reasonably compelling case for clemency existed. The evidence may have been legally sufficient to sustain the jury verdict, but was it strong enough to justify extinguishing a man's life? Even ardent proponents of Becker's prosecution harbored doubts. Becker also had something he might be able to trade: information about high-ranking corrupt police officials. But an insurmountable obstacle stood in the way. The governor was the very same Charles Whitman who had prosecuted Becker. Capitalizing on the popularity of the Becker case, Whitman successfully ran for governor in 1914 and was regarded as a leading GOP candidate for president in 1916.[25]

Manton pointed out the obvious unfairness in Whitman's deciding Becker's fate under these unusual circumstances. He called for Whitman to delegate the Becker pardon decision to the lieutenant governor. Meeting with Whitman in Albany, Manton proposed, as an alternative, that the governor appoint a prominent citizen of unimpeachable integrity, such as Elihu Root, to rule on Becker's plea. As yet another possibility, Manton suggested that the decision be turned over to a special commission made up of former Court of Appeals judges. All of Manton's proposals fell on deaf ears. "To turn [this responsibility] over to another man would be shirking my duty," Whitman self-servingly explained. Unsurprisingly, Whitman disagreed that Becker deserved a pardon or a commutation of sentence. "There never was a case more perfectly proved in the history of jurisprudence," he said in a laughable overstatement that served only to highlight his lack of objectivity and political motivations.[26]

There is little doubt that Charles Becker was a corrupt cop who took money from the gamblers he was supposed to be locking up. Manton himself acknowledged that Becker did not testify in his own defense because "when he was asked if he had grafted" Becker would have had "to refuse to answer on the ground that he might incriminate himself."[27] More than a century later, however, there remains considerable doubt that Becker was actually guilty of Herman Rosenthal's murder.[28] Entire books have been written parsing the evidence and concluding that Becker was innocent of that crime, and that his life was sacrificed on the altar of Charles Whitman's political ambitions and the public's fevered desire to strike a blow against police graft. Manton felt the intensity of the public's wrath, receiving letters threatening him with bodily harm if he kept Becker from the electric chair. A stranger seized his arm on the street and told him that if he did not give up the fight for Becker he would be killed.[29]

On the afternoon of July 29, 1915, word reached Manton and Cockran that Governor Whitman had turned down a last-ditch personal plea from Becker's wife to save her husband's life. The two lawyers rushed in a taxicab to Sing-Sing. Manton spent more than two hours in the death house with Becker, followed by Cockran. They said goodbye to their client for the last time and took the train back to Grand Central.[30] The next morning Becker was electrocuted, the first policeman to receive the death penalty in American history.

* * *

If Manton rendered some legal services to Becker for free, he could afford it. He and Eva now lived in one of the "superb residences" on Brooklyn's tree-lined Ocean Parkway, modeled on Baron Haussmann's grand Parisian boulevards.[31] The Mantons were in need of larger quarters. Unable to conceive a child after eight years of marriage, they decided to adopt. David, born in 1915, came first, followed three years later by an orphaned girl they named Catherine, Manton's mother's name.[32]

The Mantons had begun splitting their time between the city and a second residence in Long Island, a practice they would keep up for three decades. In 1910 Manton purchased the Bedell House in Sayville, which had sixteen bedrooms, a stable, and shaded grounds. He thoroughly remodeled the inside and sold it off in 1916, upgrading to a much larger property, "Liberty Hall," located on South Ocean Avenue in Bayport, the seaside town due east of Sayville. Liberty Hall was a forty-acre estate fronting the Great South Bay on which sat a "castle-like mansion" built in 1897 by a New York City stockbroker, Joseph H. Roppani. Roppani needed to sell. He had just been convicted of grand larceny and sentenced to two years in prison. In the spring of 1916, Manton bought Liberty Hall for $30,000 and rechristened it "Fairacres."[33]

Manton had developed quite an appetite for real estate. Real estate records from 1908 to 1916 are replete with references to Manton buying, selling, and giving mortgages on dozens of properties, mainly in Brooklyn and Suffolk County. In 1910 Manton became a director of a real estate investment firm headed by Joseph Doolittle, a Queens realtor. In 1911 Manton and his brother formed a real estate company with a Brooklyn building contractor, P. J. McCauley, with $10,000 in capital. McCauley-Manton Co. won local government contracts worth hundreds of thousands of dollars in Brooklyn, Passaic, New Jersey, and Baltimore, Maryland.[34]

By the time he was appointed a federal judge in 1916, Manton was a millionaire (meaning he was worth more than $25 million in today's dollars).[35]

* * *

He had wealth, fame, smarts, oratorical skill, a Columbia law degree, a facility for partisan combat, an athletic build, and a face whose features were not unpleasing. It was just a matter of time before Manton would be talked about for electoral office. That time first came in the summer of 1908, when Manton turned twenty-eight and Brooklyn papers reported that Democrats might nominate him as a candidate for Congress. Although recognized as "a lawyer of high standing," "well liked by the leaders of both [party] factions," "eloquent on the stump," and (less accurately) "a great football player and runner in his day," Manton did not get the party's nod.[36] Two years later Manton was again rumored to be considering a run against an incumbent Republican congressman in Brooklyn. The nomination appeared to be his for the asking. But "at practically the last minute" Manton "declined to take the risk" and withdrew, leaving Democratic leaders scrambling to find a replacement.[37]

Strong for Woodrow Wilson in 1912, Manton presided over an enthusiastic mass rally for the Democratic presidential nominee held by the Irish-American Municipal Union in Brooklyn.[38] Manton planned to attend Wilson's inauguration along with other Brooklyn Democrats, but "lost his voice while pleading a case in the Long Island City Court House."[39] Manton's Wilsonian progressivism worked to loosen his bonds with Tammany. Tammany had thrown its support to Wilson's rival, House Speaker Champ Clark, at the Democratic National Convention, and Wilson and his chief political adviser, Colonel Edward House, "were determined to break the power of Tammany if they could."[40]

Shortly after taking office Wilson made it known he wanted to displace Tammany leader Charles Murphy and his sometime alter ego in Brooklyn, John H. McCooey. Wilson elevated the profile of a young anti-Tammany Democrat named John Purroy Mitchel, appointing him commissioner of customs in New York, the top federal patronage job in the city. Mitchel soon jumped into the mayoral race on the third-party reformist Fusion ticket. He trounced the lackluster Tammany candidate by twenty points. Manton actively supported Mitchel's candidacy, contributing money and giving speeches on Mitchel's behalf. He perhaps sensed a kinship with the ambitious Irish-Catholic progressive just one year older than him (the two had briefly overlapped at Columbia). The Fusionists toyed with the idea of nominating Manton to the Surrogate's Court in Brooklyn as an "independent Democrat" who was "favored by the anti-Tammany elements on the Fusion committee" and also "said to be acceptable to the Republicans." Mitchel wanted to appoint Manton to run the city's law department in Brooklyn, but his corporation counsel favored another candidate.[41]

After these opportunities did not materialize, Manton considered another run for Congress from Long Island. The incumbent, Lathrop Brown, was an anti-Tammany Democrat. Franklin Roosevelt's roommate at Harvard and lifelong friend, Brown came from money and married up, to a Boston heiress, settling down on a one-hundred-acre estate on St. James Harbor on the North Shore, where he raced motorboats, played polo, and shot partridge and pheasants. "Bored by his millions," the strikingly handsome twenty-nine-year-old bounded into Long Island Democratic politics in 1912. Most observers did not give Brown much of a shot; the potato farmers, cranberry growers, and oyster haulers who populated the district generally leaned Republican. But, clinging close to Wilson, Brown bested both the favored GOP candidate and the candidate of the Progressive Party—Manton's law partner, W. Bourke Cockran.[42]

Two years later Manton decided to run for the same seat. Why he did so is unclear. Serious, hard-working, and of modest roots, Manton may have been repelled by Brown's mix of noblesse oblige and dilettantism: Brown missed half of all House votes during his term.[43] Manton, though claiming to be part of no faction, chose to ally himself with the Tammany-affiliated Democratic Party regulars still smarting from the beating Brown had administered in 1912. At a dinner at Hall's Chop House in Centerport at the end of July 1914, a faction of 250 organization Democrats "boomed" Manton as their candidate to take on Brown in the primary.[44]

In a campaign photo Manton struck a youthful, confident profile: trim, clean-shaven, with sharply parted, carefully combed hair and pince-nez glasses perched atop a slightly bulbous nose, lips curled into a frown, meant perhaps to project gravity, and a fashionable bowtie completing an image of meticulousness and modernity. Manton's lack of facial hair exemplified a shift in early twentieth century America away from the bushy mustache or long beard (or often both) common among older men and the prior generation of politicians. The mustache wearer—such as Manton's opponent, Brown—"was much more his own man: a patriarch, authority figure or free agent who was able to play by his own rules." By contrast, a clean-shaven man emphasized sociability over autonomy, signaling his "commitment to his male peers and to local, national or corporate institutions."[45]

A bitter September 28 primary contest loomed between Brown, the maverick, and Manton, the institutionalist. Organization Democrats stewed over Brown's refusal to play ball on patronage appointments. "We are going to make the fight of our lives to nominate Manton for Congress," pledged one party leader.[46] Manton was not working so hard himself. He appears to have lacked the single-mindedness of purpose necessary for success in politics. Right after his "boom," he and Eva headed off for a month-long vacation out west that took them through the Great Lakes and all the way to Montana.[47] When they returned, the primary was less than four weeks away.

Two weeks later, Manton abruptly withdrew from the race. This announcement was "declared to be the most important single occurrence in Suffolk County politics in years." Manton's motivations immediately came under suspicion. Some believed Manton withdrew to ensure party unity, as he claimed in a publicly released letter to Brown, others that he bowed to the reality that the "Brown men would knife him" at the general election if he beat Brown in the primary. Others thought Manton simply got cold feet. "The fact is that Manton refused to run," one paper reported. "No one pulled Manton out of the race but Manton."[48]

Cynics smelled a political deal. They claimed vindication a few months later, when Manton's brother Michael was named postmaster of Sayville. "Nothing which has happened for a long time has created such a commotion in Sayville" as the news that Michael Manton—who had lived in Manhattan for the past fifteen years and "was practically unknown to the people of Sayville"—had procured this coveted post, in those days a presidential appointment requiring US Senate confirmation. Politicians of both Democratic Party factions were reportedly "up in arms" and attacked the "bargain" as "a shame and a reproach."[49]

The political horse-trading may have been on a grander scale than even the cynics suspected. According to an FBI report prepared in connection with Manton's trial, President Wilson, who had "a high regard" for Brown, asked Manton to withdraw, and "Manton acceded to the President's request."[50] Two years later, Wilson was in a position to reward Manton for his pliancy.

* * *

In February 1916, E. Henry Lacombe, the second judge ever to serve on the US Court of Appeals for the Second Circuit, retired. Manton immediately let it be known he was interested in the seat. The year before, Brooklyn Democrats had nearly nominated him to run for Brooklyn district attorney, or for a State Supreme Court judgeship, but neither prospect panned out.[51] Although Manton never seemed to warm to electoral office campaigning, he proved supremely skilled at working political and legal contacts behind the scenes to promote himself for a judicial appointment.

In May 1916, under the front-page headline "Manton Is Backed For U.S. Court of Appeals," the *Brooklyn Daily Eagle* reported that the Wilson Administration was being "strongly urged" to name Manton to the Second Circuit. Both John H. McCooey, the Brooklyn Democratic leader, and Edwin S. Harris, the chairman of the State Democratic Party, actively lobbied in Washington on Manton's behalf. Yet not everyone agreed the Circuit Court was the right spot for Manton. Some local Democrats felt Manton should go on the federal district court instead. From that place, they reasoned, Manton could dole out lucrative patronage appointments: receivers, referees in bankruptcy, commissioners in admiralty, special masters in equity, and court clerks. Manton "is said to have made it plain, however, that he would consider no appointment but that to the Circuit Court of Appeals."[52]

Tammany Hall, it was reported, would push no candidate of its own and would not object to Manton's appointment. Tammany had bigger fish to fry than controlling a post on the Second Circuit, "which, from a patronage standpoint, was worthless." Manton, who had been a vocal proponent of keeping the Brooklyn Democratic Party independent of Tammany's control, must have been relieved that he would not face opposition from that influential quarter. Despite Wilson's initial anti-Tammany inclinations, the administration more recently was keen to mend fences with New York's Democratic machine, in advance of the approaching 1916 presidential election.[53]

To further his cause Manton sought help from his old law school friend, Louis Levy, now a lawyer in private practice in Manhattan. Manton wanted Levy's partner, John B. Stanchfield, to endorse Manton's candidacy. Stanchfield, a well-known lawyer and prior unsuccessful Democratic candidate for governor and US Senate in New York, broke with Tammany to support Wilson at the 1912 Democratic National Convention.[54] While reluctant at first, since he did not know Manton personally, Stanchfield agreed to recommend Manton once Levy assured him that Manton was "a decent fellow" who "has come a long ways" and "would make a very good man."[55]

Wilson's attorney general, Thomas W. Gregory, was looking for a candidate who would be acceptable to Tammany and anti-Tammany forces alike and would reflect the administration's policy views on antitrust and other regulatory issues.[56] Manton fit that description, but as the summer wore on, his chances seemed to fade, irritating both Manton and his allies. In early August McCooey went to Washington to intercede with the president, but got only as far as Treasury Secretary William G. McAdoo, who already backed Manton. At a Democratic Party conference in Saratoga, McCooey also lobbied Wilson's young assistant secretary of the navy from New York, Franklin D. Roosevelt. With hope for a Second Circuit appointment nearly abandoned, McCooey moved to his backup plan. Manton, it was reported, would now be tapped to run for Brooklyn district attorney against the Republican incumbent.[57]

When Brooklyn Democratic leaders assembled on August 14 to choose their slate of local candidates for the fall, "Manton's name was on everybody's lips." A "well-defined rumor" circulated that "word had come from Washington that his chances of appointment [to the Second Circuit] were very good, after all," which was Manton's own preference. The organization withdrew Manton's name from consideration for district attorney and nominated someone else for that office.[58]

This reading of the Washington tea leaves proved only partly prescient. Attorney General Gregory was ready to make Manton a federal judge—but not on the Second Circuit. For that spot Gregory chose Southern District judge Charles M. Hough who, while a Republican, was considered sympathetic to economic regulation. Hough's elevation to the Circuit left a vacancy in the Southern District. Gregory decided to make Hough's appointment palatable to McCooey and other New York Democrats by nominating Manton to fill that vacancy. On August 15, 1916, President Wilson simultaneously announced the appointments of both Hough and Manton.[59]

Gregory's compromise met with "much surprise" in political circles in New York. At first it was unclear if Manton would accept the president's nomination. "In some quarters the impression prevailed that Manton would decline the post," the Brooklyn Citizen reported. But on August 17 Manton did accept. In fact, Manton wrote Cockran, his appointment caused him to live in a state of "atmospheric joy for several days where my mouth has watered with but a sweet taste."[60]

The following week Manton traveled to Washington as the US Senate decided whether to approve his nomination. Two objections had been lodged. Francis M. Curran, a lawyer and minor player in Brooklyn Democratic politics, wrote a "vicious" letter, which Manton claimed was simply sour grapes over having lost to Manton in a will contest. A more credible objector, the Wall Street firm of Stern & Gotthold, submitted a lengthy protest attacking Manton as an "ambulance chaser." Stern and Gotthold's opposition puzzled Manton. "I don't know the gentlemen," he wrote Cockran, adding "but hope to see them often hereafter"— meaning, presumably, that he planned to exact revenge when Stern & Gotthold appeared in Judge Manton's courtroom. The protests were not "of any consequence," according to Sen. James O'Gorman, chairman of the Senate Judiciary subcommittee handling the nomination. The Senate unanimously confirmed Manton on the night of August 23 before he had even arrived in Washington.[61]

Less than a month past his thirty-sixth birthday, Manton was now the youngest federal judge in the nation. The local Suffolk County paper cheered the "rapid rise of [the] young Sayville lawyer," whose appointment to the federal bench was "a source of pride to his townsmen." "One of the ornaments of the local bar," the *Brooklyn Citizen* called the new judge, and the *Brooklyn Daily Eagle* agreed that "Mr. Manton's standing at the bar [cannot] be impeached." *Bench and Bar*, a lawyer's magazine, "confidently" predicted that Manton would "discharge his new duties with credit to himself and to the court in which he now sits." Manton "will grace the bench," concurred the *Brooklyn Daily Times*.[62]

Although Manton was largely a denizen of the New York state courts, the press, misled by the biographical materials he supplied, lauded his "extensive" experience in federal court, his "instrumental" role in prosecuting antitrust cases, and his "considerable" practice in admiralty law.[63] In fact, so far as the historical record reveals, Manton had handled only two antitrust cases and no admiralty cases unrelated to his negligence practice. Nor had he been involved in any known patent litigation (a big chunk of the federal docket at the time) or any federal criminal cases. Of

139 reported decisions in which Manton served as counsel, 133 were in the New York state courts and only six were in federal court, and all of the latter appear to have been personal injury suits.[64]

Federal district court judges at the time were paid $6,000 per year, much less than what Manton earned in private practice. The *Brooklyn Citizen* commended Manton's "willing[ness] to sacrifice a lucrative practice for the honor of a seat on the bench." "Lawyers of profitable practice are not mercenary when they take appointments on the federal bench," the *Brooklyn Daily Eagle* wrote admiringly when Manton was appointed. "They must be moved by other and higher considerations."[65] Manton, active in civic and public affairs, may well have been moved by such considerations. But by this time he also was a very wealthy man. And he had no intention of abandoning his money-making pursuits just because he was now a federal judge.

CHAPTER FIVE

"Within an Ace"

To the Second Circuit, and Almost Beyond

PROMINENT LAWYERS AND POLITICIANS FETED MANTON ON HIS appointment to the bench at a dinner at the Hotel Claridge in Times Square. Guests included Cockran, Stanchfield, Senator O'Gorman, New York state senator (and future US senator) Robert F. Wagner, 1904 Democratic presidential nominee Alton B. Parker, and Dudley Field Malone and Stuart G. Gibboney, Democratic attorneys who acted as liaisons for the Wilson Administration in New York. Also in attendance, though likely not in as festive a mood, were all three of Manton's new Southern District colleagues, Judges Learned Hand, Julius M. Mayer, and Augustus N. Hand.[1]

The Hand cousins, in particular, were apprehensive about Manton's arrival. Gus found Manton's selection "very surprising," he wrote Learned. At a dinner at the Century Club right after the announcement, Arthur Gotthold, the Wall Street lawyer who protested Manton's nomination, showed Gus one of Manton's printed circulars listing his verdicts in negligence cases, given to one of the lawyer's clients by a runner. "It certainly made the whole thing seem most cheap" to the Harvard-educated Gus, who had also practiced on Wall Street. Nevertheless, a Brooklyn State Supreme Court justice at the club, Frederick E. Crane, vouched for Manton as "a very agreeable fellow" with "excellent habits" and a "clean life." Gus told Learned that he, too, hoped that Manton "may after all turn out well" and, in that spirit, had written Manton a short letter of congratulations. "I had not the face to do more, and thought I should not do less."[2]

Learned, a philosophical skeptic, likely did not share Gus's optimism. He seems to have never wavered in his view that Manton was nothing more than a Democratic clubhouse politician. It probably did not escape his notice that, within two weeks of his confirmation as a federal judge, Manton accompanied McCooey and other Brooklyn Democrats to the political ceremony at which President Wilson formally accepted the Democratic Party's nomination to run for a second term.[3] Yet Learned too was willing to give Manton the benefit of the doubt; in his view, the gossip about Manton's shady practices as a lawyer did not amount to proof of conduct "dishonorable in the more serious sense."[4] As the Southern District's now-most senior judge, Learned sent Manton a polite note welcoming him to the court, wishing him success, and suggesting he take at least a month off before commencing his judicial duties. Manton replied appreciatively and pledged his "devoted service to the duties of this high office."[5]

Manton seemed happy in his new station. He got so giddy listening to a fellow speaker at a meeting of the New York County Lawyers' Association in early January 1917 that he created a "sensation," captured by the New York Times' headline: "M.T. Manton of Federal Bench Laughs So Heartily He Falls Out of His Chair." Manton, "leaning far back in his chair to laugh with more leisure, tumbled off the platform and disappeared behind a pair of violently agitated curtains," the paper reported. "Fortunately the platform was not high, and Judge Manton emerged from behind the curtains somewhat upset as to his judicial dignity, but not injured."[6]

Such gaiety soon fell into short supply. The United States entered World War I. Much of the new judge's caseload grew out of conflicts at home generated by the hostilities abroad. The Wilson Administration aggressively prosecuted conscientious objectors, antiwar protestors, and others who undermined the war effort. Swift justice was dispensed in Manton's courtroom to a Socialist who failed to register for the draft: a two-hour trial, a two-minute jury deliberation, and a prison sentence immediately pronounced.[7] Manton also meted out the maximum sentence for Selective Service officers who took bribes to grant exemptions from the draft, rejecting their argument—similar to one he would make in his own defense two decades later—that the men from whom they took money were physically unfit and would have been exempted anyway.[8]

Manton presided over the retrial of journalists from the *Masses*, a radical antiwar magazine, charged with sedition. To Max Eastman, the magazine's top editor, Manton was "hard, brisk, and mean-looking, unpossessed of dignity, and always in a hurry, as though he had larger interests elsewhere." Yet Manton allowed Eastman to deliver a summation to the jury extolling socialism and the newly formed Russian Soviet Republic. "International socialism was argued in court," an astonished John Reed, the most famous of the defendants, later wrote, "thanks to the curiosity and the fair-mindedness of Judge Manton." Reed also praised Manton for giving a jury charge that "vindicated" free speech principles by explaining that the defendants had the right to criticize the government so long as they did not intend to discourage recruiting or cause disobedience in the armed forces. The jury deadlocked.[9]

By the time of the *Masses* trial, Manton technically was not a district judge anymore. Before he could barely warm his lower court seat, an opportunity for advancement arose.

* * *

In early 1917, Second Circuit judge Albert C. Coxe announced his retirement. Manton felt confident that, this time, the Wilson Administration would pick him for the Court of Appeals. Even before Coxe's resignation was public knowledge, Assistant US Attorney John Knox was in Manton's courtroom watching a fellow prosecutor try a case when, during a break, Manton beckoned Knox up to the bench. Leaning over, Manton told Knox that Coxe was resigning and that Manton thought he would be named as Coxe's replacement. What's more, Manton felt he might be able to name his own successor. "How would you like to be a district judge?," Manton asked Knox, who had gotten his job in the US Attorney's Office through his Tammany political connections but was considered an able lawyer in his own right.[10]

Ultimately, both of Manton's predictions were vindicated. But it took a full year for President Wilson to act. Furious jockeying for Coxe's seat took place in the interim. Learned Hand, eight years older than Manton and a Southern District judge since 1909, believed the position should be his. Hand had many influential supporters in Washington. He enlisted leading Progressive intellectuals like Walter Lippmann, Herbert Croly, and Felix Frankfurter to promote his cause. Other friends such as George Rublee, Wilson's FTC chairman, and New York lawyer and civic leader Charles Culp ("C. C.") Burlingham were also busy "intriguing" on Hand's behalf.[11]

Attorney General Gregory, again mediating between different factions, had his own ideas. The Second Circuit did not have a seasoned patent lawyer on the court, and Gregory decided to recommend New York lawyer Thomas Ewing, currently serving as commissioner of patents. Ewing was backed by former senator James O'Gorman of New York. News of Ewing's rise left Manton "a good deal chagrined." Wilson, however, rejected Ewing, who was "far from being a loyal supporter of the administration."[12]

Later in the summer, Hand too gave Wilson cause to doubt Hand's loyalty to the administration. In a prelude to the government's indictment of the *Masses* editors, the postmaster general, acting under the newly enacted Espionage Act of 1917, barred distribution of the magazine through the US mail. The *Masses* brought suit challenging the ban, and the case was assigned to Hand. Hand ruled in favor of the magazine, narrowly construing the Espionage Act against the backdrop of an original and unusually speech-protective interpretation of the First Amendment. Suppression of hostile criticism of the government cannot be based on its predicted effects (the then-prevailing judicial view), Hand postulated; only direct incitement to illegal action warrants punishment.[13]

In time, Hand's "incitement" test proved to be a landmark in free speech jurisprudence, influencing Justice Holmes's stirring dissent in *Abrams v. United States* two years later and eventually becoming, in substance, the law of the land. In the short term, however, with American troops fighting and dying on French soil, Hand's defense of antiwar radicals met with widespread condemnation, including from the Second

Circuit, which swiftly overturned his ruling.[14] Hand knew the case could sink his opportunity for promotion to the Circuit. Nonetheless, he wrote his wife, he had no choice but to "do the right as I see it" and render a decision "absolutely devoid of any such considerations." "[I]f I have limitations of judgment," he continued, "I may have to suffer for it, but I want to be sure that . . . I have none of character."[15]

No such scruples impeded Manton's path to the Second Circuit. His published decisions during his brief tenure on the district court, workmanlike and conventional, steered clear of controversy and caused no stir. Generally though not invariably, Manton sided with the government. One month after the United States declared war on Germany, Manton gave a speech lauding Wilson as "the greatest peace President our country has had in its history" and as destined to become "the greatest war President" too.[16] And he enjoyed the active support of both the Brooklyn Democratic organization and Tammany Hall.[17] With Ewing out of the running and Hand fading, Manton emerged as the frontrunner in late 1917.

The prospect of a Manton appointment sickened Hand and his allies. "I can't believe that Manton will be appointed," Frankfurter wrote Hand. To Hand, Manton seemed the least competent of his Southern District colleagues, someone who "spent more time with his political cronies and on self-promotion than on preparing adequate opinions." Hand tried to foment opposition to Manton, telling Lippman that Justice Louis D. Brandeis "might be willing to raise a hand" to block a Manton appointment. Even after learning, in January 1918, that he had been eliminated from contention, Hand expressed the hope to Frankfurter that Gregory "will select a better man than Manton." A few days later, Hand heard "on pretty good authority" that Gus Hand would replace Coxe. "That will be a splendid appointment," he wrote Frankfurter with cousinly pride, adding, with a burst of Schadenfreude: "I suspect our friend M.T.M. is out of it and it seems to me he is exhibiting some signs of uneasiness."[18]

In the end, Hand was triply disappointed: the post did not go to one Hand or the other, but to Manton. Gregory preferred a faithful Democrat with strong party support and a reputation as a proponent of vigorous enforcement of the antitrust laws. The Brooklyn Democratic organization was reportedly "pleased." On March 12, 1918, President Wilson announced Manton's appointment, along with Knox's to the district court.[19] Just as he had been the nation's youngest federal district judge, now Manton, still only thirty-seven, was its youngest judge on the circuit court level. He was, and still is, the youngest judge named to the Second Circuit in its history.

* * *

In the early twentieth century, a federal judgeship could serve, for those so inclined, as a platform for patronage. The Democratic apparatchiks who in 1916 urged that Manton be named to the district court rather than the circuit court, to maximize his patronage potential, knew what they were talking about. Addressing the American Bar Association as its newly elected head in 1913, former president William H. Taft decried the "patronage that [federal] judges have exercised" and focused, in particular, on the "[a]buses [that] have grown out of appointments to receiverships and to other temporary lucrative positions." Separate bankruptcy courts and bankruptcy judges had yet to be established. When a business declared bankruptcy, a federal judge typically would appoint a receiver to handle its affairs. These assignments, which could generate tens of thousands of dollars or more in fees, were doled out to private lawyers or other private citizens selected by the judge in his sole discretion. "It would be well if possible," Taft somewhat tepidly recommended, "to relieve judges of such duties."[20]

Federal judges had not been relieved of those duties by the time Manton came on the bench in 1916, and he exercised them in the manner that local Democrats expected. A review of Manton's receivership appointments reveals dozens and dozens of instances in which he chose Democratic politicians, politically connected lawyers, business associates, friends, and even family as recipients of his largesse. These appointments were not shrouded in secrecy; leading New York City newspapers reported on federal receiverships daily. "Within a few months" of becoming a judge, the FBI's subsequent investigation in 1939 discovered, Manton came under criticism for "the manner in which he appointed bankruptcy receivers." But these criticisms "had no effect" on his rise to the Second Circuit.[21]

Manton's very first receivership when he assumed the bench in September 1916 went to State Senator Robert F. Wagner, who was among the guests at the dinner at the Hotel Claridge celebrating Manton's appointment.[22] As co-receivers for Continental Public Works, a major contractor, Manton named Stuart G. Gibboney, who also attended the Claridge dinner, and Joseph A. Flynn, the dinner's host, who had supported Manton's candidacy for a judgeship.[23] Manton also handed out multiple receiverships to a different Democratic state senator who later married the stepdaughter of Tammany boss Charlie Murphy;[24] another Democratic state senator who would be convicted of grand larceny in 1934;[25] and a top Murphy aide and advisor to Tammany's successful mayoral candidate in 1917, John H. Delaney.[26] Delaney and Manton were also friends and business partners. Just before being named a district judge in 1916, Manton invested $20,000 in a milk bottling company, Atlantic Bottle Co., of which Delaney was a principal shareholder.

Manton managed to continue making receivership appointments after his promotion to the Second Circuit. In this he was not unique. What was unusual was the extent to which cronyism and nepotism colored Manton's selections. George V. S. Williams, a former public service commissioner and "Brooklyn lieutenant" of Tammany boss Charlie Murphy, was a co-owner with Manton in a laundry business; he got no fewer than eight receiverships from Manton.[27] Samuel L. Reis, a non-lawyer, got nine receiverships from Manton at the same time he served as an officer and director of a Manton real estate entity and the leasing agent for Manton's real estate properties.[28] Manton also named Daniel E. Lynch a receiver five different times in 1922, the year before Lynch became president of the Forest Hills Terrace Corp., another Manton real estate investment vehicle.[29]

Perhaps most notable (and front-page news in the Brooklyn press) was the receivership Manton gave a twenty-one-year-old John H. McCooey Jr.—son of the Brooklyn Democratic boss—only two months after he graduated law school and the same month he became a member of the bar.[30] McCooey Jr.—who was "far from a brilliant lawyer"[31]—got four more receiverships from Manton the following year.[32] For good measure Manton named Leader McCooey's younger son Herbert, who was not even a lawyer yet, as receiver for another firm.[33]

Manton also rewarded Thomas B. Felder, a former solicitor general of Georgia known for his political connections in Washington. Felder apparently helped engineer Manton's elevation to the Second Circuit. When Manton asked John Knox if he wanted to become a district court judge, he told Knox to go see Felder, whom he described as "something of a lobbyist."[34] After Manton moved to the Second Circuit, Felder practiced law with W. Bourke Cockran. Manton named Felder as a receiver at least four times, including for some major companies, and as a special master in a copyright case.[35] In 1925 Felder's influence-peddling finally caught up with him when he was convicted in federal court in Manhattan of taking $65,000 to bribe President Harding's attorney general, Henry Daugherty, to dismiss mail fraud charges brought against a group of stock swindlers. Manton testified as a character witness at Felder's trial (and then had to be prodded by the prosecutor into recusing himself from hearing Felder's appeal). When Felder died three years later, his will appointed Manton trustee for a fund to be used for the benefit of Felder's son.[36]

Those closest to Manton benefitted the most. Fellow Brooklynite John B. Johnston worked with Manton on the Charles Becker trial. Although only three years out of law school at the time, Johnston was close in age to Manton and the two became good friends. Johnston continued to practice with Cockran's firm after Manton's appointment to the bench. A Democrat, Johnston was elected to Congress from Brooklyn in 1918 but served only one term. Before, during, and after Johnston went to Washington, Manton funneled him a steady stream of receiverships: at least two dozen over five years.[37] This cozy relationship attracted attention from the press, which reported in 1924 that Johnston had reaped more than $133,000 from Manton's appointments. Later, when Johnston ran for the State Supreme Court, Republicans used this as an attack line, claiming that all the money Johnston was making from Manton's appointments explained why he had showed up in Washington for only one-third of the votes taken when he was a congressman.[38] Johnston won the Supreme Court election anyway and served as a state court judge for the next quarter-century.

The single largest beneficiary of Manton's largesse was Thomas H. Matters Jr., named a receiver more than thirty times between 1917 and 1922.[39] Although the Nebraska-born Matters graduated from Harvard Law School in 1911, he had not been practicing law in New York for very long. But Matters held one strong qualification in Manton's eyes: He was Manton's brother-in-law, married to Eva's sister Amy. Matters had been invited to join Cockran & Manton in 1916, but Manton's appointment as a judge spoiled that plan.[40] Manton, perhaps, felt he needed to find another way to help his brother-in-law earn a good living.

Or perhaps Manton meant to profit personally. When he formed Forest Hills Terrace Corp. in 1923, his brother-in-law became one of its largest investors. Surely at least some of the $37,000 Matters plowed into Manton's enterprise came from the fees he reaped from Manton's receivership appointments. By the end of the year Matters had transferred his shares to Eva Manton, seemingly for no consideration (based on a 1939 FBI summary of corporate records).[41] Johnston too bought over $15,000 of Forest Hills Terrace stock in 1924; this "investment" may also have simply been a way to funnel receiver fees back to Manton, judging from Johnston's failure to recall it when interviewed by the FBI years later.[42] It does not take an overly active imagination to wonder also if shady lawyers such as Felder kicked back to Manton a slice (say, 10 percent) of their receiver fees, or if Manton, when working out financial arrangements with business associates he appointed as receivers (e.g., how he and Williams divided up profits in their laundry ventures, or what he paid Reis, his real estate agent), negotiated more favorable terms for himself in consideration of the fees he had put into their pockets.

Federal authorities investigating Manton in 1939 heard another disturbing account from those days. In 1921, Manton had installed two of his business partners, Williams and James J. Sullivan, as co-receivers for the Carl H. Schultz Corporation. When Walter T. Kohn, a lawyer representing parties seeking to purchase the bankrupt company's assets, pressed Manton to adopt his clients' plan over the receivers' plan, Manton angrily threatened to hold him in contempt. Later that evening, Sullivan paid a visit to Kohn's office to explain the source of the judge's ire. Kohn "was bucking Manton himself," Sullivan told Kohn, as Manton was personally "interested" in Carl H. Schultz and the receivers were "working for Manton." Kohn got the message. He dropped the case because "he did not wish to jeopardize any future practice which he may have in the Federal Courts."[43]

Contemporary observers also doubted whether Manton was deciding cases purely on their merits. Root Clark, the prestigious white-shoe law firm, filed a motion on behalf of stockholders of a company in a bankruptcy proceeding before Manton. According to a report in *The Bull*, Root Clark's in-house publication, a firm lawyer named Henderson believed the motion would succeed on its merits. Familiar with Manton, Emory Buckner, one of the era's greatest lawyers, had a different view. "Mr. Henderson thinks our motion will be granted. Mr. Buckner thinks otherwise. Mr. Henderson knows the law and Mr. Buckner knows the judge."[44]

In 1919 the Consolidated Gas Co. challenged a New York State law imposing a price cap on gas. The City of New York sought to intervene in the case. Southern District judge Julius Mayer denied the City's motion and the Second Circuit upheld Mayer's ruling. But Manton brought the proceedings to a halt by granting a stay pending the City's application to the Supreme Court.[45] As Gus Hand read the situation, "that hound of a Manton" must have been doing the bidding of Tammany-backed Mayor John Hylan. "Nothing but the kind of politics played by a 'pie faced mut[t]' like Hylan could make [Manton] grant stays as he has in the Consolidated Gas case," he wrote his cousin Learned. "I hope we shall live to see him get out for he is a Bad one."[46]

Eyebrows rose higher after Manton's unusual intervention in a high-profile case involving the comptroller of the City of New York, Charles L. Craig. Craig, swept into office along with Mayor Hylan in a Tammany wave in 1917, had harshly criticized a ruling by Judge Mayer in a case involving the city's subway system. In February 1921, a thin-skinned Mayer held Craig in contempt of court, saying his comments were "intended to play on human frailty and to deflect and deter the Court from the performance of its duty."[47] When Craig refused to retract his comments as the judge expected, Mayer sentenced Craig to sixty days in jail. As the marshal took Craig into custody, his lawyer assured reporters that "we'll have him out of this in five minutes." Whereupon the lawyer went upstairs to Judge Manton's chambers and obtained a writ of habeas corpus.[48]

Two months later Manton, acting as a single judge, overturned Mayer's contempt order. "There is no divinity about the office or duties of a judge which makes him free from criticism," Manton decreed, not insensibly[49]—but wholly without authority, as both a three-judge panel of the Second Circuit and the Supreme Court would later determine. Individual circuit judges have no power to issue writs of habeas corpus, those courts ruled.[50] Privately Chief Justice Taft denounced Manton's peculiar action as a "breach of judicial comity" that "revealed the characteristics that he was known to have at the Bar."[51]

In the conventional understanding of our legal system, the one in which the Hands saw themselves operating, judges decide cases based on neutrally determined facts and legal rules that transcend the particular dispute and the particular parties. In this idealized conception, the parties enter the courtroom shorn of their identities; in the language of the law they are the "plaintiff" and the "defendant," the "party of the first part" and the "party of the second part," the "creditor" and the "debtor," abstractions that can sometimes work injustice but are designed to immunize judicial decision-making from impurities. Manton did not approach the business of judging in that same way. Transactional considerations of the kind that typify the political process, anathema to the Hands and most other judges, were acceptable to Manton. In March 1919, he wrote Learned Hand about Henry Malkan, a bookseller who employed Manton when he was a student at Columbia. Malkan's creditors had forced his bookstore, once the largest in the city, into bankruptcy at the end of 1918, and the case was before Judge Hand.[52] "Will you see [Malkan] and listen to his troubles," Manton asked Hand, explaining that "[w]hen I needed a job very badly while working my way thru college" the man had given him one. Manton would appreciate "whatever kindness you may show him."[53] Almost certainly Manton saw nothing improper in this overture, despite its open suggestion that Hand treat a litigant more favorably than he otherwise would because of Manton's personal relationship. Almost certainly Hand viewed it as another manifestation of Manton's unsuitability for the federal judiciary.

* * *

On September 5, 1922, the White House released word that Supreme Court justice William R. Day planned to retire. Inconceivable as it may seem in today's hyper-partisan climate, the Republican administration of Warren G. Harding looked to replace Day with a Democrat. According to then-prevailing political custom, at least three members of the Supreme Court should hail from the minority party.[54] Harding had just replaced one of Wilson's three appointees, John H. Clarke, a Democrat, with a Republican, leaving only two Democrats remaining (Justices Brandeis and James Clark McReynolds). "I very much wish to avoid the accusation of being unduly partisan," Harding explained to Columbia University president Nicholas Murray Butler.[55]

Religious and geographical considerations also factored into the administration's calculus. The Court's lone Catholic, seventy-nine-year-old Justice Joseph McKenna, was expected to retire soon. With qualified Republican Catholics in short supply, Harding preferred to name a Democratic Catholic now. The time also seemed propitious to plug a gap created by Charles Evans Hughes's resignation from the Court in 1916: the absence of any justices from the nation's most populous state, New York. Age mattered too. Harding wanted a younger man who could serve for decades.[56]

Martin T. Manton met all of Harding's criteria: a Democrat, a Catholic, a New Yorker, and at forty-two younger than any justice at the time of appointment since before the Civil War. Further, and despite his relative youth, Manton could claim six years of prior federal judicial experience, more than any current member of the Court at the time of appointment save for Taft and Willis Van Devanter. Manton mobilized a range of powerful and influential supporters to lobby Harding on his behalf. His advocates began with the Roman Catholic Church. A faithful Catholic—"Praying Manton," outside the courtroom—Manton was a generous contributor to the Church and active in Catholic organizations.

Archbishop Patrick Hayes of New York, the leading Catholic prelate in the nation, visited the White House and pushed hard for Manton. Through the bishop of Brooklyn, Manton lobbied Boston's Cardinal William H. O'Connell to put in a "good word" for him with Massachusetts senator Henry Cabot Lodge, the Senate majority leader. The entire Church hierarchy in the East was "solid behind him."[57]

Leading businessmen offered secular support. Two steel magnates, both good friends of Harding, Elbert H. Gary of U.S. Steel and Charles M. Schwab of Bethlehem Steel, issued strong recommendations to the president on Manton's behalf. Newspaper publisher Frank A. Munsey, who had endorsed Harding in 1920, assured the president that Manton's appointment "would be strategically wise." "Friends of the party" in New York also favored Manton, a US senator told Harding. One of these was Harry B. Rosen, a "warm friend" of Manton influential in Republican circles because of his prowess as a fundraiser. Dubbed "the finance king of films," Rosen had helped Harding's campaign manager and first postmaster general, Will H. Hays, land a lucrative job as head of the newly formed Motion Picture Producers and Distributors Association. Now Rosen prevailed upon Hays, who remained a Harding confidant, to write the president to press for Manton's appointment.[58]

Not only Rosen, but many "Jews of influence" went to bat for Manton, according to Learned Hand, who found this "very [curious]." "How he got such a backing I don't know. One must credit him with the most amazing astuteness," a mystified Hand wrote Felix Frankfurter. Hand expected Frankfurter to be "chagrined to learn" of Manton's Jewish support, and Frankfurter wrote back that he was, indeed, "chagrined." "What is the secret," the future Supreme Court justice wondered, "why should 'influential Jews' be for him particularly. But then—influential Jews are like 'influential' other guys." Other men of influence like Thomas Felder, to whom Manton had given multiple receiverships, also weighed in. Felder's friend Attorney General Daugherty was said to be "very favorabl[y]" disposed to Manton's candidacy.[59]

Unfortunately for Manton, a nearly three-hundred-pound, seemingly immovable obstacle stood in the way of his ambitions.[60] Harding had appointed former president William H. Taft as chief justice the year before, and he leaned heavily on Taft for advice on who else to name to the high court. Perhaps sensing Taft's influence, Manton had tried to get in Taft's good graces. In the summer of 1922, invited along with others by the *New York Times* to list the twelve greatest living American men, Manton had ranked Taft second, behind only his political hero Woodrow Wilson. Heaping praise on "America's foremost jurist" in language as inelegant as it was unctuous, Manton hailed Taft for bringing to the Court "a statesmanship which, combined with an excellent training and equipment, will do much to fashion the judicial decrees of that court, with a view to progressive rules for human society."[61]

Taft, however, loathed Manton. In Taft's view, Manton was "an utterly unfit man for our Court," a "shrewd, cunning, political Judge" lacking in the basic "moral qualities" indispensable to serve in such a high position. Manton's selection would "embarrass" the president and be "deplorable" for the country. Indeed, "Taft felt that [Manton] never should have been appointed to the bench in the first place—and would not [have] been if Wilson and Tammany Hall had not put him there." Taft's contempt for Manton mirrored that of many members of New York's legal establishment, including Taft's former attorney general, George Wickersham, and his brother Harry Taft, partners in the Wall Street firm of Cadwalader, Wickersham & Taft.[62]

As Manton's candidacy gathered momentum, the establishment lawyers banded together to block it. Meeting in Harry Taft's home, the Judiciary Committee of the Association of the Bar of the City of New York resolved unanimously to "do everything possible to prevent the appointment of Manton." Wickersham kept Taft apprised of Manton's machinations. "I understand Manton is pulling every wire he can," he wrote Taft on October 10. He fed Taft ammunition to use against Manton. "Appalled by the English in one of Manton's opinions," Wickersham sent a marked-up copy of the opinion to Taft along with his verdict that "composition of this order" would not "enhance the prestige of any judicial tribunal."[63] Elihu Root confirmed that Manton was "one of Wilson's worst judicial appointments" and lacked "the confidence or respect of the bar" in New York. "He is purely a product of intrigue and if the people get that idea of the Supreme Court they will smash the whole outfit." Root,

Wickersham and John G. Milburn, of the Wall Street firm of Carter, Ledyard & Milburn, summoned Columbia president Nicholas Butler to a luncheon at the Downtown Club of New York. "In no restrained language" they cajoled Butler, who was on intimate terms with the president, into seeing Harding and protesting Manton's appointment.[64]

But a suitable alternative from New York that fit the administration's profile—young, Catholic, Democratic—proved elusive. Taft wooed former solicitor general John W. Davis, a Democrat and Wall Street lawyer, but Davis was a Protestant and, in any event, not prepared to take the necessary pay cut. New York Court of Appeals judge Benjamin N. Cardozo, a fifty-two-year-old Democrat, came highly recommended from multiple sources, and Taft agreed that Cardozo was "the best judge in the State of New York." But Cardozo was a Jew and "it would not do to have two Jews on the Supreme Court," sniffed Wickersham, whose family arrived in America in 1700. What's more, Taft disparaged Cardozo as "what they call a progressive judge," the wrong philosophy for the conservative chief justice. Taft similarly dismissed Learned Hand, although of "proper age" and an "able judge" (appointed by Taft himself), as "a wild Roosevelt man and a Progressive" who, if promoted to the top court, "would most certainly herd with Brandeis and be a dissenter." Various New York Republicans who merited consideration were rejected because they were in their sixties.[65]

Expanding beyond New York, Taft's gaze landed on Pierce Butler, of St. Paul, Minnesota. Although a midwesterner, Butler, a fifty-six-year-old Democrat and Catholic, hit the administration's other sweet spots. Even better, he was a steadfast legal conservative. Butler mainly represented railroads, often defending them against government regulation, and as a University of Minnesota regent had lambasted "radical" left-wing professors.[66] In his disdain for self-promotion (he made a point of assuring Taft that he "did nothing directly or indirectly to suggest the thought to anyone or in any way to reinforce the suggestion"), Butler was the anti-Manton. For Taft, Butler represented the best hope of derailing Manton's candidacy. Working through his allies and Butler's friends, Taft rallied support for Butler from Catholic leaders in the Midwest and West to counter the New York church hierarchy that, Taft felt, was part of the "conspiracy" backing Manton.[67]

"Archbishop Hayes," Taft wrote Butler, "should be ashamed of himself for pressing Manton." The Catholic Church would deserve the "condemnation it ought to have were it to be successful in procuring the appointment of a man like Manton." Taft also vented at the influence brought to bear by other supposed conspirators like Rosen, who had "made himself useful politically to Republicans" through his campaign donations—and, Taft added, wholly gratuitously, was "a Jew." (Ironically, Taft dropped this aside in a letter that elsewhere touted his purported belief that a Supreme Court nominee's religion was a matter of indifference to him.)[68]

Up until the end, Harding nearly picked Manton nevertheless. The White House was flooded with telegrams and the president, a politician and not a lawyer, was impressed by Manton's vigorous and influential support from the Church, businessmen, and political figures. "Strong pressure recently has been brought upon the President to appoint Judge Martin T. Manton," the *New York Times* reported on October 27, 1922. Over the next two weeks came published reports from "well informed circles" that Manton "likely" would be named Day's successor. The Reverend John J. Wynne, S.J., editor of the Catholic magazine *America*, induced R. J. Cuddihy, editor of the *Literary Digest*, to back Manton, lobbied a "mercantile friend who has influence with the Cabinet," and called at Taft's home in Washington to urge Manton's appointment, "a matter which I have much at heart." On November 18, newly elected Governor Alfred E. Smith of New York telegrammed Attorney General Daugherty that "it would be most gratifying to me if Judge Martin T. Manton was appointed to the Supreme Bench."[69]

By this time, however, Taft and Daugherty had prevailed upon Harding to appoint Butler, not Manton. On November 22, the president signed Butler's nomination and forwarded it on to the Senate.

The New York legal establishment breathed a collective sigh of relief. "We New Yorkers," as C. C. Burlingham put it, "are all much pleased with the appointment of Butler and the elimination of 'M.'" Learned Hand counseled Frankfurter not to be too hard on Butler, despite the railroad lawyer's conservative reputation, for "[w]hatever he may turn out to be, he certainly saved us from Manton, and he will be welcome for that. I know whereof I speak and there is no shadow of doubt that till a few days before the appointment Manton had it." Manton, as Supreme Court justice Robert H. Jackson later put it, "had come within an ace of being appointed to the Supreme Court at the time of the appointment of Pierce Butler."[70]

* * *

What if Manton had secured a seat on the Supreme Court? As historian Daniel J. Danelski has speculated, Manton "still might have been 'the Corrupt Judge,' only on a grander scale."[71] A corruption scandal involving Supreme Court justice Manton rather than senior circuit judge Manton would have inflicted exponentially more damage to US institutions. Fortunately, the Court has remained free from this kind of blemish. Abe Fortas's greed as a Supreme Court justice in the late 1960s comes the closest, but Fortas never took money from litigants, was never the subject of a criminal prosecution, and wound up tarnishing his own reputation rather than the Court's.[72] Taft and others who worked to stave off Manton's appointment thus emerge as the heroes of this slice of American political and judicial history, the saviors of the Supreme Court from a uniquely pernicious form of defilement.

But there is good reason to doubt that Manton would have engaged in financial misconduct on the Supreme Court. Motive and opportunity supply the oxygen for most crimes, and the rarified air of the high court may have deprived Manton of both. Living in Washington, Manton may have avoided the business entanglements and corresponding financial reversals that placed him in a compromising position when the Great Depression hit. The incentives on the part of litigants and their lawyers to grease his palm may also have been much diminished—not because the cases were less important, but because the would-be corrupters could not necessarily be assured of getting enough bang for the buck. On the Supreme Court Manton would have been one of nine votes rather than one of three. In a case with a badly fractured Court, one vote could be decisive, but such divisions were rare in patent and commercial disputes where Manton tended to misuse his authority in the Second Circuit.

While Taft and Manton's other adversaries genuinely, and justifiably, questioned Manton's moral fitness, ideological considerations also stoked their opposition. Resolutely conservative, Taft could live with Harding's desire for a Democrat, provided the nominee was of "sound" views. With his pro-business background, Pierce Butler fit the bill. He was a Democrat "of the [Grover] Cleveland type," Taft noted, approvingly, in recommending Butler to Harding. In other words, Butler was not a Wilsonian progressive like Brandeis, whose nomination Taft fiercely opposed in 1916 (calling it "an evil and a disgrace"), or a liberal like Hand and Cardozo, two supremely qualified and irreproachably ethical jurists whom Taft rejected for promotion. Manton lacked the intellectual depth of these liberal giants, or their commitment to civil rights and liberties, but he had made a career of fighting big business and, as his judicial record during the New Deal would confirm, supported government intervention in the economy. This was unacceptable to Taft, who counted his conservative Supreme Court appointments as "the proudest deeds of his presidency" and was "determined to secure replacements to carry on the conservative tradition and to maintain the judiciary as the final bulwark in the defense of property."[73]

Which raises an even more intriguing "what if" question: how a Justice Manton would have affected the Supreme Court's reaction to the New Deal. Butler, one of the notorious "Four Horsemen" of reactionary justices (along with Van Devanter, McReynolds, and George Sutherland), opposed every New Deal measure to come before the Court, and became, in H. L. Mencken's phrase, "the chief demon in [the liberals'] menagerie."[74] "A bully, a pugilist, a man who had lifted himself out of poverty and disdained those who could not manage the same," Butler clung to the belief that laissez-faire individualism was frozen in place by the Constitution.[75] Almost certainly Manton would have voted with the three liberal justices (Brandeis, Cardozo, and Harlan F. Stone) to uphold the Roosevelt Administration's economic reforms.

While many of the Supreme Court's controversial decisions during this period were 6–3, with Chief Justice Hughes and Justice Owen

Roberts joining the Four Horsemen, the conservatives sometimes issued 5–4 decisions, such as Butler's 1936 opinion for the Court in *Morehead v. Tipaldo* invalidating New York's minimum wage law for women. Moreover, scholars have questioned whether Chief Justice Hughes would have actually voted to cripple the New Deal and defy the will of the American people if his had been the critical swing vote rather than part of a six-justice majority, as it would have been had Manton sat on the Court rather than Butler. It has been suggested that Hughes sided with the conservatives more to foster public acceptance of the Court's decisions (a 6–3 ruling seeming more authoritative than a 5–4 one) than out of fidelity to his constitutional principles.[76] If Hughes had been pulled within the orbit of a four-justice liberal bloc that included a Justice Manton, there would have been no sweeping judicial renunciation of New Deal programs, no epic clash between the Court and the Roosevelt Administration, no Court-packing plan proposed by FDR to resolve that conflict, no "switch in time that saved nine." Our constitutional history today would look very different indeed.

It may well be that in blocking Martin T. Manton from serving on the Supreme Court, William Taft saved the Court from terrible embarrassment. It may also be that Taft's decision helped precipitate the greatest constitutional crisis in the Supreme Court's history.

CHAPTER SIX

"Material Things"

Manton's Roaring Twenties

THWARTED IN HIS HOPES OF ADVANCEMENT TO THE SUPREME COURT, Manton stayed put in New York and focused on making money as well as law. It was a good time to be business-minded, especially for those, like Manton, interested in real estate. The 1920s were "the most spectacular decade of building in the city's history." From late 1921 to the Crash of 1929, a new building rose in New York every fifty-one minutes.[1] Prices for high-end Manhattan properties doubled over the same period.[2]

In early 1923 Manton acquired a sixty-acre plot of land in Forest Hills, Queens from the heirs of an Omaha businessmen in a transaction brokered by his Nebraskan-born brother-in-law, Thomas H. Matters Jr. Forest Hills's proximity to an LIRR stop, only a fourteen-minute ride to Penn Station, made it an attractive new neighborhood for middle-class commuters. Manton's company, the Forest Hills Terrace Corporation, developed the land into cooperative apartment buildings and single-family and two-family homes.[3] Manton later formed a separate company, Marian Realty Co., that bought up two-family houses on Exeter Street in Forest Hills.[4]

From the considerable profits generated by his Forest Hills investment, Manton, together with a real estate developer named Stuard Hirschman, purchased an even larger tract of land in Queens. Measuring some 206 acres, the parcel stretched from Bowery Bay in North Astoria down to Jackson Heights almost as far as Northern Boulevard. It housed one of New York's first small airports, Holmes Airport, which opened in 1929. Manton envisioned it as the site of the city's major commercial airport and for years tried to find financial backing for the project. Those efforts did not succeed, but Manton's idea had merit. Another small airfield in Queens, located just a mile to the northeast, was subsequently purchased by the city and turned into what is now LaGuardia Airport.[5]

In Brooklyn Manton owned a four-story commercial building in a prime location on Washington Street extending through to Fulton Street. His tenants included haberdashers and the Brooklyn branch office of the *New York Times*.[6] Landlord Manton attended the opening of the *Times'* branch office along with top Brooklyn Democratic and Republican politicians and Brooklyn newspapermen. The following year Judge Manton, acting as an arbitrator, delivered a sweeping victory to the *Times* and New York's other dailies in a dispute with the pressmen's union over wages and working conditions, deciding nearly every point in favor of the publishers. The "Manton Award," as it came to be known, lengthened the workers' hours and decreased their earning capacity by 35 percent, according to the union's president.[7] Manton sold the Brooklyn building in 1926 for a "huge profit," nearly five times what he had paid for it in a foreclosure sale a decade earlier.[8]

Manton invested most actively in Manhattan real estate, both residential and commercial properties. These were typically short-term plays rather than long-term investments. The Turin, an apartment house at 331 Central Park West that Manton invested in with his partner Joseph Doolittle, was held for two years and then sold for $1.3 million. It took Manton less than a year to flip a $1.3 million fourteen-story apartment building on Seventh Avenue and 54th Street. A sixteen-story loft and commercial structure at Fourth Avenue and 28th Street held in the name of his secretary, Marie Schmalz, was sold just a month after it was bought for $1.25 million.[9]

Upper Manhattan, and especially Washington Heights, then attracting droves of Irish and other first- and second-generation immigrants escaping from overcrowded conditions downtown, caught Manton's eye as well. He bought and sold a newly constructed six-story apartment building on Broadway between 169th and 170th Streets. In less than two months, one of his firms flipped a $900,000 architecturally award-winning apartment complex on Fort Washington Avenue. Manton accumulated eight other apartment houses in Upper Manhattan and the Bronx, containing 337 apartments, that he sold as a package for $2.3 million in 1926. These properties later came back to him, apparently because the buyer (later convicted of forgery) defaulted on a purchase-money mortgage.[10]

The crown jewels in Manton's portfolio were two luxury "apartment hotels" on the Upper West Side. Apartment hotels offered full-time residents and transient guests amenities such as restaurants and housekeeping services, dispensing with the need for kitchens and servants. In 1925, Forest Hills Terrace Corp. paid nearly $3 million for the Hotel Alamac at an auction sale. The Alamac, located at Broadway and 71st Street, had gone into receivership mere months after it opened in 1923. It featured Japanese-inspired décor, a Japanese grill on the second floor, and a restaurant and dance floor on the twentieth floor called the "Congo Room," with tables designed as African huts, wall murals sporting exotic flora and fauna, and its own "Hotel Alamac Orchestra."[11] Around the same time Manton acquired the fourteen-story Hotel Esplanade a few blocks away, on Central Park West and 74th Street. Completed in 1921, the Esplanade was "one of the most modern of the uptown multi-family structures" and "command[ed] extensive views of the Hudson and Palisades."[12] Manton borrowed heavily to buy these hotels, incurring millions of dollars of mortgage debt.

Manton did not handle the day-to-day operation of these properties himself. He relied mainly on his business associate James J. Sullivan. Sullivan was the president of the Alamac-Esplanade Corporation, which held title to the two hotels and Manton's apartment houses, although Sullivan's ownership interest in the company was minimal. Sullivan also presided over the Sulmar Realty Corporation, the managing agent for the properties. Sulmar was a combination of Sullivan's last name and Manton's first name. The economic interest in the company was not so evenly divided: Manton owned 81 percent and Sullivan held 19 percent.[13]

Real estate represented only one dimension of Judge Manton's outside business interests. In 1919, together with Sullivan and former public commissioner George V. S. Williams, he acquired a laundry business in Brooklyn, whose newspaper ads promised to put an end to "wash day drudgery in Brooklyn homes."[14] In 1923 Manton and Sullivan started a carpet cleaning business, Modern Carpet Cleaning and Storage Corp., located in Upper Manhattan ("By our scientific process we guarantee to restore to your rugs their original freshness, with added lustre").[15] Two years later Manton, Sullivan, and Williams invested $100,000 in a Pennsylvania coal company, Harleigh Coal Co. They lost their entire investment when the coal company went belly-up shortly thereafter. But Manton could afford setbacks like this. Around the same time he sold off his interests in several Brooklyn laundries reportedly for a profit of $250,000.[16]

In 1927, Manton and Sullivan formed National Cellulose Corp. to acquire a paper mill located in Baldwinsville, New York, near Syracuse. Cellulose fiber bundles in wood pulp act as the base for a wide variety of paper products. National Cellulose's leading product would be facial tissues, sold under private brand names in department stores, drugstores, and variety chains. The company also would enter the nascent sanitary napkin industry, competing with the likes of Kotex. Sullivan served as president of National Cellulose, working out of its executive offices in Manhattan. Manton was the principal stockholder. Not visible in the company's capital structure were minority stakes held by two prominent Wall Street lawyers whose interests were disguised and unknown until becoming part of Manton's corruption scandal a dozen years later.[17]

Rarely did Manton pass up an opportunity to make money. In his native Sayville, he owned and operated a working farm. There, he raised and sold swine and boars, along with potatoes, turnips, cabbage, and other vegetables. In newspaper ads "Judge Martin T. Manton, Owner," invited Long Islanders to bid on "Pure Bred Duroc Hogs" and hawked potatoes whose "steaming aroma will tell you before tasting that they are full-flavored and fresh from the fields."[18]

Manton's net worth grew steadily. By the end of the decade, he was worth more than $2.7 million, or over $45 million in today's dollars.[19]

* * *

Unlike his great-uncle "Hermit Manton," Manton did not hoard his wealth. Like others during the 1920s, Manton consumed liberally, and sometimes conspicuously.

In 1924, the Mantons moved to New York's most fashionable street, Park Avenue.[20] This was the decade when Park Avenue cemented its status as the premier address for New York's upper class, a mix of the old-money elite, who were abdicating their grand nineteenth-century Fifth Avenue mansions, and the hordes of nouveau riche created by the booming economy. Between these two groups Park Avenue housed "the most stupendous aggregation of multimillionaires which the world has ever seen," wrote economist and social critic Stuart Chase in the *New Republic* in 1927. It was "the end of the American ladder of success. Higher one cannot go." A north-south pedestrian promenade cut through each strip of its grassy, landscaped median, forming a nearly forty-block linear park that gave the avenue its name.[21]

Manton's building, 471 Park Avenue, stood at the southern base of the storied thoroughfare, on the southeast corner of 58th Street. Designed by architect Charles W. Buckham, 471 Park Avenue was known for its duplex apartments, majestic cornice, and entrance porch carried on six massive carved pillars. "In a metropolis where individual houses are becoming impossible and undesirable," an architectural critic wrote with specific reference to 471 Park Avenue upon its completion in 1908, the duplex apartment was "a New York creation," where a family "can live as much by themselves as in an Italian palace—but more comfortably."[22] The duplex apartments at 471 Park opened into a studio living room, or salon, that extended the full two stories, more than twenty feet high, with wide double-height windows. A foyer hall, library, dining room, kitchen, and pantry filled the lower floor; a staircase led to three bedrooms above. The apartment rooms were "of an exceptionally large size, . . . more on the order of those found in a private house."[23] Occupying those rooms were dozens of the city's most illustrious citizens, listed in the "Blue Book," a list that now included Martin and Eva Manton, who leased one of 471 Park's duplex apartments.[24]

Manton's primary residence remained his Fairacres estate on Ocean Avenue in Bayport. In 1924 he purchased additional shorefront property adjacent to his own fronting on to the Great South Bay, prompting the local newspaper to note: "Judge Martin T. Manton Now Has Finest Property in Bayport."[25] He and Eva lived in Bayport from the spring until October, when they would shutter the house and move back to the city. "Servants galore" attended to the family's needs in both locations. The children were enrolled in private schools: David was sent off to the elite Westminster boarding school in Simsbury, Connecticut, while Catherine attended Catholic girls' schools in New York.[26]

Manton kept a stable of top-line cars in Bayport, including a Reo coupe, a Cadillac sedan, a Ford station wagon, and a Pierce-Arrow. He also kept a chauffeur to drive him around in these vehicles. Motorboats were another high-speed hobby. The judge could be seen out on Great South Bay in his new thirty-foot mahogany speed runabout, "Frolic." Manton's Dodge Watercar, the "Motor Car of the Sea," gave him such "constant enjoyment" that he wrote a letter praising its "speed, efficiency and endurance," which was reprinted in magazine ads by the manufacturer as an endorsement from "a well-known judge."[27]

Every two years or so, when the Second Circuit shut down for the summer, Manton, together with Eva and the children, would board a much bigger boat, one of the luxury ocean liners of the day, for a transatlantic voyage. Author Donald L. Miller has described the now-forgotten summer ritual for the "patricians of Park Avenue" who, with their "mountains" of luggage, embarked from Chelsea Piers on ships that "looked incredibly romantic, floodlit and overrun with people in evening dress."[28]

The Mantons sailed first class on the three flagships of the United States Lines, all of which had been seized from Germany during the Great War. In 1922 the Mantons left for a six-week European trip aboard the SS *America*, which a decade earlier, as the SS *Amerika*, had futilely signaled the doomed *Titanic* about approaching icebergs.[29] Their next two voyages, in 1924 and 1926, were aboard the SS *Leviathan*, considered the world's largest and fastest ship, which featured the "prewar splendor of Edwardian, Georgian and Louis XVI styles now merged with modern 1920s touches."[30] In 1928 the family embarked on another expensive European vacation, this time on the SS *Washington*, whose sumptuously appointed first-class public rooms included murals commemorating the life of America's first president and a dining saloon, topped with a gilded dome, that spanned the width of the ship.[31]

While the Mantons did not participate in the speakeasy culture of the 1920s—Manton being a teetotaler as well as a federal judge—the society pages captured the Mantons from time to time at more staid venues. They could be seen at charitable events such as the annual Emerald Ball held at venues like the Waldorf-Astoria, seated in a box belonging to one of Manton's business associates, Eva decked out in "amethyst velvet, gold cloth and diamonds." Manton and Eva also formed part of the "representative assembly of society folk" that attended the opening of the opulent French Renaissance dining room at the Savoy-Plaza Hotel, "decorated in pastel shades of green and gray, trimmed with gold leaf and paneled mirrors," its translucent dome giving a "golden glow at night."[32]

At the same time, the Mantons gave generously of their time to a variety of Catholic and other charitable causes. Manton was on the Board of Trustees of the South Side Hospital, and Eva served as chair of its Bayport Ladies' Auxiliaries Committee and treasurer of the Bayport Red Cross. In the city, Manton was elected president of the Catholic Club, considered the country's leading Catholic laymen's organization. He was the only North American lay trustee of the International Eucharistic Congress, and was a founder and the first president of the Catholic Association for International Peace. Eva, too, served on the boards of the Catholic Settlement Association, the Catholic Women's Association, the Catholic Young Women's Club, and the New York Circle of the International Federation of Catholic Alumnae.[33]

In July 1924, Manton received the highest honor offered by the Catholic Church to a layman. While in Amsterdam addressing the International Eucharistic Congress, Manton learned that Pope Pius VI had bestowed upon him a Knighthood in the Order of Saint Gregory, in recognition of Manton's service to the Church.[34] "It is most important to find a layman at the head of a great business, a family, a profession who has been touched by the spirit of charity," Archbishop Ryan said at a Catholic Club dinner later that year honoring Manton and other recipients of the Knighthood.[35]

Manton saw no inconsistency between the materialism of the age and his religious convictions. At the International Eucharistic Congress in 1926, held in Chicago, Manton spoke about prayer, "man's first duty to his Maker, and his chief resource and consolation in distress." The "prayers of savages," Manton noted, often involved petitions for "material prosperity or gain." But this "is also a prominent characteristic of all higher religions," he reminded his audience in the Chicago Coliseum. "The truly civilized being prays for material things" too, albeit "with a spiritual motive."[36] Up until the last few months of 1929, Manton would have been justified in believing that his "civilized" prayers were being answered.

* * *

Partisan politics occupied as much of Manton's time off the bench as his religious and charitable pursuits. Having been "a confidant and political ally of McCooey, the Tammany leader of Brooklyn," Chief Justice Taft seethed in one of his anti-Manton diatribes during the appointment fight in 1922, Manton "is now a politician on the Bench," whose "consultation room is always full of men of that kind."[37]

To a degree that would be unimaginable today, Manton remained active in Democratic politics while serving on the Second Circuit. He donated money to the local Democratic organization and publicly endorsed Tammany-backed candidates in judgeship and district attorney races.[38] He was "credited with still wielding much influence in Kings County" political affairs and regularly attended both local and national political functions, including the quadrennial Democratic presidential nominating conventions.[39] In early 1928 Manton was even named as a delegate to the Democratic National Convention by the Thirteenth Assembly District Democratic club in Brooklyn. That designation reportedly puzzled Tammany Brooklyn boss McCooey and his subordinates, who "questioned whether a Federal Judge is eligible to attend the convention in the official delegate's role," and it was quickly rescinded and blamed on "overenthusiastic friends" of the judge.[40]

No mere spectator at such events, Manton endorsed particular presidential candidates and promoted their candidacies. At the San Francisco convention in 1920, Manton actively "work[ed] for" William G. McAdoo, the former Wilson treasury secretary who led on the first ballot but ultimately fell to Ohio governor James Cox.[41] Switching teams four years later, Manton helped bankroll New York governor Alfred E. Smith's challenge to McAdoo at the 1924 convention in Madison Square Garden. Then, after the deadlocked delegates instead turned to lawyer John W. Davis as their nominee, Manton offered advice to Davis and made speeches on his behalf.[42] At a dinner of the Columbus Italian-American Society three weeks before the election, Manton ripped into President Coolidge for his administration's "vicious Immigration Law" that had greatly restricted Italian immigration. The law "should quickly be repealed," Manton urged, but "[w]e have no promise" of that from "the party in power." Manton's "attack on the honesty of the President," a Brooklyn Republican bitterly countercharged, better befit "a cheap spellbinding street corner political stump speaker than one holding the exalted position of a United States Circuit Judge."[43]

In 1928, Manton enthusiastically supported Smith, who became the first Catholic nominated for president by a major party. After Smith's nomination in Houston, Manton sent a congratulatory message conveying his "every good wish for assured success" which was reprinted in the *New York Times*. Writing to Smith's campaign manager, John J. Raskob, while on holiday at the Grand Hotel Brufani in Perugia, Italy, on July 23, 1928, Manton pledged "to add my full effort in furtherance of this cause" and invited Raskob "to command my every effort." Disembarking from the SS *Washington* upon his return, Manton predicted a Smith victory. "I expect to see Governor Smith elected," Manton told reporters, unpresciently. During the campaign, Manton financed nationwide advertisements protesting anti-Catholic bigotry.[44]

Manton was even briefly rumored as a possible gubernatorial candidate in 1922 and a possible mayoral candidate in New York in 1925. Mayor John Hylan, the Brooklyn Democrat coming to the end of his second term in 1925, had fallen out of favor with the Tammany machine. Tammany wanted to exile him to a state court judgeship. As the machine "scurr[ied] around" looking for a replacement, Manton's name was floated as one possibility. Given Manton's distaste for electoral politics, he probably did not do much to pursue the opportunity. McCooey, the Brooklyn Democratic leader, publicly threw cold water on the idea, predicting that Manton would not be receptive to it and suggesting that, as a Bayport resident, Manton would be ineligible in any event.[45] Ultimately Tammany threw its backing behind a colorful state senator, Jimmy Walker.

Today, the Code of Conduct for United States Judges prohibits federal circuit court and district court judges (it does not, surprisingly, apply to Supreme Court justices) from engaging in political activity, and specifically political speechmaking, public endorsements, and campaign contributions. The Code was not adopted until 1973, however, and Manton's conduct was not so obviously improper as it would be considered in more modern times. Still, the American Bar Association's Canon of Judicial Ethics of 1924 advised that judges "should avoid" partisan politicking, including participating in party conventions. Manton's activities undoubtedly raised some eyebrows among his colleagues, especially the big bushy ones belonging to Learned Hand, who viewed Manton as "preoccupied with his political cronies."[46]

* * *

Manton also became a popular toastmaster, commencement orator, and after-dinner speaker, before audiences of lawyers and non-lawyers alike. Why this was is hard to say; his speeches tended to be as turgid and unilluminating as his judicial opinions. But on occasion he would address politically fraught legal issues of the day.

Manton spoke out against the wave of nativism that swept the nation in the 1920s. He denounced the new immigration quotas imposed by the Republicans in control of Congress and the White House. "The success and growth of this country has depended upon its immigration," he said in a Columbus Day address in 1923. More immigration meant more laborers helping American industry reach new heights. "No greater asset ever entered any port than a pair of calloused hands," Manton asserted.[47]

The newly ascendant Ku Klux Klan also drew Manton's ire. Speaking at commencement exercises at a Catholic women's college in 1923, Manton called attention to a recent Klan gathering in a Suffolk County cornfield called to protest a "fancied grievance," the supposed outsized influence of Catholics in government affairs. How could it be, he wondered, that "in this enlightened age, there are found some thousands of American citizens masked and in the dark, practicing the trades and conduct of men ashamed of their acts and declarations?" They represented "a menace to our freedom of worship," he warned, and threatened a return to "the history of the dark ages."[48]

The defining political and legal issue of the decade was Prohibition. "Soaking-wet" New York soon became "the center of lawlessness," according to US Assistant Attorney General Mabel Willebrandt, the energetic enforcer of the Volstead Act. Tens of thousands of speakeasies flourished in hidden nooks and crannies across the city. Liquor flowed so freely at the 1924 Democratic National Convention that McAdoo, leader of the party's "dry" wing, complained that "some of my best men have been hopelessly drunk since they landed in New York." Law enforcement was overwhelmed. "The great United States Court in the Southern District of New York had degenerated" into something even seedier than a "police court," sniffed Manhattan US Attorney Emory Buckner, overrun with a "seething mob" of "bartenders, peddlers, waiters, bond runners and fixers" along with "bootleggers, speakeasy operators, crooked druggists, fake rabbis, fallen priests, alky cookers, and various other violators dragged into court" on the authority of the Volstead Act.[49]

Surprisingly for an Irish-Catholic New York Democrat—the constituency that had blocked McAdoo's bids for the Democratic presidential nomination in 1920 and 1924 precisely because of his support for Prohibition—Manton was a "dry." When the Wilson Administration elevated Manton to the Second Circuit in 1918, Methodist bishop Horace Mellard DuBose, a leading figure in the temperance movement, effusively praised the appointment of a man of such "character, loyalty, and devotion to ideal."[50] Writing in the *Christian Advocate*, DuBose reprinted a letter he received from a fellow Methodist church member and New York lawyer active in lobbying for passage of the Eighteenth Amendment. According to this lawyer, Manton "was born in Long Island in 1880 of very poor and humble parents," "drove a coal truck in Brooklyn" to put himself through college, and became "essentially the attorney of the people," who made it a point of principle "never to represent a corporation" and "especially devoted his talents to fighting" the trusts.

Of course, to DuBose, an individual's character was measured against a single yardstick—fidelity to the temperance cause—and his unidentified correspondent assured him that Manton was firmly on the side of the righteous:

> *This brave, clean young man has never taken an intoxicating drink in his life, never smoked a cigar or cigarette—in fact, never used tobacco in any form—and has never once taken the Lord's name in vain. His charities and philanthropies are broad. He is married to a charming Christian woman, and this relationship has existed happily for more than a dozen years. . . .*
>
> *Notwithstanding the fact that it is not considered ethical for judges to dabble in politics, yet in the long drawn-out fight that we had in Washington City I took occasion to call upon him frequently for his potential intervention in the prohibition cause, and he always responded cheerfully and with alacrity. If the prohibition amendment is ever adopted at Albany, he will have been as much responsible for the result as any fifty men in America.*

On the bench Manton did not shy away from enforcing Prohibition. In 1922 he ordered that Reisenweber's, a legendary restaurant and cabaret on West 58th Street and Eighth Avenue near Columbus Circle and the place where jazz is said to have been invented, be shuttered for persistently violating the Volstead Act. The US attorney hailed Manton's "courageous action" as "the greatest step forward for law enforcement and restoring respect for the law" since the Volstead Act went into effect. Prohibition authorities were looking to make an example of Reisenweber's; dozens of agents had burst into the massive restaurant just after midnight on New Year's Eve, sending hundreds of revelers fleeing in their evening clothes and leaving others with summonses in their hands when alcohol was discovered at their tables.[51]

Manton proved somewhat less judgmental when liquor was discovered at his own table later that same year. At a dinner sponsored by the

Brooklyn Riding and Driving Club, Manton was seated at the speaker's table next to the Reverend James E. Crowther, a well-known Philadelphia pastor and staunch Prohibitionist. The reverend did a double take when he spotted a bottle of Scotch whiskey at his table and the other tables in the room, and grew increasingly alarmed as a waiter repeatedly attempted to fill his glass with the forbidden liquid. When other men in the room, who had no compunctions about downing the whiskey they were served, burst into song and started throwing dinner rolls across the room, Crowther had had enough. He left before his turn to speak. Meeting with the press upon his return to Philadelphia, Crowther denounced the evening's events to reporters as a "feast of Belshazzar," an "open and official violation of the Constitution of the United States," and "my most painful experience in twenty years of public life in America."[52]

Because Reverend Crowther also faulted Judge Manton for taking no action, Manton felt compelled to respond, triggering a week-long contretemps in the press. "I failed to see what he claims to have seen," Manton told reporters. "Personally I never drank anything alcoholic in my life, and I didn't on that occasion. Moreover, I know of no one who did."[53] In a statement, Crowther conceded that Manton himself did not have anything to drink, but claimed that "the judge expressed to me before I left his deep concern over the growing tendency toward the disregard and violation of fundamental law, as evidenced by what was taking place." Manton in turn denied that he had told Crowther any such thing.[54]

Now the reverend got hot, issuing a blistering, sarcastic reply that essentially called Manton a liar. "It is truly remarkable what the Judge could not see," the pastor retorted. "Perhaps he did not see the quart of whiskey within reach of his hand, nor the waiters carrying out empty bottles under his nose, nor the waiter responding to my energetic demand that he take away the glass of whiskey he had poured for me." Men "in high places" should not encourage disrespect for the law, Crowther chided. Recognizing that it was unwise to fuel more headlines pitting his word against a minister's—on the subject of whether he was fully, or only dimly, aware of violations of law taking place right in front of him—Manton refused to comment further.[55]

Prohibition, a test of the power of law to change behavior, wound up deeply corroding public respect for law and giving birth to rampant criminality and corruption. "Political corruption had been baked into the system almost from the beginning."[56] The temptations were simply too great. In New York City, police officers routinely collected protection payments from bootleggers and speakeasy owners, to the point where operators of several of the swankier Midtown booze joints formed a sort of bribery collective to pay off authorities from a common pot of money. "It is clear," the Justice Department's Mabel Willebrandt tartly observed, "that if the police of New York City, and some of the politicians who control their appointments, are not collecting at least one hundred and sixty thousand dollars a day or sixty million dollars a year from the speakeasies alone, they are either very honest or very stupid."[57]

Federal officials were not immune. One of the first federal Prohibition directors in New York, a former state court judge, was under indictment within a year of assuming his post, after hundreds of liquor withdrawal permits mysteriously disappeared from a locked cabinet in his office and wound up in the hands of bootleggers. His replacement did not last any longer before he too resigned, under suspicion of taking a $100,000 loan from a bootlegger and allowing illegal withdrawals of liquor from bonded warehouses.[58] The Volstead Act, maintained the *New Republic*, was such a "ruinous source of corruption" that it "brought into active opposition to law forces so powerful that federal officials of justice as of the treasury became accomplices in its degradation."[59]

The depths of this degradation came into public view at a federal trial in 1926 of William "Big Bill" Dwyer, a well-known racetrack owner, hockey promoter, restaurateur, and Broadway personality who led a second and secret life as the nation's biggest bootlegger. Dwyer kept on his payroll dozens of Coast Guard seamen, captains, and senior officials, who not only looked the other way as Dwyer's smugglers ferried massive quantities of liquor into New York harbor, but sometimes carried the contraband themselves on their government vessels. The outraged district judge sentenced Dwyer to the statutory maximum and denied him bail pending appeal.[60] But the "King of the Bootleggers" found a friendlier ear in the teetotaling Manton, who released Dwyer on bail and then voted, in dissent, to overturn Dwyer's conviction. Thirteen years later, a jailhouse informant told the FBI that Manton had been paid off to set bail for Dwyer and had done so upon returning from a trip to Europe. The informant's account was never corroborated, but his chronology checks out: Manton heard Dwyer's bail application on August 18, 1926, two days after arriving back in New York on the SS *Leviathan*.[61]

* * *

He did not drink or smoke or swear. He was devout and philanthropic and a papal knight. He had adopted two infants and given them a home. He was a federal judge. When Manton took the stage at Fordham University Law School in June 1926, he and his audience no doubt believed he spoke with moral authority. Fordham was honoring him with a doctor of laws degree and the keynote address at its graduation ceremony. It was one of five honorary degrees conferred on Manton between 1921 and 1936 (the others were from Manhattan College, NYU, the University of Vermont, and St. Bonaventure College).[62]

To the eager young graduates Manton stressed the "importance of personal principle" and "sound moral training" in their upcoming professional lives. "If [a young lawyer] lacks this," Manton said, "let him not attempt to practice law, for he will fail." Not just that: he will "probably land in the penitentiary."[63] Some of the Fordham students may have thought this warning a bit extreme. None would have expected their commencement speaker himself to become living proof of it.

PART TWO

A CARNIVAL OF CORRUPTION

CHAPTER SEVEN

"Surprising to the Point of Shock"
The Subway Fare Case

IN APRIL 1927, CHARLES HOUGH, THE SENIOR CIRCUIT JUDGE FOR THE
Second Circuit, succumbed to a heart ailment. His death thrust Manton,
at the relatively tender age of forty-six, into the role of "senior" Second
Circuit judge. Younger than the two other remaining Second Circuit
judges, Learned Hand and Thomas Swan, he nonetheless had served on
the court for longer than either of them. Manton also became the youngest member of the Conference of Senior Circuit Judges. Virtually all of
his colleagues were in their sixties and seventies.

The following year, and likely because of his status as senior circuit
judge, Manton participated in a case of enormous practical consequence.
The case involved a constitutional challenge to New York City's longstanding five-cent subway fare. Before the city took it over in the 1940s,
New York's labyrinthine network of underground and elevated railway
lines was privately operated. The main operators were the Interborough
Rapid Transit Corporation (known as the IRT or the Interborough) and
the Brooklyn-Manhattan Transit Corporation (B.M.T.). Ever since an
1894 state law authorizing construction of the rapid transit system, and
as agreed by the operators in various contracts over the years, the fare
was fixed at a maximum of five cents. From today's vantage point, the
nickel fare looks like a pretty sweet deal for commuters, both cheap (the
equivalent of less than a dollar today) and convenient (just drop a nickel
into the slot). No wonder that each day, approximately three million New

Yorkers boarded the city's subways and elevated trains, packed together so tightly that the *Daily News* habitually referred to them not as riders but "sardines."

The Interborough and the B.M.T., along with their stockholders, did not view the five-cent fare in the same positive light. For many years they had been agitating for a fare increase. City officials, the State Transit Commission, and elected state-court judges had all been unwilling to support such a politically unpopular request. "[I]t can surely be said that no local political issue generated quite so much fire and bluster in New York during [the interwar] period as did the matter of preserving the nickel fare."[1] Maintaining the nickel fare was, in effect, the third rail of New York City politics. "I'd sooner cut off my right arm than do anything that would increase the fare!" exclaimed Jimmy Walker on the day Tammany nominated him to run against incumbent mayor John Hylan, himself a fanatical defender of the fare.[2]

There were those who believed the transit operators would succeed in raising the fare. One of those optimists was Thomas L. Chadbourne, an influential corporate lawyer in New York and a large stockholder in both the Interborough and the B.M.T. He ran Chadbourne, Stanchfield & Levy, a legal powerhouse created when Chadbourne teamed up with John Stanchfield and Louis Levy, Manton's law school classmate. The law firm, later known as Chadbourne, Parke, remained one of New York's most venerable until its 2017 merger with UK-based Norton Rose Fulbright. Chadbourne's rise to the top of the legal profession was fairly remarkable considering that he was expelled for misbehavior from virtually every school his parents sent him to and never attended college or law school. When Chadbourne was nineteen his father, a Harvard-educated lawyer, kicked him out of their Michigan home, having concluded that his 6' 7" rebellious son was "not fit for a profession or any other work in life that calls for mental effort." Chadbourne relocated to Chicago, became a cop, apprenticed for a Chicago lawyer, passed the bar exam, and practiced in Milwaukee and Chicago before heading to Manhattan in 1902.[3]

Assured, affable, astute, and ambitious, Chadbourne grew fabulously wealthy acting as a dealmaker and consigliere for corporate titans. He acquired residences in the St. Regis Hotel in New York, in Greenwich,

Connecticut, and in Palm Beach, Florida, along with a 175-foot yacht christened "Jezebel" with a crew of twenty-eight. Unusually progressive for a Wall Street lawyer, and able and willing to write large checks, Chadbourne also became a confidant to leading Democratic politicians of the day. He claimed to have raised the bulk of the Democratic campaign fund in 1916, and was one of William McAdoo's main financial backers in 1920 and 1924.[4]

Chadbourne also donated generously to New York governor Alfred E. Smith—and not just to Smith's campaigns. When Smith was re-elected governor in 1922, he complained to Chadbourne about the pay cut he would have to take, and Chadbourne decided to ensure that Smith's standard of living would not suffer. Over the next six years Chadbourne gave Smith more than $400,000 in cash and stock options, an astonishing sum that remained a secret until Chadbourne's autobiography was discovered more than forty years after his death. Even then Chadbourne's chapter on his payments to Smith was deleted from the published autobiography at the insistence of the Chadbourne law firm and became public knowledge only after its sensational contents were leaked to the *New York Times*. In his memoir Chadbourne claimed his payments to Smith sprung from "altruistic motives." "I was a great believer in Smith as a public servant," he wrote, "and was glad to put him in a position where he could afford to return to office without bread and butter worries."[5]

Yet at the same time, Chadbourne acknowledged that he expected Smith to support a two-cent increase in the nickel subway fare. That would have greatly increased the value of Chadbourne's holdings in the Interborough and the B.M.T., both of which were publicly traded. By mid-1927 Chadbourne held roughly $4.5 million worth of B.M.T. stock, or about 10 percent of the total, and he was a close friend of, and advisor to, B.M.T. board chairman Gerhard M. Dahl. Chadbourne's stake in the Interborough was more complex and opaque. He held $375,000 worth of Interborough shares in his own name, but when combined with interests held by the B.M.T., entities controlled by Dahl, and relatives of Chadbourne, he and Dahl collectively held in excess of 10 percent of the Interborough's stock.[6] The newspapers began referring to Chadbourne as the "traction king" or the "traction baron," "traction" being tabloid shorthand for the city's rail and bus system.[7]

Chadbourne's influence brought him into the crosshairs of the Transit Commission and its special counsel, Samuel Untermyer. Untermyer was also a longtime fixture on the New York legal scene and every bit an outsized personality as Chadbourne. Born into a German-Jewish family in Lynchburg, Virginia, Untermyer moved with his family to New York after the Civil War. Later in life Untermyer would reminisce about his Virginian upbringing, claiming that his father, proprietor of a clothing store, owned a tobacco plantation with twelve hundred slaves and served as an officer in the Confederate army, stories that historians have determined were untrue.[8] Untermyer graduated from Columbia Law School at age twenty and, together with another Lynchburg refugee, Randolph Guggenheimer, started what became the only Jewish Wall Street law firm. A fierce cross-examiner and feared trial lawyer, Untermyer discovered that there was more money to be had in corporate law and investing than in litigation. Like Chadbourne, he became adept at both, amassing a fortune estimated at $50 million, in part by taking stock rather than cash in payment for his legal fees. Also like Chadbourne, Untermyer was very active in Democratic Party politics, a strong supporter of President Wilson and proponent of government regulation who helped draft the Federal Reserve Act, the Clayton Act, and the Federal Trade Commission Act.[9]

At the end of 1926, the Transit Commission tapped Untermyer to prepare a "unification plan" that would bring the Interborough, the B.M.T., and other subway lines under one system of ownership and operation. Untermyer held a public hearing at which he sought to expose the greed of the traction industry and defend the five-cent fare. One of the main witnesses he summoned was Chadbourne, "the real power in traction affairs," in Untermyer's view.[10]

Over two days in May 1927, Untermyer thrust and Chadbourne parried. Calm and smiling where Untermyer was intense and prosecutorial, Chadbourne simply refused to answer several of Untermyer's questions as "not pertinent," such as when he acquired his B.M.T. and Interborough stock and how much he paid for it. Chadbourne expressed confidence the five-cent fare would soon be a thing of the past. In fact, he said, his belief in the unsustainability of the nickel fare is what prompted him to take such large positions in the B.M.T. and the Interborough in the first place. "Your idea was that you could take this stock until you could get the rider to pay more fare?" Untermyer asked. "Yes," Chadbourne replied unapologetically. "I had no doubt about it then and I have no doubt about it now."[11]

Chadbourne also made clear how he expected this change would come about: through the courts. When he decided to invest in transit stock, Chadbourne testified, "I knew that the day would have to come when the stock would reflect the real values of the properties, because I knew, in the final analysis, the courts would give a fair return on a fair value, and when they did the stock would get the benefit of it."[12] Chadbourne's language invoked a particular legal doctrine then part of the US Supreme Court's substantive due process jurisprudence. Public utilities, the Supreme Court held in those days, were entitled to a "fair return" on the "fair value" of the property they used for the public convenience.[13] State rate-setting that deprived the utility of the right to earn a "fair return" was deemed "confiscatory" and, hence, a violation of the utility's Fourteenth Amendment right to due process.

Railroads, gas and electricity companies, and other public utilities typically filed such due process claims in federal court, where they could expect a warmer reception. A federal statute, Section 266 of the Judicial Code, provided for a special three-judge court to hear cases like these seeking to enjoin state statutes or regulations on constitutional grounds. Earlier in the decade, the Southern District of New York had invalidated a New York law setting a maximum rate for gas in a suit brought by the Consolidated Gas Co., and the Supreme Court had affirmed that ruling.[14] But it was not clear if the New York City transit lines could bring themselves within the protection of the Supreme Court's case law. B.M.T.'s earnings, Chadbourne cheerfully admitted to Untermyer, were "advancing very handsomely," although he felt growth should be more along the lines of 8 percent per year rather than 6 percent. The Interborough's counsel acknowledged at the same hearing that it too was making money. Nevertheless, he predicted that unless the five-cent fare was raised, the Interborough would eventually be forced into bankruptcy.[15]

* * *

On February 1, 1928, the Interborough put into motion the legal strategy Chadbourne had prophesied. The transit company filed a seven-cent fare schedule with the Transit Commission for its subway and elevated lines, stating that it was prepared to go to court if its request was refused. After the Transit Commission took no action and Untermyer and Mayor Jimmy Walker announced their implacable opposition to a fare increase, the Interborough commenced a lawsuit in the Southern District of New York alleging that the five-cent fare was "confiscatory."[16]

The case was assigned to district judge William Bondy, a Republican appointed by President Harding, and a three-judge court was convened. Under Section 266 of the Judicial Code, one of the judges had to be either a Supreme Court justice or a Circuit judge, and in the Interborough case that spot went to Manton. Southern District judge John C. Knox rounded out the trio of jurists. Untermyer, representing the Transit Commission, and the City's lawyer, Charles L. Craig, probably felt good about this draw. Manton and Knox were both progressive Democrats, and Manton had briefly intervened in the City's favor in the Consolidated Gas confiscation case and had overturned Judge Mayer's contempt citation of Craig earlier in the decade. As senior circuit judge, Manton could be expected to take the lead in the court's deliberations and might command a certain degree of deference from his junior colleagues, and especially from Knox, who owed his judgeship to Manton.

To Untermyer, the dispute was, at its core, a simple contract case. The Legislature had effectively delegated to the City the power to set rates with the transit lines, and the City had proceeded to do that in its contracts with the Interborough, including the latest contract entered into in 1913. The Interborough had obtained substantial benefits from the contract negotiations, including guaranteed annual income of $6.4 million for forty-nine years. The Interborough, Untermyer argued, was therefore bound by the five-cent fare to which it had agreed as part of its contract. The Transit Commission had no statutory authority to authorize a higher fare even if it wanted to. In fact, according to Untermyer, since Interborough's gripe all boiled down to a matter of the interplay between the relevant state statutes and the Interborough's contracts, the federal court lacked jurisdiction to decide the case.[17]

It did not take long for Untermyer's confidence to slip. At the first hearing of the statutory court, over which Manton presided, Manton announced that the Transit Commission and the City's jurisdictional objections had been overruled. When Untermyer insisted that the case involved only a question of contract and was not a rate matter, Manton cut him off, saying: "This is nothing but a rate case now."[18]

If he heard about it, Untermyer may have been even more unsettled by a bar association speech Manton gave on April 27 in which he assailed critics of the federal courts. "The view that Congress or the States may pass what laws they will and the judiciary must lend its aid to the usurpation, even though contrary to the mandatory prohibitions of the Constitution," Manton said, "finds no willing adherence with men who have the most elementary knowledge of our own democracy and its fundamental law."[19] This was an era when critics of judicial activism tended to be those on the left upset by decisions of federal judges using the Constitution to protect property rights of corporations. Manton's defense of the federal courts echoed themes invoked by lawyers for the property owners who benefited from those decisions.

Five days later, on May 2, 1928, Manton delivered the unanimous opinion of the three-judge court. It was a complete victory for the Interborough, upholding "practically every contention of the Interborough lawyers."[20] Manton rejected the Transit Commission and the City's argument that the New York Legislature had effectively delegated the rate-setting function to the city and that the Interborough had contracted away the right to challenge the five-cent fare by entering into contracts with the city at that rate.[21]

And, Manton found, the five-cent fare was indeed confiscatory, as the Interborough claimed. The Interborough was earning a return of only about 2.5 percent on the value of the property in use, far below the 8 percent level that Supreme Court precedent seemed to set as a minimum level of a "fair return." To reach this finding, Manton included in the denominator the value of all property utilized in the transit line's operations, including that contributed by the City, rejecting Untermyer and Craig's argument that the City's property should be excluded from the calculation.

Manton's ruling sparked extra-large front-page headlines and a public furor. "Surprising to the point of shock," the *Brooklyn Daily Eagle* called the "momentous" decision. The federal court, noted the *Daily News*, "reached its hand into the pockets of Father Knickerbocker's straphanging 'sardines' yesterday and lifted $28,749,793 annually"—the additional revenues expected to flow to the Interborough from the two-cent fare hike. Mayor Walker immediately announced that he had decided to run for re-election so that "there may be no doubt of the sincerity of the city administration in its determination to uphold the 5 cent fare." Even the normally pro-business *New York Times* agreed that "Mayor Walker is fully warranted in his determination to carry the case promptly to the Supreme Court."[22]

The general public, the *Daily News* editorialized, would find one particular aspect of the decision "incomprehensible": how the US courts had become arbiters of what was "a strictly local dispute." "The net effect of this decision," the paper wrote, "is that the federal statutory court becomes the actual transit operating commission in and for New York City." This "continued encroachment of the federal judiciary" was "dangerous" and "one of the most alarming tendencies of the present century."[23] Manton's bar association speech the week before, of course, seemed to anticipate this line of attack, and his ruling similarly declared that the court had taken jurisdiction "not as a matter of discretion or comity, but as a matter of duty."[24]

Stockholders of the Interborough—and of the B.M.T., which was expected to follow in the Interborough's footsteps and seek approval for its own seven-cent fare—rejoiced. The stock prices for both firms had been rising steadily since the litigation began, in anticipation of a favorable decision. Interborough stock had doubled since the start of the new year, and the B.M.T.'s stock price was above its annual low by 43 percent.[25] For Thomas Chadbourne, that meant that his stock holdings in the two companies were worth millions of dollars more. Chadbourne decided it was time to cash in his chips; as he disclosed in his autobiography, during the lead-up to and following Manton's decision, he and his friends sold off their transit stock.[26]

* * *

What the general public did not know, and would have found even more incomprehensible had it known, was the financial relationship between the author of the five-cent fare decision, Judge Manton, and one of its principal beneficiaries, Thomas Chadbourne. That relationship remained a closely guarded secret until January 1939, the year after Chadbourne's death, when reporter S. Burton Heath broke the story in the *New York World-Telegram* as part of the overall Manton scandal.

At the end of 1927, Manton asked Chadbourne if he wanted to invest in National Cellulose Corporation, the paper manufacturer Manton and Sullivan had just formed. Chadbourne and his partner Louis Levy, Manton's law school classmate, agreed to invest a total of $75,000—over $1.2 million in today's dollars. Chadbourne fronted the entire investment, with Levy reimbursing him for Levy's share a couple of years later. But neither Chadbourne nor Levy would be listed as shareholders in the company's books and records. Rather, the subscribers for their two blocks were shown as Frank F. Knapp and Jessie McLardy. Knapp worked as a clerk at Chadbourne, Stanchfield & Levy; McLardy was a stenographer at the firm. Dividend checks were sent to Louis G. Bissell, a lawyer at the Chadbourne firm, and then endorsed by Knapp in favor of Thomas Chadbourne, and by McLardy in favor of Levy.[27]

National Cellulose's board of directors formally allotted the $75,000 of stock, in two equal tranches, to Knapp and McLardy on January 23, 1928—eight days before the Interborough launched its legal battle on February 1.[28] Thus, at the time Manton sat on the three-judge court and issued his decision in the Interborough's favor, he was effectively a business partner of Chadbourne, one of the Interborough's (and the B.M.T.'s) largest stockholders.

The ruling by the statutory court was subject to review by the US Supreme Court, and the Transit Commission and the City immediately announced they would appeal. Chadbourne's decision to sell off his transit stock holdings before the Supreme Court weighed in—despite his professed confidence in the strength of the Interborough's legal position—was a characteristically canny one. In April 1929, the Supreme Court overturned Manton's ruling by a 6–3 vote.

The Supreme Court held that the statutory court had erred in deciding for itself the long-disputed question of the effect of the Interborough contracts on the Transit Commission's ability to set a different fare. This, the Court held, depended on the proper construction of "complicated state legislation" and was a matter for the state courts to decide in the first instance. Further, the Court found, considering the probable fair value of the subways, "no adequate basis" was shown for the Interborough's claim that the five-cent rate was confiscatory. Manton's view that the value of property owned by the city should be considered in the fair return calculation was "unprecedented" and "ought not to be accepted" without firmer support in the record. All in all, according to Justice James C. McReynolds's majority opinion, Manton's decision "was improvident and beyond the proper discretion of the court."[29]

Thus was the nickel fare saved from extinction. It would remain the cost of hopping on a New York subway for another nineteen years.

* * *

Was the $75,000 investment in National Cellulose an attempt by Chadbourne to purchase Manton's assistance in overturning the five-cent fare—in short, a bribe? The episode, well beyond the applicable statute of limitations, was not part of Manton's criminal trial in 1939. Testimony about the investment was elicited when Louis Levy was brought up on federal and state disciplinary charges after Manton's conviction, but the matter was peripheral to the charges and no factual findings about its relationship to the Interborough case were made.

At first blush, any charge of influence-peddling must account for the fact that the investment was made before the Interborough litigation was filed, let alone before Chadbourne knew that Manton was assigned to hear the case. Moreover, Section 266 of the Judicial Code provided that the district judge to which the case was assigned "shall immediately call to his assistance" the two other judges, suggesting that it was Judge Bondy who decided that Manton should be part of the statutory court.[30]

Yet Chadbourne and Manton cannot be let off the hook so easily. As his May 1927 testimony before the Transit Commission makes clear, Chadbourne anticipated, prior to the National Cellulose investment, a due process challenge in the courts attacking the five-cent fare as confiscatory. As a savvy lawyer, he also would have expected the lawsuit to be filed in federal court and heard by a three-judge panel that would include a Second Circuit judge. Moreover, despite the language of Section 266, Judge Bondy almost certainly did not unilaterally decide what Second Circuit judge would sit with him. He would have consulted with the Second Circuit, and logically the person he would have consulted with was the senior circuit judge—Manton. It seems likely, therefore, that Manton picked himself to be the Second Circuit's representative on the panel, shortly after receiving $75,000 through Chadbourne.

Chadbourne and Levy's use of nominees to conceal their investment in National Cellulose also bespeaks an improper motive that required concealment. Moreover, Chadbourne and Levy paid virtually no attention to the investment after it was made, remaining silent even when they learned, years later, that National Cellulose funds had been diverted into Manton's real estate investments—suggesting that the $75,000 was as much a gift as a bona fide investment.[31] Still further evidence of consciousness of guilt comes from Manton's testimony at Levy's state disciplinary proceeding in 1940, in which Manton claimed that he and Chadbourne had never discussed the five-cent fare. That testimony was contradicted by Chadbourne's "personal man," who testified that when he was employed by Chadbourne, Manton was a frequent visitor to Chadbourne's apartment and that the two men discussed a fare increase and Chadbourne's interest as an Interborough and B.M.T. stockholder.[32]

Indeed, in the omitted chapter of his posthumously published autobiography, Chadbourne admitted that he and Manton talked about the subway fare case itself. While the case was pending, Manton had a conversation about it with Governor Smith in the private dining room of millionaire contractor William F. Kenny, Smith's close friend since boyhood and largest campaign contributor. The room was filled with bronze and stuffed tigers and was famously known as the "Tiger Room" because, as Kenny explained, "I am a good Tammany 'tiger.'"[33] Smith, making clear his own view that "a contract is a contract" and the Interborough should be held to the agreement it signed with the City, asked Manton how he intended to rule. Manton replied that, while he was still studying the law and did not know how he would come out, "I am inclined to think" that the Interborough had the better of the argument. Manton relayed this conversation to Chadbourne, along with his observation that Smith seemed to backtrack and "deceiv[e] Kenny about his attitude on the fare question" when Kenny (who, like Chadbourne, had investments in transit stocks and was hoping for an Interborough victory) joined the conversation later. It appears Manton wanted to apprise Chadbourne of Smith's hostility to an increase in the nickel fare, which contradicted Smith's assurances to Chadbourne that he supported an increase.[34]

The Tiger Room dinner also underscores the peculiarity of Manton's ruling in the subway fare case in the context of his general political and ideological leanings. In their private conversation, once Manton indicated his inclination to rule in the Interborough's favor, Smith urged him to delay the decision until after the November election. When Manton replied that "that wouldn't be possible," Smith accused Manton of disloyalty: "You are going straight against the party. We don't want any seven-cent fare in this city before this election."[35] Manton was, indeed, a committed Democrat and would be a vocal and committed supporter of Smith's presidential run that same year. But none of those political ties dissuaded Manton from striking down the nickel fare. Ordinarily that would speak well of Manton's judicial independence, but in the circumstances it appears only to signify that those political ties were not as strong as Manton's financial ties to Chadbourne.

Siding with the Interborough over state and city regulators, with the consequence of enriching the transit lines at the expense of the public, also is hardly what would be expected from a Wilsonian Democrat and so-called "attorney of the people" who built a practice suing railroads. Of course, political beliefs play a relatively minor role in most decision-making by inferior federal judges; the facts and law often compel the judge to reach a decision that may not be in accord with his or her sense of good policy. That was hardly true in the Interborough case, however. The suit's outcome pivoted on a number of unresolved issues that called for the exercise of judicial discretion: whether to defer to the state courts, how to analyze the interplay between the various New York statutes and the contracts between the Interborough and the City, what property to include in the determination of fair value. On all of these issues Manton exercised his discretion in favor of the transit line.

The Supreme Court's reversal of Manton's decision is, in this regard, quite telling. Even such ardent defenders of the property rights of corporations as Chief Justice Taft and Justice McReynolds felt that Manton had gone too far in invoking federal judicial power to free the Interborough from purportedly oppressive state regulation. Manton's opinion found favor only with the three dissenters, Justices Van Devanter, Sutherland, and Butler, the Court's most deeply conservative members. As the judicial controversies of the 1930s would confirm, Manton normally occupied a position on the ideological spectrum diametrically opposite from this bloc of justices.

Long before Manton's financial ties to Chadbourne were revealed, Felix Frankfurter smelled something rotten in how Manton "threw the authority of the federal courts on the side of the Interborough" and "cavalierly brushed aside the applicability of the five-cent contracts."[36] The Supreme Court's ruling, Frankfurter noted in an unsigned essay in the *New Republic* in 1933, showed the "impropriety of Judge Manton's action in depriving the state courts of an opportunity to pass upon questions of state law peculiarly meet for their decision." When those questions of state law did come before the state courts, all thirteen judges to hear the case, at the trial level, on the intermediate appellate court, and on New York's highest tribunal, unanimously ruled, as Frankfurter put it, that "Judge Manton was wholly wrong and that the five-cent contracts were controlling."[37]

Perhaps it was a coincidence that, in the one politically charged case where Manton acted more like a conservative Republican than a Tammany Democrat, he happened to have surreptitiously received $75,000 from an interested party with a strong rooting interest in an Interborough victory. The weight of the evidence suggests this is not the most persuasive explanation.

CHAPTER EIGHT

"Venal and Corrupt"

The American Tobacco Litigation

MANTON BUILT HIS REAL ESTATE EMPIRE UPON PILLARS OF DEBT. THAT left him in a precarious position when the Great Depression struck. Manhattan real estate values plunged 67 percent by the end of 1932. For highly leveraged investors like Manton, this meant their properties were now worth less than the mortgage. Manton found himself buried under more than $6.5 million of mortgage debt encumbering his crown jewel properties: the Alamac and Esplanade hotels on the Upper West Side and the Holmes Airport property in Queens. Efforts to sell the hotels fell through, as the Crash also dried up the pool of available purchasers.[1]

Signs of Manton's financial strains surfaced publicly. At the end of 1930, a run on the Bank of the United States, New York's third-largest commercial bank, led to the bank's collapse and a cascade of other bank failures across the country. Investigators sifting through the financial wreckage discovered numerous unsecured and outstanding loans to prominent New Yorkers, Manton among them. Manton had guaranteed loans for $69,000 to the Camala Corp., which owned the two apartment hotels, and for $70,000 to Forest Hills Terrace Corp. Simultaneously it was revealed that Manton co-endorsed two notes totaling $200,000 held by the recently closed Chelsea Savings Bank, also related to his real estate investments. All the notes "will be met at maturity," Manton assured the *New York Times*.[2]

To keep his real estate creditors at bay, Manton would soon engage in the single most lucrative corrupt act of his career and the history of the American judiciary—even as, all around him, dozens of Tammany judges and politicians were losing their jobs for abusing their office for financial gain.

* * *

At a Democratic banquet at a Bronx restaurant in December 1929, the guest of honor, Magistrate Albert H. Vitale, rose to speak when masked gunmen barged in, lined the diners up against the wall, and dispossessed them of their money and jewelry. A police detective present at the dinner surrendered his revolver without a fight. Within hours, Magistrate Vitale somehow managed to round up and return all the stolen money and jewelry, as well as the detective's revolver. Vitale did not explain how he managed this feat, but it lent credence to suspicions that he was connected to organized crime.

The city bar association commenced an investigation and found that Vitale had misused his office to obtain a $20,000 loan from the late gangland figure Arnold Rothstein. Two weeks later, Vitale dismissed a larceny charge brought against one of Rothstein's associates. In March 1930, a New York appeals court ousted Vitale from the bench because of the Rothstein loan—only the second removal of a city magistrate since Manton's ex-client Henry Furlong. At his trial Vitale admitted that in four years on the bench he had amassed $165,000, while being paid only $12,000 annually as a judge.[3]

Calls for a broader investigation now rang out from the usual anti-Tammany quarters: establishment lawyers like Henry Taft and C. C. Burlingham, Republican politicians, socialist leader Norman Thomas, Protestant and Jewish clergy, and the press. At first Mayor Jimmy Walker and Governor Franklin D. Roosevelt resisted, but Roosevelt, mindful of how he could be tarred by association with Tammany in a presidential run in 1932, quickly relented. Ex-judge Samuel Seabury, with whom Manton sparred at Lieutenant Becker's retrial, was appointed to launch an inquiry into the magistrates' courts.[4]

Seabury's investigators gathered evidence that the various denizens of the magistrates' courts—bail bondsmen, clerks, assistant district attorneys, defense lawyers—were profiting from payoffs in vice and gambling cases. Worse, Seabury found, the magistrates who presided over this "distortion of law to illegal ends" were "sitting back and permitting this outrageous spectacle to be enacted before them day in and day out." Seabury also laid bare the magistrates' dependency on loyalty to Tammany Hall for their appointments, which he condemned as "a scandal and a disgrace." Tammany district leaders routinely interceded with magistrates in pending cases on behalf of constituents and told Seabury frankly that they saw nothing wrong with this. "That is the way we make Democrats," one Bronx district leader explained.[5]

Rather than undergo Seabury's scrutiny, a number of magistrates headed for the exits. Just a few months into the probe, the roster of city magistrates had been "shot to bits by resignations, removal proceedings, and sudden sickness," the *Daily News* reported.[6] By contrast, Magistrate Louis B. Brodsky chose to stand and fight. The "millionaire magistrate," as he was dubbed by the press, held interests in numerous real estate companies and speculated massively in the stock market. He had given a power of attorney over one of his many brokerage accounts to the son-in-law of the Tammany politician responsible for his appointment as a magistrate. Brodsky also kept $40,000 in cash in a "tin box" at home. Seabury charged that Brodsky's outside business interests violated a state law that prohibited judges in New York City from "engag[ing] in any other business or profession" that could detract from the full-time performance of their judicial duties. A New York appeals court disagreed and exonerated Brodsky.[7]

After the Brodsky ruling, Republican legislators in Albany sought to amend the law to prohibit city judges from serving as officers and directors of companies. Governor Roosevelt claimed to agree. "It is repugnant to our sense of the proper administration of justice that judges should be permitted to engage in business during their terms in office," Roosevelt told the Legislature. In fact, Roosevelt felt so strongly about this principle that he could not accept limiting it to "one city alone"; rather, he insisted that the same restrictions apply to upstate judges—most of whom, of course, were Republicans. As Roosevelt must have expected, if not intended, Republican legislators balked at broadening the amendment in this way. The net result: no change was made and the status quo was preserved.[8]

Seabury's mandate, meanwhile, expanded beyond the magistrate courts. Named as counsel to a state legislative commission to investigate corruption in city government, Seabury held a series of sensational public hearings, revealing personal fortunes of numerous city officials out of all proportion to their government salaries. New York County sheriff Thomas M. Farley, a Tammany sachem, had accumulated nearly $400,000 in six years on an annual salary of $8,500. Asked by Seabury to explain the source of his wealth, Farley, like Judge Brodsky and other Seabury targets, credited a cash-stuffed "tin box"—"a wonderful box," he called it—he kept in a safe at home. Farley never, however, explained how the cash magically appeared in the box to begin with. After a hearing in Albany, Governor Roosevelt removed Farley from office.[9]

Shortly thereafter, Seabury bagged the biggest prize of all: the charismatic, high-living, seemingly untouchable Jimmy Walker, decisively re-elected mayor in 1929 with 61 percent of the vote. Seabury's investigators discovered that Walker, too, had amassed a fortune as mayor. Beginning when Walker first took office, the bookkeeper from his former law firm, Russell T. Sherwood, maintained a secret joint safe-deposit box for Walker at a brokerage firm. Over five years Sherwood deposited $750,000 in cash to the box. As investigators closed in, Sherwood decided it was a good time to get married and take a honeymoon in Mexico, beyond reach of Seabury's subpoena power.[10]

Just as damning were several other peculiar sources of income discovered by Seabury's investigators. A newspaper publisher, who owned half of a company trying to sell subway tiles to the city, contributed nearly $250,000 to a joint brokerage account he held with Walker. A senior partner of a Wall Street brokerage firm—which held a large interest in Checker Cab, dependent on city regulation—delivered $26,000 in cash to the mayor at City Hall representing profits from the sale of an oil company investment to which Walker had contributed nothing. And when the mayor vacationed in his typical high style in Paris in the summer of

1927, more than $10,000 of his expenses were paid out of a slush fund maintained by a group of businessmen and politicians behind a company that hoped to take over all of the city's bus lines.[11]

Even Walker's preternatural charm could not extricate his political career from a muck of greed this deep. For New Yorkers suffering through the third and most brutal year of the Depression, the mayor's good-natured knavery was wearing thin. In June 1932, Seabury forwarded the results of his investigation to Governor Roosevelt, who had the authority to remove the mayor from office. Already dogged by accusations he was too cozy with Tammany Hall, FDR did not want to be seen as doing Walker any favors at the same time he was vying to be anointed the Democratic presidential candidate. Roosevelt decided to hold a hearing in Albany to determine Walker's fate, similar to the course that had led to Sheriff Farley's removal.[12]

Behind the scenes, according to one account, Tammany leader John F. Curry and his Brooklyn sidekick John McCooey of Brooklyn tried to protect Walker by enlisting the aid of a high-ranking federal judge: Manton. Acting as their emissary, Manton approached Roosevelt with a proposal: If FDR agreed to acquit Walker, Curry and McCooey would ensure that the all-important New York delegation at the Democratic National Convention would support Roosevelt over his rival, ex-governor Al Smith. This, at any rate, was the claim made by Manton's friend, former New York congressman Joseph J. O'Connor, in a 1958 letter to the *New York Times*.[13]

"That was just too raw a deal for Roosevelt" to go along with, according to O'Connor. After securing the nomination without Tammany's backing, Roosevelt proceeded to preside over what amounted to a public trial of Walker in Albany. Midway through, on the eve of questioning about the Sherwood safe-deposit box, Walker gave up the fight and resigned. He set sail a week later to meet his paramour, a former member of Ziegfeld's Follies, in Italy and hide out in Europe for a while. Observers interested in the consequences of corruption may have taken note that once Walker resigned, his legal troubles ended. Roosevelt shut down the Albany hearing, public attention subsided, and the now-former mayor never faced prosecution.[14]

While Samuel Seabury was shining klieg lights on the overstuffed tin boxes and bank accounts of municipal officials, Richard Reid Rogers was performing a similar function exposing corporate gluttony. In 1931, Rogers launched a double-barreled legal assault on cash bonus and stock subscription schemes at the American Tobacco Company that had showered more than $10 million on the company's top executives.

The nation's leading cigarette manufacturer, American Tobacco was led by George Washington Hill, who succeeded his father as president in 1926. With "a single-mindedness indistinguishable from monomania," Hill nearly doubled the company's market share in five years. His "plump face, piercing eyes and beetling brows" fixed above an ever-present bowtie, Hill was "the brassiest, most flamboyant operator in all of U.S. business." Within the company's headquarters in Manhattan's Flatiron District, where he "ruled like a paranoid dictator," Hill was known as "God." A bronze statue of Bull Durham (the name of the company's roll-your-own tobacco) adorned the garden of his Westchester County estate, and tobacco plants filled the flowerbeds. Even Hill's dachshunds were named "Lucky" and "Strike" after the firm's flagship brand.[15]

Behind the firm's turnaround was Hill's fanatical focus on marketing. "An advertising man at heart," Hill "spent more money advertising a single product than anyone in history" at the time. He hired public relations guru Edward Bernays to smash the cultural taboo against smoking in public by women. Bernays promoted smoking as a form of feminism, hiring a cadre of attractive young women to light up Lucky Strikes during New York City's Easter Day parade in 1929, one of whom explained to reporters that she was "lighting the way to the day when women would smoke on the street as casually as men." Slick advertising campaigns, produced by the man considered the founder of modern advertising, Albert D. Lasker of the Chicago-based Lord & Thomas agency, hammered home this theme. Lucky Strikes, one ad proclaimed, were removing the "ancient prejudice" that held women to be inferior and too meek to smoke. Other ads conceived by Hill and Lasker urged female consumers to "Reach for a Lucky instead of something sweet" and smoke Luckies in order to "keep a slender figure." For millions of American women lured in by these messages, the health effects would prove tragic. For Hill it was "like opening a new gold mine right in our front yard."[16]

Much of this newly mined gold went into Hill's pockets. In 1912, the company had adopted a bonus plan providing for 10 percent of net profits in excess of the firm's net profits in 1910 to be distributed to top executives. This turned out to be quite a sinecure once cigarette consumption, and American Tobacco's profits, mushroomed following World War I. Hill raked in $1.6 million in bonus payments during the 1920s, and for 1930 alone was entitled to a bonus of over $840,000.[17]

But Hill and American Tobacco's other officers still felt underappreciated. On July 28, 1930, American Tobacco adopted a new Employees' Stock Subscription Plan that gave its directors plenary power to dole out stock awards to company personnel. When the directors (the majority of whom were Hill and his vice presidents) activated the plan in January 1931, they chose to allocate most of the shares to themselves, at a price of $25 per share. At the time, the market price of American Tobacco's stock was $112 per share, creating an immediate enormous paper profit for the recipients. For Hill this amounted to $1.1 million; for the directors collectively the haul neared $3 million. Hill now stood to earn more than $2 million for 1930—this just one year after a raging public debate about whether any corporate chieftain was worth even $1 million a year.[18]

It was all too much for Richard Reid Rogers, a New York lawyer and substantial stockholder of American Tobacco. Rogers did not fit the mold of a typical plaintiffs' lawyer. A genteel Kentuckian, educated at Princeton and the University of Virginia Law School, Rogers ambled on the upper crust of Kentucky society before moving to New York shortly before the turn of the century. He practiced law with what became Cravath, Swaine & Moore, the quintessential Wall Street law firm, until President Theodore Roosevelt in 1906 appointed him general counsel of the Isthmian Canal Commission, the agency responsible for building the Panama Canal. While stationed in the nation's capital, Rogers and his wife hosted elegant parties attended by the cream of Washington society. As a federal judge later said, by the time he instituted the American Tobacco litigation, Rogers "had attained real eminence at the bar."[19]

Rogers filed separate lawsuits, removed to federal court in Manhattan, challenging the bonus plan and the stock subscription plan. The stock subscription case, *Rogers v. Guaranty Trust Co.*, was assigned to Southern District judge Robert P. Patterson, a Hoover appointee and former Wall Street lawyer. In February 1932, Judge Patterson dismissed the case on jurisdictional grounds. American Tobacco was incorporated in New Jersey, and Rogers asserted that the subscription plan violated several New Jersey statutes. To Patterson that meant the legality of the subscription plan was "a matter for determination in the first instance by the New Jersey courts."[20]

Rogers's challenge to the bonus plan, *Rogers v. Hill*, was assigned to Southern District judge Francis G. Caffey, a transplanted Alabaman who had been US attorney in Manhattan during the Wilson Administration. Ruling in March 1932, Judge Caffey found that he was bound to exercise jurisdiction over the suit but engaged in a curious form of passing the buck. Citing the "exigencies of performing other court duties" that prevented him from "complet[ing] [his] study" of the "interesting and important" issues involved, Caffey confined himself to expressing his "tentative" "impressions" that the bylaw authorizing the bonus plan was invalid. He issued a preliminary injunction barring further bonus payments, hoping this disposition would "put the case in shape for immediate review by the Circuit Court of Appeals."[21]

Barely before the ink was dry on Judge Caffey's preliminary injunction, American Tobacco appealed the ruling to the Second Circuit.[22] Meanwhile, Rogers had already filed his own appeal seeking to overturn Judge Patterson's jurisdictional ruling. The appeals were briefed with unusual expedition. On May 3 and 4, 1932, in the Old Post Office Building near City Hall, a Second Circuit panel consisting of Judges Manton, Harrie Chase, and Thomas Swan heard oral arguments in both appeals.[23]

Arrayed against Rogers was a phalanx of formidable defense lawyers. Chadbourne, Stanchfield & Levy acted as chief counsel for American Tobacco and its executives. For the Second Circuit oral arguments, Chadbourne brought in even more firepower. John W. Davis of Davis, Polk, Wardwell, Gardiner & Reed, the former solicitor general in the Wilson Administration, argued the appeal in the stock subscription case.

Former New York governor Nathan L. Miller, who had also served as a judge on New York's highest court, opposed Rogers in the bonus plan appeal. None of this legal talent would have intimidated Rogers, who did not lack for confidence. What would have concerned Rogers more, had he known, was the behind-the-scenes assistance rendered by two other partners of the Chadbourne firm, which had nothing to do with their legal acumen.

* * *

One morning in April 1932, a few weeks before oral argument in the American Tobacco cases, Manton met up with his friend Louis Levy of the Chadbourne firm. Although Levy's full-time residence was in Dobbs Ferry, he like Manton also maintained a home in Midtown Manhattan, at the Ritz Tower hotel on Park Avenue and 57th Street, adjacent to Manton's apartment's building. The two friends and former law school classmates often walked partway downtown together on their way to work, as they did on this particular morning.[24]

Levy and Manton talked about their ongoing efforts to develop the Holmes Airport property in Queens into a major airport. The Chadbourne firm represented several major aviation companies, and Levy had arranged several meetings with potential partners and financial backers for the airport project. Levy never charged Manton a fee and even arranged for the Chadbourne firm to pick up $3,000 in expenses for the project.[25] Thomas Chadbourne, too, had recently done Manton a favor by trying to persuade the president of Manufacturers Trust Company (of which Chadbourne was a director) to give Manton an extension to repay an outstanding note.[26]

Levy and Chadbourne's beneficence, along with their stockholdings in Manton's National Cellulose Corporation, were reason enough for Manton to have disqualified himself in cases where the Chadbourne firm represented a party, or, at the very least, to have disclosed his financial ties to two of the firm's name partners. That was especially true for the American Tobacco litigation: Levy personally participated in the litigation, appearing as counsel on the papers filed by Chadbourne in the district court, and Levy held in his name, for the benefit of the Chadbourne firm, shares worth over $85,000 (or over $1.7 million in today's dollars) issued under the American Tobacco stock subscription plan under challenge.[27]

As severe as these conflicts of interest were, they were about to be eclipsed by a far more serious one. During their walk downtown, Manton mentioned to Levy that his business partner, James Sullivan, the National Cellulose president, was in need of a loan. Manton asked Levy: "Do you have any clients who would be interested in making a loan to Sullivan?" Levy told Manton to have Sullivan come down to the Chadbourne firm and "we will see what we can do for him."[28]

Chadbourne and Levy did indeed have a client they thought would be interested in arranging a loan to Sullivan: American Tobacco. Chadbourne telephoned Paul M. Hahn, George Washington Hill's thirty-seven-year-old chief assistant. Chadbourne and Levy were well-acquainted with Hahn. A graduate of Columbia Law School, where he had been on the law review, Hahn practiced law at the Chadbourne firm for six years. He so impressed Hill with his work on American Tobacco matters that Hill poached him away in 1929, hiring him to work full-time at the company at a salary of $50,000.[29]

"I would like to ask you to do a favor for me," Chadbourne said to Hahn. Chadbourne explained that a friend and client of his—Sullivan—was looking for a loan of $250,000, to be secured by National Cellulose stock. Chadbourne would have loaned the money to Sullivan himself, but sadly it was not "convenient" at the moment for him to do so. But Chadbourne had an idea to bounce off Hahn. "You know Albert Lasker very well, don't you?" he asked, referring to American Tobacco's advertising man at Lord & Thomas. It had "occurred" to Chadbourne that Lasker might be interested in making the loan because Lasker was familiar with the cellulose products business.[30]

"I will appreciate anything you can do to help this along," Chadbourne told Hahn. "I am very much interested in Sullivan getting this loan." About to set sail for Europe, Chadbourne left it to Levy to follow up. Levy too assured Hahn that "Sullivan is a thoroughly responsible man" and that "this loan is wanted for only a short time and it will be repaid promptly." Hahn consulted with Hill, who blessed the request.[31]

A week after the oral argument in the Second Circuit, Lasker and the president of Lord & Thomas, Ralph Sollitt, visited with Hill and Hahn at American Tobacco's office in New York to discuss the company's advertising plans. As the meeting ended, Hahn pulled Lasker aside into an adjoining room. "I want to speak to you on a matter that Mr. Hill is embarrassed to speak to you about," Hahn said by way of preface to asking Lasker to lend $250,000 to Sullivan.[32]

Despite its considerable heft—$250,000 in 1932 is roughly $5 million today—the request was a hard one for Lasker to turn down. American Tobacco was his biggest client. The account had grown to $19 million a year, representing about one-third of Lord & Thomas's overall billings and generating $2.8 million in commissions for the agency.[33] It was the largest single advertising account in the world. Sure, Lasker responded to Hahn, "we would be glad to accommodate you," on the understanding that the loan would be repaid in four months. On May 11, Sollitt met with Sullivan at Lord & Thomas's New York office near Grand Central Station and handed him a check for $250,000.[34]

Manton claimed that his brief talk with Levy was "all I had to do with" the loan and the amount discussed was only $25,000. Levy claimed he never spoke with Manton about the loan and blamed it all on Chadbourne (who conveniently had died by the time of Levy's testimony). Two judges concluded they were both lying, finding that "a scheme was concocted between Manton and Levy whereby Manton could obtain $250,000," that Sullivan was "little more than a conduit" through which the loan proceeds "flowed into Manton's depleted reservoirs," and that Levy "knew that Sullivan was a dummy acting for Manton" and "in mind, heart and action, was venal and corrupt."[35]

Those findings drew sustenance from a letter dated April 26, 1932 that Levy received from "Sullivan" just a few days after his walk with Manton. In that letter, "Sullivan" explained why "we" were endeavoring to place a $250,000 loan through Levy: to pay outstanding debts on the Esplanade Hotel, including $115,000 in arrears of interest and taxes, and to fund needed improvements on the property. Manton and the corporations he controlled owned 94 percent of the preferred stock and 99½ percent of the common stock of the Alamac Esplanade Corporation, which owned the Esplanade. Manton held the overwhelming majority of the economic stake—about 79 percent—with Manton's friends owning roughly 14 percent and Sullivan a comparatively paltry 7 percent. And while the April 26 letter bore Sullivan's signature, it was not signed by him or prepared at his office. If one looked closely enough, as investigators later did, a US government watermark—a spread eagle—was visible. Manton's secretary, Marie Schmalz, typed up the letter on her office typewriter. She then signed Sullivan's name to it.[36]

Within a few weeks after the loan was made, the vast majority of the money—$205,000 at the least—was deployed for the benefit of Manton's companies. Disbursements were made at Manton's direction to pay down the taxes and arrears on the first mortgage on the Esplanade Hotel and to pay off the second and third mortgages, just as "Sullivan's" April 26 letter contemplated. Other funds went to Forest Hills Terrace and the Astoria-Riker Corporation (which held the Holmes Airport property)—companies in which Sullivan had no interest whatsoever—as well as to Sulmar Realty, owned 80 percent by Manton, and Manton's carpet cleaning companies. Some of the checks bore Schmalz's handwriting (excepting Sullivan's signature).[37] All of this had been masterfully engineered under the cloak of a transaction between a lender (Lord & Thomas) and a borrower (Sullivan) neither of whom, on the surface, had anything to do with any cases pending before the Second Circuit.

* * *

As the Second Circuit mulled what to do in the American Tobacco cases, thousands of World War I veterans were descending on Washington, DC, pitching makeshift tents on the banks of the Anacostia River near the Capitol. Rendered jobless and near destitute by the Depression, this "bedraggled and bearded" mass of hungry men were demanding early payment of bonuses for their military service promised them by Congress in 1924. The payments would amount to about $1,000 per man, a far cry, dollar-wise, from the bonuses at stake in the American Tobacco litigation, but quite possibly the difference between subsistence and starvation for the veterans and their families. On June 17, 1932, the hopes of the seventeen-thousand-strong "Bonus Army" were dashed when the Senate voted down a House-passed measure to accelerate delivery of the bonus payments. The next month, on orders of President Hoover, US troops commanded by General Douglas MacArthur, advancing with tear gas, fixed bayonets, and tanks, forcibly evicted the bonus seekers and burned down their encampments.[38]

George Washington Hill and his "bonus squad" fared much better in their pleas to the Second Circuit. On June 13, 1932, the Second Circuit ruled in their favor in both appeals, in opinions written by Judge Manton and joined by Judge Chase over dissents by Judge Swan. Manton's rulings did not simply go against Rogers; they drove a stake through the heart of both of Rogers's cases.

In the stock subscription case, *Rogers v. Guaranty Trust Co.*, Manton essentially ignored the issue of jurisdiction, which had been the basis for Judge Patterson's ruling. Without ever saying that Patterson was wrong or explaining why he was wrong, Manton simply noted that American Tobacco's principal office, chief executives, board meetings, and corporate records were all in New York, and then dove into the merits, endorsing all of the defendants' arguments. The directors "had no self-interest" at stake when they approved the subscription plan in June 1930, even though a few months later they voted to allocate most of the shares issued under the plan to themselves. The re-election of the directors by the stockholders, after the allocations were announced, "justified the claim" that the stockholders thought the awards were a good idea. Simply put, American Tobacco's stock plan "was a matter of internal management of the corporation's affairs," with which the courts had no right to interfere.[39]

Dissenting, Judge Swan believed the stock subscription plan could not be squared with the relevant New Jersey statute (which Manton's opinion barely discussed). The statute required that the directors first "formulate" a plan for the stockholders to approve or disapprove, but the American Tobacco plan contained no formula at all; instead it simply conferred upon the directors unfettered discretion to make any sort of allotment of shares they thought desirable. The directors only formulated the actual plan later. Swan questioned whether "the board would have had the temerity to submit to the stockholders in advance a plan which on its face so largely benefited themselves."[40]

For Rogers, the majority's ruling was the worst outcome imaginable. Had the Circuit simply affirmed Patterson's ground for dismissing the case, Rogers would have had to refile the suit in New Jersey—an annoyance, and not the battleground on which he wished to fight—but the substance of his claim would have remained intact. Manton, however, went much further, indeed as far as he could possibly go: He declared the battle over and American Tobacco's executives the victor.

Manton's disposition of the appeal in *Rogers v. Hill*, the bonus case, followed a similar trajectory. He took what had been a temporary loss for the American Tobacco executives—Judge Caffey's preliminary injunction stopping further bonus payments—and converted it into a final victory in their favor. The 1912 corporate bylaw that mandated the bonus payments, Manton held, was "lawfully passed" and was "valid, effective, and controlling in the allotment of additional compensation to officers of the corporation." "It became part of the contract of employment," a "promise which the corporation must keep until the by-law is repealed or changed." The bylaw "is neither ultra vires, fraudulent, nor illegal, and, since it is not, courts must refuse intervention because they are powerless to grant it."[41]

Judge Swan again found Manton's approach overly deferential. He would have affirmed the preliminary injunction, viewing Hill's "bonus" of $840,000, in relation to his fixed salary of only $168,000, as "presumptively so much beyond fair compensation for services as to make a prima facie showing that the corporation is giving away money, and a by-law which sanctions this is prima facie unreasonable, and hence unlawful." Even if the bylaw was valid when originally adopted, "it does not follow that it will remain valid for all time," Swan wrote. "If a bonus payment has no relation to the value of services for which it is given, it is in reality a gift in part, and the majority stockholders have no power to give away corporate property against the protest of the minority."[42] These were strong words from the normally understated Swan, "an old-fashioned Yankee" and former *Harvard Law Review* president, business lawyer, and Coolidge appointee who was far from a progressive firebrand.[43]

Not satisfied with merely safeguarding their legal rights, Manton portrayed Hill and his cohorts as morally deserving of the unprecedented sums lavished upon them. Sounding more publicist than jurist, Manton's opinions lauded the "most unusual commercial success" of American Tobacco, which he attributed to "the skillful management of these able men" and the "extraordinary and unique" services they had rendered. He cited the company's $43 million in net earnings, nearly $30 million in dividend payments, and $150 million it had paid in taxes, by comparison to which its executives' compensation seemed modest. He singled out "[Hill's] management" for turning American Tobacco into "the leader in the cigarette industry." Hill, who knew good advertising copy when he saw it, must have smiled when he read Manton's tributes. As Felix Frankfurter put it in an anonymous essay for the *New Republic*: "President Hill himself could not have been more righteous in his accents of approval, or more deferential to the great captains of industry, than was Judge Manton in sanctioning these luscious windfalls of the American Tobacco Company."[44]

* * *

Unfortunately for Hill, he was about to discover what the IRT learned in the subway fare case: a Manton-led court was not a court of last resort. Unprepared to surrender, Rogers sought review of Manton's decision in the bonus case, and in October 1932 the Supreme Court agreed to hear it. The stock subscription case initially went back to the district court, but that court found that the case had to be dismissed based on Manton's unequivocal rejection of Rogers's legal arguments. The Second Circuit (Manton, Swan, and Gus Hand) agreed that Manton's decision was binding, but Hand said in a concurrence, "With the matter open I should reach a different decision." With Manton's ruling now opposed by two well-respected members of his own court, the Supreme Court agreed to review the stock subscription case as well.[45]

The Supreme Court reversed both of Manton's rulings, without a single justice agreeing with Manton's disposition of either case. In the stock subscription case, decided by a 5–3 vote in January 1933, all the justices believed Manton had erred in deciding the case on the merits in favor of the executives. The majority held that Judge Patterson had been right all along in refusing to assert jurisdiction in light of the general rule that matters involving the internal affairs of a corporation should be decided by the courts of the state of incorporation.[46]

In a lengthy and impassioned dissent, Justice Stone said that he, like Manton, would have reached the merits; but, unlike Manton, he would have ruled in Rogers's favor, condemning the "wholesale gratuities which the directors . . . bestowed upon themselves" and their "unconscionable conduct." Echoing Swan, Stone charged that it was "a misuse of words" to call the open-ended stock subscription proposal presented to stockholders a formulated "plan." And even if it could be called a "plan" as contemplated by the New Jersey statute, the directors' action in allotting stock to themselves, "in violation of their duty as fiduciaries, exceeded the authority conferred upon them by the stockholders, and was, therefore, ultra vires."[47]

Although the views of Stone and his fellow dissenters, Cardozo and Brandeis, did not carry the day, they breathed new life into Rogers's now-revived challenge to the stock subscription plan. Newspaper accounts focused on their "vigorous" and "sharp" dissents. The "righteous indignation" and "stern words of the supreme court justices should have a broadly beneficial effect in truing up corporate ethics," a Chicago paper editorialized. Rogers refiled his suit in New Jersey in early February 1933. That same week, in a letter to stockholders citing the dissenters' criticisms of the plan, Hill renounced his own stock allotment.[48]

Then, in May 1933, the Supreme Court unanimously reversed Manton's ruling in the bonus case. It was Judge Swan's dissenting opinion, the Court held, that had correctly stated "the applicable rule": If a bonus payment has no relation to the value of the services rendered, it is "in reality a gift." Stockholder approval of the plan could not justify payments of sums "so large as in substance and effect to amount to spoliation or waste of corporate property." Further proceedings were warranted to determine whether the bonuses constituted "misuse and waste of the money of the corporation."[49]

The Supreme Court's ruling emboldened a growing movement to curb what was seen as excessive levels of executive compensation during the early 1930s. Hill was now targeted as the poster boy of corporate greed. Not only did Hill's compensation package resemble a raid on the corporate treasury at the expense of stockholders, it contrasted jarringly, if not obscenely, with the meager or nonexistent wages of most Americans. Hill's millions "would buy an awful lot of smokes," an Indiana paper pointed out, and effectively drove up the cost of smoking, "which gives a lot of comfort to fellows out of work." A Democratic congressman from Missouri fumed that Hill's reported $1.6 million salary for 1932 was simply "too much for any one man—while others starve."[50]

Faced with the unappetizing prospect of defending against Rogers's lawsuits in this environment, American Tobacco threw in the towel. The company reached a settlement with Rogers to put an end to both cases, agreeing, among other things, that virtually all the stock under the 1930 plan slated to go to the directors would be returned to the company.[51]

Ironically, not only were both American Tobacco decisions issued by the same predominantly conservative Supreme Court that would shortly block the New Deal, they were authored by Pierce Butler, the Minnesota railroad lawyer chosen over Manton by President Harding in 1922. The irony was not lost on Felix Frankfurter. "The reprimand of Judge Manton's view of corporate morality, as practiced by the American Tobacco Company," Frankfurter wrote in his *New Republic* essay, "was all the more decisive in that it was pronounced by Mr. Justice Butler, the most uncompromising conservative on the Court."[52]

* * *

Chadbourne, Levy, Hill, and Hahn thus never got the final judicial victory they hoped for. And Albert Lasker never got his money back. He tried, up to a point; but he ultimately and understandably concluded that this was not a matter in which, practically speaking, he had any legally enforceable rights.

After multiple letters to Sullivan went unanswered, Lasker began importuning Hahn to help him get paid. But Hahn returned with only vague assurances from Chadbourne that the loan would be repaid "soon." Then, in December 1935, Sullivan suffered a fatal heart attack in his office. Manton, named as one of the two executors of Sullivan's estate, called and wrote Lasker, asking for a meeting to discuss how to resolve the $250,000 debt. By this time, Lasker must have sensed there was something seriously amiss—and that he should not be negotiating directly with a federal judge who decided two critically important cases in favor of the same company that asked Lasker to make the loan. Refusing to return Manton's calls, Lasker retained a well-known New York lawyer, Max D. Steuer, to deal with Manton on his behalf.[53]

Manton may have been surprised and a little alarmed when Steuer showed up in his chambers. A famous trial lawyer and legendary cross-examiner, Steuer was shrewd, pugnacious, and a keen judge of human nature. But Steuer's client for this particular assignment did not want to unleash Steuer's usual aggressiveness. Fiercely independent yet simultaneously pragmatic (he kept close ties to Tammany Hall), Steuer may not have chafed, too much, at being kept in check. He averaged at least one Second Circuit appearance per year. Antagonizing the senior circuit judge would not help him win those appeals.[54]

"I have a great proposition for [Lasker]," Manton told Steuer. National Cellulose manufactured a sanitary napkin called "Puritas," and Lasker was invested in the company that produced Kotex; perhaps Lasker would be interested in buying out National Cellulose and merging the two firms? Steuer spoke with Levy, who thought the idea had merit, and the Chadbourne firm even paid for an independent auditor's report of National Cellulose. The report, however, showed that National Cellulose "was not particularly thriving" and was worth less than what Lasker was owed. That put an end to the potential merger of the two sanitary napkin brands.[55]

Steuer then pressed Levy's partner, George W. Whiteside, reminding him that Lasker had made the loan on the faith and credit of Hahn and Hill, not Sullivan. Whiteside agreed fully that Lasker should be repaid. Nonetheless, he told Steuer, "neither Hill, Hahn, nor the Tobacco Company would recognize any responsibility for the money advanced to Sullivan."[56] Having gone to great lengths to keep Hill's, Hahn's, and American Tobacco's fingerprints off the Sullivan-Lasker transaction, the senior partners of the Chadbourne firm were not about to let them now repay the loan directly.

Instead, Whiteside advanced a series of proposals to make Lasker whole surreptitiously in ways that would involve falsifying the books and records of Lord & Thomas and American Tobacco. For instance, White-side suggested, American Tobacco could throw additional advertising to Lord & Thomas at higher rates, or Lord & Thomas could charge a special commission for Lasker's prior advice about a radio advertising program. These proposals, too, were rejected by Lasker, afraid of becoming "an ex post facto participant in events that were obviously shady in the extreme."[57]

As the Chadbourne lawyers and Hill no doubt were fully aware, Lasker and Steuer had no real leverage in these negotiations. Lasker was not going to pursue Lord & Thomas's legal remedies against Sullivan's estate and thereby bring public attention to the sordid circumstances behind a sizeable loan made for no apparent business purpose to an individual with whom neither he nor his firm had any prior relationship. Nor could Lasker afford to play hardball with American Tobacco, his biggest client.

Lasker, in short, was "caught in a trap." In early 1938 Steuer, his hands tied, withdrew and the statute of limitations on Lord & Thomas's claims expired without any legal action being filed. No payments of principal or interest on the $250,000 "loan" had been made, nor was there any prospect of repayment, when the Manton scandal was exposed in 1939.[58]

CHAPTER NINE

"Judicial Shenanigans"

Milking Bankruptcies for Patronage and Profit

THE WEEK AFTER DECIDING THE AMERICAN TOBACCO CASES, MANTON picked a fight with his judicial colleagues in the Southern District of New York that would heighten suspicions about his integrity and earn him yet another rebuke from the US Supreme Court. The fight was over a subject dear to Manton's heart and, even more so, his pocketbook: the appointment of receivers in bankruptcy cases.

At the end of the 1920s, the patronage-plagued system of appointing politically connected lawyers as receivers finally brought scandal to the federal judiciary in New York. Several lawyers, appointed as receivers, were indicted for embezzling funds from bankrupt estates. Some had ties to Southern District judge Francis A. Winslow, who was accused of favoring a small "ring" of bankruptcy lawyers. One of them, Marcus Helfand, boasted of his influence with the judge, telling colleagues and clients, "I can get Judge Winslow to sign any order I submit to him." To prove he was not just blowing smoke, Helfand invited skeptics to watch from afar as he took the judge out to dinner and the theater.[1]

US Attorney Charles H. Tuttle convened a federal grand jury to examine the allegations against Winslow. While concluding there was insufficient proof of personal corruption, the grand jury issued a report accusing the judge of "serious indiscretions." Under pressure from the bar, the Southern District's senior judge, John C. Knox, initiated an investigation by the court itself. Winslow's activities also caught the eye of then-congressman Fiorello H. La Guardia, Republican of New York, who introduced a formal resolution calling for Winslow's impeachment. Winslow resigned, taking the wind out of the sails of the various investigations against him.[2]

Meanwhile, a separate impeachment inquiry was initiated in the House against a second federal judge, Grover M. Moscowitz of the Eastern District of New York. Judge Moscowitz stood accused of bestowing receiverships on a former law partner and his associates while maintaining a business arrangement with the former partner. The House ultimately condemned Moscowitz's conduct as "unethical" but did not impeach him. Moscowitz continued to serve on the Eastern District bench until 1947.[3]

As the investigation of the lawyer-receivers picked up steam, the judges of the Southern District instituted a major reform. Henceforth, Senior Judge Knox proclaimed, a single bank—the Irving Trust Company—would act as receiver in all bankruptcy cases.[4] Despite his Tammany roots, a decade on the bench had convinced Knox that the existing system "gives every opportunity for favoritism" and, worse yet, "opens the door to crookedness."[5] The group of judges he led was dominated by former Wall Street lawyers and stout Republicans like Thomas D. Thacher, a graduate of the Phillips Academy and Yale, member of Skull & Bones, and son of a founding partner of the white-shoe Simpson, Thacher & Bartlett—the type of men who viewed patronage as dirty.

Martin Manton was not that type of man and not that type of judge. Having mastered the use of receiverships for patronage, Manton took a visceral dislike to the Southern District's new rule. So too did much of the New York bar; after all it was lawyers, by and large, who were being displaced by Irving Trust. The stakes were high. Irving Trust was overseeing thousands of bankrupt businesses at any one time. Opposition to the Irving Trust monopoly deepened once the Depression began biting into lawyers' incomes. Bankruptcy filings soared, and lawyers looked on with dismay as Irving Trust pocketed fees they felt should have been theirs.[6]

The profession's resentment crested at a dinner of the Federal Bar Association of New York, New Jersey, and Connecticut on June 14, 1932. The Southern District judges, claimed a speaker, Charles H. Hyde, had struck "the severest blow ever received by the legal profession." It was wrong, Hyde maintained, for US courts to appoint "a corporation without a soul" to any position where "human responsibility and personal integrity" were essential. As for the 1929 bankruptcy scandal, Hyde insisted that "compared with the fraudulent bankers, the number of lawyers who have been accused of any wrongdoing, no matter how slight, is mighty small."[7]

Senior Judge Knox replied almost immediately, defending the Southern District's rule. "From my personal observation," Knox said, "the work of the Irving Trust Company has been satisfactory and has served the purpose I thought it would serve." In his estimation, Irving Trust "gives a better administration than when receiverships were given out among a variety of individuals with varying talent." Supporting statistics were cited: According to Irving Trust, administrative costs for the receiverships it administered averaged about 29 percent of the total assets realized, compared with 43 percent in cases administered by individual receivers.[8]

As this debate played out in public, lawyers for the Fox Theatres Corporation approached Judge Manton. The company and one of its creditors were organizing a "friendly" equity receivership application, and it wanted to avoid the appointment of Irving Trust as receiver, which it claimed was conflicted. Manton agreed to intercede, and on June 21 spoke with the Southern District judge on duty, Manton's former law school classmate John M. Woolsey. According to Manton, he urged Woolsey to appoint a receiver other than Irving Trust but Woolsey refused, dismissing out of hand Irving Trust's claimed conflict.[9] In private correspondence, Woolsey stated that Manton's account was "not the true version" of their talk. Instead, Manton wanted Woolsey to appoint Fox Theatres' own president as the receiver, which Woolsey refused to do.[10]

But Manton was prepared to give Fox Theatres what it wanted. In March 1930, Manton had entered an order giving him the power to designate himself to act as a district court judge whenever necessary or needful in the public interest. Invoking that authority, Manton appointed his own receivers for Fox Theatres, including its president, John F. Sherman. Manton entered this order on June 22, 1932, and headed off a few days later to the Democratic National Convention in Chicago.[11]

* * *

When Manton returned from Chicago, he was reading the *New York Law Journal*, the daily chronicle of court rulings, orders, calendars, and goings-on for the New York legal community, when an item caught his eye and raised his blood pressure.

In his absence, the judges of the Southern District had rebuffed Manton's incursion onto their turf. On June 30, 1932, the judges voted to revise the court's General Rules to provide that any judge designated to sit in the Southern District "shall do such work only as may be assigned to him by the senior district judge," Judge Knox. In case that was not clear enough, the rules were also amended to provide that "[a]ll applications" for the appointment of receivers in bankruptcy cases "shall be made to the judge assigned to hold the bankruptcy and motion part of the business of the court"—by definition, one of the Southern District's own judges—"and to no other judge."[12]

Manton dashed off a letter to Knox objecting to the new General Rules as not simply unwise but unlawful. Manton claimed the Southern District's rules were trumped by a higher authority—federal statutes. One statute gave the senior circuit judge the power, "if the public interest requires," to "designate and assign any circuit judge of a judicial circuit to hold a district court within such circuit"; another statute confined the rulemaking authority of district courts to those rules that were "not inconsistent with any law of the United States."[13]

Simultaneously, Manton issued a statement to the press insisting on the superiority of the lawyer-receiver: "All integrity, honesty and understanding have not left the bar just because of the so-called bankruptcy scandal. Lawyers give to bankruptcy cases their individual personal attention—their humane consideration. They are efficient and competent and, I believe, can handle the exigencies of bankruptcy situations more satisfactorily than a banking corporation."[14] In Washington, Brooklyn Democratic congressman Emanuel Celler gave Manton's argument a populist twist, charging that Irving Trust, "like most corporate bodies, is ruthless and cruel, devoid of human sympathies," and "endeavors to coerce poor and indigent bankrupts into making settlements."[15]

It did not take long for Manton to prove to Judge Knox and his colleagues that he meant what he said. The opportunity arrived courtesy of the same Interborough Rapid Transit Company that Manton had favored four years earlier in the subway-fare case. Facing an impending default on its public notes, the Interborough decided to seek the protection of a "friendly" equity receivership to reorganize its financial affairs. This would be one of the most consequential business failures of the Depression: The Interborough delivered a vital public service, employed more than eighteen thousand workers, and had been entrusted with hundreds of millions of dollars in capital from the city and private sources. Toward the end of August 1932, counsel for the Interborough and one of its creditors paid Manton a visit in his chambers and asked him to appoint a receiver other than Irving Trust, claiming the bank could not adequately manage a transit system of the Interborough's size and importance. Interborough's counsel, not surprisingly a fan of Manton's ruling in the subway fare case, regarded him as a judge who "had courage" and "seemed to act according to his conviction."[16]

Manton happily obliged. On August 25, without even consulting the Southern District duty judge or Judge Knox, Manton designated himself as a district judge to hear and determine all applications and proceedings in the Interborough matter. On the next day, Manton appointed Victor J. Dowling and Thomas E. Murray Jr. as temporary receivers—"loyal Tammany men" and, like Manton, both Knights of St. Gregory. As counsel for the receivers, he appointed a law firm he also was quite familiar with: Chadbourne, Stanchfield & Levy. On September 6, Manton extended the receivership to cover the Manhattan Railway Company, whose affairs were intertwined with those of the Interborough, and appointed its president as receiver.[17]

Manton's imperiousness and disrespect for his Southern District colleagues outraged those members of New York's legal establishment who had long disdained him. Reproducing Manton's Interborough orders in a September 5 letter to his friend Felix Frankfurter, an appalled C. C. Burlingham, part of the resistance to Manton's Supreme Court bid a decade earlier, exclaimed, "Well, what do you think of that!" Burlingham, known as the "first citizen" of New York for his many civic engagements, answered his own question: Manton's "brazen" actions were an "affront which the District Judges should resent."[18]

Burlingham highlighted one particularly peculiar justification Manton gave for his intervention. Manton claimed that he was acting in part pursuant to Section 23 of the Federal Judicial Code, which authorized the senior circuit judge to decide how to assign cases where the district judges in a particular district "do not . . . agree." Of course, there was no disagreement among the eight Southern District judges themselves, who unanimously had voted to bar Manton from unilaterally appointing receivers. Nonetheless, Manton reasoned that, having appointed himself to hold a district court, his own disagreement with how receivership cases were assigned created a deadlock that he was empowered to break as the senior circuit judge. In other words, as Burlingham put it to Frankfurter: "A C.J. [Circuit Judge] makes himself a D.J. [District Judge] to disagree with his fellows + then steps in as a C.J. to settle a disagreement of his own making." "It is like the Mikado," Burlingham added, referring to Gilbert and Sullivan's operatic farce satirizing illogical legal reasoning.[19]

Burlingham sought to excite opposition to Manton in influential quarters, lobbying the Association of the Bar of the City of New York, the organization favored by the legal elite; the *New York Times* and other newspapers; and Chief Justice Charles Evans Hughes and Justice Harlan F. Stone (who was responsible for the Second Circuit). But, Burlingham observed to Frankfurter, Manton had insulated himself from criticism by assuming "the posture of champion of the needy lawyers vs. Irving Trust Co."[20]

Burlingham succeeded in galvanizing the irrepressible Frankfurter into action. Frankfurter, then still a Harvard Law School professor, published a letter in the *New York Times* excoriating Manton's Interborough orders as an "abuse of judicial authority." Echoing Burlingham, Frankfurter mocked Manton's reliance on Section 23 of the Judicial Code with his own Gilbert and Sullivan reference, comparing Manton to the lord chancellor in *Iolanthe*, who twisted the law to serve his own personal ends.[21]

In Washington for a lunch with recently retired Supreme Court justice Oliver Wendell Holmes Jr., Frankfurter and DC circuit judge

Billie Hitz explained "the whole Judge Manton situation" to the ninety-one-year-old jurist. In his diary, Frankfurter recorded Holmes's reaction to Manton's Interborough antics: "All of his old-time alertness became engaged—he has for a long time been wholly uninterested in matters legal—his mind became focused and he said as he was wont to of old: 'I'd think I'd find some way of undoing such an outrage.'"[22]

Naturally, Manton's actions also "stirred much resentment among members of the District Court" in Manhattan.[23] Southern District judge Alfred Conkling Coxe Jr., whose father Manton replaced on the Second Circuit, wrote Frankfurter that he was confident "the thing will straighten itself out right" in due course, "as I cannot and will not believe that such tactics will ever permanently succeed among the lawyers in New York City." Coxe, former district judge Tom Thacher, who was now US solicitor general, and Burlingham met at Burlingham's weekend estate on the Connecticut shore one Saturday in September to discuss how Manton's power-grab could be challenged. Thacher felt the issue should be presented to the US Supreme Court.[24]

The difficulty, as Coxe pointed out, was in finding "the right kind of litigant" to mount the legal challenge. The City of New York, which eyed Manton's involvement warily in light of his subway fare ruling, decided not to intervene. But shortly before a scheduled September 22 hearing before Manton, Benjamin F. Johnson, a Manhattan Railway stockholder, and Lillian Boehm, another stockholder who also owned Interborough bonds, stepped forward and filed a suit objecting to Manton's appointments as illegal and void under the Southern District's rules. At the hearing, Manton ignored those objections, made Dowling and Murray's appointments permanent, and put himself in charge of the Interborough and Manhattan Railway cases for at least three years.[25]

It fell to Judge Woolsey, presiding over their separate suit, to rule on Johnson's and Boehm's objections. On October 13, 1932, Woolsey issued a blistering decision assailing Manton as a "mere usurper of judicial power" and declaring all of his orders in the Interborough cases "wholly void and of no juridical effect."[26] (As harsh as that sounded, Woolsey confided privately to Frankfurter that he had been tempted to use "something very like" Frankfurter's Gilbert and Sullivan analogy in his opinion and "say some other things which I think would have been quite to the point," but decided it was best to leave out "all embroidery.")[27] Mounting a full-throated defense of the Southern District's prerogatives, Woolsey maintained that he and his brethren must be "masters in their own house" if they "are going to function at their best." Woolsey shredded Manton's claim that he was merely resolving a "disagreement" among the district judges, observing that "the domestic economy of this court was wholly tranquil" before Manton intervened. "The whole matter may be summed up," Woolsey wrote, "by saying that, when a Circuit Judge is designated to hold a District Court, and proceeds to sit therein, he is acting as a District Judge and must obey its rules."

Manton's rejoinder came less than a week later, in a lengthy opinion attacking Woolsey's "erroneous" decision and instructing Dowling and Murray to promptly take an appeal.[28] Manton used the occasion to submit what was, in effect, his own brief to the Second Circuit. It was uncharacteristically tightly reasoned and felicitous in style. Frankfurter, writing to Woolsey, remarked that "[i]f Judge Manton is the author of that memorandum, then he has literary versatility to an extraordinary degree. In the course of business I have been reading his output in the past, and this is different. It moves along smoothly and at times deftly." As Frankfurter implied, and Manton's trial would prove, Manton was not above asking private lawyers to ghostwrite opinions for him, so perhaps he did that here, or perhaps he simply was moved to greater rhetorical heights by the unusually personal nature of the dispute.

Manton wisely dropped his weakest argument (that he was merely resolving a "disagreement" among the district judges) and focused on the broad language of Section 18 of the Judicial Code authorizing the senior circuit judge to designate circuit judges to sit as a District Court. He emphasized that his predecessors as senior circuit judge had repeatedly relied on that statute to appoint themselves to handle particular cases in the District Court, including the appointment of receivers. So had senior circuit judges elsewhere in the country, according to Manton's survey of them. Cleverly using these other jurists as a shield against Woolsey's criticism, Manton wrote that it was "little short of preposterous" for Woolsey to claim that "these learned and distinguished Senior Circuit Judges" were "'usurpers' of judicial power and that all the orders they made were 'wholly void and of no juridical effect.'"

In a unanimous ruling on December 7, 1932, the Second Circuit agreed with Manton. Neither Judge Learned Hand, who authored the decision, nor Judges Swan and Chase, who joined it, were happy with that result. In pre-conference memoranda, Swan said that he was voting to reverse Woolsey "[w]ith regret" because "I deprecate a circuit judge being able to select special cases to be tried before himself in the District Court," and Chase said there "was in fact no basis" for Manton's finding that the "public interest" required his self-designation. But the law, they felt, gave them no choice. Because the objections to Manton's appointments came in the form of a "collateral attack," i.e., via a separate and independent lawsuit and not in the case in which Manton's decrees were issued, the question was not whether Manton was right or wrong. Rather, Judge Hand wrote, the question was whether Manton's decrees were "so far without color of authority that they might be ignored as a futility, or vacated by another judge in another suit." Manton's "disregard" of the Southern District's rules—even assuming those rules were valid and should have been followed—did not go that far, Hand concluded; Manton's orders were still "a judicial act, unassailable collaterally," not "the empty words of a mere intruder."[29]

The battle did not end there. The Supreme Court agreed to hear the case. On May 29, 1933, the Supreme Court unanimously affirmed Manton's orders—as a strictly legal matter. Echoing Judge Hand, Justice Van Devanter's opinion for the Court stressed the collateral nature of Johnson and Boehm's attack and found they had not met the high standard required. But the Supreme Court also endorsed more of Manton's reasoning than Hand could bring himself to do. For example, Justice Van Devanter agreed that the practice of Manton's predecessors and of senior circuit judges in other circuits was highly significant. He also agreed with Manton that the Southern District's rules interfered with the senior circuit judge's discharge of his duties under Section 18 of the Judicial Code and were, to that extent, inconsistent with that statute and thus invalid.[30]

But Van Devanter had "something more" to say. His postscript began with the observation, "The possession of power is one thing; the propriety of its exercise in particular circumstances is quite a different thing." The power of a senior circuit judge to assign himself to sit in a particular case in the District Court should be "sparingly exercised," Van Devanter cautioned, especially in the context of a receivership matter as large, complex, and delicate as the Interborough. Manton, Van Devanter concluded in what amounted to a sternly worded censure, had acted unwisely and improperly—even if lawfully—in exercising that power in the Interborough matter:

The difference of opinion, between the Senior Circuit Judge and the District Judges, respecting the relative fitness of individuals and trust companies as equity receivers, was not a proper ground for taking the cause away from the District Judge before whom it ordinarily would come, and bringing it before the assigning Senior Circuit Judge. Granting that the latter was most sincere in what he did, there was yet no compelling reason for assigning himself. Had he reflected he probably would not have made such an assignment; but he acted hastily and evidently with questionable wisdom. This action has embarrassed and is embarrassing the receivership. If he were now to withdraw from further participation in the receivership proceedings the embarrassment would be relieved; and the belief is ventured here that, on further reflection, he will recognize the propriety of so doing and, by withdrawing, will open the way for another judge with appropriate authority to conduct the further proceedings.

Any other federal judge would have immediately obeyed such an admonition from the Supreme Court. Not Manton. In an extraordinary opinion issued a month later, Manton announced that, "[a]fter the most anxious and self-critical consideration, I am convinced that I was fully justified" in taking jurisdiction over the Interborough receivership. Declaring, as if he sat in judgment of the Supreme Court rather than the other way around, that Justice Van Devanter's opinion was based on a "misapprehension," Manton said he would not follow the Court's direction after all. His "profound convictions" would not allow him to.[31]

Manton's reasons for disregarding the Supreme Court were strained and unconvincing. The Court's alleged "misapprehension" was that "the sole ground" on which he had acted was his belief that individuals made better receivers than trust companies, when in fact the determining factors were the "far-reaching and extensive public interests" involved in the Interborough receivership. But neither in this opinion nor his earlier ruling did Manton explain why the unusual importance and complexity of the Interborough situation required his oversight as opposed to that of a district judge. The duty judge at the time of the Interborough application was Robert P. Patterson, not only a gifted lawyer but a highly skilled administrator who founded his own major law firm and would play a critical role in mobilizing the US military for World War II as undersecretary (and later secretary) of war.

Manton also sought refuge in the longstanding principle, most famously articulated by Chief Justice John Marshall in *Cohens v. Virginia*, that a federal court has "no more right to decline the exercise of jurisdiction which is given, than to usurp that which is not given." Manton intimated he was doing nothing more than fulfilling his duty under *Cohens* when the Interborough receivership papers "were presented to me," despite "the exceptionally onerous labors and the exceptionally difficult judicial duties likely to be involved," and that this same sense of duty impelled him to continue his sacrifice and remain in charge. The passivity of this self-portrayal stood in stark contrast with Manton's very public campaign virtually inviting litigants to come directly to him for the appointment of receiverships. It also begged the critical question of why it was necessary for Manton to assume this burden rather than the Southern District's duty judge, who literally did have a duty to take on the case.

"In effect," wrote the *New York Herald Tribune*, Manton decreed that "the Supreme Court did not know what it was talking about." Or as Felix Frankfurter put it in an acerbic unsigned essay in the *New Republic*, "The worthy judge thinks very much better of his own opinion than he does of the Supreme Court." Frankfurter's essay, "Judge Manton and the Supreme Court," gave vent to his long-held animosity toward Manton. It presented Manton's "judicial shenanigans" in the Interborough case as of a piece with Manton's earlier rulings—both roundly rejected by the Supreme Court—in the subway fare and American Tobacco litigations. The future Supreme Court justice could not believe that Manton's "moral obtuseness" in the Interborough case and decision to "thumb his nose at the Supreme Court" would go unchallenged.[32]

It did not go unchallenged. The Manhattan Railway, controlled by a new group of stockholders and directors, had grown concerned that Manton was favoring the interests of the Interborough at the expense of its own. In early August 1933, it declared it would refuse to recognize Manton's rulings, and its counsel filed an "affidavit of prejudice" seeking Manton's withdrawal, which sensationally charged that Manton had a "strong personal bias against the interests of the Manhattan Railway Company" and was "motivated by political and ulterior purposes inimical to Manhattan's welfare." Manton swiftly and angrily denied this application as untimely, legally insufficient, and the product of bad faith, and threatened to hold the Manhattan's lawyer in contempt.[33]

The fight now returned to the Supreme Court. Manhattan Railway, having been told by a Second Circuit judge to proceed directly to the high court, filed a petition for a writ of prohibition claiming that Manton's continued control over the receiverships "threatens to destroy the public faith and confidence in the Federal courts generally and in the Federal courts of the Southern District of New York particularly." Privately, as C. C. Burlingham advised Chief Justice Hughes, "many lawyers think it is up to the Supreme Court to deal with the situation," as the "unseemly spectacle" of a "largely personal" conflict between Manton and the Southern District, along with Manton's "flouting of the Supreme Court," had "already done great harm." Burlingham pleaded: "Cannot something be done to set things right?"[34]

On September 21, 1933, from his summer home in Maine, Justice Stone signed an order restraining Manton from taking any further action in the Interborough receivership pending the Supreme Court's resolution of the writ of prohibition. With the stage set for another rebuke from the nation's highest court, Manton decided it was time for him to surrender. He did so with a characteristic lack of grace and candor in a short written opinion that made no mention of Justice Stone's order or the pending

Supreme Court proceedings, boasted that the Supreme Court's prior opinion had "completely sustained" his construction of the law, pretended he had been planning to retire from the case since July, and attributed his withdrawal to the sudden realization that "[t]he task of supervising these receiverships," added to his other duties as senior circuit judge, "is too onerous to continue another year."[35]

* * *

It was not just a philosophical disagreement with his Southern District brethren, or even party loyalty, that animated Manton's actions in the receivership dispute. C. C. Burlingham sensed this at the time. Manton was "not acting politically" in assuming control over the Interborough receivership, Burlingham told Frankfurter. "What he wants is personal power and patronage which will help him financially in the end."[36]

In due time the publicly available facts caught up with Burlingham's hunch. Thomas E. Murray, one of the Interborough receivers appointed by Manton, was a "well-respected figure in the New York Irish community" and a successful inventor, engineer, and businessman "worthy of the confidence of any judge or court."[37] He was also, unbeknownst to the public or any of the courts that passed on Manton's receivership appointments, an investor in Manton's Forest Hills Terrace Corporation.

In May and July 1932, just weeks before his Interborough appointment, Murray wrote two checks totaling $22,500—roughly $450,000 in today's dollars—to purchase a 16 percent interest in Forest Hills. Manton used the money to reduce Forest Hills's debt to the Bank of the United States, whose liquidator was pressing him for payment. As of the time of Manton's trial seven years later, Murray had not received any dividends or other benefit from his investment. The stock was likely worthless, or nearly so, when he bought it. Which is not to say, when viewed from a different angle, that Murray made a bad investment. Over the life of the Interborough receivership, fees for the receivers exceeded $300,000, and Murray presumably collected around half of that.[38]

The other Manton-appointed receiver, Victor Dowling, drew criticism even at the time. While Dowling had spent two decades as a respected state appellate judge, his affiliation with the Chadbourne law firm raised questions about his independence in light of Thomas Chadbourne's influence in transit affairs. It was not until Dowling swore he had severed his ties to the Chadbourne firm that Manton overruled the objections to Dowling and allowed him to continue as receiver.[39]

Public criticism forced the Chadbourne firm itself to bow out as counsel to the Interborough receivers. As a result, the firm lost out on the more than $400,000 in legal fees that the Interborough receivership wound up generating for successor counsel. That would have been a generous judicial "thank you" for Chadbourne and Levy's help in arranging for Lord & Thomas to pump $250,000 into Manton's real estate ventures.[40]

FBI files reveal another, previously undisclosed abuse of the Interborough receivership: a secret kickback scheme that enriched Manton family members and cronies. Dowling and Murray needed a new insurance broker to handle the Interborough's fire insurance business, which generated $100,000 in annual premiums, the biggest such account in the city. They selected John Eckert & Company, a logical choice since Eckert was one of the largest and best-qualified brokers in town. But there was a string attached: Eckert had to split its commissions, 50/50, with another brokerage firm that was seeking the business, Kennedy Sullivan Corp. Kennedy Sullivan, a tiny operation, had no real qualifications for the job. But two of its three shareholders had strong connections to the judge overseeing the receivership: Edward W. Sullivan, the brother of Manton's business partner James Sullivan, and Mary E. McKenna, a widow and Manton's sister.[41]

Over six years, Eckert surreptitiously kicked back some $43,000 of its commissions (worth over $900,000 today). About half of this money went to Mary McKenna and her daughter Ruth, Manton's niece, who worked for Kennedy Sullivan and took over her mother's ownership stake when the business later merged with Steinreich & Company, owned by Evelyn Wagner, the niece of Senator Robert F. Wagner. The payments, Eckert's president Alexander Heid understood, were "Judge Manton's way of taking care of his widowed sister." The funds received by Wagner facilitated a more direct personal benefit to Manton: They began flowing the same month her husband, Kenneth Steinreich, guaranteed premium payments on a life insurance policy that Manton pledged in order to borrow $50,000. Some of Eckert's kickbacks went to another firm owned by the brothers of James A. Farley, FDR's postmaster general and longtime political advisor, when they, with Murray's blessing, muscled in for a piece of the action.[42]

None of the recipients of the kickbacks did any actual work for the Interborough. When asked by the FBI why he paid them anyway, Heid explained that the reason was obvious: in New York, it was "not what you know but who you know that counts."[43]

* * *

Manton exploited the Fox Theatres receivership in much the same way, and for longer; unlike the Interborough, Manton never relinquished control over Fox Theatres. The receivers awarded insurance business to Kennedy Sullivan and also to Ruth McKenna, Manton's niece, after she went to work for a new employer.[44] As in the Interborough matter, Manton's hand-picked receivers knew who buttered their bread. John F. Sherman, the co-receiver, had previously expressed interest in buying the Alamac and Esplanade hotels from Manton, which helped Manton borrow $345,000 on the hotels from the Ungerleider Financial Corporation in 1929.[45]

When Sherman died in 1934, Manton replaced him with Milton C. Weisman, who was then acting as Manton's personal lawyer. Immediately before his appointment, Weisman had wrapped up a favorable settlement of Manton's debts to various banks. Notably, at his trial, Manton could not recall if he ever paid Weisman's bill for his work on the settlement, and admitted he at most paid Weisman a "small fee." Weisman would not have minded; his firm collected $122,500 in fees from the Fox Theatres receivership. Returning the favor, Weisman later deposited significant amounts of Fox Theatres funds with a Brooklyn bank in order to facilitate the bank's making sizeable loans to Manton. Weisman also introduced Manton to a client of his, a garment center businessman, who gave Manton a $25,000 interest-free loan.[46]

Weisman was not the only Manton crony who benefited from the Fox Theatres receivership. On January 30, 1939, in what was Manton's last official act before resigning from the bench, Manton appointed Kenneth Steinreich—the same individual who had guaranteed his life insurance premiums—as Weisman's co-trustee to implement Fox Theatres' liquidation plan.[47]

Even more significantly, in 1937 Manton approved the sale of a valuable Fox-owned movie theater and other properties to the Skouras Theater Corp. for a seemingly low price of $155,000. The sale was backed by Weisman and opposed by Fox creditors, who did not know that Skouras was paying another $25,000 in the deal—to Manton. The payment was made through Harvey B. Newins, a realtor and longtime Manton friend. After Manton's conviction, George P. Skouras and Newins were indicted for bribing Manton with a total of $30,000 in "loans." The case against Skouras was mysteriously dropped in 1944; according to a previously undisclosed FBI memo, this was because the US Army deemed Skouras "indispensable to the success of certain Army Air Force missions which were thought would contribute materially to the early end of the war." Although Skouras escaped criminal prosecution, he agreed, in the face of a civil lawsuit by Fox creditors, to rescind the tainted sale and pay back rent.[48]

* * *

But for the Supreme Court's intervention in the Interborough case, Manton undoubtedly would have taken control of other receiverships during the Depression. The official history of the Cravath, Swaine & Moore law firm relates another, albeit unsuccessful, attempt shortly after the Second Circuit's ruling in the Interborough case. As Paramount Pictures was heading into equity receivership in January 1933, an individual "who was later implicated in transactions resulting in" Manton's conviction "suggested that he could arrange to have Judge Manton take the case, and assure the Paramount of easy sailing in the reorganization." This unnamed individual insisted that the Cravath partner in charge of the Paramount representation go see Manton. "After evasive double talk," Manton "urged adoption of the mechanics used in the criticized then current IRT receivership, viz., that Judge Manton would designate himself to act as a district judge to take the matter." The Cravath partner declined the suggestion and reported the offer to Senior District Judge Knox.[49]

Manton found ways to manipulate receiverships for his benefit even without directly exercising jurisdiction over the case. With a receivership looming for Fox New England Theatres, Inc. (owned by the already-bankrupt Fox Theatres), Manton cut a deal with Jacob Handelsman, a Manhattan money broker. Handelsman located a motion picture magnate willing to buy Fox New England's theaters at what Manton assured him would be a favorable price. In exchange, Handelsman agreed to buy Manton's Alamac Hotel, and cut a $10,000 check to Manton's Forest Hills Terrace Corporation as a down payment. At Handelsman's request, Manton called Judge Edwin S. Thomas of the District of Connecticut, where the Fox New England receivership was being filed, and instructed him to install a lawyer friendly to the magnate as one of the receivers.[50]

A year later, Manton raised another $10,000 for Forest Hills Terrace through another bankruptcy reorganization. Judge Clarence G. Galston of the Eastern District of New York had appointed Manton's business associate, James J. Sullivan, as one of the trustees for Kings Brewery, Inc. Sullivan, in turn, utilized the services of another Manton associate: William J. Fallon, who was instrumental in carrying out Manton's corrupt schemes and, when the scandal broke, was dubbed Manton's "bag man."

Roughly the same age as Manton, Fallon also grew up on Long Island, on the North Shore, the son of an Irish-American Civil War veteran. Manton first encountered Fallon in 1907, when he called Fallon as a character witness at the murder trial of Dr. James Simpson. The two men renewed their acquaintance at the end of the 1920s when Fallon tried to sell Manton stock in an encyclopedia company.[51]

"Portly" and "silver-tongued," Fallon had tried and largely failed in a variety of different enterprises as a banker, theater ticket agent, zipper manufacturer, coal plant operator, and radio station owner. His ticket agency, Tyson Company Inc., was forced into receivership in 1925 by a group of angry stockholders, who accused Fallon of diverting company funds for his personal benefit. Fallon raised $300,000 from three hundred blue-blooded investors that included the likes of J. Pierpont Morgan,

Otto H. Kahn, several bank presidents, and "a host of others whose names are known to the Social Register readers and to every first class hotel clerk in town." When Tyson stopped issuing annual reports and an examination of its books disclosed it was insolvent, the investors reacted with less than a sense of aristocratic good cheer.[52]

After reconnecting with Manton, Fallon established himself as a useful intermediary to raise money for the judge. This is what Fallon did in the case of the Kings Brewery. Fallon approached Charles A. Rogers, an insurance broker, and asked him for a $10,000 loan. The note, he said, would be endorsed by Judge Manton. In exchange, Fallon promised that Rogers would get Kings Brewery's insurance business from Sullivan. Rogers insisted on meeting with Manton personally, and after doing so made the unsecured loan to "Sullivan," obtaining Manton's endorsement on the note. The proceeds of the loan were plowed into Forest Hills Terrace Corporation. The insurance business promised to Rogers, however, never materialized. Rogers sent Manton a letter threatening to expose the transaction. The loan was then repaid.[53]

The reorganization of the Prudence Company, a major real estate investment firm, offered Manton a smorgasbord of opportunities. At Manton's request, Eastern District judge Grover M. Moscowitz—the same judge who been censured but not impeached by Congress in 1929—appointed John N. McGrath, a vice president of Sterling National Bank, as one of three co-trustees. McGrath, in turn, gave Fallon a job as an "investigator" and a large office in Prudence's building at 43rd Street and Madison Avenue. From that perch Fallon would hold many meetings with Second Circuit litigants and their representatives to negotiate loans and payments to Manton.[54]

Fallon and McGrath tapped into Prudence's coffers to help Manton financially. In addition to the sums deposited by Milton Weisman as receiver for Fox Theatres, Prudence, too, opened accounts and deposited funds at the Brooklyn bank that made a personal loan to Manton. Prudence also purchased some $50,000 of carpets from Manton's Modern Carpet Cleaning Company to install in the Essex House and other of its hotels. Prudence hotels even purchased chickens from a broiler farm business Manton operated at his Fairacres property in Bayport. Fallon also obtained a $5,000 loan for Manton from a businessman in negotiations with Fallon to acquire property in Newark controlled by Prudence.[55]

McGrath, the Prudence trustee, expressed his gratitude to Manton directly. Sometime in 1937, Manton went to see McGrath for a loan. McGrath said that as a matter of policy his bank did not make loans to public officials. But, McGrath said, he would be happy to personally loan Manton $12,000 (nearly a quarter of a million dollars today). On May 28, 1937, the same day McGrath received $32,000 in fees for his service as a Prudence trustee, McGrath gave Manton a cashier's check for $12,000. This "loan" was unsecured and memorialized only in a promissory note reflecting no interest rate. As of the time the Manton scandal broke in January 1939, nearly two years later, Manton had made no payments of principal or interest to McGrath.[56]

CHAPTER TEN

"Inequitable Conduct"

The Cigarette Lighter Case

In September 1932 Alfred F. Reilly found himself in a tough spot. Reilly was the president and controlling stockholder of the Evans Case Company of North Attleboro, Massachusetts, then known as "Jewelry City" for its profusion of jewelry producers. Adept in jewelry design and electroplating (the process of coating metals with a film of silver or gold), Reilly made his mark devising silver-plated vanity cases that became immensely popular with young women after World War I. Evans Case's product array also included costume jewelry, pocket flasks, handbags, and—with smoking becoming more socially acceptable, and even fashionable, among women—cigarette cases and cigarette lighters. Novel, decorative design elements, such as cloisonné enamel, textured metal, pastel colors, and Art Deco flourishes, helped Evans products stand out and reel in their female clientele. Even after the Depression began, it remained a "fast growing concern," launching new products eagerly awaited by the trade press and sold exclusively in stores like Saks & Co. on Fifth Avenue in New York.[1]

The business itself was not what was troubling Alfred Reilly in September 1932. His worries arose from an arena about which he knew little and could control less: litigation.

The litigation concerned two of the company's cigarette lighters: the "Evans Automatic Lighter" and the "Evans Roller-Bearing Lighter." The exteriors of the lighters, sold widely throughout the United States, bore the telltale signs of Reilly's craftsmanship. Their innards, however, did not rightfully belong to Reilly or Evans Case at all—or so claimed Art Metal Works, Inc. in a patent infringement suit it filed in 1930 against one of Evans Case's customers, the Abraham & Straus department store of Brooklyn. Both Evans lighters, the suit contended, infringed a 1928 patent on a cigar lighter issued to Louis V. Aronson, the owner of Art Metal.

The patent boosted Art Metal's sales of lighters under its popular "Ronson" brand name—a name derived from that of its owner, modified just enough to obscure his Jewish roots. The precocious son of German-Jewish immigrants, Aronson graduated from the New York City public schools at the age of twelve and proceeded, in a very literal sense, to set the world ablaze. He was a magician of ignition, inventing a "Wind-match" that would light in adverse weather, a kitchen match that greatly reduced the risk of accidents, a non-phosphorous match that won an award from the Belgian government, and a fuse used to detonate bombs during World War I. He founded Art Metal while still in his twenties, patented the first Ronson pocket lighter in 1910, and built the business into the industry leader, which it remained for decades. Reportedly Aronson rose at 5:00 a.m. and sometimes slept in the office, yet still found time to be prominent in Jewish philanthropy and Republican politics. He was also a cofounder, director, and officer of a Newark bank. Aronson, in short, was a force to be reckoned with.[2]

Reilly's day of reckoning now felt close at hand. As the manufacturer of the allegedly infringing lighters and, therefore, the real party in interest, Evans Case stepped in for Abraham & Straus to defend against the Art Metal suit. The case was filed in federal district court in Brooklyn and heard by Judge Clarence G. Galston. With so much at stake, the litigation was, the judge later observed, "conducted in a spirit of bitter controversy." Handing down his decision in October 1931, Judge Galston reached a mixed verdict: The Evans Automatic Lighter infringed Aronson's patent; the Evans Roller-Bearing Lighter did not.[3]

All things considered, Reilly could live with the district judge's decision. Evans Case had already discontinued making its Automatic Lighter; the real money was with the Roller-Bearing Lighter, and as to that product Evans Case had prevailed. Aronson, however, would not leave well enough alone. He was determined not simply to win the litigation, but to crush Reilly and eliminate Evans Case as a competitor, according to Reilly's later testimony in the case. Shortly after Judge Galston's ruling, Reilly met Aronson for lunch at Aronson's private suite at the Newark Athletic Club. Playing the role of the benevolent victor, Reilly metaphorically offered his adversary a peace pipe. "I think we would be better off making lighters than fighting," he told Aronson, hoping to initiate a settlement dialogue. Aronson responded by metaphorically taking Reilly's peace pipe and breaking it in two. "It is unfair to say that you have won the suit," he snarled, "because we are going to appeal it." He added (Reilly claimed), "There isn't room for two of us in the lighter business," and made clear he expected to be the survivor. Reilly challenged Aronson to "take me, if you can."[4]

Aronson could, and did. On August 23, 1932, the Second Circuit reversed Judge Galston's ruling in a unanimous opinion by Augustus Hand, joined by Manton and Thomas Swan, and held that the Roller-Bearing Lighter did indeed infringe Aronson's patent.[5] For Reilly, the Court of Appeals' decision spelled disaster. Not only would Evans Case be enjoined from future sales of its lighters, but it also faced a potential damages award for past infringement in the hundreds of thousands of dollars.

On top of all this, Aronson sought to exploit the Second Circuit's ruling to undermine Evans Case's standing with the trade. Within days of the ruling, Art Metal dispatched its salesmen and flooded the country with telegrams, telegraphs, circulars, and advertisements in trade journals to spread the news of its "sweeping victory" and to threaten retailers with damages suits if they did not return their existing stock of Evans Case lighters. One retailer wrote Reilly that a Ronson salesman called at his store and "put the fear of God into everyone around here stating we were liable if we offered anything for sale." A Detroit merchant claimed that his Ronson salesman told him that Aronson "was out to break Reilly" and "would fight to the finish to get Reilly."[6]

"They were practically putting [me] out of business," Reilly later testified.[7] But Reilly was about to discover that, in the world of New York City litigation in the 1930s, it helped to have friends in high places.

Reilly explained his predicament to a longtime friend, Morris White—
"[a] particular friend," as Reilly would call him at Manton's trial.[8] Morris
White epitomized how rapidly business fortunes could rise and fall in
early-twentieth-century America. Arriving in 1903 from a village near
Odessa, Russia, as a thirteen-year-old "tousled, curly haired stripling,"
White stayed in school for all of ten days before landing a job in a hand-
bag factory in New York. By the age of nineteen, with $50 in capital, he
went into business for himself, selling cheap handbags off a pushcart. By
the age of forty he was worth $20 million, hailed as "the Henry Ford of
handbags" for his mass-produced line of bags made out of pin seal leather.
His firm, Morris White, Inc., was the largest manufacturer of ladies'
handbags and fancy leather goods in the world.[9] But when the Depression hit, customer orders for White's handbags plunged, and White's real
estate ventures began hemorrhaging money. By early 1931 both White
and his firm were bankrupt.

By the end of 1931 White was an experienced Second Circuit
litigant. Manton wrote an opinion overruling most of the objections
lodged by creditors to White's plan of reorganization.[10] Along the way it
appears White learned something of Manton's proclivities—information
he could now use to help Reilly. White brought Reilly to see Milton
C. Weisman, who had helped advocate for the Morris White Inc. plan
of reorganization and would later serve as Manton's personal lawyer.
Weisman's legal qualifications were unclear: He was not a patent lawyer.
Nonetheless, by the end of the meeting Reilly had retained Weisman as
his new lawyer for the Art Metal case for $10,000 in cash and another
$10,000 in notes.[11]

The next day, Reilly entered White's factory on Sixth Avenue between
18th and 19th Streets, greeted by the smell of leather wafting from the
hides arrayed in the well-manicured production area. In his office White
had someone else to introduce Reilly to: William Fallon. Fallon and
Reilly walked outside into the unseasonably warm late September air and
hailed one of the long taxicabs of the era, so roomy there was little risk
a conversation between passengers in the backseat could be overhead by

the driver in the front. In the cab, Fallon said to Reilly: "Morris tells me you are in a tough spot." "Yes," Reilly confirmed. He explained that the Court of Appeals "has just reversed a decision on me, and has placed me in a very difficult position." "Stop worrying," Fallon assured Reilly. "I am a great friend and associate of Judge Manton, and I am going to see him sometime this afternoon. If you would have lunch with me tomorrow, it will be a pleasure, and I will tell you what he has to say."[12]

The next day, September 23, Reilly and Fallon met for lunch at the Hotel Astor in Times Square. Lunch was served to gentlemen only, in the Hunting Room, "the hub of hubbub," a favorite haunt for Broadway bigwigs and other important figures in the entertainment world.[13] Fallon reported that, as promised, he had a talk with Judge Manton about the Art Metal patent litigation—indeed, a talking-to. Fallon claimed that he "gave [Manton] the dickens for giving [Reilly] such a tough break." As if to defend himself, Manton told Fallon that the Evans Case attorneys "had made a very poor presentation of the case, and that he had not taken a great deal of interest in it and signed it [the opinion] as a routine matter." His interest reawakened, Manton summoned the records of the case. Alas, Judge Galston's decision still seemed "very well written" to him.[14]

Fallon, however, proceeded to tell the judge about the aggressive methods that Art Metal had been using to exploit the Second Circuit's ruling. This gave Manton an idea. Coincidentally, just two weeks earlier, in an unrelated case from Connecticut involving a patent on finger rings, Manton and two other Circuit judges had granted a petition from the infringers seeking leave to amend their answer to allege "inequitable conduct" on the part of the patent owner "in publishing and disseminating misleading statements said to be false regarding the decision of this court." Evans Case's attorneys, he suggested, should seek the same relief.[15]

Inequitable conduct was, and is, a legal doctrine that enables those accused of patent infringement to turn the tables on their accusers. Patent infringement cases call upon the court to employ its equitable powers to protect the patent owner's rights. Applying the maxim that "those who seek equity must do equity," courts have long recognized that a patent owner's own inequitable conduct can disqualify it from the law's protection. The doctrine typically involves misconduct in the procurement of the patent, such as a misrepresentation to the Patent Office, but can also include misconduct during the patent litigation itself. But under Manton's suggestion, Art Metal's conduct *after* winning the litigation could erase that victory, leaving it without a remedy for an adjudicated violation of its rights. In football terms, it would be as if the punishment for excessive celebration of a touchdown was to take the seven points off the board, rather than a 15-yard penalty on the ensuing kickoff.

Reilly heeded Manton's advice. His legal team—now including Milton Weisman—successfully petitioned the same panel of Second Circuit judges for permission to apply to the District Court for leave to assert the defense of "inequitable conduct" by Art Metal.[16] The case was sent back to Judge Galston. What was already a highly contentious litigation grew even nastier. Seeking to press his advantage even further, Aronson had Art Metal file a second suit claiming that a new Evans Case lighter, known as the "Trig-a-Lite," also infringed his patent. Reilly fought back on this new front and simultaneously pursued the inequitable conduct defense as aggressively as he could, collecting evidence from dozens of big department stores and other retailers across the country about how Art Metal portrayed its Second Circuit victory.[17]

In July 1933, Judge Galston issued a lengthy opinion sifting through the evidence and concluding that Evans Case had failed to establish that Art Metal acted in bad faith. Some of Art Metal's telegrams and notices, and some of Art Metal's salesmen, may have been guilty of "linguistic inadequacy" and of even using "bad" language that was "not justified by the facts" or that, when "read literally," might have "caused a false impression to be drawn by the trade." But none of these communications, Judge Galston found, justified an inference that Art Metal set out with "evil intent" to deliberately misrepresent the scope of the Second Circuit's decision.[18]

By now Reilly had learned well the lesson that the District Court's ruling is not the last word. And he had good reason to think that Evans Case could win the case on appeal, irrespective of the merits of Judge Galston's ruling.

* * *

In February 1933, when Reilly and Fallon were together in New York, Fallon asked Reilly for money. "Al," he said, "I am in terrible need of a couple of hundred dollars. Could you lend it to me for a couple of weeks?" Reilly cut a check for $200. It was the first of many such requests. In the first half of 1933 Reilly or James Nolan, his general manager and assistant treasurer, gave Fallon a dozen or so checks, all made payable to the "Allied Rediscount Corporation." In all they totaled $3,900, a reasonable annual wage for a middle-class worker in 1933. The advances all represented "loans," but Fallon never repaid any of them, and Reilly never asked him to.[19]

In June 1933, as Judge Galston neared his ruling on Evan Case's inequitable conduct defense, Fallon began asking for money for Judge Manton. Manton's doctor had ordered him to take a sea trip for health reasons, Fallon explained to Nolan, and "it would be a nice gesture on the part of the Evans Case Company if they provided the funds"— $1,000—"with which this trip could be made." A couple of months later, Fallon told Nolan, "It would be a nice thing if the Evans Case Company purchased a box for Judge Manton's use at the World Series" for $500. Then in October 1933, Fallon explained that Manton "was in a very bad way financially, and hard pressed about some taxes that were due." Again, Fallon thought it would "be a nice thing" if Evans Case could provide $3,350 to help the judge pay his taxes.[20]

Each time Reilly coughed up the requested funds, but he wanted to put a stop to Fallon's seemingly never-ending requests for money. He told Fallon that from now on, he would put Fallon on the Evans Case payroll, at a "salary" of $100 per week.[21] That no-show job would continue for three and one-half years, from October 1933 to March 1937. One more sizeable payment, though, was still to come.

* * *

In the early part of 1934, Reilly met Fallon again in New York. Fallon asked for a loan of $10,000 for a zipper business that he was involved with, called Liberty Tool & Die, in Providence, Rhode Island. "It's impossible," Reilly replied. A few days later Fallon was back with another proposal. Now, Fallon was asking Reilly for a $15,000 loan—to Judge Manton. Reilly said that this, too, was simply a financial impossibility.[22]

"Well," Fallon countered, "suppose your cases turn out okay?" Reilly's resistance evaporated. "Well, that would be a different story." And so it was agreed. Fallon, however, said that he needed to show Manton written proof of Reilly's commitment. This, he suggested, should take the form of a letter in which the loan would be disguised as an investment in Fallon's zipper business. This letter, drafted by Nolan and dated February 19, 1934, prattled on about "the research information" and "the research work" that Fallon's organization had supplied; "the numerous other occasions on which we have been able to employ the services of your organization"; Evan Case's "desire to continue the arrangements which have been in existence during the past months"; and so forth—all "camouflage" and "subterfuge," as Nolan and Reilly later testified.[23]

A different form of camouflage was deployed when Evans Case's appeal was heard on April 3 by a panel consisting of Judges Manton, Learned Hand, and Chase. While Art Metal's lawyer was addressing the court, Milton Weisman, who appeared for Evans Case, jumped up and interrupted—something that is never done at appellate arguments. This drew a severe censure from Manton of Weisman's unprofessional conduct. The whole scene had been prearranged in advance by Manton and Weisman, in order to "make it appear that [the judge] was unfriendly toward Weisman."[24]

On April 30, 1934, Fallon telephoned Reilly from New York with some very good news: "We ha[ve] a favorable decision."[25] The Second Circuit, in a 2–1 ruling, had reversed Judge Galston's ruling on the inequitable conduct issue. Art Metal would get no damages for Evans Case's past violation of its patent rights, and no injunctive relief preventing Evans Case from further infringement. Art Metal's suit was dismissed. So too was Art Metal's second suit: In a separate decision issued the same day, the Circuit unanimously agreed with Judge Galston that Evans Case's Trig-a-Lite lighter did not infringe the Aronson patent. The opinion for the Court in both appeals was written by Judge Manton, with Judge Hand the dissenter in the inequitable conduct case.[26]

Along with this good news Fallon had a demand to make of Reilly: Manton needed his money, and he needed it right away. The judge was, Fallon explained, "in bad circumstances." Reilly met up with Fallon the next day at the Biltmore Hotel in Providence, Rhode Island, and delivered $10,000 in cash along with three checks for $500 apiece, short of the promised $15,000. However, Reilly reminded Fallon of the $3,350 check delivered the prior October to help pay Manton's taxes, and argued that the check should be credited toward the $15,000. Fallon reacted sourly. "I don't think the Judge intends you should deduct the tax money," he said. Reilly said he was sorry but he was tapped out.[27]

Apparently Manton was satisfied, for although the $15,000 loan was never repaid, Reilly was not asked for more money either. Reilly got to meet the judge that summer at the Belle Terre Hotel in Port Jefferson, Long Island, where Fallon introduced them. Reilly and Manton even struck up a friendship; Reilly golfed with Manton a few times, went dancing with him and Eva, met him for lunch in Bayport and the City, and dined with the Mantons at the St. Regis and the Waldorf-Astoria.[28]

Thanks to Manton's rulings, Evans Case came back from the brink. By early 1937 the business had seven hundred full-time employees and announced bonuses and salary hikes. It was able to take full advantage of an explosion in cigarette lighter sales during the 1940s. Evans Case also began producing innovative leather handbags, equipped with matching cigarette cases, combs, mirrors, perfume atomizers, and, of course, lighters. Reilly would introduce each year's new line at widely covered fashion shows held in New York City hotels. "Evans is elegance," became the company's slogan.[29] The nearly $40,000 in payoffs that Reilly had shelled out, not so elegantly, to Manton and Fallon proved a worthwhile investment.

The year 1934 proved to be a dreadful one for Louis Aronson. The month before Judge Manton's rulings put an end to his patent infringement litigation, Aronson's wife of forty-three years, Gertrude, died of pneumonia. Art Metal asked the Supreme Court to review Manton's decision, but the high court declined. Making it all worse, Aronson knew he had likely lost because of foul play. Back in the fall of 1932, Morris White—just days after setting up Reilly with Milton Weisman and

Fallon—told one of Aronson's good friends that, at a dinner in Washington, DC, Reilly had blurted out that he was not worried about the case because "Judge Manton will take care of it." Shortly thereafter, White asked for a private meeting where he warned Aronson that Reilly was a "skunk" who would use "unfair means" to win the litigation and who had already "taken steps" to get Manton to reopen the case after Art Metal's initial victory. Why White chose to stab his "friend" Reilly in the back in this way is unclear. Very possibly he hoped (or was asked) to spark a bidding war between the two litigants; he cryptically offered to "do anything he could" to help Aronson. If that was bait, Aronson did not take it. Years before Aronson had been solicited for a bribe by a New Jersey state banking commissioner. Unlike Reilly, Aronson resisted the temptation and later testified about the incident at a legislative committee hearing in Trenton.[30]

Two years later, Fallon unwittingly confirmed Aronson's suspicions. "A night-club habitué," Fallon "liked to drink, and he liked to talk while drinking."[31] One night at the Essex House, Fallon struck up a conversation with an advertising executive attending a trade show. Drinking heavily, he boasted to his new-found acquaintance how he had been "the power behind" the decision in an "important case"—the Art Metal case. This was accomplished, he indiscreetly intimated, through a payoff to Judge Manton. Unbeknownst to Fallon, the advertising executive used to work for Art Metal and promptly reported the conversation to his former employer (though without, at the time, revealing Fallon's name).[32]

Aronson no doubt felt vindication when, in 1939, after Manton's conviction, the Second Circuit reheard the Art Metal cases and overturned both of Judge Manton's rulings.[33] Judge Hand's dissenting opinion from 1934 now became the ruling of the Court on the inequitable conduct issue. Unfortunately, Aronson did not have much time to savor the triumph. A year later he was dead, at the age of sixty-nine, after an illness of several months. His patent, scheduled to expire in 1945, was given new life in 1944 when Congress extended the patent term by seven years, the same period of time Manton's ruling had wrongfully deprived Aronson of its use.[34]

* * *

Manton was not a man much given to irony, yet his main opinion in the Art Metal litigation, considered in light of his own inequitable conduct, fairly drips with it. In finding that Art Metal had forfeited its right to judicial relief for Evans Case's adjudicated infringement, Manton emphasized the special nature of a "court of equity," which "acts only when its conscience commands" and must never be "the abetter of iniquity." "Courts," Manton righteously intoned, "cannot permit unfair practices to go on to harass or obstruct a business rival."[35]

It was in these highly moralistic terms that Manton evaluated Art Metal's conduct following its litigation victory in August 1932. He condemned Art Metal's "determination to eliminate the Evans Case Company as a competitor" in the lighter business, citing the Aronson-Reilly *mano-a-mano* at the Newark Athletic Club. Where Judge Galston saw only a genuine belief by Art Metal as to the implications of the Second Circuit's decree, coupled with some instances of sloppiness, Judge Manton saw only bad faith, a "campaign of misrepresentation" and a "policy of molestation" designed to "intimidate" and "coerce" Evans Case's customers and "driv[e] [Evans Case] out of business." And unlike Galston, Manton insisted that the actions of Art Metal's salesmen in the field were attributable to their employer.[36]

All this left Learned Hand quite befuddled. Hand could find "not even the proverbial scintilla of evidence" of conscious wrongdoing by Art Metal. Assuming the truth of Reilly's account of his conversation with Aronson, Hand saw nothing unlawful in it: The very point of a patent monopoly is to give the patent holder the "power to stop others' activity." Manton's moralism seemed to evoke a standard of behavior from a bygone era, at odds with the modern world of competitive capitalism, and Hand mocked it with biblical imagery in his inimitable style. Aronson may have sought to "press [his] advantage to the full," may have acted "ruthlessly," may have "threaten[ed] the defendants' business with extinction"; yet Hand "kn[e]w of no doctrine" requiring, or even permitting, courts "to temper the wind to the shorn lamb."[37]

Hand assumed that the salesmen, "being a zealous folk, not sensitive, and perhaps not scrupulous," bent the truth; but he was "not much concerned with what the salesmen did say," for he believed their acts did not tarnish the company's good faith. The majority erred, Hand argued, in applying principles of tort law—which generally hold an employer liable for damages caused by its agents and employees—to reach the "monstrous" conclusion that "the sins of those he employs" should be grounds for denying a patent-holder the protection of the court.[38]

Commentators were also perplexed. Hand's dissent "appears to be well founded in precedent," said the *George Washington Law Review*. The *Columbia Law Review* agreed, and added that even if Art Metal did engage in inequitable conduct, "the action of the court seems especially drastic." The *Yale Law Journal* similarly called Manton's opinion a "deviation from precedent" that "appears harsh" in its consequences.[39]

Yet it is hard to say that Manton's decision lacked foundation, or necessarily would have come out differently but for Reilly's financial inducements. There certainly was evidence that Art Metal misstated the scope of the Circuit's prior decree and that Evans Case's customers were misled (as Galston and Hand acknowledged). The critical question thus became whether Art Metal intended that result or not, and there was some evidence to support both views. Indeed, Hand avoided a finding adverse to Art Metal on that issue only by refusing to hold the company accountable for the statements by its salesmen. To a twenty-first century lawyer, it is Hand's view—that the salesmen's conduct could not establish the company's culpability—that sounds odd to the ear.

Then too, it must be remembered that Manton could not have decided the appeal in Evans Case's favor without Judge Chase's agreement. Chase did not have the sturdiest of judicial backbones, or the intellectual faculties of a Learned Hand; the Vermonter "preferred his outings on the golf course to his struggles with arguments and judicial opinions."[40] Though respected by them, Chase was not part of the "intimate" inner circle formed by the Manton-loathing Hands and Swan, and was closer to Manton than they were.[41] Still, there is no reason to believe that Chase did not truly believe that Art Metal acted in bad faith or that the proper remedy for that misconduct was to take away its right to injunctive relief and damages.

Probably the most that can be said from an objective perspective is that the result in the Art Metal case seems disproportionate and unjust in relation to Art Metal's conduct, and that most impartial judges would likely see it that way most of the time. But that, in a way, is precisely what makes judicial corruption like Manton's so insidious. In litigation there is usually no easily discernible single right answer; most cases are horse races that either horse could win and that both riders feel, with justification, they should win. Were the answer free from doubt the parties rationally would not incur the expenses and burdens of litigation in the first place. For these same reasons, it is virtually impossible to detect from the judge's decision itself the contrivance of a corrupt hand—and all the more important that such extraneous factors not be a hidden thumb on one side or the other of the scale.

* * *

Some six weeks after his ruling in the Art Metal case, Manton sat down in a conference room in Lower Manhattan to have his deposition taken by the attorney in charge of the liquidation of the Bank of the United States. The deposition amply corroborated Fallon's statement to Reilly, in their April 30 telephone conversation prior to their meeting in Providence, that Manton was in "bad circumstances." Manton testified that his assets amounted to $6,250 and his $12,500 annual salary, and that his liabilities exceeded $500,000. Asked if he had any other personal assets, Manton swore: "I know of none." Manton also was asked if, up through May 1934, he had repaid one of his creditors, Central Hanover Bank & Trust, $15,000—coincidentally, or not, the same amount Fallon had asked Reilly for in the April 30 call. Manton replied that he had repaid Central Hanover only $10,000—coincidentally, or not, the same amount of cash Reilly actually gave Fallon.[42]

The attorney did not ask where Manton got the $10,000 from.

The federal courthouse at Foley Square in Manhattan, 1936. Wikimedia Commons

A promotional photograph of Manton
as a young lawyer. *Brooklyn Daily
Eagle*, Brooklyn Public Library, Center
for Brooklyn History

Manton pictured after an argument
in the murder case of NYPD
lieutenant Charles Becker, 1915.
Wikimedia Commons

The US Court of Appeals for the Second Circuit during Manton's tenure as senior circuit judge: (from left to right) Augustus N. Hand, Learned Hand, Martin T. Manton, Thomas W. Swan, and Harrie B. Chase. Courtesy of the Office of the District Executive, US District Court for the Southern District of New York

The Manton estate in Bayport, Long Island (family photo). Courtesy of Vicki Kirshner

Eva and Martin Manton out riding (family photo). Courtesy of Jeff Denning

Manton with his two children, David and Catherine, in the early 1920s (family photo). Courtesy of Jeff Denning

Delegates at the 1932 Democratic National Convention react to William G. McAdoo's call to throw their support to FDR. Wikimedia Commons

"Good old McAdoo!" FDR cheered upon hearing of McAdoo's conversion. Manton was said to have acted as FDR's go-between with McAdoo. Wikimedia Commons

George Washington Hill, president of the American Tobacco Company, which engineered a $250,000 "loan" for Manton's benefit while it had major litigation pending before his court. AP Images

Albert D. Lasker, head of the advertising firm Lord & Thomas, made the $250,000 loan at American Tobacco's request. Bettmann/Bettmann Archive via Getty Images

Wall Street lawyer Thomas L. Chadbourne returning with his family from a trip to Egypt. Chadbourne facilitated the American Tobacco loan and held a secret investment in a Manton company. Bettmann/Bettmann Archive via Getty Images

Louis S. Levy (left, with his attorney John W. Davis) was disbarred for his "venal and corrupt" participation in the American Tobacco loan. Bettmann/Bettmann Archive via Getty Images

These Men KNOW CHICKS

MR. A. B. HALL
President

When Mr. A. B. Hall and his brother, Mr. L. C. Hall, started this business back in 1911, it was realized from the start that, eventually, continued sound growth would depend largely upon the ability of buyers of HALL'S chicks to make money with them. For 31 years we have kept this in mind. As our business has grown, we have enlarged our field organization, both to sell and to service a wider and wider field.

These are trained men, each a specialist in his field: Two former University Extension Men, a former County Agent, honor graduates in Poultry Husbandry and Business Administration. We require our field representatives to have: *First*, a scientific groundwork in poultry culture; *Second*, practical experience on one or more poultry plants; and *Third*, an intensive training with us, which will enable them to be of the most help to any of our customers who may need help. Some work from our hatchery as headquarters, some are continuously out in the field.

We never forget that our success depends upon the success of our customers to make money with Hall's Chicks.

Connecticut chicken farmer Almon Blakeslee ("A.B.") Hall bribed Manton to win a patent infringement suit over an egg incubator used to hatch chicks. Courtesy of the Wallingford, Connecticut Historical Society

Archie M. Andrews bribed Manton to prevail over his business rival, Col. Jacob Schick, in a patent infringement suit in the nascent electric razor industry. AP Images

William J. Fallon (left), Manton's "bag man," leaving court after pleading not guilty. Fallon later admitted the charges. Ed Jackson/*New York Daily News*

John L. Lotsch, a lawyer and banker, bribed Manton to get a criminal case against him dismissed. Bettmann/Bettmann Archive via Getty Images

Louis "Lepke" Buchalter, one of
New York's most feared gangsters. Lepke reportedly arranged
for a bribe to Manton so he and
his partner, Jacob "Gurrah" Shapiro, would be released on bail.
Bettmann/Bettmann Archive via
Getty Images

DAVIS further informed that LEVEY was the intermediary in the
SHAPIRO BUCHALTER payoff in which MANTON received $25,000 for the release
of those two gangsters on bail and for the subsequent reversal of conviction against one. Further, that LEVEY of his own initiative, inas-
much as he was very close to MANTON, was instrumental in securing the
release on bail of these two individuals because of his close connection
with SHAPIRO and BUCHALTER . DAVIS related that after LEVEY'S proposition
of a reversal for $25,000.00, which was to be paid to Judge MANTON, that
BUCHALTER had conversed with DAVIS about the proposition and BUCHALTER
claimed that LEVEY could not do what he claimed for him; that LEVEY was
so sure that he would be able to do this that he even pawned his wife's
jewels for twenty or twenty-five thousand dollars, which was paid over
to the Judge and that subsequently after the reversal BUCHALTER reim-
bursed LEVEY. DAVIS felt that the jewelry had been pawned with some
large loan outfit in New York, probably the PROVIDENT LOAN COMPANY.

J. Richard "Dixie" Davis, a turncoat Mob lawyer, told the FBI how Nat Levy, a
Brooklyn racketeer, funneled Lepke's payoff to the judge. National Archives and
Records Administration (Declassification Authority NND 921071)

After being freed by Manton, Lepke and Gurrah began "killing all the witnesses" against them. George "Whitey" Rudnick was hacked to death with an ice pick. Burton Turkus Papers, Lloyd Sealy Library, John Jay College of Criminal Justice/CUNY

Tammany boss and underworld ally Jimmy Hines reportedly said of Manton: "He's the only federal judge left in New York we can use to get people out of jail." Irving Haberman/IH Images/Archive Photos via Getty Images

Burt Heath, a crusading anti-Tammany reporter, won a Pulitzer Prize for his exposés on Manton's peculiar business activities. Published with permission of The E. W. Scripps Company

Manhattan District Attorney Thomas E. Dewey. Dewey's investigation of Manton culminated in a report to Congress and spurred the federal prosecution of Manton. AP Images

John T. Cahill, who prosecuted Manton, being sworn in as US attorney in Manhattan in March 1939 by US District Judge John Knox. Bettmann/Bettmann Archive via Getty Images

JUDGE MARTIN T. MANTON, INC.

An editorial cartoon published in the *St. Louis Post-Dispatch*. Daniel Robert Fitzpatrick Editorial Cartoon Collection, P0077, The State Historical Society of Missouri–Columbia Research Center

Manton declares his innocence at a press conference on January 28, 1939. AP Images

Manton (center) after the jury found him guilty on June 3, 1939. Bettmann/ Bettmann Archive via Getty Images

The portrait of Judge Manton that the Second Circuit hoped would disappear.
Courtesy of the Office of the District Executive, US District Court for the Southern
District of New York

CHAPTER ELEVEN

"Judge Manton Has Requested That We Prepare a Draft Opinion"

The Car Parts Cases

IN EARLY 1933, WHILE JUDGE GALSTON WAS DEALING WITH THE ART Metal case that the Second Circuit had sent back down to him, another patent case, *Cinema Patents Co. v. Warner Bros. Pictures*, bubbled up from the Eastern District of New York. The plaintiff claimed that Warner Brothers was infringing patents issued to Leon Gaumont, a French inventor and film industry pioneer, for developing, fixing, washing, and drying motion picture film. Eastern District judge Marcus B. Campbell decided the case in Warner Brothers' favor, finding no infringement of the Gaumont patents.[1]

A panel consisting of Judges Manton, Swan, and Chase heard oral argument on May 5–6, 1933 on Cinema Patents' appeal. On July 20, 1933, two days before Manton set sail on his therapeutic voyage funded by Evans Case, Manton went to see Harry M. Warner, the president of Warner Brothers. The two men had met at political functions and various dinners over the years, but Warner "in no way considered himself intimately acquainted" with the judge. Nevertheless, Manton asked Warner for a $50,000 loan to meet his real estate obligations. Warner agreed on the spot to lend Manton $25,000, and said he would provide the balance if Manton needed it.[2]

On September 11, 1933, while the Cinema Patents appeal was still pending, Manton called on Warner again asking for the other $25,000. Warner gave Manton two more checks for $12,500 each, drawn out of trust accounts for Warner's daughters. Both of Warner's loans were unsecured, and they totaled over $1 million in today's dollars.[3]

The day after the September 11 loan, the Second Circuit decided the Cinema Patents appeal. The opinion, written by Judge Swan, was unanimous and in Warner Brothers' favor, affirming Judge Campbell's finding of no infringement. The Circuit also ruled against Cinema Patents in a companion case filed against a manufacturer.[4]

Whether or not Manton did anything to influence the result in the Cinema Patents appeal—and it does not appear he needed to—he made good use of Warner's $50,000, depositing all the checks to a bank account for his financially strapped Forest Hills Terrace Corporation. He repaid one of the loans in June 1934. But the other loan was never fully repaid; Manton still owed Warner $10,000 when the transaction was exposed by District Attorney Dewey in January 1939.[5]

The day after that disclosure, Warner issued a statement to the press to try to quell the furor. Warner claimed it was just a coincidence that he loaned Manton $50,000 at the precise time his company had an appeal pending in the Second Circuit that had been argued before Manton. "At the time the loan was made I did not know of the existence of the Cinema Patents case," Warner asserted. "The first time I ever heard of the case was when [one of Dewey's prosecutors] mentioned it to me at our interview."[6] However implausible that assertion seems, interviews by federal investigators of Warner's subordinates and lawyers failed to generate evidence contradicting it, and the Warner loan did not form part of the charges at Manton's trial.

Warner's statement also made a point of stressing that the loan "was made out of personal funds" rather than corporate assets, as if that made a difference. Manton echoed that meaningless distinction during his cross-examination, noting that the loans were negotiated "with Harry Warner individually, the case in the court being Warner Brothers Company, a corporation."[7] It is not credible that Manton actually believed this was a real justification when he approached Warner for a loan in 1933.

Whatever Warner did or did not know, Manton unquestionably was aware that Warner's company was a party to a pending case before him.

It was life imitating art, Manton channeling the cynicism of *Lawyer Man*, a popular Warner Brothers movie that year about rampant corruption in New York's legal system. "Every guy for himself . . . Fight, cheat, deal from the bottom," observes the lead character, a jaded lawyer played by William Powell, looking down from his skyscraper office on the hurtling masses below. "That's what it takes to make good here, and that's what I'll give 'em."[8]

* * *

Manton's corruption docket included several other patent infringement cases. That was no coincidence. If Manton and Fallon had put together a formal business plan for their off-the-books venture, patent litigation would have featured prominently in it. There was ample supply: The Second Circuit handled more patent cases than any of the other federal judicial districts. The cases tended to be for high stakes and between relatively well-heeled corporate litigants. Patent law was supposedly one of Manton's specialties; he testified before Congress on patent legislation and authored dozens of patent opinions as a district and circuit judge.[9] This may have boosted his customers' confidence that he would be able to shepherd his colleagues toward the desired result.

In fact, Manton and Fallon affirmatively sought out customers in patent litigation cases. In 1935, they found one in John L. Lotsch, a partner in the Manhattan law firm of Schechter, Lotsch & Sulzberger. The "bald, melon-headed" Lotsch was one of the leading patent lawyers in New York City. Lotsch's stable of clients included phonograph companies, cigar banding manufacturers, purveyors of baby pants, and the Yellow Checker Cab Company. Adding to his luster, Lotsch was tapped to serve as editor for a respected treatise on patent law, *Walker on Patents*, winning praise in the *Columbia Law Review* for his "very thorough, sympathetic and comprehensive revision" of the subject.[10]

Lotsch maintained offices in the fashionable sixty-floor Art Deco office tower located at 500 Fifth Avenue, between 42nd and 43rd Streets. Home remained his native Brooklyn, where he lived in an elegant large

Georgian-style home on Ocean Avenue. The Lotsches decorated their home in grand style, with Louis XV and Louis XVI gold furniture, oil paintings, chime hall clocks, Royal Napoleon vases, marble statuary, Persian and Chinese rugs, and a gold baby grand piano. They summered at rented estates in Westchester and Greenwich.[11]

Like Manton, Lotsch found the practice of law too confining. He was heavily involved in Republican politics in Brooklyn and was the longtime president of the Flatbush Republican Club. Lotsch's ambitions once aimed higher. He ran, unsuccessfully, for Congress in 1928. Lotsch was no patrician Republican. "Snobs and high hats have been the principal faults of the Republican Party," he lamented at a gathering of fellow Brooklyn Republicans in 1930. After Hoover's election, Lotsch's supporters were rumored to be lobbying for his appointment as a federal judge in Brooklyn, but no call from the White House ever came.[12]

In the bustling economy of the 1920s, Lotsch embarked on business ventures together with his brothers, including a metal engraving firm and a candy manufacturer. At the height of the boom, in early 1929, he helped form Fort Greene National Bank, a new bank on Flatbush Avenue in Brooklyn. Lotsch was chairman of the board and the largest stockholder. Toward the end of April 1935, one of the bank's directors, Henry L. Glick, suggested that Lotsch meet William Fallon. From his buddy Benjamin Tabenhouse, a recent litigant in the Second Circuit, Glick understood that Fallon was "a close personal friend" of Judge Manton. Glick felt Lotsch should get to know Fallon "especially as [Lotsch] had a lot of patent work."[13]

As it happened, at just this time, Lotsch was at work on a Second Circuit appeal in a patent case. Lotsch's client, P & D Manufacturing Co., had been sued in federal court in Brooklyn. The Ohio-based plaintiff, Electric Auto-Lite Co., supplied electric ignition systems to automobile manufacturers, composed of numerous smaller parts. A significant part of its revenues came from providing replacement parts to mechanics and car owners when the originals wore out. Electric Auto-Lite claimed that P & D was illegally muscling in on its business by copying these smaller parts and then marketing them as suitable replacements for Auto-Lite parts.[14]

This was a test case: A number of Auto-Lite's other competitors were doing the same thing as P & D, and Auto-Lite hoped to put the kibosh on all of them. Over one hundred similar cases were pending all across the country. Lotsch had been retained by a group of manufacturers to defend their interests.[15] New car sales fell by 75 percent in the first three years of the Depression. Yet people were not giving up their cars; car registrations dipped by only 10 percent during the same period.[16] With old cars staying on the road longer, and inevitably breaking down, grabbing a bigger share of the repair market became a matter of great importance, if not competitive survival, for parts makers.

The Auto-Lite case was assigned to Judge Robert A. Inch, still in the first third of what would become a thirty-eight-year judicial career notable more for its longevity than its contributions to the law. An avid competitive golfer, Inch was a workhorse on the bench, once presiding over nine nonjury trials in a single week—at age eighty-two.[17] But he was a below-par jurist in the estimation of many lawyers and Second Circuit judges. Learned Hand, in particular, "found little to praise and much to condemn in Inch's rulings." "How well named he is," Hand chided in caustic internal memos to his Second Circuit colleagues, belittling Inch further by rechristening him "Judge Millimeter."[18]

Judge Inch's ruling in the Auto-Lite case would not have altered Hand's assessment. Long and meandering, Inch's opinion managed to mangle both the English language and the law. One of its more impenetrable utterances: "The unwarranted interference in an industry by courts or government leads to trouble and uncertainty, but wise regulations of business by government and adaptability by the courts of its equity power, so that justice and fair dealing may obtain in an industry in accordance with the growth, change of conditions, purpose, etc., is concerned, requires that the court be alive and flexible source of power to promote the progress of that industry and those who are consumers in it; that is, in this case the consuming public, i.e., the car owner." Whatever the meaning of this sentiment, it translated into a victory for the plaintiff. Not because its patents had been infringed; Inch found that only the overall Auto-Lite ignition system was protected, not the individual parts. P & D was free to copy those parts and sell them as its own. But P & D was not free, he found, to advertise that its own parts "fit" Auto-Lite devices or could "replace" Auto-Lite parts. This constituted "unfair competition" and an affront to "old ideas of honest dealing."[19]

Both sides appealed. Shortly after the appeal was docketed, Lotsch walked the one block from his office to the Prudence Company at 43rd Street and Madison Avenue, where Glick introduced him to Fallon. "I'd like to introduce you to Judge Manton," Fallon told Lotsch. "I think Judge Manton could be of help to you with your cases in the Second Circuit—if you can secure loans for Judge Manton."[20]

At a meeting in Manton's chambers in the Old Post Office Building, Manton asked Lotsch for a loan of $25,000. If he could arrange such a loan, Manton told Lotsch, "it would redound to [Lotsch's] benefit"— though Manton did not expressly mention the Auto-Lite appeal—and Fort Greene Bank would receive "substantial deposits" from the bankrupt Prudence Company and Fox Theatres Corporation. Both firms were run by Manton-installed receivers, John McGrath and Milton Weisman, respectively.[21]

Lotsch went to see Colonel Casper V. Gunther, the Fort Greene Bank president. Since Manton was unwilling to provide a financial statement, Gunther was only willing to lend Manton $10,000, but he did not rule out making an additional $15,000 loan in the future. On May 10, 1935, Lotsch returned to Manton's chambers in the Post Office Building. There, Manton signed a promissory note for the unsecured loan, a signature card and a letter stating, "This is to certify that my net worth is upwards of $750,000"—despite the fact that less than a year earlier he had sworn under oath that his liabilities exceeded his assets by at least $500,000. When Lotsch reported the loan to Fallon, Fallon said that he would see to it that a decision would be rendered in the Auto-Lite appeal favorable to Lotsch's client.[22]

* * *

In June 1935, the Auto-Lite appeal was argued before a panel of Judges Manton, Swan, and Gus Hand. Joining Lotsch in the argument was his co-counsel, Theodore S. Kenyon of Kenyon & Kenyon. Kenyon's firm was one of a handful of law firms specializing in patent law. Kenyon's father and uncle founded the firm in the late nineteenth century. After graduating from Harvard and Columbia Law School, Kenyon joined the Army, helping General John J. Pershing pursue Pancho Villa in Mexico and then winning medals for his valor in combat in World War I. He and his brother took the helm for the next generation of Kenyon & Kenyon. Their sister, Dorothy, became a lawyer too. "Why not, my dear?," her enlightened father responded when, as a little girl, she asked if that was possible. She went on to become a New York municipal court judge and an outspoken advocate for women's rights and civil liberties.[23]

Kenyon and Lotsch split the oral argument, with Lotsch leading the charge on Judge Inch's unfair competition ruling and Kenyon defending the judge's dismissal of the patent infringement claims. For appellate advocates, the most agonizing part of the process is not the briefing (as many late nights and weekends as it may consume), not the preparation for the oral argument (as fretful as that can be, trying to anticipate the curveballs that may be thrown), not even the argument itself (as anxiety-producing as any litigation event). It is what comes after the argument—the immediate aftermath spent drenched in regret, over opportunities missed and arguments mangled, as superior and more finely articulated answers spring, too late, to mind; and then the days or weeks or months waiting for the court's decision. Once the argument concludes, the curtain is drawn, and the judges retreat into a private cloister of internal conferences and memoranda, accessible only to themselves and their clerks. At that point the advocate has lost what he or she treasures most, which is control, or more accurately the idea of control, the perception that what the lawyer says and does will actually influence the outcome of the case.

In the Electric Auto-Lite case, Lotsch and Kenyon were spared the usual uncertainty. Days after the argument, Fallon summoned Lotsch to his office. He told Lotsch that "I should arrange to get an additional loan promptly or immediately for Judge Manton, and that there would be a favorable decision, and that he [Fallon] wanted $5,000." Fallon had one other request: that Lotsch "draft the opinion for the Court of Appeals." Lotsch went to see Kenyon in the latter's office in downtown Manhattan. "We have won the case," Lotsch reported. "The Judges have had their conference and have decided in our favor on all of the issues." He also said, "Judge Manton has requested that we prepare a draft opinion," and asked Kenyon to prepare the draft. Unfazed by this exceedingly strange request, Kenyon did so, and gave it to Lotsch, who in turn delivered it to Fallon.[24]

On July 8, 1935, the Second Circuit issued its unanimous ruling, written by Judge Manton. It was, as Fallon said it would be, a complete victory for P & D. "There is no deception or unfair competition in copying a part of an unpatented article and selling it as such," Manton declared. Nor is it "unfair to use the name of a well-known article and label a repair part if it be used in a fair way and simply to indicate that the part is made to fit the article." P & D's use of the phrase "to fit Auto-Lite" in marketing its parts was therefore permissible.[25] Unlike his opinion in the Art Metal case, Manton's decision would be favorably cited in the future, despite its tainted origins, and the law as he stated it remains the law today.[26] Even when the Second Circuit, after Manton's conviction, revisited the case in 1940, it found "we need add nothing to what we said before" on the unfair competition point and endorsed Judge Manton's decision.[27]

After Manton's ruling, Lotsch went back to Fort Greene for another $15,000 loan to Manton. The board of directors was "rather cool" to the idea, until Lotsch explained that if the loan were made, Manton "would exert influence and direct the trustees in large bankrupt estates to deposit with the [bank] funds to the extent of $100,000"—a fact he stressed must be kept "sub rosa." The loan was made on July 19, 1935, just eleven days after Manton's ruling. Around the same time, as Manton had promised, Milton Weisman deposited $50,000 with Fort Greene Bank on behalf of Fox Theatres, and John McGrath deposited $25,000 on behalf of Prudence (followed by another $25,000 three months later). Lotsch also made sure Fallon got his $5,000, almost all in cash.[28]

* * *

Two days after resolving the Auto-Lite case as a judge, Manton submitted an extraordinary brief as a lawyer—representing himself. Manton was mired in a dispute with the Bureau of Internal Revenue (as the IRS was then known) over the amount of capital gains tax he owed on the sale of his stock in a milk bottling company in 1930. The Bureau had slapped him with a $21,518 deficiency notice. Manton addressed his submission to the agency's assistant general counsel, Robert H. Jackson, the future US solicitor general, Supreme Court justice, and Nuremberg war crimes prosecutor. Manton had first met with Jackson in Washington, on the same day he visited President Roosevelt in the White House (a fact one imagines Manton did not keep secret from Jackson). Manton explained to Jackson that he felt he could not litigate the issue because, as a judge, he frequently passed on tax questions involving the Bureau. Therefore, Manton believed that the Bureau should more carefully examine the issue before arriving at a final decision. Jackson agreed.[29]

Before going on the bench, Manton invested $35,000 in the Atlantic Bottle Company, whose president was a fellow Bayport resident, Edward F. Glacken. In ensuing years, the company issued dividends to Manton in the form of stock, increasing his ownership stake. In 1930, Atlantic Bottle was acquired by Owens-Illinois Co. for $2 million. The Bureau of Internal Revenue claimed that Manton owed capital gains tax on the difference between what Owens-Illinois paid for his stock and the $35,000 he paid for his original investment. Manton took the position that the value of the stock dividends he received should also form part of his cost basis, lowering his capital gain and, hence, the tax on that gain. Referring to himself in the third person as "the taxpayer," Manton's six-page, single-spaced, dry-as-dust submission amounted to an assault on a 1920 Supreme Court decision, *Eisner v. Macomber*, that held that stock dividends did not constitute income to the recipient—a curious argument from a judge whose job it was to follow Supreme Court precedent.[30]

With "high regards and good wishes," Jackson diplomatically notified Manton that he was having Manton's issue "analyzed from the Bureau's point of view." Jackson referred the matter to a five-person committee, which soon came back with its answer: The committee was "unable to find any basis for taxpayer's contention." Manton's position, Jackson's subordinates reported, was "thoroughly unsound" and "probably not even advanced in good faith." "What taxpayer really asks," the committee tartly observed, "is that having escaped tax on the issuance of the stock dividend shares, he should again escape a tax on his true gain when those shares are disposed of as if *Eisner v. Macomber* never existed."[31]

On August 29, 1935, Jackson delivered the bad news to Manton. Manton's brief, Jackson wrote, was "carefully studied by a committee of our staff," and then reviewed personally by Jackson, but "[t]he conclusion is that we could not accept your position." One can imagine Manton's face creasing into a scowl as he read these words sitting at his desk in chambers. Mentally he made a note to get even with Jackson. A Bureau lawyer and revenue agent reported to Jackson that, when they spoke with Manton to close out the case, Manton fumed that Jackson "will someday regret it" for "sticking [me] with that tax."[32]

Manton had other debts coming due in the fall of 1935. In October 1931, he provided Samuel Ungerleider with preferred stock in the National Cellulose Corporation to secure the $345,000 loan he received from the Ungerleider Financial Corporation in September 1929. Manton promised to repurchase the stock no later than October 26, 1935 at a price of $361,283. In the spring of 1935, with this deadline fast approaching, he convinced the Reconstruction Finance Corporation to agree to loan $250,000 to National Cellulose. But RFC chairman Jesse H. Jones, at a meeting with Manton in Washington, refused to allow the loan proceeds to be used to pay off preferred stockholders and the loan was aborted. Manton then negotiated a settlement with Ungerleider, reducing the amount he owed to $125,000.[33]

Manton was not without means to raise the funds needed to satisfy this obligation. For one thing, John Lotsch was back before the Second Circuit with another patent infringement case arising from another dispute between car parts manufacturers.

* * *

General Motors Corp. v. Preferred Electric & Wire Corp. was a close cousin to the Auto-Lite case. GM held patents on ignition devices and parts, which it used in its own cars and sold to other car manufacturers. Like P & D, the defendant, Brooklyn-based Preferred Electric & Wire, sold to car dealers and repair shops imitation parts for use in GM and other cars, advertising that these parts fit the systems made by GM. Preferred purchased the imitation parts from a number of other companies, including P & D. GM claimed that this business infringed upon its patents. Lotsch and Kenyon, as part of their broader retention by the group of copycat car part manufacturers, represented Preferred. After a trial, Judge Grover Moscowitz of the Eastern District of New York agreed with GM and, in a June 1935 ruling, found either direct or contributory infringement by Preferred of six separate GM patents.[34]

Judge Moscowitz's ruling created considerable consternation on the part of Lotsch and Kenyon's group of car parts manufacturers. GM had filed a number of similar cases in the Southern District of New York against them, and now, on the strength of the Moscowitz ruling, it was moving in those cases for preliminary injunctions stopping defendants from selling their parts. To avoid that result, Lotsch and Kenyon asked Judge Moscowitz to stay his ruling pending Preferred's appeal to the Second Circuit. After an extended argument, Judge Moscowitz refused a stay.[35]

Lotsch knew what to do: "I went in to see Judge Manton." This was July 24, 1935, less than a week after Fort Greene had loaned Manton $15,000, on top of the $10,000 loan extended in May. Alone with the judge in his chambers, Lotsch asked Manton to block GM from pursuing a preliminary injunction in one of the Southern District cases, citing Manton's own freshly issued decision in the Auto-Lite case. Manton granted Lotsch's application and afterwards enjoined GM from prosecuting any of its patent suits pending Preferred's appeal.[36]

The appeal was argued in the morning of October 7; that afternoon, Manton called Lotsch at his office. Lotsch, who by now likely had little doubt about why Manton was calling, visited Manton in his chambers the next day. Manton wanted another loan, this time for $25,000. With $25,000 in unsecured loans already extended, Lotsch doubted his ability to get Fort Greene to double-down on its Manton credit, and he told Manton that. Lotsch suggested that if the loan could be made to a third party, and if collateral could be posted, he "might be able to put that through" at the bank.[37]

Manton had just the man for the job: his dependable nominee, James J. Sullivan. Fort Greene, Manton suggested, could make the loan to Sullivan, and the loan could be secured by Manton's preferred stock in National Cellulose Company (of which Sullivan remained president). Manton would personally guarantee the loan as well for good measure. Lotsch agreed, and secured Colonel Gunther's approval.[38]

On October 21, 1935, Lotsch, Manton, and Sullivan met at National Cellulose's offices on Fifth Avenue and 35th Street. Manton suggested that Lotsch bring him a certified check for $25,000, but Lotsch told him that "was not a good thing" because the bank's certified check records would then reveal Manton's name. Instead, on Lotsch's recommendation, the check was made to Sullivan's order, and then endorsed by Sullivan to Manton, so that "nobody would know to whose order it was made."[39]

The check, bearing Manton's endorsement underneath Sullivan's, was deposited to an account of the Ungerleider Financial Corporation. With that $25,000, along with $25,000 in cash that Manton borrowed from Brooklyn brewery owner Nat Levy, another $25,000 in cash borrowed from another brewery owner, $15,000 borrowed from a New York lawyer, and $50,000 borrowed from the Pennsylvania Exchange Bank, Manton managed to corral enough funds to make the $125,000 settlement payment due and owing to Ungerleider in October 1935.[40]

Manton issued his opinion for the Court on November 4, 1935, reversing the injunction against Preferred in its entirety. As for GM's claims of contributory infringement, Manton found his decision in the *Electric Auto Lite* case to be controlling. As for GM's claims of direct infringement, Manton marched through each one and rejected them all as involving no true invention worthy of protection under the patent laws.[41] As in the Auto-Lite case, when the Second Circuit reheard the case in light of Manton's conviction, with Learned Hand substituting for Manton, it found no reason to overturn Manton's ruling.[42]

So Manton apparently reached the right result in the car parts patent cases, if not necessarily for all the right reasons. He also did right by Fort Greene Bank—he repaid, in full, the $50,000 he and Sullivan had borrowed during the pendency of the two appeals. Notably, though, Manton did not repay most of the debt until 1937, two years after the loans were made. It may not be a coincidence that, in the interim, the

FBI commenced an investigation of unrelated conduct at the bank by Lotsch and others.[43]

As 1935 drew to a close, John Lotsch should have been in a celebratory mood. He had, in quick succession, scored two major litigation victories in the second-most important appellate tribunal in the land in cases of great significance for a crucial sector of the economy. But as over one million New Yorkers piled into Times Square in "one of the most delirious welcomes to a New Year" in memory—their "[h]appier faces" and "heavier spending" signaling, "beyond all doubt, a definite return of mass confidence"[44]—Lotsch's spirits, and prospects, were spiraling downwards.

CHAPTER TWELVE

"Judge Thomas Wants $10,000"

The Perversion of Criminal Justice

IN DECEMBER 1935, DAVID S. KANE, THE LAWYER FOR THE DEFENDANT in a patent infringement case in Brooklyn, called the Justice Department to report a crime. The court-appointed special master in the case, John Lotsch, had just solicited him for a bribe. At a meeting in Lotsch's office at 500 Fifth Avenue, Lotsch told Kane he was about to issue a ruling in favor of Kane's client. "That decision should be worth five thousand smackers to you and your client," Lotsch said, demanding $500 for himself. Kane thought he was joking, but Lotsch persisted, explaining he had judicial "connections" he could tap to help Kane going forward. At the FBI's request, Kane set up a meeting with Lotsch at the City Club in Midtown Manhattan and handed him an envelope with $200 in marked bills, whereupon Lotsch was arrested.[1]

After he was indicted, Lotsch went to see Manton in his chambers. By this time Manton had relocated to the new federal courthouse in Foley Square in Manhattan. Foley Square, the site of several important federal and state government buildings, is named after a turn-of-the-century Tammany Hall district leader and local saloon owner. Square-shaped and standing over six feet tall, Thomas F. "Big Tom" Foley embodied the best of Tammany's brand of machine politics. A quiet man who shunned city-wide office, he catered to the needs of his constituents "as English squires looked after the welfare of their country villages," spending each day at the Downtown Tammany Club "listening to the cries for help" and demanding nothing in return for the favors he dispensed other than "a straight Democratic vote." "I don't know the value of money and I don't care anything about it," Foley once said, uncharacteristically for a Tammany politician.[2]

Flanking the county courthouse just to the south, the new federal courthouse was designed by Cass Gilbert, the eminent architect whose many other creations include the Woolworth Building and the US Customs House in downtown Manhattan and the US Supreme Court building in Washington, DC. The Foley Square Courthouse did not win universal acclaim. A "supreme example of pretentiousness, mediocrity, bad design, and fake grandeur," scoffed Lewis Mumford, the notoriously irascible architecture critic for the *New Yorker*. Architecturally the whole enterprise was, in Mumford's view, "nothing short of a major crime."[3] But to the judges and prosecutors who inhabited the reviled Post Office Building—"Never was there a dirtier, noisier, uglier, more uncomfortable or more crowded building"[4]—the move to Foley Square was a godsend.

Manton, who had worked hard to secure congressional funding for this new home for the Second Circuit and Southern District of New York, attended the groundbreaking ceremony on July 20, 1932, along with Mayor Walker and numerous dignitaries of the bench and bar. After the usual speeches, it was Manton who "climbed aboard the digging machine" and, "at the controls of a massive steam shovel, lifted the first earth" from the site. Exuberance exceeding skill, he then chose, unwisely, to continue, endangering those around him with his inaccurate aim, until "one of the cables slipped off the pulley, which made him decide to return to writing opinions," as recounted in the house publication of the US Attorney's Office.[5]

In hindsight, perhaps Manton had been unnerved by an unintentionally prophetic joke in Mayor Walker's address. Walker noted that the groundbreaking coincided with the construction of a new prison on Riker's Island, and that the price tag for each facility was roughly the same. "It dawned upon some one of us," the mayor quipped, "that it would be a good thing to make our judges at least as comfortable as the men they sent away." If, despite the 87-degree sultry July heat, the image of a judge behind bars sent a chill coursing through Manton—who just one month before had issued his ruling in the American Tobacco case after finagling a $250,000 "loan" arranged by the company and its lawyers—the sensation did not last long.[6]

* * *

Among the favors "Big Tom" Foley dispensed was helping constituents who had been arrested. Consciously or not, Manton reprised Foley's role when Lotsch came into his chambers and asked for help with his criminal case—except that Manton's assistance, unlike Foley's, came at a price. Manton could not descend from his appellate perch to take direct control of Lotsch's case in the district court, as he had done in the IRT receivership. But as senior circuit judge, he had the power to influence which district court judges would hear which cases. And so when, in early February, Lotsch's case was set down for trial in March, the judge who would preside over the trial was a matter still undetermined, and within Manton's control.

It speaks well of the integrity of the judges then sitting in the Southern District of New York that Manton had to look beyond them to find his man. In 1936, the Southern District bench remained stocked almost entirely with Harding, Coolidge, and Hoover appointees, as well as Manton's now adversary, John Knox. Manton told Lotsch that he would reach into the District of Connecticut (also part of the Second Circuit) and assign Judge Edwin S. Thomas to sit in the criminal part in the Southern District in March 1936. White-haired and distinguished-looking, a graduate of Yale Law School and an authority on patent law, Thomas, like Manton, had been active in Democratic politics and was appointed a federal district judge by President Wilson.[7]

Thomas had aided Manton's financial machinations before; he was the district judge Manton called to install a friendly co-receiver for the Fox New England movie chain at the request of Jacob Handelsman. When Handelsman's deal to buy the Alamac Hotel fell through, he asked Manton to return his $10,000 down payment. Manton suggested Handelsman get the money from the receiver, who was expecting a $25,000 fee. But the receiver refused to share. "All right," Manton reportedly told Handelsman, "I'll see that he gets nothing out of that receivership."

Manton called Thomas again, and Thomas slashed the receiver's fee to $7,500.[8]

It was not unusual for Thomas to come down from Norwalk to help out the perpetually overburdened trial judges in the Southern District, the nation's busiest federal court. Entering 1936, the Southern District had only eight full-time judges to handle more than eight thousand pending criminal, civil, and bankruptcy cases.[9] "Our judges . . . are overworked and forced to drive themselves constantly to physical and mental impossible tasks, doing night work and giving up their holidays, and Sundays," said a 1934 bar association report prepared by a committee of distinguished practitioners, including John Lotsch.[10]

Thus did Thomas find himself meeting with Manton at the Hotel Edison in Times Square on Sunday, March 1. Manton then met up with Lotsch in the lobby of the Hotel Commodore at Grand Central Station, a "veritable marvel of beauty" laid out on the plan of a grand Italian garden or courtyard. The two men passed through arched doorways leading to the Grand Central shop corridor, where they sat down at an ice cream parlor and ordered ginger ales, which had become popular as a substitute for alcohol during Prohibition. Over this incongruous libation in this incongruous setting, Manton told Lotsch what it would take to fix his case.

"I saw Judge Thomas," Manton explained. "He'll take care of your case. But he wants $10,000. You've got to pay before the trial."[11]

Ten thousand dollars was a big lift for Lotsch in early 1936. Burdened with debt and no longer able to generate income from his legal practice, he was about to sell his mansion on Ocean Avenue and auction off its valuable furnishings. He did not want to wind up like a prior owner of 940 Ocean Avenue, a Tammany congressman convicted of illegally accepting money from a federal contractor in 1904.[12] Lotsch did not balk at Manton's asking price.

The next morning, March 2, Lotsch scrambled to procure a $10,000 loan from Fort Greene. He did this over the telephone, because he had to be in court in the event his case was called. The loan was arranged through his brother's company. As Lotsch waited inside the Foley Square Courthouse, his brother, together with a company vice president and a

Fort Greene bank official, rushed from Brooklyn and delivered the bribe money around 10:00 a.m. Lotsch took the cash and rode the elevator to Manton's chambers on the twenty-fourth floor. There, he handed over $5,000 to Manton, falsely claiming that he had only been able to raise this amount, even though he actually had a total of $12,500 in cash on him. Manton stood firm. "You have to get the other $5,000," Manton instructed. "Judge Thomas wants it. You have to get it before the trial starts." Accepting the $5,000 from Lotsch, Manton dialed open his safe—that important tool of his peculiar trade had made the journey from the Old Post Office Building over to Foley Square—and stuck the cash inside.[13]

* * *

Having begun his day by disregarding the biblical injunctions against corrupting justice—"And you shall take no bribe," commands Exodus 23:8, "for a bribe blinds the clear-sighted and subverts the cause of those who are in the right"—Manton ended it by lecturing young lawyers about the importance of adhering to religious and moral values. That night he traveled to Brooklyn to speak at a meeting of the Catholic Lawyers Guild at St. Joseph's College for Women. Commending the Guild for its oversight of the unprecedented gush of federal legislation issuing from the New Deal, Manton declared that "it is the duty of the Catholic lawyer" to make sure that statutory law is infused with "true Christian morality." An important lesson of the Depression, he observed, is "to pay more attention to the natural rights of man rather than lay too much stress on the protection of his property rights."[14]

This was not the first or last time during the economic crisis that Manton preached an end to avarice. "The great good that will come from this depression," he said at Temple Emanuel Synagogue in Manhattan in January 1933, "is the message that tells us that all life's efforts should not be directed to piling up our individual mountains of gold."[15] Later, in a commencement speech at City College, Manton credited "the restraint and moderation shown by all elements of the populace" as the reason why "the city has passed successfully through the depression."[16]

The morning after his speech to the Catholic Lawyers Guild, Manton, showing little restraint or moderation, continued to add to his pile of gold. (And perhaps Judge Thomas's as well; it was never revealed how the two judges split the bribe proceeds from Lotsch.) Lotsch, who must have gotten a chuckle if he read the account of Manton's talk in that morning's *Brooklyn Daily Eagle*, returned to Manton's chambers. He delivered the remaining $5,000 in cash, which Manton duly tucked inside his safe.[17]

* * *

When Lotsch's trial got underway later that week, Judge Thomas was on the bench. Lotsch's lawyers presented Judge Thomas with a motion to dismiss the indictment because of a legal defect. Specifically, they argued that Lotsch had never taken the oath prescribed by statute for serving as a special master, and therefore could not be found to have violated that oath. On Monday, March 9, Judge Thomas granted the motion and directed that a judgment of acquittal be entered in Lotsch's favor. This ended the case against Lotsch, because the government, then as now, has no right to appeal a judgment of acquittal entered after a jury has been impaneled and before the jury delivers a verdict.[18]

Lotsch's ordeal was not over, however. Before he left the courtroom, he was arrested again, this time on the charge—arising out of the same facts—that his conduct constituted the separate crime of extortion by an officer of the United States. Undoubtedly the prosecutor, Charles J. Nager, thought this was a clever move. But Nager did not know about Lotsch's very good friend in a very high place. After he was released on bail on the new charge, Lotsch rode the elevator up to Judge Manton's chambers once again. Lotsch's lawyers felt he had a good argument that the new charge was barred by principles of double jeopardy. Enlisting the judge as an unofficial member of his legal team, Lotsch asked for his opinion. Manton concurred.[19]

Relying on the double jeopardy argument, Lotsch's attorneys sought a writ of habeas corpus dismissing the indictment. This was denied by District Judge Henry W. Goddard. Lotsch appealed, and the case was argued before a panel consisting of Judges Manton, Gus Hand, and Chase. After the argument, Manton summoned Lotsch and recommended that he file a supplemental brief making an additional argument: that a special master was not an "officer" of the United States within the meaning of the extortion statute at issue. Lotsch heeded Manton's advice and instructed his lawyers to prepare and file the supplemental brief.[20]

The next time Lotsch saw Manton was not in the courthouse; it was in the parlor car of the Patchogue Express, the train from Long Island that originated near Manton's Fairacres estate in Bayport. Manton had called Lotsch the day before and asked that Lotsch meet him on the train at 8:15 a.m. Parlor cars were a haven for well-to-do train passengers, where "all of the people are clean and do not smell badly," in the words of H. L. Mencken, in contrast to the "revolting" "stinks" pervading ordinary coach cars.[21] Yet this particular parlor car on this particular day in 1936 was redolent with the aroma of corruption. Manton was giving Lotsch an advance peek at the Second Circuit's opinion in Lotsch's own case. He handed Lotsch a draft of the court's ruling. Reading it through as the train clattered toward Manhattan, Lotsch was no doubt pleased to see that the opinion called for a reversal of the district court's ruling. The Court of Appeals was ordering that the second indictment against Lotsch also be dismissed. And the ground for that decision was the one that Manton had promoted: a special master was not an "officer of the United States" within the meaning of the statute.[22]

Nonetheless, Lotsch was not entirely happy with some of the language in the draft opinion. He asked Manton to remove the offending passages, and Manton agreed to do so. When Lotsch testified to this fact at Manton's trial, the trial judge did a double-take, as if he could not quite believe that a federal appellate judge would actually cede editorial control over the court's work product to one of the parties. "Did you say that it was agreed that certain things that you objected to . . . should be taken out?" he asked Lotsch to confirm. In one respect, though, Manton overruled Lotsch's *ex parte* objections. Although completely unnecessary to its holding, the opinion made clear the Court of Appeals' view that Judge Thomas's original ruling, dismissing the case against Lotsch because he never took the oath as special master, was wrong. Lotsch objected to this gratuitous criticism of Judge Thomas's ruling, recognizing that it would be read to mean that he was unjustly acquitted (indeed, it was the only part of the Second Circuit's ruling that the *New York Times* would quote). But Manton refused to remove it, assuring Lotsch that "his colleagues would not stand for it."[23]

The Circuit's ruling in November 1936 finally put an end to Lotsch's special master saga. It was to prove but a short-lived reprieve. The next summer, Lotsch was arrested again and charged, this time in federal court in Brooklyn, with accepting commissions from businesses seeking loans from Fort Greene National Bank. The borrowers never repaid the loans, which was becoming a common event at Fort Greene: In August 1937, the bank collapsed and closed its doors.[24]

Lotsch too seemed on the verge of collapse. At his trial, Lotsch delivered the closing argument on his own behalf, "in a voice which at times became hysterical as he sobbed and wept," claiming that the government was "out to get me" and had made him a "scapegoat" for the bank's failure. When he was finished, Lotsch, who "had strangely developed a leg injury overnight," then "staggered backwards from the jury box and almost fell." He "returned to his chair and wept continuously" while the prosecutor made his closing argument. The jury was unmoved by Lotsch's tears, antics, or arguments; it found him guilty on all three counts.[25]

Lotsch's luck had run out. He was sentenced to a year in prison, the statutory maximum.[26] Disciplinary proceedings soon resulted in Lotsch's disbarment, leaving him without either a bank to run or a profession to practice. Lotsch appealed his conviction and, once again, sought Manton's guidance. Manton offered encouragement, predicting that "the case would be reversed in the Court of Appeals, when it was reached, because of certain errors that were committed at the trial." This time Manton was wrong. He was no longer in a position to help. As Lotsch's appeal was proceeding, District Attorney Dewey's investigators were closing in on Manton. When Lotsch and his lawyers showed up to argue his appeal on January 27, 1939, Manton was not there. Three days later he resigned. A panel of the two Hands and Judge Chase affirmed Lotsch's conviction, characterizing Lotsch as "plainly guilty."[27]

* * *

Morris Renkoff was a character of a different sort. Gaunt with a thick head of wavy dark hair, in contrast to the chubby, tremulous, melon-headed Lotsch, Renkoff easily took honors as the most entertaining government witness at Manton's trial. A Polish-born Jew, "Moisha" to his wife, Renkoff had a lengthy arrest record for crimes ranging from burglary and grand larceny to dealing in stolen securities and concealing bankruptcy assets. The garrulous Brooklynite, fifty-three years old at the time of trial, gave testimony "in a sort of breathless rush of words," as if he were relating a story to friends at the local deli, and with a commensurate level of precision.[28] For instance, Renkoff claimed to be "in the real estate business," but this assertion of fact quickly dissolved on cross-examination into a statement of mere aspiration:

Q. Are you now in the real estate business? A. Yes, sir.

Q. Where is your office? A. Well, I now live at the Concourse Plaza.

Q. Is that where your real estate office is? A. No.

Q. Where is it? A. I have property but I am not engaged in the real estate business, not right now.

Q. Have you been since you came out of jail? A. No.

Q. So that is not your business at this time? A. Probably will be in the future.[29]

Renkoff also said he was in "real estate" when he was arrested in 1931 for helping an international counterfeiter and alien-smuggler named Vasile Murgulescu escape from federal custody on Governors Island. Murgulescu promised his prison guard, Colonel Alfred G. Bral, who happened to be a former comrade from the French Foreign Legion, hundreds of thousands of dollars if he allowed Murgulescu to escape. Disguised in a new suit of clothes and a wig supplied by Bral, Murgulescu was whisked off the island in a motor boat operated by his confederates. Bral never got his payoff; he was questioned, confessed, court-martialed, and sentenced to a year and a half at hard labor. He identified Renkoff as among those who plotted Murgulescu's escape.[30]

That charge against Renkoff did not stick, but within months he landed in hot water again. Some $131,000 worth of bonds issued by the government of Italy was stolen from the mail aboard the SS *Leviathan*. By the spring, Renkoff was exhibiting samples of the bonds and, with his confederates, trying to sell the whole lot of them, for a substantial discount, to a prospective buyer in the Bronx named Cohen. Unfortunately for Renkoff, Cohen was an informant working with US postal inspectors, who were tapping Renkoff's telephone. Renkoff realized that Cohen was "a rat" and relocated to Paris, but in 1934 US authorities arranged for his extradition and he was convicted at a trial in the Southern District of New York in January 1936. Describing the evidence of Renkoff's guilt as "overwhelming," the trial judge, Robert P. Patterson, sentenced Renkoff to three years in prison.[31]

Renkoff appealed. His legal arguments were not the strongest. But two brothers, Jack and Charlie Rich, who helped Renkoff fence stolen bonds, offered the prospect of extra-legal assistance. The Rich brothers had been acquainted with Manton since he called them both as defense witnesses in the Becker case in 1914. Jack Rich had initially been indicted for participating in Herman Rosenthal's murder, and then for bribing a witness in a separate police graft investigation, but neither prosecution was pursued. Born Jacob Reich, he achieved a measure of fame under the name "Jack Sullivan" as a boxer, a self-described "King of the Newsboys," and one of New York's most prolific racetrack gamblers. Rich became good friends with Manton and was a frequent visitor to his chambers.[32]

"If you listen to me, I will get you out of this trouble," Jack Rich promised Renkoff at a goulash restaurant owned by Rich on the Upper West Side, which doubled as a card-gambling den. First Rich took $750 from Renkoff to get Manton to lower Renkoff's bail. Then Rich told Renkoff that for $10,000 he could buy a reversal of his conviction; Renkoff negotiated the amount down to $7,500. Concerned that Rich would gamble away the money before it ever reached Manton, Renkoff insisted on giving the $7,500 to Rich's brother Charlie. Charlie told Renkoff the money had been delivered to Manton, and showed Renkoff a note as proof. Don't worry, Charlie assured Renkoff—his conviction would be reversed.[33]

It did not turn out that way. On June 22, 1936, a Second Circuit panel consisting of Judges Manton, Gus Hand, and Chase unanimously affirmed Renkoff's conviction. The court did not bother to explain its reasoning; it simply affirmed without opinion. This made Morris Renkoff a very unhappy customer. He "made a big holler about it" with Charlie Rich. "Morris, you will get your money back," Rich assured him. "Judge Manton could not help it. The other two Judges wouldn't go with him. Therefore, he had to go with the other two." While Renkoff did not get his conviction reversed, he at least got his money back. Rich refunded him the full $7,500.[34]

Unrequited in one attempt to woo Manton, Renkoff tried another. When Renkoff had been extradited back from Paris, he ran into two friends, Abe and Frank Silinsky, disgraced former Wall Street brokers with prior convictions for defrauding investors. The Silinsky brothers introduced Renkoff to Bill Fallon. Fallon, Abe Silinsky said, "has got the biggest connection" in New York: "Anything you want of Manton in case you are in trouble, this is the man to handle it." Meeting at the Prudence Company, Renkoff now asked Fallon for his help. "You were a damn fool," Fallon chastised. "If you were to come to me in the beginning your case would have been thrown out because the money that you gave was not delivered in full. I could have done it for less."[35]

For $1,000, Fallon said, Manton would write an opinion in support of Renkoff's pending motion for rehearing, which would increase the odds of the Supreme Court taking Renkoff's case. In the meantime, he asked Renkoff for a loan because "the Judge is going to Europe and he needs money." Around July 13, 1936, Renkoff, accompanied by the Silinskys, delivered $2,500 in cash to Fallon at Fallon's apartment in Midtown Manhattan. Manton arrived shortly thereafter to pick up the cash from Manton, and two days later, he and Eva embarked for Europe on the SS *Manhattan*. Manton, however, did not deliver the promised opinion. Instead, all Renkoff got was another refund, this time of his $2,500.[36]

Renkoff, who in the meantime had brought a businessman named Archie Andrews to Fallon to fix a patent infringement case, tried again.[37]

He complained that he had gotten nothing out of the Andrews deal and asked Fallon, "What are you going to do for me?" Fallon came back with another idea: Manton could arrange for Renkoff to get a suspended sentence, so long as Renkoff "can show something he can hang his coat on." Renkoff had a hook: an affidavit from a witness purporting to show that Renkoff was "framed." Fallon took the affidavit to show to Manton. Fallon promised Renkoff that Manton would talk to Judge Patterson. Fallon said he was "positive" that Patterson would give Renkoff a suspended sentence on the strength of the affidavit.[38]

Once again, Renkoff was to be disappointed. At a hearing, Judge Patterson reviewed the papers filed by Renkoff's attorney, went back into his chambers, reemerged, and announced that he could not grant Renkoff any relief. Infuriated, Renkoff walked out of the courtroom and across the street to Schleifer's restaurant on Lafayette Street, where Fallon was waiting for him. A popular hangout for lawyers and judges, Schleifer's recently had been the target of racketeers hoping to coerce its owner, Arnold Schleifer, into paying dues to a "restaurant owner's association."[39]

At Schleifer's Renkoff unloaded on Fallon, "start[ing] to give him hell." Fallon cut him off. "Wait a minute, Morris, don't get excited," Fallon protested. "Something has gone wrong. I will go up and see the old man and find out." Renkoff, about to be hauled off to prison, was running out of time and patience. He warned Fallon not to come back without a stay of his sentence, so he could remain free while pursuing a pardon application with the Department of Justice in Washington. Renkoff had another demand as well: He wanted Manton to support his pardon application. If Manton refused to help, Renkoff threatened, he would "go to the newspapers and expose the entire proposition." "Don't do that," Fallon pleaded. Fallon went across the street to talk to Manton. When he returned, Fallon assured Renkoff that he would get a stay of his sentence and a letter from Manton supporting his pardon application.[40]

Renkoff's lawyer met with Alexander Holtzoff, the pardon attorney at the Department of Justice, and suggested that Holtzoff ask for Judge Manton's views on Renkoff's petition. Holtzoff did so, and on December 22, 1936, Manton sent Holtzoff the following response on Manton's official court letterhead:

Dear Sir:

Answering your inquiry of December 15th as to Morris Renkoff who was convicted in the United States District Court for the Southern District of New York on the charge of receiving stolen bonds and sentenced to three years imprisonment and whose conviction was affirmed by the Circuit Court of Appeals, I may say that I presided on the appeal from that conviction. It became necessary for me to review carefully the evidence in that record and the errors assigned and argued on appeal. After reading the record, I was satisfied that Renkoff's guilt was of considerable doubt. We could not reverse because we are without authority to review the weight of evidence. There were no substantial errors committed which would justify our reversing, and therefore the conviction was affirmed.

But in view of my own doubt as to his guilt, and in answer to your inquiry, I unhesitatingly say I think he is entitled to executive clemency.

Respectfully,

MARTIN T. MANTON Circuit Judge.[41]

Perhaps Holtzoff sensed there was something wrong with this extraordinary entreaty by the tenth most important federal judge in the country on behalf of an obscure trafficker in stolen bonds. Perhaps Holtzoff had heard rumors about Manton's corruption. Whatever the reason, Holtzoff denied Renkoff's pardon application. For the third time, Manton had swung and missed: He was unable to engineer either a reversal of Renkoff's conviction, or a suspended sentence, or a pardon. For the time being, however, Manton's efforts succeeded in stopping Renkoff from blowing the whistle on his dealings with the judge. Renkoff went off to the federal penitentiary to serve his sentence, in silence—until the Manton scandal publicly erupted in early 1939.

* * *

Lotsch and Renkoff's were the only criminal cases mentioned at Manton's trial. But, as FBI files reveal, the Manton racket did a brisk business in the criminal realm. Investigators found, as FBI director J. Edgar Hoover later put it, that "ex-convicts and even crooks still confined in prisons used Judge Manton's name with familiarity."[42]

After Leonard Weisman was convicted of mail fraud and sentenced to 15 years in prison in January 1936, his lawyer—according to what Weisman later told the FBI—suggested he meet with Frank Cohen, "the right-hand man" of Judge Manton. A shady New York insurance executive, Cohen had been helping Manton seek federal funding for his Holmes Airport property in Queens as well as his financially brittle National Cellulose Corporation. Cohen rebuked Weisman's lawyer for not seeking his assistance earlier; if he had, Cohen would have gotten Manton to "call in another judge from another part of the country and everything would have been taken care of."[43]

Meeting with Weisman in prison, and sensing Weisman's wealth from their negotiations (in fact, Weisman had $700,000 in cash stashed with his attorney), Cohen said Manton needed "50 G's" to reverse Weisman's conviction. The first installment was a $7,500 check dated March 2, 1936—the same day John Lotsch paid the first installment of his bribe in Manton's office so that his case would be "taken care of" by a judge from another state called in by Manton. Weisman supplied another $2,500 check, which Cohen said was needed to make a premium payment due on Manton's life insurance policy, followed by $20,000 in cash. Yet it was not enough. Weisman never delivered the $20,000 balance, and hence he received no judicial favors. Manton denied Weisman's bail application, citing the presence of reporters in his chambers, and the Second Circuit then affirmed Weisman's conviction. This is what happens, Manton remarked to Cohen, to "persons who make much money and get in difficulty and then don't want to pay over a certain part of it to prevent their difficulties."[44]

Weisman never testified about this scheme, but he did provide copies of the canceled checks made out to his lawyer, and prison records confirmed that Cohen visited Weisman seven times. Weisman's wife also corroborated her husband's account; in fact, she said she met with Manton in his chambers to discuss her husband's bail application, and shared with the FBI a contemporaneous memo describing the meeting along with a map depicting the layout of Manton's chambers.[45]

Albert N. Chaperau (born Nathan Shapiro), a pal of Morris Renkoff with a criminal record almost as long, learned of another path to Manton. A lawyer, Albert Rubien, told Chaperau that if he knew of any cases that needed "fixing" he should call Rubien and they could both make some money. Rubien's entree to the judge was through George M. Spector, an insurance broker who shared office space with Rubien and who would later stand trial as Manton's co-defendant. In March 1938, Chaperau brought Rubien and Spector a customer, a friend named David Dubrin, imprisoned for committing stock fraud. Dubrin paid $1,000 to get his bail lowered by Manton. He agreed to pay another $4,000 to get his conviction reversed, but backed out of the deal at the last minute, telling Chaperau he "didn't have any confidence in the situation because everybody seemed to claim they had a contact with Judge Manton." Dubrin's conviction was affirmed.[46]

Chaperau himself, a smooth and dapper self-styled diplomat and "friend of everybody in Hollywood," was arrested later in 1938 for smuggling high-priced jewelry into the country for a slew of high-profile clients. Rubien and Spector offered to get his bail reduced for a payment of $3,000. Chaperau's case was still before the district court, not on appeal. Manton nonetheless could deliver a lower bail, Spector said, by calling the assistant US attorney handling Chaperau's case, Joseph Delaney—the son of Manton's former business partner, John Delaney. "The old man will do anything I tell him," Spector assured Chaperau. Chaperau declined the offer. He decided instead to cooperate with the government against his co-conspirators, who included the comedians Jack Benny and George Burns and the wife of a New York state court judge, all of whom pleaded guilty in the case.[47]

So widespread was Manton's reputation in the Federal Detention Center that one convict fabricated a claim of paying off the judge just to bolster his standing with his fellow inmates. Jack "Yahsa" Katzenberg, a prison buddy of Chaperau, told Chaperau that he had paid Manton $3,000 through George Spector. When the FBI visited him, Katzenberg readily admitted that he had told this story to Chaperau—but also said he had made it all up. The reason, Katzenberg explained, was that other inmates were giving him the "silent treatment," because they suspected he was cooperating with narcotics investigators (which Katzenberg was in fact doing). Katzenberg tried to change the narrative by spreading word, through Chaperau, that he was seeking to reduce his sentence by bribing Manton. He threw in Spector's name because "it was known at the [detention center] that Spector was a contact man for Manton."[48]

The trick worked. The silent treatment Katzenberg had been receiving "was relaxed to a great degree." None of the other inmates, it seems, doubted for a moment that he was bribing Manton. Within New York's criminal community in the late 1930s, Manton's corruptibility was a matter of common knowledge.

CHAPTER THIRTEEN

"We Realized There Was Something Wrong with the Guy"

Manton and the Mob

MANTON'S ACTIONS IN OTHER CRIMINAL CASES HAVE CAST AN EVEN more sinister shadow over his legacy. They suggest Manton corruptly used his judicial powers to serve the interests of the ruling Tammany political machine, and, even worse, its confederates in the underworld. While not part of his criminal trial, and never proven in any court of law, these allegations drew the attention of investigators at the time and echo down to today. Manton has his own entry in *The Mafia Encyclopedia*, a reasonably respectable source, which accuses the judge of taking "mob money." Joseph Borkin, the sober-minded former Justice Department official who wrote a book chronicling the misconduct of Manton and two other federal judges, testified before a US Senate subcommittee in 1968 that "Murder, Incorporated had a direct line to Manton." Manton wrote so many "weird" decisions that "made racketeers happy" that he was like an "angel to the underworld," according to Burton B. Turkus, the renowned Brooklyn prosecutor of the Murder, Inc. gang.[1]

Fueling these charges is an incident involving Louis "Lepke" Buchalter and Jacob "Gurrah" Shapiro, "two of the cheapest and most vicious gorillas New York rackets have bred," as a newspaperman of the time described them. Children of Russian-Jewish immigrants, Lepke and Gurrah met on the Lower East Side while robbing the same pushcart vendor. "Lepke" was short for "Lepkeleh," meaning "Little Louis," a Yiddish term of endearment used by Buchalter's mother; "Gurrah" was supposedly how Shapiro, in a thick Yiddish slur, pronounced "Get outta here!" to those whose presence he no longer desired. There were many such people, and Lepke and Gurrah had a knack for making them disappear, often permanently.[2]

Starting off as "free-lance sluggers who sold their services in industrial disputes to the highest bidder," Lepke and Gurrah became protégés of the gangster Arnie Rothstein, best remembered for his alleged role in fixing the 1919 World Series. After Rothstein's death in 1926, the two thugs murdered their way to the top of his organization. Slim, handsome, and businesslike, Lepke was the brainier member of the team, and Gurrah—coarse, crude, beefy, and bull-necked—brawnier, "the exclamation point at the end of Lepke's every sentence," author Rich Cohen wrote in *Tough Jews*. Lepke is credited with creating Murder, Inc., essentially an efficient system of contract killing "as groundbreaking, as effective, as influential, as Henry Ford's assembly line." Italian and Jewish crime syndicates employed Murder, Inc. to eliminate hundreds of rivals, turncoats, and would-be witnesses. Through infiltration of labor unions and intimidation of business owners, Lepke and Gurrah built "a vast labor racketeering empire" especially dominant in the garment district, the bakery industry, and the trucking business. "Their names became a legend," Thomas Dewey wrote. "Whenever a gorilla called on a businessman and said, 'I am from L & G,' the victim asked no questions. He paid whatever he was asked to pay."[3]

By the mid-1930s, Lepke and Gurrah were household names in New York and raking in more than $2 million in profits a year. In one of his first acts upon being named special prosecutor in 1935, Dewey publicly announced that he would seek an indictment against "the leaders of the most dangerous outfit in New York City—Lepke and Gurrah." As Dewey's team sought to pry testimony from understandably reluctant witnesses, the federal government charged Lepke and Gurrah with, of all things, misdemeanor violations of the antitrust laws. Despite their limited bite (which reflected the modest anti-racketeering tools then available to federal prosecutors), the charges brought to light one obscure corner of the Lepke-Gurrah criminal enterprise: The two men, it was alleged, orchestrated a reign of terror against non-unionized fur dressers and thereby restrained trade in the rabbit skin industry. After they were convicted in November 1936, Southern District judge John C. Knox imposed the maximum sentence possible, two years for each defendant, while lamenting it was only a "slap on the wrist." Dewey hailed the verdict as "a first step in breaking the underworld power of these two important criminals and the racket dominated by them."[4]

Unknown to the public, Dewey was about to take another, far more important step toward that goal: indictments on state extortion charges that could send Lepke and Gurrah to prison for the rest of their lives. Dewey was "sure that Lepke and Gurrah, if they were at liberty when the indictments were handed up, would then become fugitives." That concern was alleviated when Judge Knox denied bail pending appeal and ordered both Lepke and Gurrah remanded to prison. But it reemerged when the two men sought bail pending appeal from the Second Circuit—meaning from Senior Circuit Judge Manton, to whom such applications were directed.

Dewey decided to go and see Manton in his chambers at the Foley Square Courthouse. Dewey explained that he was about to indict Lepke and Gurrah and that if the prosecution was successful "[i]t would remove the worst remaining mob from the New York scene." He asked Manton to deny bail until the indictment could be completed, or at least to fix bail at a high enough level to keep the defendants held. "Manton was cordial and gracious, as always," Dewey recalled. Manton "assured me that he certainly would not like to see Lepke and Gurrah escape, and that he would bear in mind all that I had said." While he had always been mistrustful of Manton, going back to his days in the US Attorney's Office, Dewey walked away believing that Manton would heed his request.[5]

The next day, Manton set bail for Lepke and Gurrah at $10,000 each—essentially a get-out-of-jail card. Sure enough, a well-heeled clothing manufacturer posted bail for both men, and they were released that same day.[6] Dewey was dumbstruck.

To make matters worse, the Second Circuit, deciding the merits of the appeal in March 1937, held in an opinion by Judge Chase—joined by Manton and Gus Hand—that the evidence failed to prove Lepke's guilt beyond a reasonable doubt. Gurrah's convictions, however, were affirmed. As Dewey predicted, when his own indictments against Lepke and Gurrah were handed down later that same month, the two men were nowhere to be found. Although Gurrah, unable to stomach life on the lam, surrendered relatively quickly, Lepke remained at large for more than two years. An intensive international manhunt led by the FBI looked for Lepke in all the wrong places: He was still in New York. Finally Lepke surrendered to FBI director J. Edgar Hoover personally on the night of August 24, 1939.[7]

While in hiding, Lepke, in his own way, was preparing his defense to Dewey's charges, by ordering the assassination of numerous gang members he feared would testify against him. The murders were carried out in a particularly gruesome manner. George "Whitey" Rudnick, a loan shark, was hacked to death with ice picks and a meat cleaver. The body of Hyman Yuran, a former business partner of Lepke, was flung into a lime pit in the Catskills. Irving Penn, gunned down in the Bronx, was an innocent businessman who had the misfortune to resemble a former gang member who lived in his building. "The Lepke mob is waging a war of extermination against its former and some of its present members," Dewey raged when announcing a Wild West–style $25,000 reward for information leading to the fugitive's capture, "dead or alive."[8]

After becoming district attorney in 1938, Dewey launched his own investigation of Manton, which ultimately would lead to Manton's downfall. Assigned to the investigation team was Lawrence E. Walsh, then a twenty-six-year-old assistant district attorney two years out of Columbia Law School, and later a partner in the Wall Street firm of Davis Polk & Wardwell, a federal district judge, and the special prosecutor in the Iran-Contra affair during the Reagan Administration. Half a century later, Walsh still recalled Manton with disgust. "He had let Lepke and Gurrah out of jail on $10,000 bail and they started killing all the witnesses," Walsh said. "We realized there was something wrong with the guy."[9]

Dewey's team developed evidence to support their hunch. In early 1938, they arrested J. Richard "Dixie" Davis, previously the lawyer for high-profile mobster Dutch Schultz (born Arnold Flegenheimer), on charges that he and Schultz oversaw the lucrative Harlem numbers racket. Schultz was not a defendant, for the simple reason that he had been gunned down in October 1935 in the bathroom of the Palace Chophouse restaurant in Newark. Ironically enough, according to gang-land lore, Schultz was killed because he was planning to have Dewey murdered; the other crime bosses, including Lepke and Charles "Lucky" Luciano, viewing Schultz's plan as a huge mistake that could lead to their destruction, decided to get rid of Schultz before he could get rid of Dewey. Dewey wanted Davis to turn state's evidence on Schultz's Tam-many connection, James J. Hines, a district leader in Manhattan.[10]

Hines, "the last of the great Tammany bosses," epitomized the fusion of racketeers and political power in 1930s New York. From his base on Manhattan's Upper West Side, Hines shimmied to the top of the Tam-many totem pole, controlling Democratic Party patronage and nomina-tions for elective office. In fine Tammany tradition, a tradition that the government programs ushered in by the New Deal would ultimately ren-der obsolete, Hines scrupulously attended to the needs of his constituents by providing them with various social services—packages of food for the hungry, buckets of coal for residents of freezing apartments, phone calls to the city marshal to prevent the eviction of down-on-their-luck tenants who fell behind in their rent.[11]

Less visibly—yet not completely shielded from view either—Hines maintained friendly relationships with various racketeers and protected them against meddlesome interference from law enforcement. This assis-tance took a variety of forms. Hines hand-picked a see-no-evil district attorney in Manhattan, William C. Dodge, who met all of Hines's qual-ifications: "stupid, respectable, and my man." (Dodge's resolute refusal to attack New York's organized crime contagion is what led to the appoint-ment of Dewey as special prosecutor in 1935.) Honest cops who showed too great an interest in pursuing racketeers found themselves reassigned, thanks to Hines's influence with the police department. And if a gang member did get arrested, the charges could be made to disappear with a simple phone call from Hines to a top-ranking police official, or to the magistrate handling the case.[12]

Among the beneficiaries of Hines's influence was Dutch Schultz, with whom Hines could be seen dining at restaurants in New York and riding horses in Connecticut. Hines even gave Schultz and his henchmen advice on how best to intimidate and bribe policemen and judges. The racketeers were only too happy to repay the favors, usually with large wads of cash; Hines received up to $1,000 a week from Schultz alone. Some of the money went to bankroll Hines's distributions of food and fuel to the needy; as a police commissioner said at the time, Hines was "a Robin Hood figure who stole from the crooks to provide services to the poor." Yet some of the money went for less lofty purposes, enabling Hines to purchase an apartment on Central Park West, send his sons to Harvard and Yale, and generally "live in a high style reminiscent of Boss Tweed," even during the Depression.[13]

Dewey had long been gunning for Hines, but he had trouble finding willing witnesses. In 1932, when Dewey was chief assistant in the US Attorney's Office, he brought income tax evasion charges against Henry Miro, who ran a numbers racket in Harlem. Dewey knew there was some illicit tie between Miro and Jimmy Hines; why else would Miro have bought Hines twelve silk shirts? But Miro refused to cooperate against Hines. "Christ, my life wouldn't be worth a nickel," he explained. For Miro, going to jail for three years was a better option.[14]

After being nabbed by Dewey's team, Dixie Davis figured that Hines would be able to work his usual magic and arrange for Davis's release. When Hines failed to come to his rescue, Davis decided he needed a new protector. He agreed to plead guilty and cooperate in Dewey's prosecution of the Tammany boss. Along with two of Dutch Schultz's former lieutenants, Davis was one of the prosecution's star witnesses at Hines's trial on charges of protecting Schultz's numbers racket in 1939. Hines was convicted and sentenced to four to eight years in prison.[15]

In his private meetings with prosecutors, Davis also shared some explosive information about Judge Manton. "When Davis began to talk with us," Dewey recounted in his memoir about his days as a prosecutor, *Twenty Against the Underworld*, "he said that Lepke's and Gurrah's people had sent out $25,000 in cash to Manton the night before he let Lepke and Gurrah go on bail."[16]

Dewey and his prosecutors apparently believed Davis's story about Manton. They clearly believed that Davis was telling the truth about Hines. At Davis's sentencing, Dewey asked for "the utmost leniency" for Davis, and assured the judge, "We found that the information provided by Davis was wholly correct." Nonetheless, however credible Davis's information about Manton may have seemed, it was not a firm enough foundation on which to build a criminal charge. As Dewey explained in his memoir, "We only had Dixie Davis' testimony and he was not a witness to the actual passage of money to Judge Manton. He just knew about the arrangement. We could never get a corroboration of this testimony, so we never used it."[17]

Dewey never shared the details of Davis's story, and they have remained secret—until now. Declassified FBI files from the federal investigation of Manton explain how Davis knew about the $25,000 payment: Lepke himself told Davis about it. Lepke also identified the intermediary for the payment: Nat Levy, a well-known Brooklyn racketeer who operated an illegal beer business during Prohibition. According to Davis, Lepke at first was skeptical that Levy could deliver, but Levy "was so sure that he would be able to do this that he even pawned his wife's jewels" in order to raise the cash. Afterwards, a surprised but pleased Lepke reimbursed Levy.[18]

This was not the only time Levy funneled a bribe to Manton on behalf of a gangster, according to Davis. When they finished talking about Levy's plan to help Lepke and Gurrah, Lepke told Davis about another incipient scheme to bribe Manton. In 1935, Dutch Schultz, Davis's former client, had escaped jail when a federal jury in upstate New York acquitted him of tax evasion charges. Despite the acquittal, the government resisted returning $75,000 in Liberty bonds that had been posted to secure Schultz's release pending trial. The government slapped a lien on the bonds to recoup Schultz's unpaid taxes. The district judge upheld the lien in part, finding that the government could keep some of the bonds but not all of them.[19]

When the dispute came before the Second Circuit—according to what Lepke told Davis—Manton advised Levy, who in turn informed Lepke, that he would turn over all $75,000 to the government unless he received a cut of either $15,000 or $20,000. Davis alerted George Weinberg, one of Schultz's lieutenants, who had posted the bulk of the bonds. (Schultz, being dead at this point, was disinterested.) Weinberg then gave the bribe money to Buchalter, who passed it on to Levy, who gave it to Manton. In March 1937, Manton issued the Second Circuit's opinion ordering that the entire $75,000 be returned to Weinberg and another individual who had furnished the bonds.[20]

The idea that Levy acted as a go-between for Manton and the Mob was far from implausible. Levy had strong ties to the underworld. Along with his four brothers, he operated the Excelsior Brewery on Pulaski Street in Brooklyn, which later became the Kings Brewery. Licensed to manufacture "near beer," a form of low-alcohol malt that remained permissible during Prohibition, the brewery instead served as a key supplier of illegal "real beer" for bootleggers and gangsters. Prohibition agents raided the brewery on multiple occasions, once discovering beer flowing through a twenty-foot underground pipe that ran across the street to two nearby garages. Among the many notorious mobsters linked to the brewery in one fashion or another were "Waxey" Gordon, "Legs" Diamond, Abe "Longie" Zwillman, and Morris "Little Ziggy" Zeig.[21]

Levy also had clear ties to Manton. He had known Manton for many years through their mutual friend, James Sullivan. In 1934, after the Kings Brewery filed for reorganization, Sullivan was appointed co-trustee of the business. Even though Levy had been publicly identified as a "racketeer" since at least 1929,[22] he was a frequent visitor to Manton's chambers. At his trial, Manton admitted to receiving two cash loans from Levy of $25,000 apiece in July 1935 and March 1936, before he let Lepke and Gurrah out on bail but while the two gang leaders were under federal indictment. Levy loaned Manton another $4,000 in January 1939. None of these loans was ever repaid.[23]

Well-connected politically, Levy also appears to have been well-schooled in the art of fixing cases. "During the lifetime of [John H.] McCooey," the Brooklyn Democratic boss who mentored Manton, Levy "was reputed to be able to handle the Police Department on anything short of murder," investigative reporter Burt Heath told the FBI. Levy knew most of the judges in Brooklyn, including the notoriously corrupt

George W. Martin, who considered Levy "a friend of mine." In 1935, Martin dismissed criminal charges of receiving stolen goods brought against two of Levy's brothers, a disposition so peculiar in light of the evidence that it later formed one of the grounds for Martin's impeachment trial in the New York Senate. Martin admitted he had given Levy's brothers "the benefit of a borderline case," but denied any impropriety.[24]

FBI files also reveal that Davis was not the only witness, or even the first witness, who claimed to know about Lepke and Gurrah's bribery of Manton. In January 1938, before Davis's arrest, the FBI interviewed Israel Brinkman, a disbarred lawyer serving a five-year sentence for bankruptcy fraud. Once a well-known, well-heeled New York attorney—before being convicted for fencing stolen securities—Brinkman had spent time in the same Federal Detention Center where Lepke and Gurrah were held prior to their release. There, Brinkman claimed, Lepke confided that he had paid $30,000 to Manton to secure his and Gurrah's release. But Brinkman did not name Levy; he alleged the money was paid through Frank Cohen, Manton's bagman for the bribe payments made by Leonard Weisman to secure his own release.[25]

When the Manton scandal broke in early 1939, another prison informant, Charles H. Greenhaus, stepped forward to provide what he called "definite information to link Manton with the underworld." Once known as "the boy wizard of Wall Street," Greenhaus was jailed in 1931 for swindling investors. Five years later, when he violated his parole, Greenhaus, like Brinkman, found himself residing in the Federal Detention Center. He claimed that Gurrah told him that the two gangsters paid off Manton—with either $20,000 total or $20,000 apiece. Greenhaus believed the intermediaries were Dixie Davis and Bill Fallon.[26]

Morris Renkoff supplied still more incriminating evidence. Lepke and Gurrah's bail application was under consideration around the same time Renkoff was negotiating with Fallon to get his own sentence set aside. At one of their meetings at the Prudence offices, Renkoff learned that Fallon was "try[ing] to fix bail through Judge Manton for Lepke and Gurrah and he was offered $15,000 but he asked for $25,000." Fallon never heard back from the racketeers' representatives. One day thereafter, Fallon and Renkoff were approaching the federal courthouse when they spotted Nat Levy coming out of the building. A lightbulb went off in Fallon's head. "Now I know why they didn't come back to me for arranging the bail," he told Renkoff. "I see [Levy] is working on it." Fallon guessed that Levy's cut would have been smaller than Fallon's.[27]

After Manton's conviction, his prosecutors received a letter from "Moe Dimples," postmarked in Brooklyn, claiming that Manton got $75,000 from Levy and that "Nat got this do[ugh] from Lepke and Gurrah to give to Manton to let these gunmen out on bail." "Moe Dimples" was the nickname of a real-life gangster, Morris Wolensky, a trusted confidant of Lepke who helped harbor the fugitive in Brooklyn. In fact, it was Wolensky who induced Lepke to come out of hiding and surrender to the FBI later that summer, assuring him that the Feds would not turn him over to Dewey (an assurance that, in the event, proved false). If Wolensky genuinely sent a letter to the FBI in his own name (though this seems unlikely), that would be further powerful proof that the Manton payoff actually happened. Whoever he was, "Moe Dimples" said that if authorities contacted Levy, "he will squeal."[28]

The FBI decided it was time to pay a visit to Levy. Arriving at his apartment on Eastern Parkway in Brooklyn on July 10, 1939, the agents found only his wife, Rose. Rose admitted that Nat pawned her jewelry, but disclaimed knowledge of his purpose. The agents came back the next day to interview her husband. Levy did not "squeal." He denied knowing Lepke or Gurrah and "absolutely" denied giving Manton money to help with their bail. Dixie Davis had predicted as much: It would be "almost useless" to talk to Levy, Davis told the FBI, because Levy would "refuse under all conditions to furnish any information." Levy was well acquainted with the dangers of crossing the wrong people. In 1929 he wound up in the hospital in critical condition after being savagely beaten by four men who, the police believed, had intended to take Levy for a "ride." Levy refused to cooperate with police on that occasion as well.[29]

Ultimately, the smoke and sparks around Manton's decision to let Lepke and Gurrah out on bail did not ignite a fire. An internal FBI memo following Manton's conviction noted that although it was "strongly rumored" that Manton had been bought, "these rumors have not been definitively established."[30]

* * *

From today's perspective, the idea that a federal circuit court judge would take bribes to help organized crime bosses escape justice may seem fantastical. To properly assess the claim, however, it is important to recreate the very different times in which Manton lived, when Tammany, organized crime, and the delicate alliance between the two were fixed features of the New York landscape, as seemingly permanent and immovable as the city's mammoth skyscrapers. "In 1935," recalled one lawyer on Dewey's team who lived through those days, "the mobs had a tremendous hold on the legitimate business life of the community. As a matter of fact you could feel it. . . . [T]here was a general feeling that the investigation couldn't succeed because the hold of the mobs on the community was so strong that you could never break it."[31]

Manton surely encountered gangsters through his law practice and business interests. The Becker trial brought him into contact with individuals who toiled in and around the underworld, such as the Rich brothers. Manton owned partial interests in laundries in Brooklyn in the 1920s (the term *laundromat* did not exist until the introduction of the coin-operated machine in the 1940s). Racketeers were particularly powerful in the industry; recalcitrant owners saw their laundry trucks go up in smoke, their employees slugged and maimed, their businesses burnt to the ground. "The laundry racket," said the Brooklyn district attorney, was "the most vicious, widespread and piratical that has ever operated in Brooklyn." Manton would not have been immune from the racket's effects. His co-owner was later a partner of Jacob Mellon, the "czar" of the Brooklyn laundry racket who was convicted on racketeering charges in 1933. It was Mellon to whom Manton sold his interests in 1925, reportedly for a profit in excess of $250,000.[32]

In 1936 or 1937, Manton had a new idea for the Holmes Airport property in Queens. He thought it would make an ideal site for a racetrack. Manton again enlisted Louis Levy's help, and Levy pitched the idea to his friend and client Joseph E. Widener, scion of a wealthy Philadelphia family and owner of Belmont Park on Long Island and the Hialeah Park in Miami. Widener seemed interested—until Levy showed him Manton's list of investors who would provide the $1 million in contemplated financing. "These men are no good," Widener told Levy. "They are the kind of men I have been trying to keep out of racetracks I am associated with." While the potential investors' names were never revealed, they included gangsters and bookmakers, according to Manton's prosecutor. One of them may have been Nat Levy, who claimed his loans to Manton were intended as an investment in the racetrack.[33]

Reformers of the time who sought to root out racketeers, and the corruption that protected them, tended to be Republican in their politics, patrician in their bearing, and idealistic in their disposition. Manton was none of these. He was never a prosecutor, on the federal or state level. While he involved himself in a number of civic causes and gave dozens of speeches and lectures on all manner of topics, not once did he address the growing lawlessness enveloping New York or call for legislative remedies or a stiffer response from law enforcement. In 1929, Tammany's sixty-nine-year-old choice for Manhattan district attorney, Thomas C. T. Crain, squared off against Frederic R. Coudert Jr., a young former assistant US attorney who was one of those idealistic patrician Republican reformers. Manton wrote Crain a letter of endorsement and allowed Crain to publish it in newspaper campaign ads, proclaiming that once the Tammany sachem was elected, the public would be "assured of a just enforcement of the criminal laws for the next four years."[34] Crain won, and like William Dodge after him, proved "singularly ineffective" and "decidedly incompetent" when it came to investigating cases against racketeers and corrupt public officials.[35]

In short, Manton was content to accept the status quo, whether because he believed it could not or should not be changed, or because it benefitted him personally. Sol Gelb, who joined Dewey's special prosecutor team and followed him to the District Attorney's Office, bumped into Manton on the street before Dewey first hired him. When Gelb, who knew Manton from appearances in the Second Circuit, told him of his plans to join Dewey's rackets investigation, Manton was unimpressed. "Oh, that's a waste of time," he said. "It won't amount to anything. In six months it will be dead." Gelb insisted that "there's a real need" for the investigation, but Manton disagreed, calling it "a lot of publicity hunting . . . and, what's more, it's overplayed."[36]

* * *

Arousing suspicion above and beyond his decision to set bail for Lepke and Gurrah, Manton wrote decisions reversing the convictions of high-powered Tammany-connected criminal defendants in two other cases. Joseph Shalleck, a diminutive and shrewd lawyer, was one of Jimmy Hines's closest friends. His loyalty to Hines "burned in him like a flame, never to be extinguished." As a young lawyer, Shalleck served as campaign manager when Hines ran for Manhattan borough president in 1921. Arriving at a polling station to check out allegations of vote fraud, Shalleck was attacked by Hines's rivals, who slugged him, shot him in the stomach, and then kicked him as he lay bleeding on the ground. Shalleck spent election night in the hospital and, "in the tradition of many of his clients, steadfastly refused to identify his attacker." Shalleck also represented some of the most colorful gangland figures of the era. These included the handsome and homicidal Owney Madden, nicknamed "The Killer," a terrifying thug who made a fortune from speakeasies and nightclubs—"so sweet and so vicious," said Mae West, his one-time lover.[37]

In 1930, Shalleck found himself in the position of defendant rather than defender. He and two other lawyers were charged with bribing a juror—using the court bailiff as a go-between—in a major stock fraud prosecution involving the Utah Lead Corporation. The lawyers were convicted in the Southern District of New York, sentenced to prison by Judge Knox, and disbarred. But their convictions were reversed on appeal, in an opinion by Manton joined by Judges Swan and Gus Hand. In overturning the conspiracy convictions, Manton relied on a legal principle known as "Wharton's Rule." Named after the author of a leading nineteenth-century treatise on criminal law, Wharton's Rule holds that no conspiracy charge can exist if the underlying crime, by its nature, requires at least two persons acting in concert. Adultery is one example. Bribery is another, Manton explained in his ruling in *United States v. Sager*. "There may not be a conspiracy founded on a crime to commit bribery between persons, one charged with the intended taking and several charged with giving the same bribe." The conspiracy convictions of the three lawyers, Manton thus held, could not stand, and so Shalleck went free.[38]

Manton's application of Wharton's Rule has since become obsolete. As the Second Circuit later made clear, the rule ceases to apply where more than two individuals were parties to the illegal agreement.[39] Of course, that was true in *Sager* too, as Southern District judge Robert P. Patterson pointed out when confirming in a 2000 ruling that *Sager* "is no longer good law." In the course of interring *Sager*, Judge Patterson, the son of the judge who replaced Manton on the Second Circuit in 1939, specifically (and, one senses, gleefully) noted that its author was "Chief Judge Manton," as if that fact itself further devalued the case as precedent.[40]

Even at the time, however, Manton's ruling was considered "a legal curiosity among lawyers" in the Second Circuit. Most courts that had considered the question previously (including a decision by a Second Circuit panel that included Manton) concluded that if there were more actors than necessary to commit the underlying offense, Wharton's Rule did not apply. That indeed was Wharton's own view. While Manton's position found support in an earlier District Court opinion—and, of course, in the concurrence of his other two panel members—Shalleck and his co-defendants must be considered the beneficiaries not of a straightforward application of a preexisting legal rule, but of an interpretation of an unsettled legal question that could easily have gone the other way.[41]

After the Manton scandal broke in early 1939, an informant explained to federal prosecutors why Manton may have been inclined to read the law in Shalleck's favor. Jimmy Hines and Dutch Schultz, the informant alleged, "raised the money necessary to pay off the persons for the securing of the reversal."[42] The informant did not provide details and is not identified in the FBI's files. But given everything else that is known about Manton's conduct and Tammany connections, the claim is more than plausible.

A similar beneficiary of Manton's malleable reasoning was Samuel Kantor, the political lieutenant of Alderman William "Billy" Solomon, a Tammany district leader whose Democratic clubhouse in Harlem also served as a hangout for the Schultz mob. Kantor and several other Democratic election workers were convicted in the Southern District of New York of intimidating voters and ringing up illegal votes in violation of federal law during the November 1932 election. According to the evidence at trial, would-be Republican voters were literally thrown out of polling stations, and a third of the signatures in one registration book were shown to be forgeries. Kantor was seen "swaggering around the polls with a pistol in his holster" and voting several times in one polling location. When a Republican inspector protested against men register-ing multiple times to vote, Kantor "stuck something hard to [his] ribs" and threatened to "punch [his] nose through" if the inspector made any trouble.[43]

Condemning these "ruthless" acts of intimidation, Judge Knox sen-tenced Kantor and his co-defendants to prison while recognizing that they were under the control of larger and more sinister forces: "In a sense these men are victims of a system exceedingly dangerous to our form of government," Knox said, "a philosophy that says political bosses are above and beyond all law and that on election day politics may run riot at the expense of the rights of the people."[44]

Yet when the case came before the Second Circuit, Judge Manton found that the government failed to prove that Kantor and his cohorts had committed a crime at all. Federal law only protected the civil rights of citizens voting in elections for federal office. Although candidates for Congress were on the ballot in November 1932, so too were candidates for New York state office (including delegates to the Electoral College). There was no proof, Manton observed, that the disenfranchised voters "attempted to or did vote for federal offices as alleged in the indictment." The court could not presume that the voters would have cast ballots for Congress; they might have showed up just to elect state officeholders. Manton also rejected the government's theory that fraudulent votes deprived those who did vote of the right to have their legitimate votes fully counted. "The statute does not include the public at large nor elec-tors within its scope. It is the individual voter who is protected," Manton wrote in his June 1935 ruling.[45]

As in the *Sager* case, Manton's opinion drew no dissent from the other panel members (Judges Swan and Chase) and cannot be said to lack any legal foundation. In the verdict of one commentator at the time, Manton's decision was "legally sound since an intent to exercise a federal right is an essential part of the government's case and should have been proven beyond a reasonable doubt." That same commentator, however, strongly criticized the second part of Manton's decision, which exonerated the defendants on the charge of ballot-stuffing, as "regrettably technical."[46]

Many years later, a union racketeer named Max Rubin, once Louis Lepke's representative in the bakery racket, identified another possible motivation for Manton's ruling. Testifying at a trial of Lepke in a Manhattan state courtroom in 1940, and again at a hearing of the New York State Crime Commission in 1952, Rubin described how Lepke had extorted money from a baking company in the spring of 1935 to call off an impending Teamsters strike. The victim delivered $10,000 in cash to Rubin and Kantor in Billy Solomon's insurance office. Kantor took a $500 commission for his role in the scheme, but, according to Rubin, when the bulk of the funds were turned over to Lepke, "Kantor pleaded that he needed more money because he was involved, at the time, in fighting a charge of election fraud brought against him by the Federal Government." This was precisely when Kantor's appeal was pending before the Second Circuit.[47]

Whether Lepke gave Kantor more money, and whether Kantor used it to bribe Manton, has never been established. For his part, Kantor vehemently denied Rubin's account. "If Mr. Rubin has testified to any such thing," Kantor told the State Crime Commission, "Mr. Rubin should be a fiction writer and is a confounded liar." That denial does not count for much. Kantor also denied engaging in voter fraud and denied knowing Dutch Schultz when he testified in his own defense at his federal trial. Kantor later admitted in his testimony before the State Crime Commission that he did know Dutch Schultz, as well as other notorious gangsters such as Frank Costello.[48]

A few months after springing Kantor, Manton received assistance from an even more prominent Tammany politician—Jimmy Hines. Or so it was alleged by Jacob Handelsman, the money broker who loaned Manton $10,000 in connection with the Fox New England case. According to Handelsman, Manton repaid part of the debt but still owed $3,150. Handelsman threatened to bring suit for the balance. Soon Handelsman was summoned to a breakfast meeting in Hines's apartment. Surrounded by four or five "strong-arm men," the Tammany power broker explained to Handelsman why suing Manton was simply out of the question: "We can't afford to have Manton in trouble. He's the only federal judge left in New York we can use to get people out of jail."[49]

Instead, Hines arranged a settlement whereby Fallon would pay Handelsman the $3,150, guaranteed by Hines, if Handelsman "would keep his mouth shut." When months went by and the balance remained unpaid, Handelsman sued Hines and Fallon in March 1937. Now, Handelsman was approached by Hines's lawyer—none other than Joseph Shalleck, who, thanks to Manton's reversal of his conviction, had regained his law license and resumed representing Hines. Drop the lawsuit, Shalleck warned Handelsman, or face prosecution for "blackmail" by Dodge, the Tammany district attorney. Handelsman dropped the lawsuit. Later, when the suit came up during Manton's trial, Shalleck assured reporters that it was all a big misunderstanding. Shalleck claimed that no settlement was ever made, no payment was ever made, and Handelsman dropped the suit because he realized he "had made a mistake."[50]

Previously undisclosed FBI files reveal that Manton may have received funding from an even more disturbing source: underworld boss Owney Madden, Joseph Shalleck's former client. Unlike Hines, who at least enjoyed a patina of political respectability, Madden was a pure hoodlum who served seven years in Sing Sing for manslaughter. In a March 1939 memorandum, FBI director J. Edgar Hoover advised US attorney general Frank Murphy: "It has also been alleged that Madden loaned Judge Manton $50,000." This allegation came from former Republican National Committee chairman Harry Blair, who was a director of Insuranshares Corporation of Delaware, which, prior to Blair's arrival, had loaned Manton $50,000 in January 1933. Blair had heard that Manton was forced to take this loan to repay a prior loan from Madden because "Madden was bringing pressure for collection."[51]

Blair's source, fellow Insuranshares director William C. Edwards, would not substantiate the Madden link. Yet the story he gave the FBI broadly aligned with Blair's account. Edwards said that he had heard that "Judge Manton owed one particular beer running outfit in Brooklyn the sum of $50,000, and in order to pay off the loan, a similar loan was obtained from the competing beer running outfit." Owney Madden had run one of the biggest beer bootlegging operations in the city (albeit centered in Manhattan). Alas, Edward's sources for this information were "unknown to him at this moment."[52]

The Insuranshares loan to Manton was itself highly suspect. It was engineered by his friend Frank Cohen, who had acquired control of Insuranshares a few months before. Cohen appears to have injected $50,000 in cash into the company for the Manton loan. A wire-puller of the first order, Cohen "bears a most unsavory reputation," FBI Director Hoover advised the attorney general when Cohen's connections to Manton first surfaced. Cohen flitted on the periphery of the underworld, but mainly he was known for orchestrating a series of complex corporate transactions that left a trail of insurance companies in financial ruin. This earned him an FBI investigation, an SEC investigation, an indictment in Atlantic City, a denunciation by the Massachusetts insurance commissioner as a "racketeer" and the "mad dog of the insurance world," and a finding by a federal judge that he was "the prime mover" in a fraud on creditors. Yet somehow Cohen managed to emerge intact from his run-ins with the law. He, too, was a regular visitor to Judge Manton's chambers.[53]

So was Jack Rich, the gambler who had even deeper ties to gangsters. Rich made a very sizeable $40,000 loan to Manton, in the form of eight $5,000 bills (no longer printed today due to money laundering concerns). Despite repeated requests for repayment from Rich, and repeated promises of repayment by Manton, the loan was not repaid before Rich's death in December 1938.[54] Tallying up the loans Manton admitted receiving from Nat Levy, the loan from Rich, the loan from Cohen, and the possible loan from Owney Madden or some other bootlegger, Manton may have received nearly $200,000, or nearly $4 million in today's dollars, from the darkest recesses of Depression-era New York.

On one occasion—according to Morris Renkoff—Manton's avarice very nearly dragged him into the vortex of the underworld. When Renkoff complained to Charlie Rich about Manton's failure to deliver a reversal of his conviction, Rich told Renkoff this was not the first "double-cross" Manton had pulled. Rich proceeded to relate to Renkoff a bone-chilling story about how "the old b******" "double-crossed my brother and my brother nearly lost his life." Jack Rich had mediated a $25,000 payoff to Manton from an "underworld combination" to throw out a case. But the case was not thrown out, leaving the "combination" angry and suspicious that Jack never delivered the money. In his inimitable style, Renkoff recounted to the FBI what happened next:

> He [Jack Rich] was taken for a ride and he suggested to the people, to the underworld people to go down to Judge Manton's home with them and prove it right in front of their face that he delivered that $25,000 to Judge Manton. They agreed to that and they went down with Jack to Judge Manton's house. They came into the house and he said that Jack wants to see the Judge and the Judge came down. He says, "What is it, Jack?" He says, "Here's the people that I took $25,000 off of, they are going to kill me if they don't get their money back." The Judge started to shake all over his body. He said, "Wait a minute, you don't have to tell me anything about this man. The money will be returned to you tomorrow."

As the thugs left Manton's house, one of them threatened the nation's tenth highest-ranking judge that "someday they will find him in the same place where they are going to find Judge Crater, if they ever find him."[55] The reference was to Joseph Force Crater, the infamous New York state court judge who vanished outside a Broadway theater one night in 1930 and whose body has never been found.

* * *

Did Manton set New York City's two most dangerous gangsters free because of a payoff? A plausible, less cynical explanation for Manton's decision exists: that he believed, on the merits, that Lepke and Gurrah were entitled to bail. Whatever the scale of their uncharged criminal conduct, in the case at hand Lepke and Gurrah were convicted only of misdemeanors and sentenced only to two years in prison. The evidence linking them to the antitrust violations was not overwhelming, as Judge Chase's opinion reversing Lepke's conviction later made clear. No judge wants to see a defendant serve time in jail if there is a good chance the conviction will be reversed.

As for Dewey's personal plea that Lepke and Gurrah remain incarcerated, Manton may have been unpersuaded by it for a number of reasons. While Manton was not exactly a paragon of legal ethics, he may have rightly viewed Dewey's visit as of dubious propriety. Decisions about a defendant's liberty are not supposed to be made on the basis of *ex parte* representations by a prosecutor behind closed doors, to which the defendant has no ability to respond. As a lifelong Democrat, Manton no doubt was no fan of the politically ambitious Republican special prosecutor. Granting bail may, in Manton's mind, have had less to do with letting Lepke and Gurrah fly and more to do with clipping Dewey's wings. The Second Circuit was Manton's fiefdom and Manton was not about to let Dewey, two decades his junior, tell him how to run things.

Nevertheless, while inconclusive, the evidence of Manton's guilt stacks up as credible and compelling. Multiple, unrelated witnesses, including Dixie Davis, a true insider, claimed to have heard about the payoff directly from Lepke or Gurrah; Nat Levy, the purported conduit, was in the perfect position to play that role; and Renkoff's conversation with Fallon outside the courthouse puts a kind of bow on the package. What makes the charge especially believable, though, is Manton's willingness to associate with known underworld figures like Levy and Rich, and his undiscriminating, open-door policy when it came to those offering him money. There is, in short, no reason to think Manton would have *refused* a payoff just because it came from a Mob source. Considering all the circumstances, it seems significantly more likely than not that Lepke and Gurrah made such an offer and that Manton did, indeed, accept it.

CHAPTER FOURTEEN

"He Is an Old Friend"

Manton, FDR, and Another Shot at the Supreme Court

ALTHOUGH THE DEPRESSION DEVASTATED MANTON'S FINANCES, INCEN-
tivizing his abuse of office, it also carried a Democrat back into the
White House, reviving Manton's hopes for a Supreme Court appointment. Despite his rejection in 1922, Manton still aspired to a seat on the
high court. When a vacancy loomed in late 1924, Manton tried again
to ignite a campaign for the Court. Friendly newspapers claimed that
Manton "is regarded as the most likely to be selected." Manton procured
endorsements from close friends of Chief Justice Taft such as Clarence
H. Kelsey, an old Yale classmate and the president of Title Guarantee &
Trust in New York, and Isaac M. Ullman, a prominent businessman and
Republican leader in Connecticut. "My friend" Manton "is very anxious"
for an appointment, Ullman advised the chief justice.[1]

Taft would have none of it. There was not "the slightest chance of
President Coolidge entertaining [Manton] as a possibility," he admon-
ished Ullman. With equal firmness he wrote Kelsey that Manton possessed "neither the qualifications nor the standing entitling him to come
to our Court," also noting Manton's "attack" on Coolidge during his
Columbus Day dinner speech in the run-up to the recent election. Taft
marveled at "the gall of the man" in trying to engineer a promotion when
"[t]he truth is he ought never to have been appointed to the place where
he is." Manton will "never" be a Supreme Court justice "in this Administration," Taft vowed.[2]

Manton must have been relieved when Taft, in ill health, resigned in early 1930. Attempting to ingratiate himself with President Hoover's choice for chief justice, Charles Evans Hughes, Manton hosted a dinner in Hughes's honor to which he invited New York's leading judges and lawyers.[3] Yet there is no evidence that President Hoover seriously considered Manton for the seat opened up by the death of Justice Edward Terry Sanford in 1930. Instead, Hoover named a dyed-in-the-wool Republican lawyer from Philadelphia, Owen Roberts. Hoover's last Supreme Court appointment, in 1932, did go to a sitting judge who was an ethnic New York Democrat. But it was the Jewish Benjamin N. Cardozo whom Hoover chose to fill the shoes of Oliver Wendell Holmes, not the Catholic Manton. Like Harding before him, it appears Hoover was warned about Manton's unsuitability for higher judicial office. One of Manton's Second Circuit colleagues reportedly paid a visit to Hoover to make certain Manton would not be appointed to the Supreme Court.[4]

With the election of fellow Democrat Franklin Roosevelt in 1932, Manton must have felt his prospects brighten. Here was a president he knew personally. Manton attended Roosevelt's first inauguration as governor of New York in 1929, and he and the new chief executive corresponded about the state's role in enforcing Prohibition.[5] At Manton's request, FDR provided a signed photograph for Manton's twelve-year-old daughter Catherine, "a great admirer of Governor Roosevelt," Manton assured him, "who she thinks is going to be the next President." ("I have heard father say such wonderful things" about you, Catherine's thank-you letter to Roosevelt carefully noted.)[6] Manton also encountered FDR at annual luncheons hosted by Roosevelt's former law partner, Basil O'Connor, on Long Island.[7] Manton was close friends with O'Connor's brother, John J. O'Connor, Tammany's choice to fill W. Bourke Cockran's seat in Congress; Cockran maintained a home in Bayport near Manton's Fairacres estate.[8]

Even more importantly, the incoming president owed Manton a very significant political debt.

* * *

As Democrats, Manton among them, gathered in a sultry Chicago for their convention in June 1932, Roosevelt's nomination was far from assured. FDR held the pole position but faced challenges from former New York governor Al Smith, who had left his working-class roots behind to become a prosperous businessman and was fearful of FDR's liberalism, and House Speaker John Nance Garner, a conservative Texan who had the backing of the California delegation, led by Manton's long-time friend William G. McAdoo. Both Smith and Garner were largely playing a spoiler's role; unlikely to win, they nonetheless could block Roosevelt from obtaining the two-thirds' majority he needed to secure the nomination. After three ballots Roosevelt remained well short of that goal, raising the prospect that the convention would turn to a dark-horse candidate. Roosevelt's political allies and operatives then undertook a concerted campaign to convince Garner to drop out and McAdoo to switch his support to FDR.[9]

One of Roosevelt's key allies in that campaign was Manton. Despite his deep allegiance to Smith during the 1928 campaign, Manton, not one to place loyalty ahead of personal ambition, had thrown in his lot with the Roosevelt forces. According to John O'Connor, to break the logjam at the convention, FDR "commissioned [Manton] to intercede with Manton's old friend, McAdoo, to go along with Roosevelt." Indeed, according to O'Connor, FDR asked Manton to go to Chicago for that very purpose. Manton supposedly promised McAdoo the vice presidency and then, when Garner was selected to be the running mate instead, the chairmanship of the Democratic National Committee—promises that, according to O'Connor, FDR had no intention of keeping. Manton's efforts paid off; McAdoo threw California's forty-four delegates to FDR, the Smith challenge collapsed, and Roosevelt won the nomination on the fourth ballot. "Good old McAdoo!" FDR cheered while listening over the radio from Albany to McAdoo's dramatic announcement at the convention.[10]

O'Connor claimed that "were it not for the efforts of Judge Martin T. Manton in behalf of Governor Roosevelt," the convention would have turned to another candidate and that Manton was "as responsible as any one man for the nomination of F.D.R."[11] While that undoubtedly exaggerates Manton's contribution—"Of the 56,000 Democrats alleged to be in Chicago," Basil O'Connor quipped to FDR after the convention, "undoubtedly 62,000 of them arranged the McAdoo shift"[12]—Roosevelt felt it was sufficiently meaningful to record his gratitude to the judge. "Ever since the Convention," FDR said in an August 19, 1932 letter to Manton, "I have been meaning to write you a note to thank you for all that you did. I appreciate it very deeply."[13]

After Roosevelt cruised to victory over Hoover in November, Manton—literally the day after the election—appointed Basil O'Connor as a special master in the Interborough receivership case. This appointment "created some surprise in transit and legal sectors, where it had been thought that [Manton] would not take further action in the Interborough case until pending litigation over his jurisdiction had been settled."[14] Manton and Eva in turn were invited to join the president-elect at a celebratory dinner at Basil O'Connor's house. A large slab of ice, molded in the shape of the White House, was set atop the dinner table. Inspired by the image to contrast his own warmth with his predecessor's notoriously icy exterior, FDR motioned to Eva and promised: "It looks cold and that's the way it has been during the Hoover years, but I will not have it so—my friends will be able to see me when I am there."[15]

The Mantons were invited to Roosevelt's inauguration and inaugural ball. Sitting underneath sinister clouds on a cold, blustery day, they heard the new president pledge to employ new methods and indomitable optimism to confront "the dark realities of the moment" that had forced millions of unemployed and underemployed citizens to face "the grim problem of existence." It seems that Manton may not have been paying close attention when Roosevelt urged "abandonment of the false belief that public office and high political position are to be valued only by the standards of pride of place and personal profit."[16]

Thereafter, Manton met with President Roosevelt in the White House on several occasions. Manton spent time with the president in February 1934, discussing a lengthy article he had supposedly authored about international finance entitled "Governmental Defaults in the Payment of Contractual Obligations." (A friend of Manton later told the FBI that the article was actually ghostwritten, for a fee, by a professor in

Miami.) If, "after reading it," the president believed he could be of assistance, a perhaps overly optimistic Manton wrote when forwarding the highly technical, seventeen-page article to FDR, "please command me."[17]

In 1935, Manton tried to help FDR defuse a growing controversy over the Mexican government's anticlerical policies. Leading American Catholics were clamoring for the president to take a stand against what they perceived as religious persecution against Catholics in Mexico. With the 1936 election season approaching, the Mexican situation loomed as a potential political liability for FDR, sapping support from an important bloc of the New Deal coalition. Manton became one of a handful of prominent Catholics publicly defending Roosevelt. He gave a speech at a conference of the Catholic Association for International Peace opposing US interference in Mexico, earning him severe rebukes from Catholic prelates, including the Archbishop of Baltimore, who denounced him as a "secondary spokesman of the Administration."[18]

Meeting with FDR at the White House on July 8, 1935, Manton "offered his own services to bring about peace in the controversy." Manton said he could broker a meeting between the Mexican president and Boston bishop Francis Spellman, an administration supporter. Roosevelt agreed, provided the Vatican was on board. But the Vatican turned down the suggestion, to the relief of the State Department, which seemed to think Manton's plan harebrained.[19]

Manton may have had a particular reason to want to impress the president with his knowledge of international affairs and international law. He had long been a proponent of the Permanent Court of International Justice, also known as the World Court, created under the auspices of the League of Nations in the wake of World War I, and was "considered very much of an authority on the subject."[20] Manton envisioned that the World Court would eventually take over the resolution of international business disputes, which would grow in number and importance as the large US banking houses, investment enterprises, and manufacturing concerns expanded their foreign operations.[21] Although the United States opted out of the League of Nations, it nonetheless had the right to name one of its own citizens to the World Court. The position was undeniably prestigious. Charles Evans Hughes had served before being named chief justice of the Supreme Court, and Learned Hand agonized over whether to leave his beloved Second Circuit for The Hague when he was approached as a possible successor to Hughes in 1930.[22]

In early November 1935, Hughes's successor on the World Court, Frank B. Kellogg, announced his resignation. Manton quickly let it be known that he would be interested in becoming Kellogg's replacement. He published a long letter in the Sunday *New York Times* weighing in on the United States's policy of neutrality amid rising tensions in Europe.[23] John Bassett Moore, Hughes's predecessor on the World Court and a renowned international scholar, received an odd visit from a lawyer who dropped off some pamphlets on international law written by Manton, which he asked Moore to read. The meaning of that entreaty became clear to Moore later when Joseph Buffington, the senior judge of the US Court of Appeals for the Third Circuit, called and asked him to support Manton's candidacy for the World Court. Moore, a law professor at Columbia when Manton was a student there and "long suspicious of Manton," rebuffed Buffington's request.[24]

On November 20, 1935, Attorney General Homer Cummings told FDR that "Judge Manton would be pleased to be named on the World Court," adding that Professor Manley O. Hudson of Harvard Law School, an acclaimed international law expert and an even greater authority on the World Court, also "is prominently mentioned in connection with this same matter." Cummings suggested that the president "bear these two names in mind," but a few days later, when asking Secretary of State Hull for his views, FDR passed along only one name: Hudson. And it was Hudson who, the following month, procured the spot.[25]

* * *

The big prize for Manton remained the Supreme Court. To have a realistic shot, Manton would need more than a personal connection with the president. Roosevelt could not afford to look at Supreme Court nominations as opportunities to dispense plum positions to political allies, or for that matter to reward pure legal talent regardless of party affiliation, as Hoover had done with the appointment of Cardozo. Ideological fealty, to the president's progressive agenda, and to the philosophy of judicial restraint, would be the essential qualification. Roosevelt was locked in a constitutional death struggle with a Supreme Court majority determined to invalidate New Deal legislation it saw as threatening the established economic and social order. Roosevelt's antagonists were the rigidly conservative Four Horsemen—Pierce Butler, Willis Van Devanter, James McReynolds, and George Sutherland—who were joined, in most instances, by two more moderate Eastern Republicans, Chief Justice Hughes and Owen Roberts.

In early 1935, the Court dealt a blow to the signature economic reform of FDR's first term, the National Industrial Recovery Act (NIRA). The NIRA created the National Recovery Administration to promulgate codes of "fair competition" drafted by voluntary industry associations that had the effect of setting legally binding standards for wages, hours, and prices. Businesses displayed a "Blue Eagle" to show consumers they were in compliance with the code. Many Americans, especially small business owners caught in the maw of industrial codes typically drafted by big business, saw in the ubiquitous Blue Eagle a symbol of government over-reach and creeping totalitarianism. In *Panama Refining Co. v. Ryan*, the Court ruled that a section of the NIRA amounted to an unconstitutional delegation of legislative power to the executive branch. While the decision did not strike at the NIRA's core, more consequential constitutional attacks were in motion.[26]

One of those, *United States v. A.L.A. Schechter Poultry Corp.*, came before the Second Circuit for oral argument in December 1934. The defendants—the four Schechter brothers and their corporations—operated kosher chicken slaughterhouses in Brooklyn. They were convicted of a multitude of violations of the "Live Poultry Code" that governed the industry in metropolitan New York. These violations included paying their employees too little, making them work too hard, and selling poultry that was unfit for consumption or had not been properly inspected. In one much-mocked allegation, the indictment accused Schechter Poultry of having "knowingly, willfully and unlawfully sold for human consumption an unfit chicken to Harry Stauber." Another transgression was allowing butchers to select which chickens they wished to purchase. This was not the most auspicious factual backdrop for the government to defend against the claim that the NIRA intruded unnecessarily in purely local affairs.[27]

The Second Circuit panel consisted of Judges Manton, Learned Hand, and Chase. When they conferenced to discuss the case, Hand and Chase voted to overturn two counts of conviction on constitutional grounds. Manton nonetheless took responsibility for drafting the opinion. When Hand read Manton's draft, he "blew his top." Manton had simply disregarded Hand's and Chase's views and written an opinion that, cribbing liberally from the government's brief, adopted its arguments "without giving one particle of the rationale of the *majority* of the Court."[28] This resulted in one of the strangest appellate decisions ever published in the *Federal Reporter*: a lead opinion (Manton's) that comprehensively addressed the issues in the case and read like a typical opinion for the court, followed by a brief "concurring" opinion (Hand's) that set forth the views of the two judges who actually comprised the court's majority.[29]

Manton's opinion, which Hand's law clerk saw as "the most outrageous example of currying favor with the President that you could think of,"[30] was an unconditional victory for the Roosevelt Administration. It painted the business practices condemned by the Live Poultry Code as a menace to the Republic, stressing the size of the New York City poultry industry (the largest in the country) and its importance in dictating prices for poultry farmers and markets nationwide. Below-cost sales, selective killing, uninspected and diseased chickens—these were depicted by Manton not just as legal violations but moral sins, "evil practices" that the NIRA was right to eradicate.

The Supreme Court did not see it the same way. Disagreeing with Manton's position in every respect, the Court unanimously overturned the NIRA as part of the trio of stunning rebukes to the New Deal it delivered on May 27, 1935, "Black Monday." Chief Justice Hughes, who authored the opinion, made clear that in believing the law could be justified by the unique dangers presented by the Depression, Manton had badly misunderstood the Court's precedents. "[E]xtraordinary conditions do not create or enlarge constitutional power," Hughes wrote.[31]

After the demise of the NIRA, Congress passed the Wagner Act, which created the National Labor Relations Board (NLRB) to protect the rights of workers to unionize and bargain collectively with employers. "Almost no one believed the act was constitutional" given the Supreme Court's crabbed view of federal power; skeptics included many in Congress who voted for the law, Roosevelt's attorney general, and Roosevelt himself. The Wagner Act's prospects looked even bleaker after the Supreme Court ruled in May 1936 that Congress was powerless to regulate labor conditions in the coal mining industry.[32]

But two months later Manton, joined by Swan and Gus Hand, swatted down a constitutional attack on the Wagner Act mounted by John W. Davis on behalf of the Associated Press. Because the AP's business was to gather and distribute news in interstate commerce, Manton held, the NLRB acted within its authority in ordering the news service to reinstate an editor who had been fired for his union activities. "The right of employees to organize has been recognized and accepted," Manton asserted in language notable for its pro-union sentiment, and "[w]hen employers attempt to destroy this right," risking a strike that could have "a direct and paralyzing effect on interstate commerce," the federal government may intervene without infringing the employer's "legitimate" rights. Manton's opinion provided "the judicial *imprimatur*" long sought by Charles Fahy, the New Deal lawyer leading the government's defense of the Wagner Act, who used it to obtain another favorable decision from a different federal circuit court.[33]

Manton sustained yet another key New Deal law, the Public Utility Holding Company Act (PUHCA), when it came before the Second Circuit in 1937 in *Electric Bond & Share Co. v. Securities and Exchange Commission*. PUHCA, enacted after a particularly protracted and bitter congressional battle, took aim at the byzantine holding company structures created by electrical utilities to evade state regulation. The law required all holding companies to register with the Securities and Exchange Commission (SEC) and limited their operations to single states. It also included a controversial "death sentence" provision that enabled the SEC to dissolve uneconomical holding companies. The Roosevelt Administration knew that PUHCA would face a pull-out-all-the-stops court challenge from the utility industry, and FDR tasked Robert Jackson, then the general counsel at the Bureau of Internal Revenue, to lead the litigation. The government prevailed in a trial on stipulated facts before Judge Julian W. Mack in the Southern District in New York.

Manton presided when Jackson argued the appeal in the Second Circuit and Jackson faced "a good many questions." Recalling Manton's threat that he would "someday regret" denying Manton's 1935 application for tax relief, Jackson worried that Manton—"an able man whom I profoundly distrusted"—would "take advantage of this case to get even with me."[34] As it turned out, Jackson's fear was unfounded. In November 1937, Manton authored a lengthy opinion turning aside the arguments of the utility industry and tracking the government's arguments closely. SEC chairman and future Supreme Court justice William O. Douglas hailed the decision as "a liberal education in public utility and finance" and "a great milestone in constitutional law."[35]

Jackson speculated that Manton's hopes for a Supreme Court appointment outweighed any desire to exact revenge: "Manton was a man of great ambition and perhaps he didn't want to be in wrong with the administration. He had come very close to being appointed to the Supreme Court once and he'd never given up the idea that he could eventually be appointed." Still, Jackson had to admit, "[s]o far as I could see, Manton decided the case as he thought it ought to be." By the time the case reached the Supreme Court, two of the Four Horsemen had resigned, and a 6–1 majority ruled in the government's favor. However, Chief Justice Hughes's opinion paid no heed to Manton's reasoning, relying instead on Judge Mack's opinion as if the case had come directly to the Supreme Court from the District Court.[36]

Manton also authored opinions approving broad investigative powers for the fledgling SEC; rejecting a challenge to the Federal Communications Commission's authority to regulate telephone companies; and upholding the creation of the Home Owners' Loan Corporation to refinance home mortgages for borrowers threatened with foreclosure.[37] Administration lawyers would have been hard-pressed to find fault with any of Manton's judicial pronouncements on New Deal legislation or the vast administrative powers the president was accumulating and exercising as he combated the Depression.

Off the bench, too, Manton voiced his support for President Roosevelt and the New Deal. In a speech at a meeting of the National Committee for Religion and Welfare Recovery at the Hotel Astor in February 1936, Manton "paid tribute to President Roosevelt for rallying the country against the fear of collapse in the Spring of 1933," according to a newspaper account. "Without trying to appear in any sense as a partisan of any political or economic doctrine," Manton said, "we must admit that the courageous standing and wise counsel of our President at that critical period of our history did more than anything else to fortify us in our struggle against the enemies of fear."[38] A few months later, in a speech before leading Catholic laymen, Manton declared the programs of the New Deal promoting redistribution of wealth and workers' rights to be "in harmony" with papal teachings.[39]

In an NBC radio address honoring Oliver Wendell Holmes Jr. one year after the justice's death, Manton took aim at the Supreme Court majority that was blocking Roosevelt's programs. Manton heaped praise on Holmes for resisting "the forces of reaction" and "the exponents of the old order" in his frequent dissents earlier in the century from "conservative majority opinions." Drawing a parallel to the current Court controversy, Manton said he had "no doubt" that Holmes "would have condemned" the "recent attempts to maintain our people chained in perpetuity to the much abused economic doctrine of unrestricted laissez faire." It was Holmes's "constitutional liberalism" that "is destined to become the dominant legal philosophy in the not distant future," Manton predicted, and he urged "Progressives of all shades of opinion" to embrace it.[40] Just to make sure that FDR was paying attention, Manton gave an advance copy of the radio address to Hugh Gordon Miller, a prominent New York lawyer who forwarded it to Roosevelt and suggested that the president listen in.[41]

* * *

No Supreme Court vacancies arose during Roosevelt's first term. Incensed at the decisions of the conservative majority that "had left much of the New Deal in ruins," and fresh off his landslide re-election victory over Republican Alf Landon, FDR began his second term in early 1937 by proposing his audacious "Court-packing plan": an increase in the Court's membership to fifteen justices that would allow him to appoint six more liberals (one for each sitting justice over the age of 70). In a single blow, Roosevelt's plan would have reconstituted the Supreme Court into the predominately liberal body that Manton envisioned in his radio address. Of course, it did not turn out that way; Roosevelt had overplayed his hand politically and underestimated the nation's reverence for the Supreme Court as an institution above such crass partisan maneuvering. Although Democrats outnumbered Republicans by roughly four-to-one on Capitol Hill, many of those Democrats quietly, and then as public opinion grew hostile, openly and adamantly, refused to support their party-leader's plan.[42]

Manton must have figured that, as a New Deal supporter and the highest-ranking federal judge in the country not already on the Supreme Court, and still, at age fifty-six, a relatively young man, the odds were pretty good that if six new justices were to be appointed he would be among them. At the height of the Court-packing fight, Manton gave another speech condemning the conservative majority's "hard-crusted theory of economic individualism" and stressing the need for a "broad and elastic" Constitution that kept pace with "modern social and economic changes"—echoing FDR's own call in a fireside chat just days earlier for justices "who understand modern conditions" and can "save our national Constitution from hardening of the judicial arteries." Manton made sure to send copies of his speech to Jackson, which Jackson regarded as "a part of Manton's plan eventually to become a candidate for the first Supreme Court vacancy."[43] In October 1937, Manton wrote FDR directly indicating that he "favors the President's Court Plan" and "would like to discuss the matter with him."[44]

While Roosevelt's Court-packing plan failed to convince Congress, it did appear to have an impact on its intended target, the Court itself. In particular, the two more moderate members of the anti–New Deal coalition, Chief Justice Hughes and Justice Roberts, began siding with the liberals and producing 5–4 outcomes in the administration's favor, upholding the Wagner Act in April and the Social Security Act in May. On top of that, Justice Van Devanter announced his retirement, further depleting the right wing's ranks.[45] In July 1937, the *Wall Street Journal* reported that Manton was being mentioned as one of several "dark horse" candidates to replace Van Devanter, highlighting his decisions in the Schechter Poultry and Associated Press cases.[46] Indeed, Manton's name appears on an internal list of potential nominees generated around this time by Attorney General Cummings.[47] A few days later, however, Roosevelt nominated Senator Hugo Black of Alabama, an unstinting New Deal loyalist in the legislative branch.

At the beginning of 1938, another of the Four Horsemen, George Sutherland, stepped down. Archbishop Patrick Hayes of New York added his influential voice to those recommending elevation for Manton, his fellow New Yorker and Catholic luminary. Roosevelt thanked Archbishop Hayes in a January 14, 1938 letter. "As you probably know," the president wrote, "he [Manton] is an old friend of mine and his name will be given consideration when I take up the matter of filling the vacancy on the Supreme Court."[48] But the next day, Roosevelt named his solicitor general, Stanley Reed, to replace Sutherland.

When Justice Cardozo passed away in the summer of 1938, Manton enlisted the backing of Charles J. McDermott, a New York lawyer, former state court judge, and, most importantly, fishing companion of FDR. McDermott told the White House that he "saw Judge Martin T. Manton and his family at lunch on August 5, and the Judge told [me] that he was hoping to be appointed to the Supreme Court vacancy." Manton's appointment would "please all who know him in New York," McDermott assured Roosevelt. Another former New York state court judge, William Harman Black, also wrote on Manton's behalf. Unlike the response to Archbishop Hayes, Black received a reply not from Roosevelt but from his aide, Martin McIntyre, who merely thanked Black for writing, without promising that Manton would receive consideration.[49] Cardozo's seat instead went to Felix Frankfurter, Manton's nemesis.

* * *

Little did Manton know that all his efforts were in vain. There was no chance that Roosevelt was going to appoint him to the Supreme Court. The Court was already overloaded with New Yorkers: Hughes, Stone, and (until his death) Cardozo. Furthermore, a Manton nomination would have resurrected politically toxic reports of FDR's links to Tammany Hall. And unlike today—eighteen of the last twenty Supreme Court justices, stretching back more than a half-century, were previously appellate judges—Manton's Second Circuit service was not an especially attractive credential to Roosevelt. Of Roosevelt's eight Supreme Court appointments, only the last one, Wiley Rutledge, had any prior experience on an appellate court.

But a far more important obstacle stood in Manton's way, which Robert Jackson explained in 1952 in an oral history for Columbia University. When Manton, in 1935, asked Jackson to review and reverse his federal tax liability arising from his investment in the Atlantic Bottle Company, Jackson discovered something odd: "I found in [Manton's] income tax returns that fifteen years after he went on the bench he was reporting income from his old law firm for work done before he went on the bench." As Jackson recalled, "[i]t was a large sum," about $40,000. Although FBI files suggest that Manton retained a financial interest in at least one substantial Cockran & Manton case that was not resolved until the 1930s,[50] Jackson could not have known that. He smelled a rat. There was, he later wrote, "an odor about [Manton's] financial affairs that was not wholesome, although I had no proof that the thing was wrong." After talking it over with Treasury secretary Henry Morgenthau and Treasury general counsel Herman Oliphant, Jackson concluded that FDR needed to be "alerted to the danger of Manton":

> *I took that information to the President because it seemed dubious to me. Manton had accounted for the income so that there was no tax question about it, but it was strange to me that long in the depression in 1932–33 he was getting payment for work done so long before. It wasn't normal for clients to wait that length of time to pay their lawyers, if ever they were to pay. He had been appointed by Woodrow Wilson before 1918.*

Once FDR learned of Manton's suspicious tax returns, Jackson recalled, Manton "stood no chance" of being appointed by Roosevelt to the Supreme Court.[51]

Morgenthau himself likely shared with Roosevelt another disturbing piece of news about Manton, also connected with the judge's unusual finances. This related to the huge tract of land that Manton co-owned in Queens, New York. After the collapse of their efforts to convert the land into an airport hub, Manton and his partner, Stuard Hirschman, explored turning it into a massive $60 million housing project that would accommodate twelve thousand families, to be financed largely by the Reconstruction Finance Corporation. Frank Cohen, Manton's unsavory friend in the insurance business, helped try to get the project off the ground. Plans for the project were hatched "with the utmost secrecy" but eventually spilled into the press in 1933, along with Manton's interest in the venture. This project, too, fizzled. A separate proposal for the City to buy the land for $7.6 million was also dropped after attracting media attention.[52]

In 1935, Hirschman and Manton came up with a slimmed-down proposal for a $10 million housing project, to be called Astoria Gardens, and sought financing from the new Federal Housing Administration. Local FHA officials in New York rejected the Astoria Gardens application in the fall. The application was then reviewed by Peter Grimm, a prominent New York City real estate broker who had just been named a special assistant to Treasury Secretary Morgenthau for housing policy. "After careful study," Grimm turned it down too.[53]

Hirschman and Manton would not take no for an answer. "Considerable pressure" was brought to bear on FHA Administrator McDonald. Together with Cohen, Manton met with McDonald at the Carlton Hotel in Washington and, according to Cohen, arranged for FDR's attorney general, Homer S. Cummings, to be present to opine on the legality of the FHA's participation. Years later J. Edgar Hoover, when he found out about this meeting, sent Cummings's successor, Frank Murphy, a confidential memorandum noting that if Cohen's account was true, Manton had "use[d] his influence to secure an opinion from Government officials in a private matter in which he was interested."[54]

After the New Year, Dwight L. Hoopingarner, a top FHA official in New York, called at the White House to discuss the Astoria Gardens project. Noting that "Judge Martin T. Manton is one of the leading stockholders," Hoopingarner explained that the project's sponsors were "anxious to have this project expedited." Apparently assuming that the administration would want the FHA to help Manton, McDonald wrote FDR aide Martin McIntyre to assure him that "the examination of this project is being pushed through as rapidly as possible" and should be brought up for final consideration within two weeks. Also approached was Stephen B. Gibbons, an assistant secretary of the treasury and the "chief patronage dispenser for the administration within the treasury."[55] Gibbons told Grimm that "Judge Manton was coming in to see" him and wanted Grimm to drop his objections to the project.[56]

Grimm laid this out in a memorandum for Secretary Morgenthau on January 25, 1936, also reporting that he would travel to New York for further investigation. After returning on January 28, Grimm submitted, "for the Treasury Department record," another memorandum outlining his latest thinking about the project "with which Judge Manton's name is connected as sponsor." Grimm now withdrew his opposition, saying the "proposition was in much better shape" than when it had been reviewed in the fall. A respected real estate developer and a real estate lawyer had both pronounced it "sound." "It is my judgment," Grimm advised Morgenthau in a carefully worded conclusion that did not go quite so far as an endorsement, "that the utmost care has been used in the study of this proposal and all the work done very thoroughly."[57]

Grimm, Gibbons, and McDonald had all misjudged Morgenthau's willingness to make Manton happy. On January 29, Morgenthau fired off a response to Grimm, focusing on Grimm's reversal of position—"I gather that you now are favoring this loan"—and Grimm's stated wish to make a written record for the Treasury Department. "For the Treasury record," Morgenthau acidly replied, "I wish to inform you that nobody connected with the Treasury should approve or disapprove any loans made by the Federal Housing Administration. That is not the Treasury's work or responsibility."[58] Morgenthau directed his next memorandum to Gibbons. He noted that, according to Grimm's memoranda, Gibbons had "interested yourself in a $10,000,000 loan of FHA to an Astoria Housing Project of which Judge Manton is sponsor." Morgenthau provided Gibbons with a copy of his response to Grimm and the following admonition: "please, in the future, inform anybody who tries to interest you directly or indirectly in bringing influence to bear upon any governmental agency that has federal money to loan, that you or anyone else connected with the Treasury will not and cannot use his position for this purpose."[59] Finally, Morgenthau took care of McDonald. In a phone call the following day, January 30, Morgenthau told McDonald: "from now on I don't want to share any responsibility with you as to whether these big projects should or should not go through. I have a particular one in mind—this one that Judge Manton's . . . Now, we can't share that responsibility with you, see?" When McDonald tried to explain that he figured Morgenthau would have wanted Grimm's imprimatur, Morgenthau cut him off: "No, no, that's your responsibility and we can't share it with you. If you go wrong we'll jump on you with both feet."[60] McDonald laughed, but he got the message. The FHA did not go forward with the Astoria Gardens project.

Morgenthau did not want the "Treasury record" to show that the agency was turning somersaults to help out a powerful federal judge in his private financial affairs. He also suspected something underhanded was going on between Manton and Grimm, a "suave, debonair and incredibly likeable man" who before joining Treasury captained William A. White & Sons, a major New York real estate brokerage firm.[61] On February 10, a "worried" Morgenthau called McDonald again to ask him about "the housing project that Judge Manton was interested in." Morgenthau wanted to know if the sponsors had selected a rental agent; "strictly between the two of us," he had been "told positively that William A. White and Son had been promised the business." (McDonald assured him that was not the case.)[62] While there is no record that Morgenthau brought Manton's influence-peddling to FDR's attention, there is every reason to believe that he, like Jackson before him, would have done so. One of Roosevelt's closest friends since the early 1920s, Morgenthau was a fierce FDR loyalist and as treasury secretary was in virtually daily communication with the president.

It is remarkable that Manton, so intent on ascending to the Supreme Court, and finally seeing a realistic path to that lifetime goal by dint of his past friendship, partisan affiliation, and ideological affinity with FDR, chose nonetheless to diminish his prospects by pressuring administration officials to promote his financial interests. Here in microcosm is the lasting leitmotif of Manton's career: greed sabotaging ambition.

* * *

FDR assuredly never told Manton that he would not be seriously considered for the Supreme Court, let alone the reasons why. The two men maintained a friendly rapport up until the time the Manton corruption scandal broke. Manton and Eva visited with the president in early 1938. Eva promised they would send FDR some "broilers" raised at the Mantons' Fairacres farm on Long Island. Manton delivered on the promise, expressing the hope, in a handwritten letter on March 7, 1938, addressed "Dear Franklin," that the president would find the chicks "nearly as good as Mrs. Manton has represented." Manton was "particularly pleased," he wrote, "in finding you looking as well with all that I read of your great burdens," and asked the president to "keep up your grand performance for the country's progress." The chicks were gobbled up immediately, according to FDR's thank-you note two days later: "Please tell Mrs. Manton the broilers were delicious. They were much enjoyed by all." Reciprocating Manton's first-name familiarity, Roosevelt crossed out "Judge" in the original salutation so that it read "My dear Martin." On behalf of Eleanor and himself, he extended to the Mantons "our affectionate greetings and best wishes."[63]

FDR had no way of knowing that Manton's broiler business figured into yet another abuse of Manton's judicial office for private gain, or that Manton's many derelictions of duty were, finally, coming home to roost.

CHAPTER FIFTEEN

"The Judge Needs the Money"

The Chicken Egg Incubator Case

ACROSS THE LONG ISLAND SOUND AND DUE NORTH OF THE MANTONS' diminutive chicken farm at Fairacres, a sprawling 100-acre commercial hatchery hummed with activity. Almon Blakeslee ("A.B.") Hall and his brother Louis Cook Hall began raising poultry in their hometown of Wallingford, Connecticut, in 1911. Twenty-five years later Hall Brothers Hatchery was the largest baby chick hatchery in the eastern United States, if not the entire country. Every week over two hundred thousand eggs, sourced from hundreds of different farmers across New England, arrived at the hatchery, where they were deposited into mahogany-finished electric incubators warmed to a toasty 99.5 degrees and capable of housing twenty-seven thousand eggs each. Some three weeks later, the baby chicks emerged from their shells amid a chorus of peeps. They were then shipped off to broiler producers, fattened up to about nine pounds, and slaughtered. Hall Brothers hatched and sold more than 4.5 million baby chicks per year. A.B. Hall once calculated that, if placed end to end, these tiny yellow furballs would stretch for 262 miles.[1]

Not that long before, production of chicken meat on such a grand scale seemed unimaginable. For most of American history, chicken consumption was scrawny in comparison to beef, pork, and wild game, due not so much to different tastes, or a lack of health consciousness, as to economics.[2] Hens could lay only a few eggs a year, and as a result, chicken meat was relatively rare and high-priced, essentially a byproduct of the egg industry. "A chicken in every pot," the Republican Party's famous campaign slogan of 1928, was that era's version of the traditional GOP promise to pursue business-friendly policies that would bring upper-class amenities within the reach of ordinary Americans.[3]

The rise of the nascent commercial broiler industry lent plausibility to the GOP vision. Science and technology powered the industry's development. Improvements in breeding in the latter half of the nineteenth century spawned new varieties of hens that produced more eggs and faster-growing, higher-quality chickens. But even more critical was the introduction of the artificial electric incubator.

In 1918, Dr. Samuel B. Smith of Cleveland patented an especially ingenious "staged incubation" device. Eggs were placed in the incubation chamber at different intervals during the twenty-one-day incubation period. Air propelled through the chamber carried heat emitted from eggs in the more advanced stage of incubation to heat-absorbing eggs in the less advanced stage, allowing for the incubator's continuous operation through the successive stages. This made it possible to increase the number of eggs in a single incubator from a few hundred to tens of thousands. Artificial incubation revolutionized poultry farming. In 1925 only about 10 percent of baby chicks came from incubators; by 1930 the proportion swelled to 73 percent. Welcoming this new age of commercialization, a leading New England poultry lecturer advised farmers that they should no longer care "for the color of the bird's feathers, but the color of the money earned by these birds."[4]

The Hall Brothers embraced the modern techniques of poultry farming. In the early 1930s they cross-bred their own new chick, dubbed the "Barred Hallcross," which "excelled in vigor, livability, growth and egg production" and was especially popular in New York's live markets, the center of poultry distribution in the early twentieth century. "1933 was our BEST YEAR YET!" Hall Brothers crowed in a poultry trade magazine, so much so that they expanded their incubator capacity to 650,000 for 1934. The Halls were quite happy with their incubators, which were similar to Samuel Smith's staged incubation devices but manufactured by the Robbins Incubator Company of Denver, Colorado. In fact, Hall

Brothers was probably the biggest user of the Robbins Electric Incubator in the entire nation.[5]

* * *

Shortly thereafter the Halls' faith in their Robbins Incubators was shaken to the core. In June 1934, Dr. Smith filed a lawsuit against the Halls in federal court in Connecticut, claiming that their use of the Robbins Incubator infringed upon Smith's 1918 patent. The suit against the Halls was one piece of a broader, unusually ambitious legal strategy composed of patent infringement actions against some 440 farmers and hatcheries in the United States. Having leveraged his patent into a multimillion-dollar manufacturing business, Dr. Smith could afford to finance a litigation campaign on a vast scale. He hired the finest lawyers to manage it, such as Newton D. Baker, a founding partner of the Cleveland-based law firm now known as BakerHostetler, who had served as President Wilson's secretary of war.[6]

Vindication for Smith arrived with a pair of Supreme Court opinions handed down in the first week of 1935 in cases originating from the Eighth and Ninth Circuits. Accepting the arguments advanced by Baker on Smith's behalf, the Supreme Court ruled in *Smith v. Snow* and a companion case that the Smith patent was valid and infringed by two rival incubators, including the Robbins incubator. Justice Stone's opinion for the Court marveled at Smith's "novel and revolutionary" invention, which "solved the major problems of artificial incubation in a highly efficient manner."[7]

Within months the Smith legal juggernaut had rolled over the Hall Brothers as well. In July 1935, US district judge Carroll C. Hincks of New Haven ruled that the Halls' use of the Robbins incubator violated Smith's patent rights.[8] Deprived of their main defense by virtue of the Supreme Court's rulings, the Halls' lawyers argued that Smith's patent was invalid for a reason never presented to the Supreme Court—namely, that a former poultryman for the US Department of Agriculture named Milo Hastings had anticipated Smith's method of staged incubation by several years. They called Hastings as a witness, pointed to articles and photographs showing prior use of the incubator devised by Hastings in

231

the early 1910s, and introduced Hastings's own application for a patent, submitted five years before Smith's, but denied by the patent examiners in a 2–1 decision. But with the Supreme Court's rulings at his back, momentum was on Smith's side. Judge Hincks rejected the Halls' argument.

Because the Smith patent reached its seventeen-year expiration point in April 1935, the Halls could not be enjoined from further use of their Robbins incubators. But they faced liability for damages, and the potential award was ruinous. Smith was asking for $250,000 plus five cents for every egg that had passed through the Halls' infringing incubators. A.B. Hall, put in the unidiomatic position of having to count his chickens after they had hatched, estimated that he and his brother had processed about twenty-five million chicks since buying their first Robbins incubator in 1928. At a nickel apiece, this meant that Hall could wind up paying Smith as much as $1.5 million.[9] For Hall it was like a horror movie in which the millions of chicks Hall had hatched since 1928 came back to life to exact their revenge.

Hall "was at a loss which way to turn." A friend and customer, Wendell S. Still, the owner of Long Island's largest poultry farm, offered a suggestion. "I've heard of a man by the name of Fallon," Still explained to Hall. Fallon was someone "who knows the answers" and "is influential politically in New York City." How could Hall get in touch with Fallon? Still did not know Fallon personally. But he did know someone who did: Forrest W. Davis, an accountant in Port Jefferson, Long Island. Fallon's younger brother, Thomas J. Fallon, also lived in Port Jefferson, and in the summer of 1935 he had introduced Davis to William Fallon at the offices of the bankrupt Prudence Company, where both brothers worked as investigators.[10]

At the end of October 1935, Hall traveled into New York City to meet with Davis. The bespectacled, slightly built accountant brought the rotund chicken mogul up to Prudence's offices, where Hall explained his troubles to Fallon. It all seemed so unfair, Hall said. Why should the patent owner be able to go after an innocent user, such as himself, who had no knowledge of patent law, rather than suing the manufacturer of the infringing machine? And it wasn't just Hall, but 439 equally ingenuous poultrymen all across America whose livelihoods were on the line. Fallon was sympathetic. He asked Hall to provide him with copies of the District Court's decision, the parties' briefs below, and the record that would be presented on appeal. Fallon needed to "take it up with a friend of his" and get back to Hall.[11]

Two weeks later, the three men—Hall, Davis, and Fallon—reconvened at Fallon's apartment inside the thirty-two-story, 525-room Hotel Delmonico on the corner of Park Avenue and 59th Street. Fallon had in the meantime conferred with his "friend," Judge Manton. By this time Manton and Fallon had an established track record they could market to potential customers like Hall. Fallon told Hall he was "quite sure he could be of assistance" to Hall, bragging that he had fixed cases for "Mr. Reilly of the Evans Case Company" and "a number of other people." More specifically, he said he would be able, through Manton, to secure a favorable decision for the Halls for a price of $75,000. Hall was "shocked and astounded"—at the price. He did not have $75,000, he explained to Fallon, and he did not know how he could raise such a sum. Haggling ensued, at the end of which Hall and Fallon agreed on a price of $60,000, payable the same day a favorable decision was rendered. The $60,000 represented a 20 percent discount from Fallon's original quote. It also was the equivalent of well over $1 million today.[12]

The familiar pattern soon played itself out. "Judge Manton is short of money," Fallon told Hall. "Would you lend him $5,000?" Hall protested that under their deal, payment was contingent on a favorable decision by the Court of Appeals, and the appeal had not even been briefed yet. "Well, the Judge needs the money," Fallon countered, "and if you will lend me the $5,000, it will be considered as a down payment on the decision." Like Reilly before him, Hall felt he had no choice. Returning to the Hotel Delmonico, Hall handed Fallon a check for $5,000 made out to Fallon's "Allied Rediscount Corporation." To document the loan, Fallon gave Hall a personal note, on the understanding Hall would return the note once the court ruled.[13]

If Hall had to go out of pocket before the court's ruling, he felt it was fair that the other principal beneficiary of his actions—John L. Robbins, the president of the Robbins Incubator Company—help him bear the burden. Meeting with Robbins in Chicago, Hall shared with Robbins "what was going on" in New York and Robbins promised to reimburse Hall for his "expenses." Later, when Samuel Smith's estate sued the Halls and Robbins for bribing Manton, Robbins publicly stated that he had known nothing of Hall's transgressions. But on the day before Thanksgiving in 1935, he wrote Hall a letter enclosing, "in accordance with our last conversation," three $1,000 bills, nicknamed "Clevelands" at the time because they bore the image of President Grover Cleveland.[14]

Fallon hit up Hall with more requests for money in December. On December 16, he asked for another $5,000 loan for Judge Manton. This time Hall insisted on notes from both Fallon and Manton promising repayment. He got them both, but in order to conceal the link between the judge and Hall, the note from Manton was made payable to Davis. As Fallon explained, the judge thought "it would look bad if it got out" that he had issued a note to a litigant with a case pending before him. Again, Hall agreed to return the notes after the Court of Appeals' ruling. He wrote a $5,000 check to Fallon's Allied Rediscount Corporation; the next day, Fallon wrote a check on his Allied Rediscount account for $5,000 payable to Manton's Forest Hills Terrace Corporation.[15]

Hall did not mind coming to New York to meet with Fallon. The married middle-aged chicken farmer was something of a serial philanderer. At the time, he was carrying on an illicit affair with a woman who lived in Greenwich Village. Hall and Davis would also hire prostitutes when they stayed in the city. One evening, Hall got "rolled" by two prostitutes, who took his money without performing any service. Hall, together with Fallon, reported the incident to the local police precinct, doing their part to ameliorate New York's crime problem.[16]

Two days after Christmas brought another $5,000 request from Fallon, another $5,000 check from Hall to Allied Rediscount, and another note from Fallon, coupled with Fallon's assurance that a favorable outcome was "a sure thing."[17] That same day, the *New York Times*'s lead story described the "systematic extortion of money from business" by racketeers detailed in a report issued by the grand jury used by special prosecutor Dewey. The city's rackets, the grand jury found, were controlled by a dozen or so major criminals mostly "totally unknown to the public" because they "operate through henchmen" whose activities were designed to disguise "the trail running to the actual leaders."[18]

* * *

Valentine's Day 1936 saw Hall back in New York for the oral argument of his appeal, navigating swirling sleet and ice-crusted streets and sidewalks, the residue of an unusually severe winter storm. By midday, as the storm subsided and temperatures reached a comparatively balmy 36 degrees, New Yorkers were unbuttoning their coat collars, and Hall too, leaving Foley Square, could relax a little. Manton was on the panel, as promised, along with Swan and Chase, and he and Chase gave Smith's lawyer a hard time. Fallon and Davis told Hall he could expect a favorable ruling in as soon as a week, three weeks at the outside. Hall did not even balk when Fallon asked him for another $10,000 check, which brought the amount of his "down payment" to $25,000.[19]

Weeks passed with no ruling, despite repeated promises from Fallon and Davis that one was forthcoming. Hall grew increasingly impatient. There were "unavoidable delays," Davis explained, in getting "all of the judges to agree on the unanimous decision." The "Smith crowd," Fallon elaborated, "had a lot of influence in the Circuit Court" and was "trying hard to block the decision." According to Fallon, Judge Learned Hand had picked up and read a copy of the draft opinion sitting on Judge Swan's desk. "Why Swan," Hand said, "you can't do this. You are reversing the Supreme Court of the United States." Fallon even claimed that Manton needed to use Hall's money to pay off the other two judges on the panel as well as the clerk of the court.[20]

Finally, in early April, Fallon told Hall that a decision "positively" would come down the next Monday. On Saturday, April 4, Hall removed $35,000 in cash he had stockpiled in a safe deposit box and brought it to his room at the Hotel New Yorker on Eighth Avenue and 34th Street, adjacent to Penn Station, where Davis helped him count the money and deposit it in another safe deposit box at the hotel. On Monday morning, April 6, Hall waited for Fallon to meet him at the hotel, probably pacing to and fro like one of his newborn chicks. Hall retrieved the $35,000 and gave it to Fallon; he also, as promised, returned to Fallon the notes evidencing the $25,000 in funds previously advanced. Since no decision had yet been officially announced, Hall also asked Fallon for a receipt for the money, just in case.[21]

Between the high stakes and the warm spring day, Hall may have been sweating as he entered the Second Circuit courtroom on the seventeenth floor of the Foley Square Courthouse and took a seat on one of the wooden benches. He must have felt a wave of relief when he heard Judge Manton utter these words in announcing the decision in *Smith v. Hall*: "Decree reversed." The decision was unanimous, and Manton was the author.[22]

Manton's opinion for the court accepted the Halls' argument that Milo Hastings had anticipated Smith's invention in all relevant particulars, including a closed chamber, forced drafts of air, staged incubation, and capacity for thousands of eggs. The chief contested point was whether Hastings had actually contemplated staging the placement of the eggs, a feature not explicitly described in Hastings's patent application. But Manton methodically marshaled several sources of evidence showing that Hastings's incubator did, in fact, utilize staged incubation. "This is the first time the prior uses [of the Hastings incubator] have been so fully presented and substantiated," Manton wrote by way of freeing himself from the Supreme Court's validation of the Smith patent and two prior federal circuit court decisions rejecting the Hastings prior use defense.[23]

In other cases where Manton accepted money from litigants, his opinions twisted the law or the facts to reach the desired result, even if within the bounds of what might be called fair advocacy. In *Smith v. Hall* Manton's reasoning rested on firmer ground. Indeed, it was soon endorsed by untainted and even higher judicial authorities. In March 1937, the Supreme Court of Canada, in a unanimous decision, held Smith's Canadian patent invalid because of the Hastings prior use. The five Canadian justices concluded that the US Supreme Court would have come out differently if it had heard the Hastings evidence, citing Manton's opinion with approval and relying on essentially the same evidence as their brethren in New York.[24] The following month, the US Supreme Court itself, by a vote of 8–0, concurred and affirmed Manton's ruling. Justice Stone, author of *Smith v. Snow*, did an about-face, explaining that "in that case the Hastings prior use was not presented or considered," but "has been developed in the records now before us more fully than in any earlier case."[25] Manton went out on a limb in *Smith v. Hall*; examples of the Supreme Court reversing itself on a question of patent validity were "extremely rare," one contemporary commentator noted, "and can be counted on the fingers of one hand."[26] Perhaps Manton did so only out of financial self-interest. But thirteen Supreme Court justices, as well as his two Second Circuit colleagues, ultimately agreed he was right.

* * *

After learning of the Second Circuit's decision in court on April 6, A.B. Hall met Fallon in the coat room and walked with him to the clerk's office to procure certified copies of the decision. Just before they stepped in the elevator, Fallon, ever vigilant against the risk of incriminating evidence, commanded, "Give me that receipt." Hall returned the receipt that Fallon had given him earlier that morning. What he did not return, or tell Fallon about, was his image of an even more incriminating document—the December 16 note signed by Manton—which Hall had brought to a professional photographer months before. That document, Hall decided, might come in handy someday. Meanwhile, it was time to celebrate. In the evening, Hall's mistress hosted a champagne party at her apartment on Sullivan Street where she, Hall, Fallon, Davis, and Milo Hastings's wife toasted Hall Brothers' litigation victory.[27]

Hall's financial dealings with Fallon and Davis were not yet over. The next day, Fallon asked him for a "commission on this deal." Mystified, Hall said he assumed Fallon was getting his cut out of the $60,000 Hall had already paid. "No, the Judge gets all of that," Fallon responded. When Hall asked how much he wanted, Fallon suggested $15,000 or $20,000. "Not possible," Hall countered. They settled on $5,000. Later in the week, Davis "came around with a sad story that he had not received any commission either from Fallon or from Manton, and he said he believed he should have something to cover his expenses." In Fallon's presence, Hall wrote Davis a check for $3,000. Davis came back the same day, without Fallon, to complain that Fallon made him fork over most of the $3,000 to Fallon. Hall cut Davis another check for $1,000, bringing his total tab to $69,000.[28]

At least Manton was still looking out for Hall's interests. In the summer of 1936, after the Supreme Court granted certiorari in *Smith v. Hall*, Fallon told Hall that Manton believed Hall's attorney, an elderly patent lawyer from Philadelphia, had "made a weak presentation" in the Second Circuit and advised Hall to obtain "a better lawyer." Hall said he did not know a better lawyer. Not a problem, Fallon assured him; "we will find one for you." Manton chose Thomas G. Haight, a former judge on the Third Circuit Court of Appeals. Like Manton, Haight had been appointed a federal district judge, and then elevated to the circuit court, by President Wilson, all while still in his thirties. Unlike Manton, when Haight realized a judge's salary failed to fulfill his material needs, he resigned after serving only six years and returned to private practice.[29]

Manton's secretary, Marie Schmalz, called Haight's office to arrange an appointment between Haight and Hall. Apparently Haight did not think it strange—or strange enough to refuse a retainer—that Manton, the judge who had authored the opinion under review by the Supreme Court, was recommending counsel for one of the parties. In fact, when Haight realized right before the Supreme Court argument that he needed to see Smith's brief in the Second Circuit, he did not hesitate to call up Manton to get a copy. After the argument, Haight dined with Manton at the Lawyers Club in New York and predicted he was going to win the case. Manton shot back, jocularly, "That is one case you ought to win."[30]

No judge likes to be reversed by a higher court. But that was not the only reason Manton continued to help the Halls even after the Halls had paid the agreed-upon $60,000. He and the Halls were also business partners, in a sense. Beginning in early 1936, Halls Brothers supplied baby chicks for the broiler business that Manton and his son ran at Fairacres. With his Second Circuit appeal still pending, A.B. Hall agreed to a price of ten cents per chick, below his usual price of twelve or fifteen cents. Since Fairacres was buying about one thousand chicks per week, those savings added up to hundreds of dollars per year. Hall helped out in other ways, too, such as recommending a new manager for the chicken farm when the Mantons lost confidence in their existing manager.[31] And so it was that baby chicks hatched in Robbins electric incubators at the Hall brothers' farm in Wallingford, Connecticut, wound up as "delicious" broilers at the dinner table in the White House.

CHAPTER SIXTEEN

"I Got the Man Who Can Reach Judge Manton"

The Electric Razor Case

CAPTURING FORTY-SIX OF FORTY-EIGHT STATES, FDR ROMPED TO re-election on November 3, 1936. A million jubilant New Yorkers waded ankle-deep in confetti and ticker tape in Times Square to celebrate the president's victory.[1] Manton surely was pleased. The Friday night before the election, Manton had joined hundreds of Democratic politicos at a campaign rally attended by the president himself at the Brooklyn Academy of Music.[2]

On November 4, 1936, Morris Renkoff arrived at an office building a couple of blocks from the Times Square festivities of the night before. Although his attempt to bribe Manton into reversing his conviction had failed, Renkoff remained at liberty while the Supreme Court considered whether to take his case. The ever-optimistic Renkoff jumped at the opportunity when an acquaintance from Paris, "Captain Schutline," promised they could "make a lot of money" with the colorful Archie M. Andrews, a once spectacularly wealthy entrepreneur who presided over a rapidly diminishing business empire from his office on Fifth Avenue and 43rd Street.[3]

Among Andrews's many current tribulations was an investigation by the SEC into suspicious "wash" and "match" trades involving the stock of Dictograph Products Company, a public company controlled by Andrews, the 70 percent majority shareholder. Andrews, the SEC believed, engaged in transactions through nominees in order to artificially inflate the price of Dictograph stock for his benefit.[4] Andrews's immediate purpose in meeting Renkoff was to enlist his help in orchestrating additional manipulative transactions in Dictograph stock. Renkoff readily agreed to the scheme.[5]

As they left Andrews's office, Schutline shared with Renkoff another of Andrews's woes. Dictograph manufactured the Packard-Lektro Shaver, an electric razor that competed with the leading brand made by the Schick company. At the end of October, Brooklyn federal judge Grover M. Moscowitz had ruled that the Packard-Lektro Shaver infringed Schick's patent. At Schutline's mention of litigation in the Second Circuit, Renkoff's eyes lit up. By this time the two men had reached the lobby of Andrews's building. "Let's go back," Renkoff suggested to Schutline. "I think I can do a lot for Andrews."[6]

* * *

Like other patent cases in which Manton took money, *Schick Dry Shaver, Inc. v. Dictograph Products Co.* was a closely watched litigation with important implications for the future of a fledgling industry. The Schick "dry shaver"—no water, soap, or shaving cream necessary—was an instant success when it was introduced in 1931. Although expensively priced at $25, the Schick razor became a popular Christmas gift and sales soon reached into the millions of dollars.[7] "The Schick device," Judge Moscowitz predicted, "will revolutionize the manner and method of shaving."[8]

Inevitably the Schick electric razor attracted not only consumers but also competitors. First out of the box was the competing model manufactured by Andrews's Dictograph Company. Personal animosity, not just economic calculus, animated Andrews's challenge. Andrews and Jacob Schick, known as "Colonel" Schick due to his military service in the Spanish-American War and World War I, were not strangers. After hawking the Schick Electric Shaver at the Chicago World's Fair in 1933, Andrews wanted to be anointed Schick's distributor in the Midwest.

Colonel Schick refused, prompting an irate Andrews to sue Schick in Chicago claiming unpaid commissions.[9]

Subsequently, a Dictograph vice president, A. Harry Aaron, happened to be present at a friend's home in New Jersey when Colonel Schick arrived and explained the operation of the Schick razor in detail. Dictograph then used that information to develop its own electric razor. In December 1935, the Packard Lektro-Shaver first appeared on the market, buoyed by an aggressive advertising campaign that featured celebrity endorsers such as the singer Al Jolson. Perhaps to get under Schick's skin even more, Andrews announced that Dictograph would set up its production facility in Stamford, Connecticut, also home to the Schick business. Within a month of the Lektro-Shaver's introduction Schick pounced with his patent infringement suit.[10]

The round-headed Lektro-Shaver looked different from the squarish Schick. It felt different, too, its cutter exhibiting a rocking motion as it sheared stubble from the face. But these distinctions were "quite immaterial," Judge Moscowitz found in his October 1936 ruling. "There is no real difference between plaintiff's device and defendant's device." The conclusion was "inescapable" that the Packard Lektro-Shaver infringed the Schick patent.

Colonel Schick heard about Moscowitz's ruling while golfing in Bermuda. As US income tax rates rose to 60 percent during FDR's first term, Schick renounced his US citizenship, moved to Canada, and formed Bahamian corporations to hold his securities.[11] Schick's maneuvers aroused the indignation of FDR's treasury secretary, Henry Morgenthau, who denounced this "most flagrant" effort to escape US tax laws. Schick "went the whole route to eliminate American taxes as far as he could," a Treasury official charged at a congressional hearing.[12]

For Andrews, Judge Moscowitz's ruling was the latest in a series of business setbacks and legal defeats. This was a stunning reversal for a man once hailed as a "Horatio Alger Hero" by the press. Andrews started out selling newspapers on frigid Chicago streets as a high school dropout, then got a job in a stockbroker's office and saved up enough money to start a brokerage firm of his own. The Charles Schwab of his era, Andrews offered cut-rate commissions in the belief that investment securities should be treated like any other commodity. Branching out, Andrews bought automobile companies in the Midwest, hotels in California, and penny scale weighing machine manufacturers in Chicago and New York. Before the 1929 crash Andrews's net worth was estimated at between $50 million and $80 million, which would put him in the billionaire category today.[13]

Andrews spent money with abandon. He bought an eighty-five-foot yacht, traded up within a year to a ninety-five-foot yacht, and then made a splash in 1927 by purchasing, from Henry Ford, a 225-foot yacht named the *Sialia* for $250,000. *Sialia* accommodated nine staterooms, each equipped with a full bathroom; a teakwood music room appointed with a Steinway piano and a Victrola phonograph; and a thirty-four-man crew, including three chefs and a radio operator who kept Andrews apprised of developments in the stock market when he was out at sea. A friend of Andrews kept a journal of one six-week cruise around the Caribbean and West Indies, describing champagne dinners, salvos of fireworks set off from the ship, Andrews's purchase of fifteen hundred different brands of cigars in Cuba, and all manner of spirits imbibed free from the constraints of the Volstead Act. "Life seemed just too wonderful" aboard the *Sialia*, the friend wrote.[14]

Golf was another favorite pastime. Andrews built a fifty-four-hole course in Pasadena, the largest in America at the time, and garnered national headlines in 1926 for playing a golf match to resolve a $50,000 dispute with another businessman.[15] In 1928, he purchased a garish ivy-covered mansion in Greenwich, Connecticut, known as "Freestone Castle."[16] He would commute from Greenwich to his New York office aboard the *Sialia*, enjoying breakfast en route and tea in the company of business friends on the way back.[17] It was the Roaring Twenties, and it seemed like the good times would never end.

Until they did. Because so much of Andrews's wealth was tied up in the stock market, the Crash hit him particularly hard. As one example, the value of his considerable interest in a car manufacturer that made the popular "Huppmobile" fell by 95 percent as the company's sales and stock price sank like a stone. Installing himself as Hupp's chairman, Andrews tried to extract whatever money from the company he could, but these aggressive tactics only earned him the wrath of the SEC and the courts. A federal judge in Detroit, declaring that Andrews had an "unbalanced and dishonest mind," invalidated lucrative bonuses and stock options Andrews had awarded himself. In a blistering administrative ruling, the SEC found "it was a flagrant breach of good faith and against good conscience" for Andrews to have sought to rake in $36,000 a year as Hupp's chairman after assuring its shareholders he would not draw a salary. Meanwhile, within just a few months of Judge Moscowitz's ruling, Andrews was on the losing end of a $540,000 damages award for breach of contract issued by a federal court in Manhattan; a nearly $100,000 verdict against Dictograph in favor of a Cornell physicist cheated out of royalties for a product he invented for the company; and a nearly $50,000 judgment in Illinois for "bad faith and fraud" against creditors in declaring a dividend to himself from a real estate concern he controlled.[18]

Overall the 1930s had been a miserable decade for Andrews. He was not, however, about to let the vortex of the Depression suck him back to obscurity without a fight. At heart Andrews shared much in common with Renkoff, the Polish immigrant and small-time con man.

* * *

Andrews's immediate concern was obtaining a stay of Judge Moscowitz's ruling pending appeal, on conditions that were not too onerous to Dictograph. He was dubious when Renkoff offered to help with the case. "What can you do?" Andrews sneered. "I have got the man," Renkoff assured him, "that if this case reaches the Circuit Court of Appeals, you will get anything you want of that Court." Specifically, Renkoff explained, "I got the man who can reach Judge Manton like this"—Renkoff snapped his fingers. Andrews, explaining his success in business, once told a reporter: "Everything is luck . . . [and] [e]veryone has luck, but not everyone knows how to take advantage of it."[19] Andrews now applied that principle to Renkoff's offer. "It would be fine if you could do that, I would appreciate it very much," Andrews said.[20]

The "man" Renkoff had in mind was Bill Fallon, to whom he had been recently introduced by Abe and Frank Silinsky, the former securities scam artists. The Silinsky brothers now described themselves as "betting commissioners"—a euphemism, in those days, for a bookmaker—taking wagers on baseball, fights, and even elections. Frank Silinsky saw Fallon and Manton regularly, including in Manton's chambers. Renkoff now asked Silinsky to take him to Fallon's office in the Prudence Building on Madison Avenue, a block away from Andrews's office.[21]

Renkoff explained Andrews's predicament to Fallon. Fallon told him he would have to take it up with Judge Manton. When Renkoff returned the next day, Fallon said he had seen Manton and that, if Andrews paid $50,000 and hired Milton C. Weisman as his lawyer, Andrews "will get whatever he wants when the case reaches the Circuit Court." Renkoff walked west on 43rd Street to Andrews's office. Andrews said "the price was too high" just for reducing Dictograph's burden in appealing; the "real money" would come later when the merits of the case came before the Circuit. Andrews was willing to meet only half of Manton's asking price, or $25,000.[22]

Renkoff shuttled back several more times between Fallon's and Andrews's offices. At this point he did not want to let Andrews deal directly with Fallon or even know Fallon's name (which could render Renkoff superfluous). Nor did he want to negotiate by telephone, having been the subject of a government wiretap that had just led to his criminal conviction. Eventually he got Fallon to agree to accept $25,000, provided that Andrews fork over $10,000 immediately—by that afternoon, in fact, when Fallon was to meet with Manton.[23]

Andrews, now sick in bed in his suite at the Ritz-Carlton Hotel, relented. For three days his lawyers and Schick's lawyers had been arguing in court over what Dictograph would have to do to procure a stay of Judge Moscowitz's ruling. Schick asked Judge Moscowitz to require a bond of $1 million. Even worse, Judge Moscowitz on his own had suggested the appointment of a special master to look into Dictograph's affairs.[24] The prospect of an outside court-appointed lawyer examining Dictograph's books and records churned Andrews's stomach worse than a rough sea ride on his yacht.

In the meantime Stanley Osserman, Andrews's chief lawyer in the patent case and a Tammany man who ran unsuccessfully for Congress the following year, arrived at the Ritz. Andrews instructed Osserman to draw up a phony agreement for Renkoff to sign, in which Renkoff would acknowledge receiving $10,000 from Andrews the month before "to buy Dictograph stock." With Fallon's deadline approaching, Andrews confessed that he did not actually have $10,000 in cash to give to Renkoff—he had scraped together only $8,000. Renkoff offered to lend Andrews the remaining $2,000. Renkoff had about $5,000 in his pocket, but rather than reveal how flush he was to Andrews, he pretended he needed to go get the money. Renkoff went downstairs, walked around to kill some time, then returned and gave Andrews two $1,000 bills.[25]

Accompanied by Silinsky, Renkoff returned once more to Fallon's office and threw the $10,000, in various denominations, on the table. "Count," Fallon directed. Helping Renkoff confirm that the pile of $1,000, $20, and $10 bills totaled the promised bribe amount, Silinsky mused about what he could have done with so much cash. "If we had had that a couple of days ago, we would have bet it on Roosevelt. We would have made some money," the "betting commissioner" remarked to Renkoff. "Hurry up, hurry up," Fallon implored, explaining that the judge "is waiting for the money."[26]

Fallon met up with Manton at a Schrafft's at Madison Avenue and 58th Street, steps away from the judge's apartment building.[27] Schrafft's might seem like an odd rendezvous site for two middle-aged men consummating a corrupt transaction. The once-omnipresent New York restaurant chain, which closed in the 1980s, "catered to ladies who wanted to dine alone or with other women in a pleasing setting," its "dainty" lunchtime offerings "useless to any male with an appetite."[28] But this particular Schrafft's location maintained a separate, segregated "Men's Grill," which likely is where Fallon handed over Andrews's $10,000 to Manton.[29]

"Everything is O.K.," Fallon assured Renkoff. "You can go ahead and tell Archie Andrews that he is going to get the decision in his favor. There will be a bond of $25,000 and no man in the business."[30] When Renkoff conveyed that message, the ever-skeptical Andrews asked Renkoff how sure he was that Manton would deliver. "I will tell you how sure I am," Renkoff replied, offering Andrews a wager: "I will bet you two suits of clothes made by the best tailor in New York, and I am going to order them right now, and if I lose, I will pay it." But, Renkoff added, "I am sure I will win."[31]

Unaware that its fate on appeal had already been sealed, Judge Moscowitz issued his decision the following Monday: The injunction would be stayed pending a report from a special master appointed to investigate the Dictograph business and upon Dictograph posting a $50,000 bond. Although Dictograph's lawyers had purported to agree to those terms, they then applied for, and obtained, an *ex parte* order from Judge Manton on November 12, nullifying Judge Moscowitz's decision. Lunching with Manton downtown, Fallon called Renkoff to let him know the decision had come down. Renkoff went over to Andrews's office to deliver the good news in person. The two men celebrated over a bottle of egg cognac.[32]

Mystified and believing that Manton must have misunderstood the facts, Schick's lawyer Abraham Tulin, together with Dictograph's counsel, called upon Manton in his chambers the following afternoon. Manton said he had, in fact, read Judge Moscowitz's order and did not like the appointment of a special master. Wielding the minutes of the proceeding before Judge Moscowitz, Tulin showed Manton where Dictograph's lawyer had consented to this condition. Taken aback, Manton ordered the lawyers to come back the next morning. A good night's rest did not change Manton's mind. "I have decided to let my order stand," Manton said when the lawyers reassembled in his chambers. "I have read the opinion of Judge Moscowitz and I don't think much of it." Tulin protested but Manton cut him off, saying he "had to hurry" to "get to a football game." There would be no special master. And Andrews bought Renkoff a new suit and overcoat, cut by one of the finest tailors in New York.[33]

* * *

Immediately after Manton overturned Moscowitz's decision, Fallon began pressing Renkoff for the additional $15,000 that Andrews had agreed to pay. Tired of playing go-between, Renkoff lifted the veil of secrecy and introduced Fallon directly to Andrews; it turned out the two men already knew one another. By Thanksgiving Andrews had coughed up the balance, but only after persistent haranguing and threats from

Fallon that Manton was getting "very angry." The following week, Manton denied an application by Schick's lawyers to modify the bond order.[34]

The $25,000 that Andrews had paid to this point only bought him favorable conditions for Dictograph's appeal. Winning the appeal would cost more money. With Renkoff headed off to prison, Fallon stood to become Andrews's direct intermediary. But the competition among Manton's multiple fixers could be intense. Charlie Rich, who had arranged Renkoff's failed payoff for his criminal case, exploded when he learned that Fallon was now working with Renkoff and Andrews. Spotting Fallon on the street outside of Andrews's office at Madison Avenue and 44th Street, Rich "got wild" and punched Fallon in the head, shouting that he was a "son-of-a-bitch." Fallon scurried away into the subway as Renkoff, worried about Fallon's bad heart, restrained Rich from continuing the assault.[35]

While Andrews did not use Rich, he did drop Fallon in favor of a different Manton intermediary, the insurance broker George Spector, introduced to him by Osserman. Through Spector, Andrews orchestrated roughly $77,000 in "loans" to Depression-stricken Manton business enterprises. Most of the money went to National Cellulose, Manton's cash-starved paper manufacturing company, which had defaulted on a $100,000 loan from the Reconstruction Finance Corporation. In December 1935, Manton summoned Wallis E. Gallagher, National Cellulose's treasurer, to his chambers and told him that Spector could be the solution to the company's liquidity problems. After Spector examined the company's less-than-attractive financial statements, Manton telephoned Gallagher to say that Spector had decided to go forward.[36]

From December 21, 1936 to January 29, 1937, Spector made a series of uncollateralized loans to National Cellulose totaling $47,000. Although the loans seemed like a huge gamble, Spector had little of his own money at risk; Andrews supplied him with much of the loan proceeds. Shortly before Spector's notes began to mature in late 1937, Manton explained to Spector that National Cellulose's financial condition remained very poor, rendering it impossible to repay Spector. Spector graciously agreed to defer National Cellulose's debt obligation until the RFC had been repaid. As of Manton's trial, two and one-half years after the loans were made, National Cellulose had not repaid any of Spector's principal.[37]

Spector also made uncollateralized loans in 1937 totaling some $30,000 to help prop up Forest Hills Terrace, Manton's failing real estate company. Some of this money went directly into Forest Hills' bank account and was used to pay off a judgment-debtor.[38] Another $22,000 traveled a more circuitous route that employed money laundering techniques more common to future generations of criminals: layering, structuring, nominees, cash, and falsification of corporate records.

First, Andrews had his wife, Eleanor, issue a series of $5,000 checks on their bank account made payable to International Ticket Scale Corporation, which was controlled by Andrews. International Ticket Scale, in turn, cashed the checks and delivered the proceeds to Spector. Both legs of this transaction were characterized as "loans" in the company's books. In other words, the company simultaneously recorded receiving a $5,000 loan from Eleanor Andrews and making a $5,000 loan to Spector. When International Ticket Scale's president, Walton Fitzgerald, asked Andrews what the purpose of these back-to-back loans was, Andrews replied, "Never mind why. I want it that way." When Fitzgerald complained that it would "clutter up our books," Andrews barked, "God damn it, I want it this way. Don't ask any questions."[39]

From there, Spector deposited the $5,000 cash installments into his bank account, sometimes in smaller increments adding up to $5,000—e.g., a deposit for $1,000 followed the next day by a $2,000 deposit followed by another $2,000 deposit a few days later. Spector then wrote checks to Forest Hills' treasurer—Manton's longtime secretary, Marie Schmalz—who deposited them into her personal bank account. Spector's checks to Schmalz were broken into two pieces totaling $5,000—e.g., $2,750 and $2,250, $2,437.60 and $2,562.40, and $2,384.34 and $2,615.66. Some of this money was used by Forest Hills but at least $4,700 of it went into Manton's personal bank account. Spector never repaid the "loans" that International Ticket Scale had made to him, and International Ticket Scale never repaid the "loans" it received from Eleanor Andrews. Nor did Forest Hills repay any significant amount of the "loans" it had received from Spector—until Spector's relationship with Manton became the subject of scrutiny of District Attorney Dewey in the summer of 1938.[40]

While Spector may not have profited from his loans to Manton's companies—years later he sued National Cellulose, unsuccessfully—he was compensated in other ways. In June 1937, a few weeks after Dictograph won its appeal in the Second Circuit, the stocky, dark-complexioned Spector walked into a neighboring office in his building "all smiles," saying he was off to Europe to sell some foreign rights of the Lektro-Shaver. He showed off a letter of introduction that he planned to use to raise capital in London. It was signed by a prominent American: Second Circuit judge Martin T. Manton. Schick, Spector explained, had brought an infringement action against the Lektro Shaver and Spector "was responsible [for having] the decision reversed" in the Second Circuit. "I put the God damn deal over all by myself," bragged the broker, perhaps puffing on one of the long, fat cigars he favored.[41]

* * *

The Dictograph case illustrates how important Manton's administrative powers as senior circuit judge were in facilitating his corruption. When Manton denied Schick's application to modify his November 12 ruling, he also set the appeal down for oral argument on January 4, 1937, when he would be presiding. Schick's lawyers, recognizing that Manton was not on their side, did their best to get away from him. They saw in the Second Circuit list of assignments that Manton was not scheduled to sit the following week. They then entered into a stipulation with Dictograph's lawyers agreeing to move the oral argument to January 11, and no doubt were quite pleased with their craftiness when Manton so-ordered the stipulation. But Manton could not be avoided so easily. As senior circuit judge, he controlled the determination of which judges sat at what times. Manton simply instructed the Second Circuit clerk to swap out Judge Learned Hand for himself for the week of January 11.[42]

Schick got another opportunity to shake loose from Manton when a new lawyer, John F. Neary, appeared for Dictograph and asked for a further adjournment. At a conference in Manton's chambers, Schick's lawyers asked for the appeal to be heard the week of February 11—a week they knew Manton would not be sitting. Manton said he would grant an adjournment to February 4—a date when he would be sitting. Oscar W. Jeffery, one of Schick's lawyers, said that date would be inconvenient for him. "Jack, will February 11th be agreeable to you?" he asked Neary. Neary, who must have been out of the loop on the bribery scheme, responded with typical professional courtesy, "Why, that would be perfectly all right, quite all right." But what was all right with the parties' lawyers was not all right with the judge. Glaring at Schick's lawyers, Manton smiled wryly and decreed: "This case will be argued on February 4th."[43]

After the argument, a Dictograph executive invited Tulin to lunch at the Engineers' Club in Midtown Manhattan and proposed a merger between Dictograph and Schick and an end to the litigation. If Schick wanted to keep fighting, the executive confidently predicted, Schick would lose in the Court of Appeals, by a 2–1 vote. Tulin rejected any sort of alliance with Archie Andrews.[44] On April 12, 1937, the Second Circuit issued its ruling. The Court reversed Judge Moscowitz's ruling, by a 2–1 vote.[45]

The majority opinion was written by Harrie Chase and joined by Manton. Chase's opinion upheld the validity of Schick's patent, despite Dictograph's contention that Schick's razor was completely anticipated by a patent issued in Britain in 1914 to one Appleyard. But as the differences between the Schick and Appleyard inventions were "rather slight," Chase wrote, "so must infringement be proved, if proved at all, within such narrow limits." Viewed in this light, the court determined that the Lektro-Packard device, "instead of being based on Schick, is nothing but an ingenious adaptation of Appleyard." Chase (and Manton) thus found "no infringement" of Schick's patent. Gus Hand, in dissent, could not agree. What the majority saw as "a skillful adaptation of Appleyard's ideas," Hand considered "essentially an appropriation of Schick's invention."[46]

Never one to miss an opportunity to gloat, Andrews took out full-page ads in about twenty newspapers announcing the Second Circuit's decision.[47] That was sweet revenge, for Schick had taken out similar ads announcing Judge Moscowitz's ruling.[48] Sales of the Lektro-Packard soon eclipsed the million mark, more than compensating for the approximately $102,000 Andrews shelled out to buy Manton's backing.[49]

* * *

Andrews, though, just as easily could have wound up as the victim of a bribery scheme. Worried about Andrews's slipperiness, the Manton racket hedged its bets and also tried to cut a deal with Schick. In late November 1936, around when Fallon was accusing Andrews of welshing on the $25,000 deal, Abe Tulin was contacted by Joseph L. Greenberg, a solo practitioner with whom he had a passing acquaintance. Meeting at night in Tulin's home, Greenberg told Tulin and his co-counsel, Samuel J. Rosensohn, that he "had been asked to pass along [a] message": if Tulin put $5,000 in escrow with a bank by noon the following day, Judge Manton would vacate his November 12 order. For an unspecified "additional payment," Schick could ensure either that Manton voted in its favor on the appeal or that Manton did not sit on the case.[50]

Tulin and Rosensohn, both graduates of Harvard Law School, World War I veterans, and prominent Zionist leaders, dismissed Greenberg's proposal out of hand. Greenberg then explored another angle. He had done some legal work for a businessman who knew an accountant named Moses Cohen who, in turn, was friends with Colonel Schick. Through the businessman, Greenberg got word to Cohen that if Schick "wants to win the patent case he can do so for a matter of $50,000." Deeming the offer "ridiculous," Cohen declined even to pass it on to Schick.[51]

Orchestrating Greenberg's overtures was Fallon, acting through a mutual acquaintance, Louis E. Felix, the longtime head of a Tammany Democratic Club. Fallon wanted to stick it to Andrews for cutting Fallon out in favor of Spector. A month after the Second Circuit's decision in April 1937, Fallon and Felix sent Greenberg back to Tulin and Rosensohn for yet another attempt to turn the tables on Andrews. Munching over sandwiches in Tulin's office, Greenberg explained to the Schick lawyers that they had indeed been the victims of a fix. Manton had reduced Dictograph's bond because of "the intervention of a certain man" whose name "you do not have to or want to know." But, Greenberg continued, this same man—Fallon—was now "madder than hell at Archie Andrews" for "run[ning] out on him" and "wants to get back at that son-of-a-bitch." If Schick made a motion for reargument and paid $25,000, the man could "get the court" to reverse its ruling.[52]

Anticipating resistance, Greenberg came prepared with a new sales pitch. The Second Circuit's decision was "lousy," Greenberg said; both the "moral position" and "legal position" were on Schick's side. Tulin and Rosensohn should not let old-fashioned values stand in the way of "correct[ing] this injustice." The Schick lawyers, explained Greenberg, who was about ten years their junior, needed to get in step with the times. "You fellows," Greenberg wisecracked, "were admitted to the Bar around 1670 or 1770, and you are living in a world that you don't know anything about. You don't know how things are done." Practicing law "ethically and honestly" was all well and good, but sometimes, Greenberg argued, you "have to fight fire with fire."[53]

Once again, Greenberg did not succeed. Tulin refused to go along with the scheme. Andrews's victory remained secure—for the time being. For Greenberg was right that Chase and Manton's opinion in the Dictograph case was "lousy." When a federal district judge in California evaluated a similar patent infringement suit by Schick against a different competitor later that year, he agreed with Gus Hand's dissent. While he had "great respect for the decision of a court of superior authority," the judge felt that Chase and Manton had attributed "too prominent a place" to the Appleyard patent. Several other courts across the country later agreed. After Manton's conviction, the Second Circuit vacated its prior ruling due to Manton's disqualification. Dictograph then capitulated, agreeing to pay Schick large damages for its admitted infringement.[54]

Jacob Schick and Archie Andrews would never learn how their court battle ultimately ended. Within three months of the Second Circuit's decision Schick died in Canada, at age fifty-nine, from complications following kidney surgery. By June 1938 Andrews too was dead at age fifty-nine. Not long thereafter, criminal investigators would be reconstructing how, in their final wrestling match, Andrews wound up on top.

CHAPTER SEVENTEEN

"Ugly Rumors"

Why Wasn't Manton Stopped Sooner?

THE SIZE, SCOPE, AND SHEER BRAZENNESS OF MANTON'S CORRUPTION seemed to ensure it would come to light eventually. Yet for a very long time it remained hidden, enabling Manton to continue to accept and extort money from litigants again and again, in case after case. This was not because the perpetrators were especially secretive or discreet. If anything, the opposite was true. Intermediaries like Fallon and Spector blabbed freely about the magical powers they wielded in the Second Circuit. Most successful business operations, rackets included, need to spread the word, in the right circles, about the services they offer to attract future patrons.

"Ugly rumors had been in circulation in New York City for many years," the *New Republic* noted after Manton's fall.[1] With scores if not hundreds of people aware that Manton was on the take, this was unsurprising. What is astonishing is that the circle of knowledge, or at least suspicion, extended to many in a position to do something about it— prominent lawyers, congressmen, other judges, even the US Department of Justice. How is it that Manton was not stopped sooner?

* * *

Aside from the many lawyers who directly participated in Manton's schemes—including ostensibly respectable lawyers like Thomas Chadbourne and Louis Levy and John Lotsch and Milton Weisman—plenty of other members of the legal community learned of Manton's penchant for corruption, yet kept their lips sealed.

Take, for example, Samuel H. Kaufman, a well-known Wall Street lawyer who had served as a special assistant to the US attorney general and would later be appointed a federal district judge in Manhattan. Kaufman, who acted as attorney for the Prudence Company trustees, was trying a criminal case when Marie Schmalz, Manton's secretary, came into the courtroom and whispered that Manton wanted to see him "about some Prudence matter." At the end of the trial day, Kaufman dutifully went up to Manton's chambers, accompanied by a twenty-seven-year-old junior lawyer in his firm, Milton S. Gould—later, one of New York's premier trial lawyers and cofounder of the legal powerhouse Shea & Gould—who waited in the anteroom while Kaufman and Manton met behind closed doors. In his memoir Gould described what happened next:

> *When Kaufman reappeared in the anteroom, all traces of amiability had vanished. He was grim and tight-lipped; he said nothing, but motioned me to follow him. When we were settled in the back of his limousine, there was none of the usual friendly discussion of the courtroom happenings that came at the end of each day. Sam was tense and preoccupied; as we neared Wall Street, the silence embarrassed me. I made some fatuous remark about the obvious regard with which he had been received by Manton. Kaufman glared at me; the words seemed to explode out of him. "He's a thief!" he said. "He just asked me to 'lend' him fifty thousand dollars. We have two Prudence appeals that are coming before him. Both are important; we should win both of them. Of course, I turned him down. Now, God knows what will happen!"*[2]

On March 1, 1937, the Second Circuit decided both of the Prudence appeals. Judge Manton sat in both cases, and wrote the opinion in one of them. Prudence lost both.[3]

Furious as he was, Kaufman did not report Manton as "a thief" to law enforcement. After the Manton scandal became public in January 1939, Kaufman did come forward and share other information with federal prosecutors about how Manton and Fallon milked the Prudence receivership, and how Manton was paid off in the Art Metal case. Even then, Kaufman said he would only divulge what he knew to the FBI "if he was approached on the theory that his name had been found in court records, and that it did not appear that he, Kaufman, had volunteered the information."[4]

Samuel E. Darby, an "eminent patent attorney," faced a similar situation.[5] Darby, who co-founded the law firm Darby & Darby, one of the nation's premier intellectual property firms until it closed in 2010, acted as patent counsel to Remington Rand, Inc. Remington had several cases in the Second Circuit, including a dispute with Archie Andrews's Lektro-Shave company involving Remington's electric shaver, which reached the Court of Appeals in the fall of 1937.

In October 1937, James H. Rand Jr., Remington's president, told Darby he had just been solicited for a bribe. According to Rand, a "Mr. G" (likely Joseph Greenberg, who solicited Tulin a few months before) arrived in Rand's office, announced he was a representative of Judge Manton, and said Rand could win his cases if he loaned Manton $40,000. To prove his bona fides, "Mr. G" read to Rand the text of the Second Circuit's draft opinion resolving a preliminary skirmish in Rand's case with Andrews—which was in substance identical to the official decision released a week later. "Mr. G" explained that Andrews had made "a deal" with Manton but "fell down" on it and Manton was now "hard up" for money.[6]

Upon hearing of the bribe offer, Darby, a former special prosecutor for the Justice Department, instructed Rand to have no further dealings with "Mr. G." What's more, he advised Rand to "refer the matter immediately to the Department of Justice or the FBI." Rand, however, declined to heed this advice. Some sixteen months later, in February 1939—after Manton had resigned—Darby went to the FBI himself. Darby told the FBI he knew Rand would be unhappy and might even fire Darby as his patent counsel, but he "felt that his duty to uphold the integrity of the legal profession exceeded his duty to his client." However commendable that decision was, there is little doubt that, had the Manton scandal never erupted publicly, Darby would have remained silent.[7]

At least Darby had better instincts than his competitor in the patent bar, Theodore Kenyon, Lotsch's co-counsel in the Auto-Lite appeal in 1935. It is curious how, despite admitting that he prepared the court's opinion in that case at Manton's request, Kenyon emerged unscathed from the scandal. The year after Manton's trial, Kenyon served as New Jersey chairman for Wendell Willkie's Republican presidential campaign. In 1941 he was named president of the New York Patent Law Association. His law practice continued to thrive and Kenyon & Kenyon remained one of the nation's foremost patent law firms for more than eighty years.[8]

At Manton's trial Kenyon claimed "the first intimation I ever heard of any suggestion of impropriety in connection with" the Auto-Lite case was after he had been visited by government investigators in 1939.[9] There is good reason to be skeptical of that self-serving claim, even assuming Kenyon was ignorant about the loans Lotsch arranged for Manton. For one thing, Lotsch testified that when he gave Kenyon the unofficial news that they had won the appeal, he identified his source as Fallon.[10] If that is true, it suggests that Kenyon knew something of Fallon's role in the affair, which should have led a seasoned litigator like Kenyon to wonder who Fallon was and why he would be privy to the internal deliberations of the Second Circuit. Clearly Kenyon was aware of that potential line of criticism, because he contradicted Lotsch on this point, claiming that Lotsch had said "Judge Manton sent him" and that "I never heard the name of Fallon until I read it in the newspaper reports."[11] But even crediting Kenyon's version, the fact that Lotsch was having such an *ex parte* conversation with a judge sitting on the case should have struck Kenyon as highly unusual.

More unusual still was Manton's request to have one of the parties draft the court's opinion. At trial Kenyon claimed that this was not the only time he had received such a request and that he had prepared an opinion for a court once before.[12] But almost certainly that court was not a federal court of appeals. Manton himself, in his trial testimony, flatly denied that he had asked for or received a draft opinion in the Auto-Lite case and made clear that even he understood that such a request would cross a line ("No one has ever had the effrontery to try that").[13]

Should Kenyon have done something more than he did when Lotsch came to him with inside information about the Court's deliberations and Manton's request for a draft opinion? Should he have interrogated Lotsch on his relationship with Manton? Refused to participate in drafting an opinion? Resigned from the case? Gone to law enforcement? These would not have been easy questions to answer, particularly in light of Kenyon's duty of loyalty to his client, P & D, to take no action to harm its interests. But it does not appear that Kenyon ever asked these questions or attempted to grapple with them. "I felt there was no alternative" he lamely explained at trial, "but to defer to the wishes of the presiding judge."[14]

A.B. Hall's patent lawyer, Arthur E. Paige, also chose to stick his head in the sand. While Paige played no part in Hall's bribe payments, Hall did tell him about inside information he was learning about the Court's proceedings from "a man who should know." Hall once slipped and identified his source as Fallon. When Paige made a note of that fact, Hall rebuked him and instructed him to "[not] make any use of that information." The sixty-seven-year-old lawyer readily complied, assuring Hall that "if he is doing anything which he should not do," Paige "does not wish to know about it."[15]

The list goes on. The wily Max Steuer, Albert Lasker's lawyer, undoubtedly understood what the $250,000 loan to "Sullivan" was all about. Abe Tulin and Sam Rosensohn, Schick's lawyers, were told in so many words that Andrews had bribed Manton and were solicited to pay their own bribe to Manton. Art Metal's lawyers, Kenneth S. Neal of Ward, Crosby & Neal and Joseph Lorenz of Lorenz & Lorenz (whose partner and brother was a former assistant US attorney), knew all about the information Art Metal received indicating it was the victim of a fix.[16] Likewise, the lawyers for Cinema Patents in its patent infringement case against Warner Brothers, one of whom was the Democratic mayor of Mamaroneck, New York, had heard that Manton could be "reached."[17] Yet none of these estimable attorneys reported these potential crimes to law enforcement until after Manton's resignation.

Toppling a jurist of Manton's stature does not happen easily. Without hard proof, some lawyers may have thought it futile to make an explosive allegation against the senior federal judge in the city, a man knighted by the Pope and with deep ties to political, business, and religious leaders. Other lawyers had more Machiavellian motives. After Manton's downfall, one young lawyer expressed surprise to a reporter that it had taken the press so long to find the story. "Most of us lawyers knew about his crookedness," the lawyer admitted. When asked why he did not do something about it, the lawyer laughed. "Oh, we wouldn't do that. We preferred to use our knowledge."[18]

* * *

It was not just lawyers who took this approach. Andrew L. Somers was a Democratic House member from Brooklyn, known as "the Boy Congressman" after his election at age twenty-nine. Like Manton, he was a protégé of Brooklyn boss John McCooey. Together with then-congressman Fiorello La Guardia of Manhattan, Somers led the effort in 1929 to impeach Federal District Judge Grover Moscowitz. Around 1932, Somers heard that Manton "sometimes had business dealings with persons involved in matters before him, or their attorneys." He compared notes with La Guardia, who had been conducting his own mini-investigation of Manton. The two concluded that their information was "too nebulous" to warrant impeachment proceedings.[19]

A few years later in 1935, over lunch with Jacob Handelsman, the money broker, Somers heard something more concrete. Without sharing the details, Handelsman told Somers "enough to make him believe that Manton was mixed up in some sort of a 'slippery deal' and possibly should be impeached." Somers, however, was having lunch with Handelsman not to do the people's business but his own. Somers wanted a loan from Handelsman for a business venture, and Handelsman wanted Somers to do him a favor in return—to ask Manton to repay Handelsman the money that Manton owed him. Somers intended to use Handelsman's information about Manton's "slippery deal" as a lever to persuade Manton that he "should take steps to pay Handelsman and keep him quiet" or otherwise run the risk that Somers would "feel obliged" to refer the information to the House Judiciary Committee for possible impeachment. In other words, when put on notice of Manton's wrongdoing, Congressman

Somers's reaction was not to start an impeachment inquiry but to wield the threat of impeachment to serve his own ends.[20]

* * *

It is the judiciary that has taken the most heat for failing to stop Manton, and in particular his Second Circuit colleagues at the time, Learned Hand, Gus Hand, Thomas Swan, and Harrie Chase.

Joseph Borkin, who wrote about Manton in his 1962 book, *The Corrupt Judge*, testified before a Senate committee that "it is incomprehensible to me that the judges of the Second Circuit during Manton's time of corruption could not have known about it, that at least he was engaged in questionable conduct or the appearance of impropriety." Asked to explain, Borkin elaborated that Manton's "conduct was so open and notorious, the curious people who kept running in and out of his office, the discussions in the circuit, in the area around the courthouse, were such that you would have to be blind not to know that a malignant influence was at work."[21] In a later private interview, Borkin claimed that while talking to people in the Foley Square Courthouse while researching his book, he found that "everybody around there *knew!*" about Manton's corruption. Manton's Second Circuit colleagues nevertheless kept silent, Borkin surmised, because "this was the old closing of ranks, community of interest, whatever you want to call it. . . . [A] crooked judge dishonors all of them, so the best thing to do is sweep it under the carpet, then it doesn't exist."[22]

Reporter Burt Heath recounted in his memoir that as early as 1934, two unidentified "high judges" traveling on a train from Albany to New York took to discussing Manton. One of them—"a man of the highest probity and, often, of much candor and courage"—said to the other: "Manton is a thorough-going crook." But when his companion asked why he did not do something about it, the judge replied: "How can I? I have to work with him every day." Learned Hand once remarked to one of his law clerks (albeit in jest, and many years after Manton's conviction): "Do you know what Judge Augustus Hand's gravestone will bear as his epitaph? 'He always knew Martin Manton was a crook, and he never granted a rehearing.'"[23]

On this score, Learned Hand (who may well have been the morally conflicted "high judge" in Heath's train story) is a special enigma. As much as he disliked Manton, whom he reportedly described as "a first class son-of-a-bitch," Hand took a pragmatic approach to relations with his court's most senior member. Hand and his wife socialized on occasion with the Mantons; when the Mantons journeyed aboard the SS *Manhattan* in 1936, the Hands sent them "lovely flowers" as a *bon voyage*. This personal association made Hand's jumbled emotions of betrayal and guilt all the more acute when Manton's misconduct came to light. Even in his dotage many years later, Hand continued to express to Second Circuit colleagues his concern over how the Manton affair reflected on Hand's own judgment. "I socialized with him, I went to his house, he went to mine, he betrayed me, it's humiliating," Hand would vent to Judge Henry J. Friendly. "What will people say about me that I socialized with him and went to his house? What will people think of me?" Finally Friendly got so tired of hearing Hand's constant complaints about Manton that he told Hand, tongue-in-cheek, "Yes, I heard someone talking about that the other day." Hand never raised the subject again.[24]

Hand even loyally, if unsuccessfully, lobbied for Manton to receive an honorary degree from Harvard. As a member of Harvard's Board of Overseers, Hand made a forceful pitch on Manton's behalf to a hostile audience skeptical of Manton's moral worth and, perhaps more importantly, opposed to Manton's progressivism. In a letter to a fellow overseer on April 11, 1934, Hand minimized the charges made about Manton's ethical shortcomings as an attorney when he was appointed to the bench in 1916, arguing that they should not overcome Manton's "outstanding service and achievement" since becoming a judge.[25]

Ironically, Hand offered this praise during the very same month he was battling with Manton over the Art Metal case. At that time, Hand not only was convinced that Manton had reached the wrong result, he also sensed that Manton had reached it for an improper reason. Five years later, when the Second Circuit reheard the case after Manton's conviction, Hand's internal bench memo, circulated to the other judges on the panel, contained the following extraordinary sentence: "I thought [in 1934] that our lamented chief was doing dirty business of some kind here, and now I know it."[26]

Exactly what kind of "dirty business" he had in mind, Hand did not say. His biographer, Gerald Gunther, insisted that "there is no indication that he suspected Manton had been bribed," and speculated that at worst Hand thought Manton had articulated such "strange patent-misuse principles" in the case because of Manton's "friendships with old political allies." That interpretation of "dirty business" seems overly charitable. Art Metal was a commercial litigation with no political overtones or connection to Manton's old political allies.[27]

Hand's admission in his bench memo is also hard to square with his testimony at Manton's trial, given just four months earlier. There, Hand swore that in the cases at issue, which included Art Metal, he did *not* observe Manton to have acted other than "according to his oath and according to the dictates of his conscience." How could that answer have been truthful if Hand thought Manton was "doing dirty business" in the Art Metal case? It may be significant that, before answering, Hand had asked Manton's lawyer for a clarification: "You mean in the conference?" It was only after being assured that the question was limited to Manton's conduct during the court's private conferences that Hand testified he did not observe anything untoward and, for that matter, did not "remember anything about the conference."[28] Perhaps whatever Manton said or did in the Art Metal case that triggered Hand's suspicions, and that Hand *did* still remember in 1939, took place outside the conference.

For his Hand biography, Gunther interviewed numerous former Second Circuit law clerks alongside fellow Stanford law professor Herbert Packer, who was researching his own, never-published book on the history of the Second Circuit. Those interviews provide substantial support for Gunther's defense of Hand. Most of the clerks said they saw nothing to indicate that Manton was taking bribes and did not believe Hand or the other judges, for all their intense criticism of Manton, were aware of or even suspected his corruption.[29]

But not all the clerks were of that view. Lloyd Cutler, the legendary Washington power broker and counselor to presidents, recalled that during his clerkship, which began months after Manton's conviction, "there was a good deal of talk about the judges having suspected for a couple of years that something fishy was going on." Bennett Boskey, Learned Hand's law clerk during the same time, recalled that, when they were working on the Art Metal rehearing, Hand remarked, "I always sort of wondered about Manton in that case." From comments like these Boskey believed "there might have been isolated occasions in the past when some thought had gone through [the judges'] minds about Manton," even if they lacked "concrete" evidence of corruption.[30]

Years later, perhaps prompted by news of Manton's death in November 1946, Gus Hand shared a revealing story with his law clerk, Lawrence Ebb. In one case, Hand told Ebb, Manton had written an opinion and the Hands "couldn't follow his reasoning." They "talked about it for awhile. We were puzzled. . . . Something about it smelled wrong." Either Gus or Learned turned to the other and said, "Say, we got to watch that fellow." The Hands, Ebb concluded, were "deeply troubled" about Manton, so much so that Ebb assumed they would have brought their concerns to the attention of the chief justice or the attorney general. He was surprised to learn from his interviewer, Packer, that "nothing of the sort happened."[31]

On the day that Manton was indicted, Learned Hand told a former law clerk who happened to drop by (and who had been suspicious of Manton since his clerkship in the late 1920s) that "he felt more guilty sitting with Judge Manton than Manton felt doing what he did." For years afterwards Hand engaged in "intense brooding" and "soul-searching" over whether he was somehow partly responsible for Manton's corruption. Gunther absolves Hand of any responsibility, but the evidence suggests that Hand's self-doubts were not without foundation.[32]

Still, there is a world of difference between suspicion and knowledge. As Borkin himself acknowledged, "no hard evidence" exists showing that Hand or Manton's other Second Circuit colleagues knew he was on the take.[33] And the charge that they "must have known" is a classic example of reasoning by hindsight. Remember that Manton's tainted rulings usually were *unanimous*, and in the rare instances where they were not, at least one unbiased judge concurred. This naturally would have allayed any suspicions his fellow panel members may have harbored. Manton was astute enough to know when to yield to his colleagues and avoid raising red flags, even if it meant giving disappointed customers like Morris Renkoff a refund. Ironically, the same fact that heightens a corrupt appellate judge's risk of exposure—the imperative for other judges to take his side—serves, when this occurs naturally, to cloak his conduct with the appearance of regularity and insulate him from detection.

In the end, the accusation that Manton's Second Circuit's colleagues knowingly countenanced his corruption seems unfair. It would be more fair to say that the possibility of Manton's corruption likely entered some or all of their minds at one or more times, only to swiftly recede given the press of business, the absence of hard proof, the implausibility of the idea, and, not least, how distasteful it would have been for them to try to do anything about it. This itself represented a failure of fortitude and of judgment sufficient to justify the bouts of guilt that Learned Hand, if not the others, experienced for years afterward about the whole affair.

* * *

Much harder to rationalize is the reaction—or rather the non-reaction—to reports of Manton's possible corruption received by the branch of the federal government actually responsible for enforcing the law: the US Department of Justice.

In May 1937, the Ungerleider Financial Corporation's substantial loans to Manton, and the $236,000 loss it took when Manton could not pay it all back, attracted press attention when they came to light at an SEC hearing. "One wonders why a judge should be in such transactions," wrote a suspicious *New Republic* reporter. "It is not healthy to have the man who sits in such important cases getting his mind mixed up with the affairs and practices and stratagems and ethical standards of the Street."[34] When the Manton scandal became public nearly two years later, syndicated columnist Ray Tucker sharply criticized FDR's Attorney General at the time of these press reports, Homer S. Cummings, for having "made no move" to investigate Manton's unusual business dealings, and intimated that Cummings' successor, Frank Murphy, found this passivity "bizarre."[35]

When the FBI eventually did look into Manton's dealings with Ungerleider in 1939, it discovered that they were even stranger than the SEC hearing revealed. Samuel Ungerleider also loaned Forest Hills Terrace Corp. a total of $240,000 in 1934, without any collateral other than Manton's note; he made other unsecured personal loans to Manton (sometimes through Ungerleider's brother Abe); and he let Manton run up a negative $5,000 margin balance in a stock trading account. Manton repaid almost none of this debt. In all, Ungerleider lost some $500,000 lending money to Manton and his companies—more than $10 million in today's dollars.[36]

The reason for Ungerleider's extreme generosity toward Manton has never been explained. It was not, however, entirely out of character for the Budapest-born financier, a Forrest Gump–like presence in major corruption scandals of the era, Republican and Democratic alike. Ungerleider earned a mention in the Teapot Dome investigation for maintaining secret margin accounts for President Harding; Harding died without having funded the accounts, saddling Ungerleider with a $170,000 loss. A few years later, Ungerleider's name cropped up in Samuel Seabury's investigation of Jimmy Walker. Ungerleider had cashed in stock for the mayor's benefit for $22,000 more than its market value, at the same time he was interested in a taxicab business seeking Walker's help in curbing the number of taxicabs on city streets.[37]

In fairness, though, there was nothing criminal, on the surface, about Ungerleider's loans to Manton. Ungerleider appears to have had no litigation in the Second Circuit and he later told the FBI that he never asked Manton for any favors. The FBI developed a "theory" that Manton fed Ungerleider tips in advance of Second Circuit rulings, which the stockbroker turned into trading profits. This seems as good a theory as any, but nothing was ever proven.[38]

But the Cummings Justice Department's knowledge of Manton's peculiar activities was not limited to the Ungerleider loans. Beginning in 1937, the Justice Department received information that unmistakably *did* suggest that Manton was engaged in criminal conduct, yet apparently did not act on that information. This is the import of a never-before-seen January 10, 1939 memorandum from FBI director J. Edgar Hoover apprising then-newly appointed US attorney general Frank Murphy of what the FBI knew about Manton.

In the spring of 1937, Hoover's memorandum notes, FBI agents investigating John Lotsch for bank bribery stumbled across the loans by Fort Greene Bank to Manton. The agents thought it odd that the bank had written off the loans even though they were not in default. They interviewed a Fort Greene vice president, who explained how Lotsch had pushed through the loans by telling the bank's directors of the "sub rosa" arrangement whereby, in return, Manton would "exert influence and direct the trustees in large bankrupt estates" to make deposits with the bank, and how Fort Greene thereafter did receive hefty deposits from the Prudence Company and Fox Theatres trustees. The agents also discovered the May 1935 letter in which Manton certified to Fort Greene that "my net worth is upward of $750,000," at about the same time he was telling Ungerleider's company, in the context of negotiating a favorable settlement of his debt, that his liabilities exceeded his assets.[39]

In early 1938, the FBI received even more alarming news. This is when "Izzie the Lawyer" Brinkman came forward with his sensational allegation that his former cellmate, Louis Lepke, had admitted bribing Manton through Frank Cohen to arrange for Lepke and Gurrah's release on bail. Brinkman also led the FBI to Leonard Weisman, who, while refusing to provide definite information, identified Cohen as someone he had been told could help him make bail in his own case.[40]

All of this information promptly made its way up to Director Hoover. Hoover, in turn, promptly alerted the Justice Department, sending memoranda about the Fort Greene loans in June 1937 and March 1938 and separate memoranda about the Brinkman and Weisman allegations in January and March 1938. Hoover addressed his memoranda to Joseph B. Keenan, the assistant attorney general for the Criminal Division.[41]

Although Hoover famously kept files on the personal lives of senior government officials, he may not have known that Keenan was "a close friend of Manton," as the press would later report in 1939. Keenan lunched with Manton and Ungerleider, and Keenan and his wife joined the Mantons on the SS *Manhattan* for their voyage to Europe in 1936. During the subsequent Manton investigation, the FBI learned of reports that Keenan "lived on the farm of Manton on Long Island during the summers."[42]

Hoover also likely was unaware that Keenan's boss, Attorney General Cummings, had met with Manton and Cohen not long before to discuss Manton's application for an FHA loan. A onetime Democratic National Committee chairman and FDR's floor manager at the 1932 Democratic Convention, Cummings "was, at heart, a genial, gregarious politician more at home in smoke-filled rooms and on the golf course." Neither Cummings nor Keenan, considered one of the "redoubtable politicos" Cummings named to top spots in the Justice Department, may have been eager to commence a corruption investigation of a Democratic judge and "very good friend" of FDR who had recently appeared on Cummings's list of potential Supreme Court nominees.[43]

For whatever reason, Hoover's multiple missives in 1937 and early 1938 about Manton—even one alleging Manton sold his office to the nation's two most notorious racketeers—stirred no apparent reaction from Cummings's Justice Department. Hoover's January 10, 1939 memorandum to Murphy notably contains no indication that a federal criminal investigation of Manton was underway by the Justice Department at that time. In an article published after Manton was convicted, Hoover made a point of praising Murphy for "act[ing] immediately" and "energetic[ally]" in response to the allegations in Hoover's January 10, 1939 memorandum—as if to damn Murphy's predecessor by implication for not responding in the same manner.[44] All of which amply justifies columnist Drew Pearson's subsequent charge that, even though "many people knew" that Manton had been "getting away with graft for years," "other Attorneys General," prior to Murphy, "had let it pass."[45]

And if it had not been for an enterprising reporter and an ambitious local prosecutor, Manton may have never been held to account at all.

PART THREE

MANTON'S FALL

CHAPTER EIGHTEEN

"All That Is Evil in Government"

The Press and the DA on Manton's Tail

BY THE SUMMER OF 1938, THE FRAGMENTED RUMORS ABOUT MANTON finally congealed into a mass solid enough to power serious investigations by a newspaper and a district attorney's office that had no reason and no desire to go easy on the judge. Perhaps unsurprisingly, these investigations were led by a pair of non-native New Yorkers, products of deeply Protestant and Republican small-town America, where the Tammany Hall political machine was regarded as distant, alien, and repugnant.

Reporter Burt Heath, of the *New York World-Telegram*, proudly called himself a New England Yankee "in every sense of the word." Heath grew up in Vermont, which, he noted in his 1940 memoir, *Yankee Reporter*, had not once voted to send to either house of Congress, the governor's mansion, or the White House anyone who was not a candidate of the Republican Party in one of its incarnations, going back to the Federalists. Heath's father, whose Republicanism was "of the same flavor as the constancy of his moral and ethical convictions," owned a milling business that was wiped out in the Panic of 1893, which he blamed on the "perversity" of Democrat Grover Cleveland's reclaiming the presidency in 1892.[1]

Gassed in France during World War I as a nineteen-year-old infantryman in the so-called Yankee Division, Heath returned to Vermont and acquired a small newspaper. As a publisher, Heath participated in internecine battles within the state's Republican Party but maintained his father's streak of Yankee moralism. Once offered a bounty of advertising in exchange for throwing his support behind a particular gubernatorial candidate, he instead published the letter containing the bribe offer while announcing that he would, for that reason, oppose the candidate. In 1927, Heath arrived in New York as a reporter for the Associated Press. He would come to admire New York, to be grateful for the opportunities it offered for professional advancement and material gain, but chose to "remain one of the great unassimilated," pining to return to "a verdure-clad hillside that overlooks lovely Lake Champlain" and the "gracious peace and homely friendliness" he had been deprived of in the noisy, busy city.[2]

The *World-Telegram*'s editor, George Wood, lured Heath in late 1932 and assigned him to a new bureau "created for the purpose of destroying Tammany Hall and building up a reform movement by turning a pitiless spotlight upon the waste and inefficiency and corruption of the Tammany regime." The paper relentlessly promoted the mayoral campaign of former congressman Fiorello La Guardia in 1933, with Heath coordinating press coverage with campaign officials. Four years earlier, Jimmy Walker had crushed La Guardia as New Yorkers shrugged off the Little Flower's sensational accusations of Tammany Hall wrongdoing. Now, with his seemingly wild charges vindicated by the Seabury investigation, the fiery Fusion-Republican candidate swept to victory over the "cruel, vicious, greedy political machine" he castigated on the stump.[3]

Thomas Dewey, Heath's partner in ferreting out Manton's crimes, also brought with him to New York "an inborn conviction that the Tammany Hall political machine was the epitome of corruption and oppression and that the Republican Party was the only worthy instrument of government." This orientation came from Dewey's paternal grandfather, "a crusader, a political reformer, a pamphleteer, a thorn in the flesh of all he believed to be wrong." Abandoning Yankee New Hampshire—the Dewey family home dating back to their arrival from England in the 1630s—for the relative wilderness of Michigan, George Martin Dewey became a successful newspaper publisher in the town of Owosso and a founding member of the Republican Party. A popular Republican orator, he once assisted New York's GOP "in the campaign against Tammany Hallism in the Empire State." Although Dewey never met his grandfather, he imbibed the family's Republicanism through his father, who took over as publisher of the *Owosso Times*. "Tammany Hall," Dewey's father taught his son, "represents all that is evil in government."[4]

Born in Owosso in 1902, four years after Heath, Dewey grew up in relative comfort and missed out on World War I. Transferring from the University of Michigan, he arrived in New York in 1923 to complete his law studies at Columbia Law School and pursue a potential alternative career as an opera singer. Discovering that his voice was better tuned for persuading juries than entertaining operagoers, Dewey finished law school and headed downtown to work for a Wall Street law firm. The future two-time unsuccessful GOP presidential candidate immediately jumped into local politics as well, vainly attempting, as a Young Republican poll watcher, to rein in gun-toting Tammany goons who materialized at voting places on election day.[5]

Much like Manton, professional success came rapidly to Dewey, who would be elected governor of New York at age forty and remains to this day the youngest presidential candidate (at age forty-two) ever nominated by the Republican Party. When George Medalie was appointed as US attorney in Manhattan in 1931, Dewey, only twenty-eight, became his chief assistant. Kinetic, self-assured, with a razor-sharp mind and equally sharp elbows, Dewey proved a relentless investigator and formidable trial lawyer. Federal authorities in Chicago had just brought down Al Capone for income tax violations, and Dewey mastered the technique. High-profile racketeers like the bootlegger "Waxey" Gordon, the numbers banker Henry Miro, and the "Artichoke King" Joseph Castaldo were all successfully prosecuted by Dewey and imprisoned for failing to report their ill-gotten gains. So too were a corrupt cop on the NYPD's vice squad and a Tammany district leader and deputy city clerk who systematically extorted payments from bridegrooms for performing marriage ceremonies at City Hall.[6]

When Medalie resigned, the thirty-one-year-old prosecutor briefly served as the youngest US attorney ever. At the end of 1933, while Dewey was packing up his office to return to private practice, Heath visited him to talk about Harold Kunstler, a municipal court judge appointed by former mayor Jimmy Walker. Prompted by a postcard from an anonymous tipster, Heath discovered several court judgments against Kunstler revealing that lawyers and litigants in cases before him were involved in his financial affairs. Heath also discovered Kunstler's close association with Charles Leef, who was known as the judge's "fixer." Leef would ply the courtroom corridor promising litigants he could straighten things out for them, then sit with Kunstler on the bench and whisper in his ear. Heath brought his information to the New York City Bar Association, which was sufficiently alarmed to seek Kunstler's ouster. Dewey agreed to prosecute the case for the Bar Association without charging a fee.[7]

Over the next several months, Heath shared his dirt on Kunstler as Dewey meticulously prepared his case. The key turned out to be Kunstler's bank accounts, which showed that, over a three-year period, the judge deposited $126,000 in funds above and beyond his judicial salary. Curiously, these deposits ceased precisely at the time Seabury announced he would be looking into the municipal courts. Kunstler could not muster a remotely plausible explanation, and his cross-examination became, in Dewey's own reckoning, a "massacre." As Dewey methodically marched through Kunstler's financial records, eliciting admissions that Kunstler took loans from Leef and from the president of an auto insurer that frequently had cases before him, "the jurist kept slumping further and further down in the witness chair." Before Dewey could finish, Kunstler resigned. As with Mayor Walker and Federal District Judge Winslow before him, Kunstler then simply faded into obscurity. Heath, who had never seen a case "so completely prepared and so devastatingly presented as Dewey's action against Kunstler," emerged with profound admiration for Dewey's talents.[8]

Dewey walked away "shocked" at the "grubby kind of judicial corruption" that Kunstler exemplified. The local judges in New York, Dewey realized, were "a different breed" from the federal judges he was used to dealing with. In the US Attorney's Office, Dewey and his colleagues had "complete confidence" in the federal judges, who generally were of "the highest caliber." There was, however, one exception to that rule, a federal judge about whom "we had an uneasy feeling that there was something wrong" but "never anything definite to go on": Martin T. Manton.[9]

* * *

Kunstler's case was Heath's "first taste of the blood of corruption" as an investigative reporter, and it proved "habit-forming." After Kunstler's immolation, Heath published muckraking stories showing how Tammany's tax assessors favored big property owners over small homeowners and how Tammany apparatchiks were kept on the city payroll at the expense of vital social services desperately needed during the Depression. "Immersed in the anti-Tammany fight," Heath had become, in his own immodest estimation, "the unofficial scourge of Tammany Hall."[10]

In July 1938, back at the *World-Telegram*, Heath received another tip about another allegedly corrupt judge. A "stranger" came into the paper's editorial offices "in a strange manner" with "a strange story" about Judge Manton. According to this source, when Manton took control of the Interborough receivership and appointed Chadbourne, Stanchfield & Levy as counsel, he was closely associated in business with Thomas Chadbourne and Louis Levy, and obligated indirectly to Levy for a financial favor. The *World-Telegram* immediately assigned Heath to spend as much time as necessary verifying the source's claim and amassing "proof of Manton's crookedness."[11]

The next day, Jacob Handelsman came into the paper's offices with his story that Jimmy Hines had once offered to pay off one of Manton's debts because Manton was "the only federal judge left in New York we can use to get people out of jail." Handelsman's financial motives cast a shadow over his credibility; he wanted the *World-Telegram* to pay him $10,000 for the story, and he had previously used the paper to force Manton to pay part of a debt Manton owed him. For these reasons, the *World-Telegram* declined to go public with Handelsman's scandalous assertion.[12]

But Heath did decide to take Handelsman's story to Dewey. It was a reprise of the collaboration that brought down Kunstler, with one key difference: Dewey was no longer a lawyer in private practice representing the Bar Association. He was the district attorney of Manhattan, the first Republican elected to the post since Charles Whitman, Lieutenant Becker's prosecutor. Dewey's case against Hines was nearing trial, and

Heath thought Dewey could use Handelsman as a witness. Dewey told Heath he did not need Handelsman for Hines. "But I am interested in the Manton angle," Dewey said. "I have been planning for some time to have Murray Gurfein"—chief of the Rackets Bureau and one of Dewey's top assistants going back to his time as special prosecutor—"begin an investigation of Manton."[13]

Heath met with Gurfein the next day. The journalist and the prosecutor came to an agreement, blessed by Dewey, that served their mutual interests: Heath would turn over to Gurfein whatever leads he had on Manton; Gurfein would look over Heath's articles and let him know if anything was inaccurate; and neither would go public with their accusations without the other's permission before January 15, 1939.[14] The hunt was on, with Manton the prey.

During the next six months, Heath worked full-time on the Manton story, poring over rapidly multiplying stacks of records in a large private room in the *World-Telegram*'s offices kept under lock and key. The paper hired an accountant to help Heath make sense of Manton's complex financial dealings. Only a handful of top editors and Heath's close friends at the paper knew what he was up to. Dewey's investigators regularly stopped by Heath's war room to collect intelligence. Heath also held meetings there with his original source, "the invaluable tipster on Manton's life history and most of his current thoughts and actions," whose name he never revealed.[15]

Part of Heath's document trove came from proceedings in the Brooklyn Surrogate Court involving James Sullivan's estate. Despite Sullivan's many business interests, the assets in his estate were eclipsed by his liabilities, in particular his unpaid $250,000 note to Lord & Thomas. Mary Sullivan, his widow, challenged whether this was truly Sullivan's debt. As co-executor of the estate, Manton listed it as such, but the other co-executor, Sullivan's brother Edward, did not agree. Edward and Mary Sullivan's lawyers had seen the bank records showing how the loan proceeds were used for Manton's benefit, had noticed Manton's role in deciding the American Tobacco cases around the time of the loan, and felt "there was something irregular and possibly illegal about the transaction." In May 1938, Mary Sullivan filed a motion—vigorously opposed by Manton and his lawyer—asking the Surrogate Court to give her accountant access to the books and records of Manton's real estate companies as well as National Cellulose and other firms in which Manton and her late husband were interested. In her supporting affidavit, she said she was "skeptical of the theory that her husband borrowed $250,000 and used $190,000 of it to protect his interest in a real estate corporation, in which he had only a five percent interest."[16]

No reporter had yet laid eyes on these incendiary documents. Heath, with the assistance of his informer and various other records, was able to piece together the role of Chadbourne and Levy in Manton's financial affairs, including how they acquired their disguised stakes in National Cellulose shortly before Manton adjudicated the Interborough five-cent subway fare case, how they arranged for the Lord & Thomas $250,000 loan, how Manton benefited from the loan, and the proximity of the loan to Manton's rulings in the American Tobacco litigation and his appointment of the Chadbourne firm as counsel to the Interborough receivers.[17]

Armed with subpoena power, Dewey's investigators had the ability to compel documents, as well as testimony, that Heath lacked. They found evidence of Manton's receipt of loans and payments from litigants in cases unknown to Heath. For instance, they sent agents up to Baldwinsville, New York, to obtain the records of National Cellulose, which reflected $47,000 in mysterious and unpaid loans from George Spector, the insurance broker who acted as the conduit for Archie Andrews. But even the power of compulsion would not be enough to pry all relevant evidence from Spector.

Called to the grand jury, Spector first claimed he kept no records at all relating to his lending activities, pointing to his head as his only "record." He said the $47,000 he lent to National Cellulose came from cash in his safe deposit box. After further prodding, Spector admitted that, although he destroyed his original records every month, he did maintain a handwritten "yellow sheet" summarizing his business transactions. But when he produced the yellow sheet it was incomplete; the left-hand margin of the page was torn off. Asked about this omission, Spector admitted that, while having coffee that morning, he had ripped off and thrown away the part of the document that showed the names of his customers because he did not want to divulge the names. Spector said he retained a duplicate list of the names at his West End Avenue apartment; he was directed to return the following day with the list. Spector did return. But he did not bring the list of names. He explained that, the night before, he had mailed the list to a friend outside the state because "I didn't want to have it in my possession anymore." Even more astonishingly, Spector acknowledged that he consulted with his lawyer before taking that action and that his lawyer advised him not to do it. A state court judge held Spector in contempt, saying, "I have never seen a more flagrant case of contumacious conduct on the part of a witness with respect to a subpoena."[18]

Dewey also could not subpoena what he could not find. In at least one instance, Manton ensured that Dewey's process-servers would fail in their mission. Once Dewey's team scooped up National Cellulose's records, it was just a matter of time before they would want to ask John Lotsch about the loan to the company from Lotsch's Fort Greene Bank. In August 1938, Manton summoned Lotsch to Fairacres.

"Dewey is making some investigation of me in connection with the Sullivan matter," Manton informed Lotsch. "I understand he is looking for you. Could you go away for a few weeks until it blows over?" Lotsch, who by this point had been convicted in the Eastern District, demurred, saying he had no money to take a vacation. But Manton had an idea. "You have a daughter living up in Connecticut. Why don't you go up to her until this thing blows over?" suggested the nation's tenth highest-ranking judicial officer, who in that same month was urging friends of the president to lobby for his appointment to the Supreme Court. And so Lotsch hid out for two weeks in Plantsville, Connecticut, with his daughter Ethel and her husband.[19]

Manton also tried to make the Lord & Thomas loan headache disappear. Edward Sullivan's lawyers were questioning Manton under oath about it, and Thomas Chadbourne, in a conversation overhead by his chauffeur, was yelling at Manton to "take care of this loan as soon as possible" and "keep me entirely out of" it. Around the same time, a district judge in Manhattan denied a motion for a preliminary injunction in a high-stakes corporate proxy fight for control of the Chesapeake &

Ohio Railway. The case headed to the Second Circuit. Manton evidently viewed this as an opportunity to, in effect, refinance the Lord & Thomas loan. Manton sent Bill Fallon to approach Robert R. Young, chairman of the Allegheny Corporation, one of the warring factions. At a meeting at the Ritz-Carlton Hotel, Fallon told Young that "for $250,000"—the same amount owed to Lord & Thomas—"[Young] could have the decision." Revealing the iron fist in his velvet glove, Fallon further explained that, although Manton believed the merits of the case favored Young, "if [Young] did not come across with $250,000 the decision would probably go to" Young's adversary.[20]

This gambit failed, however. A corporate maverick dubbed "the Populist of Wall Street," Young was not one to capitulate to extortion. He immediately consulted with his counsel, William J. Donovan, cofounder of the white-shoe Donovan & Leisure law firm. Donovan arranged for the next meeting with Fallon to be recorded, and then, according to Young's friend and biographer Joseph Borkin, "submitted the entire matter to the authorities, who had already begun an investigation of Manton"—presumably Dewey, though he never publicly revealed this aspect of his investigation. Meanwhile, Young reached a compromise with his adversary so that regardless of how the Second Circuit ruled, it did not affect the proxy fight (with Manton on the panel, the court ultimately did rule against Young). Such were the precautions that Second Circuit litigants needed to take in the age of Martin T. Manton.[21]

* * *

By all public appearances, Manton remained untouched by the swirl of investigations. In a speech he ironically lauded the "independence" of the federal judiciary, which he described as chiefly responsible for the strength and stability of the federal government. He presided at a memorial service for Benjamin Cardozo, paying tribute to the late justice's recognition that when social relationships are "changing fast in the minds of the majority of the people, the law must keep the same tempo." Manton may have hoped that his New Deal–friendly eulogy would resonate with President Roosevelt and his advisors as they considered Cardozo's successor. Indeed, Heath heard "persistent" rumors from credible sources that Roosevelt was considering naming Manton to replace Cardozo. But these rumors were almost certainly untrue, given what FDR had already heard about Manton's strange finances from Robert Jackson. Around this time prominent leaders of the New York bar such as C. C. Burlingham were also warning the president "never to give [Manton] any honors."[22]

If his dreams of advancement to the Supreme Court were thwarted, Manton at least could remain sanguine about his material circumstances. Buoyed by the loans and gifts extracted from litigants and friends, Manton managed to keep afloat through the worst of the Depression. He suffered plenty of setbacks; despite the massive infusion of funds courtesy of the American Tobacco Company and Lord & Thomas, the Alamac and Esplanade Hotels fell into foreclosure in 1938.[23] But Manton never appeared to face a risk of personal bankruptcy. His major creditors, like Samuel Ungerleider, proved surprisingly accommodating and never moved to make good on the personal notes Manton signed to guarantee the loans to his companies.

Manton was a magician at raising cash from individuals who had reasons to curry his favor. As one example, in September 1936, Manton conjured up a $15,000 interest-free loan from Milton Speiser, a leading personal injury lawyer, whose brother and partner had just been arrested for ambulance-chasing, and who would be arrested himself the following month for bribing witnesses. From another lawyer, who had no pending cases in the Second Circuit but had appeared there on several past occasions, Manton obtained a series of loans totaling $23,000 over the course of 1937 and 1938. Then, in part to pay off his balance to that lawyer, he made another $15,000 loan appear, from a different lawyer who had won two appeals before him in the past year and a half. Manton also procured two loans totaling $6,500 from Fortune Gallo, a famous opera impresario and head of an opera company; in between, Manton interceded with Gallo's bank, which was pressing Gallo about an outstanding debt.[24]

Manton even commoditized clerkships. He hit up Charlie Rich for a $4,500 loan after promising to hire Rich's son as a law clerk, and another $7,500 loan while the son was clerking. Not even the shoe shine man was immune. As senior circuit judge, Manton approved the shoe shiner's right to offer his services in the Foley Square Courthouse. In return, Manton "always got his shoe-shine free."[25]

With such sums steadily pouring into his coffers, Manton and his family were able to maintain their comfortable lifestyle. Manton's son David graduated from Columbia in 1937 and went to work for National Cellulose in Syracuse.[26] Manton's daughter Catherine entered Marymount College in the fall of 1935. In the summers, Catherine was a fixture in the South Shore social scene and competed in horse shows and regattas.[27] In early January 1936, her parents threw a supper party for the vivacious eighteen-year-old and more than two dozen of her friends at the Central Park Casino, considered "*the* place for rich, fabulous, and socially and politically connected citizens" to party during Prohibition. Shortly thereafter, bulldozers tore down the pricey restaurant at the direction of parks commissioner Robert Moses, who considered it obscene that the city's most important public park hosted a venue for the wealthy to gorge themselves when so many other New Yorkers were unable to feed their families.[28]

On July 15, 1936, Manton boarded the SS *Manhattan* at Pier 60 on the Hudson River. He and Eva were off for another three-week summer vacation in Europe, but this time their fellow passengers were not just other middle-aged members of the city's upper crust. Over 320 "lean, lithe, full-chested, flat-stomached, steel-muscled young men" and about a dozen equally fit young women—the main body of the 1936 US Olympics team, on their way to Berlin—joined them for the crossing. "So far," Eva wrote Learned Hand and his wife Frances four days into the journey, "our trip has been perfect—a beautiful, complete calm—charming people and plenty of entertainment from the hundreds of Olympians on board." The athletes used the voyage to work out and keep in shape. "Every morning the decks bristle with activity of their sports," Eva reported.[29]

With their children grown, the Mantons moved from their duplex apartment on Park Avenue one block west on 58th Street to the Hotel Madison.[30] The Madison was an "apartment hotel," a popular choice for well-heeled New Yorkers who, like the Mantons, spent much of the year living outside the city. Apartments typically did not include full kitchens; meals would be taken at the on-premises dining room, or could be sent up to the resident's apartment via a dumbwaiter. Cleaning services also were provided by the building. Residents could grab cocktails at the "fashionable" hotel's two ornately decorated bars, the "Red Bar" and the "Green Bar," featuring gilt-edged mirrors and chandeliers and frescoed ceilings.[31]

On Christmas Day 1938, the society pages announced the engagement of Manton's son David. Long shunned by the WASP establishment, Manton probably felt not only fatherly pride but also a measure of social acceptance. David's strikingly attractive fiancée, Betty Halsey Brown, traced her bloodline to an English Puritan gentleman, Sir Thomas Halsey, who emigrated to America in 1637 and was an original settler of Southampton, New York. The Mantons celebrated by throwing a New Year's Eve supper party in the Madison's dining room.[32]

* * *

Word of Dewey's investigation began to seep into New York's legal community. Manton's Second Circuit colleagues doubted the investigation would amount to much. "The cloud still hangs over Manton," Learned Hand wrote to his wife on New Year's Day 1939, but Hand guessed that "the longer nothing breaks, the less likely any break is. He will, I think, come through with smirches, but nothing more." Gus Hand urged his cousin and Thomas Swan that "*we* ought to do something" to help Dewey's investigation, but Learned thought there was "nothing to do."[33]

Heath shared Hand's skepticism that the long arm of the law could reach Manton—at least not Dewey's arm. As a local DA, Dewey had no jurisdiction to prosecute bribery and corruption by federal officials. To find a legal hook justifying his investigation, Dewey turned on its head the technique he learned in the US Attorney's Office. Just as he had once gone after corrupt local officials and gangsters for violating federal income tax laws, now he would investigate whether Manton, a federal official, had illegally evaded New York state income tax. That was the only indictable crime Dewey's team considered. But it carried a short two-year statute of limitations, and it would not be so easy to show that loans made to Manton were actually unreported income. Shortly after New Year's, over lunch with Heath's editor, Dewey said he was still investigating and asked the *World-Telegram* to hold off publishing its story.[34]

On Tuesday, January 24, Heath got a call from his inside source. "Manton is planning to resign," the source reported. Heath was shocked. He and his editors believed it imperative to print their findings while Manton was still on the bench; if he resigned, they believed, it would be harder for official action to be taken against him. Heath immediately went to see Murray Gurfein, who initially scoffed at the idea that Manton would retire. Friends of the judge, through an emissary, promised Gurfein that Manton would resign if it meant an end to the investigation, but Dewey had summarily nixed that idea. The next day, however, Gurfein telephoned Heath: "You were right" about Manton's impending resignation, he said. "Only it is closer even than you thought."[35]

In fact, earlier that day, US attorney general Frank Murphy had met with Manton in New York. Installed as attorney general just three weeks earlier, Murphy learned of the swirling rumors about Dewey's investigation. He asked for a summary of the FBI's own long-ignored dirt on Manton, which director J. Edgar Hoover provided in his January 10, 1939 memorandum. At Murphy's request, Assistant Attorney General Keenan called Manton on January 12 to ask about the rumors and whether "there was going to be any embarrassment." Not surprisingly, Manton assured Keenan that he had been informed the investigation "was about over" and that Dewey had confided to someone that he "had nothing" on Manton. Keenan—Manton's friend—seemed to accept this at face value, advising Murphy he saw "no basis to proceed any further" in questioning the judge.[36]

Murphy, though, who felt Manton had "no moral sense," decided he needed to take action—but not by commencing an investigation. Murphy's meetings with Manton on January 25, which included both breakfast and lunch at the Ambassador Hotel on Park Avenue and 51st Street, a few blocks from Manton's apartment, served no investigative purpose. Rather, Murphy came to New York to urge Manton to resign from the bench. Manton promised Murphy he would do so.[37] Undoubtedly Manton—and very likely Murphy—expected that Manton's resignation would obviate any need for a criminal investigation, as was the case with Mayor Walker, Judge Winslow, Justice Kunstler, and so many others.

Fearing that Manton's transgressions were about to be swept under the rug, Gurfein came up with an idea: He was bringing Spector before a state court judge later that day, and he planned to put on the record that Spector's records were needed in connection with an investigation of Judge Manton. That way, Manton would be placed in a position where it would seem he was resigning under fire, which might force him to reconsider. But Gurfein's plan was foiled when, at the court appearance, the judge (a former Tammany district leader who was not the judge who had held Spector in contempt) barred any mention of Manton's name.[38]

So instead Heath began writing, quickly. All day Thursday and Friday morning, under the watchful eyes of the paper's top editors and its libel lawyer, who checked "every word, every phrase, every sequence, and every innuendo," Heath banged out the first installment of his Manton expose. "The story was torn to pieces and put together again and again." By Friday afternoon it was ready. It would come out in the final afternoon edition, on the front page under two eight-column lines of inch-high type. While Heath started writing the next installment, a veteran *World-Telegram* reporter was dispatched to Manton's chambers with a first copy of the paper to get a comment from Manton. In all his years in journalism, the reporter said, he "had never seen a man so stricken in appearance as the judge."[39]

Heath's bylined, copyrighted articles in the *World-Telegram*, loaded with details about Manton's byzantine business empire and the $250,000 loan to Sullivan, had their intended effect. From Washington, Attorney General Murphy released a statement on Saturday, January 28 announcing that the Justice Department "has been making an investigation into allegations" against Manton "to determine whether there is basis for action by Federal authorities." The acting US attorney in Manhattan, Gregory F. Noonan, was summoned to meet with high-level Justice Department officials in Washington. Rep. Hatton W. Sumners (D-Tex), chairman of the House Judiciary Committee, responsible for initiating impeachment proceedings against federal judges, also said he had taken note of the *World-Telegram*'s reporting, but that the committee had not yet received any complaints or requests for action.[40]

For his part, Manton held two press conferences in his chambers on Saturday. Reporters expected a rebuttal of the *World-Telegram*'s charges; Manton had promised to issue a statement that would "satisfy the public that there is nothing wrong or immoral about anything I have done." But on second thought, he said, he would refrain from making a statement until the entire series of articles had been published. Still, Manton "was in a jolly mood," according to one reporter, and "appeared unconcerned over the investigation." He was "glad to hear" that the Justice Department would be conducting an investigation, Manton said. All the fuss, he suggested, could be dispelled with a single rhetorical question: "Hasn't a judge a right to buy stocks and bonds?"[41]

Manton also took a swing at his accuser. The *World-Telegram* "has had it in for me for a long time," he charged, not inaccurately. At the outset of his press conference, the judge looked at the *World-Telegram* reporter and asked him to leave. Why?, the reporter asked. Because "you are publishing these stories which you know better not to do," Manton said. But when the reporter asked if he was saying the *World-Telegram*'s articles were untrue, Manton replied quickly, "I haven't said that."[42]

Meanwhile, Dewey, who felt that "it would not be in the public interest to leave this situation without public exposure," hatched his own plan for publicizing the findings of his investigation. In the midst of the retrial of Jimmy Hines, one of their most important cases, Dewey and his team halted their preparations over the weekend to prepare a lengthy letter to Congressman Sumners, taking up his invitation for a complaint that might warrant an impeachment proceeding. In plain prose unadorned with argument or commentary, Dewey's letter laid out the facts his investigation had uncovered. "If, upon the foregoing facts, the House of Representatives should assume jurisdiction of this matter," Dewey offered, "I am prepared to present evidence before your committee in support thereof."[43]

Dewey's letter revolved around six specific incidents, extending well beyond the *World-Telegram*'s revelations, in which Manton received loans from litigants or others with business before the Second Circuit. They included: (i) the $250,000 loan from Lord & Thomas to Sullivan; (ii) the $77,000 in loans from Archie Andrews and George Spector while the Schick electric razor case was pending; (iii) the $50,000 in loans from Harry Warner at the time of the Warner Brothers appeal; (iv) Manton's $37,500 in indebtedness to Fort Greene Bank at the time that John Lotsch's appeal of his criminal conviction was pending; (v) the $12,000 loan from John McGrath, the Prudence trustee; and (vi) the $10,000 loan from Charles Rogers in exchange for the Kings Brewery insurance business. All told, this added up to more than $435,000 in loans flowing to Manton and his companies, only a small fraction of which had been repaid. And, Dewey tantalizingly suggested, "there are a number of other matters in character similar to the foregoing which cannot be fully set forth at this stage of the inquiry."[44]

On Sunday afternoon, an assistant to Dewey traveled to Washington to deliver the letter to Congressman Sumners. Later that day Dewey held a press conference where he handed out the letter to reporters.[45]

Plastered across the front page of newspapers nationwide the next morning—the New York Times gave it a three-line, three-column headline[46]—Dewey's letter landed like a bombshell. It was one thing for charges to be made by a quasi-partisan newspaper, quite another for them to be echoed and expanded upon by the nation's most popular prosecutor. While Dewey would never get to prosecute Manton himself, his letter, and Heath's reporting, made it professionally and politically untenable for federal authorities to do anything other than pursue their own full and complete investigation.

CHAPTER NINETEEN

"You Should Take That to Your Grave"

Manton Under Federal Investigation

ON MONDAY, JANUARY 30, 1939, MANTON ANNOUNCED HIS RESIGNA-
tion from the court he had joined more than two decades before as the
youngest judge in its history. "The man who goes up like a rocket always
goes down like a stick," Manton had advised a graduating law school class
the year after ascending to the Court of Appeals.[1]

This time it was a weary-looking Manton who greeted reporters in
his chambers, "ill at ease" with "a forced smile on his face," speaking "in a
tone so low as to be almost inaudible at times." Sarcasm, clipped answers,
and hints of despair replaced the relaxed jauntiness of Saturday, even as
Manton continued to insist he had done nothing wrong or even anything
of which he was "in any way ashamed." Manton claimed he had been
planning "for some time" to retire anyway, but if that were true he seemed
curiously unprepared for his post-judicial career. Maybe he would "try to
build up some of these big industries I'm interested in," he deadpanned.
When one reporter asked a question about his corporate records, Manton grimly jibed: "Ask Dewey. He wants the publicity." When another
reporter questioned whether he was being investigated in connection
with his federal or state income taxes, Manton retorted with a wry grin:
"In connection with Mr. Dewey's ambitions."[2]

Manton's prompt resignation put an end to any threat of an impeachment proceeding. Despite grumbling from some Republicans in Congress, Chairman Sumners announced that, consistent with past practice,

the judge's voluntary departure made impeachment, and its remedy of removal from office, unnecessary. To the argument that impeachment could still expose Manton's wrongdoing and ensure he never again held federal office, Sumners replied, in his Texas drawl, "Why kick at the place where the fellow used to be?"[3]

Manton had dodged the impeachment bullet, and for all his menacing Dewey, given his tenuous jurisdiction, essentially was firing blanks. Dewey privately "admitted to pals that so far not one iota of evidence has been found that could be pressed against Judge Manton under state criminal statutes," the columnist Walter Winchell reported. But the feds were now on the scene, and whatever Attorney General Murphy's prior inclinations, they were not going to hold their fire now. Murphy immediately issued a statement underscoring that Manton's resignation, far from obviating the need for a federal criminal investigation, "will facilitate the thorough investigation of charges against the jurist and protect the administration of justice by keeping the courts completely above suspicion." US Attorney Noonan pledged that "this investigation . . . will continue," and that discovery of any "criminal activity in violation of Federal statutes over which we have jurisdiction" will be handled in the "usual course." The following day, on Murphy's orders, the US attorney began presenting witnesses to a grand jury in Manhattan.[4]

Murphy had little choice, both because of the threat the allegations posed to public confidence in the federal judiciary, and because of the political implications. Murphy, the *New York Times* reported, issued his pledge to continue the investigation after being "urged to do so by Administration political advisers who had an eye on the 1940 Presidential race," as Dewey had now "surged to the front" of the pack of potential Republican nominees for president.[5] Democrats "trembled" to think how Dewey could use the Manton scandal as a "powerful club" if Dewey became the Republican candidate; Republicans, meanwhile, were "jubilant over the situation."[6] Whatever loyalty Murphy's boss may have felt toward his "old friend" who helped sway the 1932 Democratic convention in his favor, Franklin Roosevelt did not reach the White House by allowing sentiment to stand in the way of his political prospects.

The president made this clear enough at his press conference on Tuesday, January 31, at which he read the text of both Manton's resignation letter and his reply. In his letter, Manton asked to remain on the bench until March 1 to wind up his judicial affairs. But Roosevelt instead gave Manton only a week, accepting the resignation effective February 7. Reporters present laughed at the snub during the president's announcement (reportedly Roosevelt wanted to accept the resignation immediately and relented only in the face of a last-minute plea from the judge). Roosevelt also added to the reply letter drafted by his staff that the earlier effective date "means of course that you will no longer sit on cases before the court."[7]

The following day, after Murphy and Roosevelt discussed the Manton matter at length over lunch in the White House, the attorney general announced that the president "has directed that vigorous efforts be made to disclose all the facts and the parties."[8] The politically astute Murphy, a former mayor of Detroit and governor of Michigan, fully appreciated that FDR could not be seen to be coddling an allegedly corrupt official tied to New York's Democratic machine.

More than this, Murphy, who prosecuted bootleggers and war profiteers as a young assistant US attorney in Detroit, and whose idealism, asceticism, and devout Roman Catholicism earned him the sobriquet "St. Francis," genuinely abhorred corruption. In his brief tenure as attorney general, he targeted crooked political machines run by both parties in Kansas City and Philadelphia. He could not have been happy as his Justice Department came under attack, even from administration allies, for its seeming passivity in the Manton scandal. "Singularly, no federal official took any steps to stop him," the *New Republic* complained. "The job had to be done by a newspaper and a local district attorney." Republicans, of course, were even harsher, with one GOP congressman intimating darkly that, but for the public disclosures by Dewey and the *World-Telegram*, "the whole matter [would] have been hushed up." Murphy resolved to change that perception and was rewarded six months later when *Life* magazine, assessing his crime-busting feats relative to the New York district attorney, gave the attorney general credit for successfully prosecuting Manton—one of Murphy's "fattest fish to date"—without even mentioning Dewey's contribution.[9]

Circumstances were conspiring against Manton in unexpected ways. "[I]f custom were followed," Berkeley law professor (and later Ninth Circuit judge) John Noonan explained in his magisterial study *Bribes*, Manton's resignation would have insulated him against impeachment or a criminal trial. But because the case Dewey developed "was too strong to be so easily disposed of," because the Justice Department "looked foolish for being so far behind," and because a Democratic administration "could not now be seen as protecting its own," Manton's resignation did not have the customary effect. Instead Manton was plunged into a fight for his freedom with an army of tenacious prosecutors and FBI agents who enjoyed the full backing of the Justice Department's leadership.[10]

* * *

FBI director J. Edgar Hoover arrived in New York to personally take charge of the Manton investigation. Some 50 FBI agents were assigned originally, led by one of the Bureau's rising stars, thirty-two-year-old Inspector Percy E. Foxworth (who would be killed in a plane crash during World War II on a secret intelligence mission). "G-men" fanned out across the city serving dozens of subpoenas at the homes and offices of lawyers, businessmen, and real estate concerns associated with the judge and seizing banking records by the barrelful. More than two dozen agents continued to work the case after the initial flurry of activity, including a bevy of accountants, who would play an instrumental role in uncovering the often-obscured money trail that connected payments from litigants to Manton's pocket.[11]

Manton's financial dealings spread so far and wide, and so sinuously, that they even tripped up the lead prosecutor, Acting US Attorney Noonan. Chief of the Criminal Division under US Attorney Lamar Hardy, Noonan became temporary head of the office after Hardy stepped down in mid-January 1939. The Manton investigation was barely a week old when Noonan made a surprising and embarrassing disclosure: Subpoenaed records showed he had been the single largest shareholder in Manton's main real estate company, Alamac-Esplanade Corp. There was an innocuous explanation for this. Back in 1925, Noonan worked as a teenage clerk in the law firm operated by Lamar Hardy and his brother, who represented Chelsea Bank & Trust Co. in negotiations with Manton over a loan. Manton pledged a large chunk of Alamac-Esplanade shares as collateral, and someone at the bank placed the stock in the young Noonan's name. Noonan claimed that he did not know the stock had been held in his name and that he never received any dividend payments. Nonetheless, to avoid any possible taint, Noonan withdrew from the Manton probe.[12]

As Noonan exited the stage, the Roosevelt Administration hastened to resolve an internal debate over Hardy's permanent replacement. Postmaster General James Farley, the president's longtime political advisor and patronage czar, favored one candidate, a "faithful but undistinguished Democratic wheelhorse" formerly on Hardy's staff. Thomas Corcoran, "Tommy the Cork," the influential New Deal lawyer, backed John T. Cahill, then serving as a special assistant to the attorney general. Corcoran and Cahill were classmates and friends at Harvard Law School and later worked at the same New York law firm as junior associates. In a sign of Farley's growing isolation within the administration (he would break ranks the following year and oppose FDR's re-election), Corcoran prevailed. On February 9, Roosevelt appointed the energetic thirty-five-year-old Cahill as the new US attorney in Manhattan. Upon taking office, Cahill told the press that Attorney General Murphy had directed him "to see to it at all costs that every angle is investigated" in the Manton matter and "to conduct this investigation with vigor and dispatch."[13]

Manton assembled his own blue-chip legal team, hiring two former US attorneys in the Southern District of New York: Martin Conboy, FDR's first appointee to the post (replacing Dewey), and Francis W. H. Adams, who filled the gap between Conboy and Hardy as acting US attorney. But Manton, the former criminal defense lawyer, had his own ideas for undermining the government's case, some of which his eminent counsel would not have countenanced.

On February 5, at the end of the week he announced his resignation, Manton and Eva attended Sunday mass in Manhattan. Afterwards they stopped for breakfast at the Savoy-Plaza Hotel on Fifth Avenue, two blocks from their apartment. Before the food arrived, Manton decided to step out and call Alfred Reilly, the president of the Evans Case Company, from the lobby. "I understand you had Bill [Fallon] on the payroll," Manton said when Reilly got on the line from his home in North Attleboro. "That will be very embarrassing for me if found out," Manton added, explaining he had "heard they [the government] intend to investigate." Manton asked: "Couldn't you pull out those pages" from the company's records? Reilly was noncommittal, professing unfamiliarity with the company's bookkeeping. "It would be very embarrassing to me," Manton repeated, if Fallon's connection to Evans Case came to light.[14]

Reilly hung up, unsure what to do. He called Frank Nolan, Evans Case's treasurer. They drove together to Boston, at first riding aimlessly around the city while they talked. Reilly asked Nolan to stop at North Station, where Reilly went into a telephone booth and called Manton at his apartment on the ninth floor of the Hotel Madison. Reilly asked Manton if it was all right to talk on the phone. "I don't think exactly," Manton answered. He arranged to call Reilly back—using an assumed name—in the phone booth in ten to fifteen minutes. Manton continued to press Reilly to "get rid of" the Fallon records. Perhaps as an inducement, he suggested that he could help Reilly with another lawsuit Evans Case faced in Boston.[15]

Reilly continued to equivocate. He called the Evans Case bookkeeper and directed him to bring Reilly all the existing records relating to Fallon's Allied Rediscount Corporation. Reilly drove, with the bookkeeper, to Reilly's camp in Taunton, intending to burn the records, until the bookkeeper persuaded him not to. A few days later, however, Reilly again instructed the bookkeeper to destroy the records, and this time the bookkeeper complied, more or less. Reilly himself destroyed the three checks made out to Allied Rediscount he had delivered to Fallon at the Biltmore Hotel.[16]

That same Sunday he asked Reilly to deep-six the Fallon payroll records, Manton placed a call to John Lotsch. Manton asked Lotsch to meet him at 60 Wall Street, where Manton had taken office space. At that meeting, Manton urged Lotsch to go see US Attorney Noonan, then still in charge of the investigation, and tell him the loans from Fort Greene Bank described in Dewey's letter were "regular business transactions."[17]

A few weeks later, a worried Lotsch met with Manton again, this time at St. Vincent's Hospital in Greenwich Village. Suffering from an old glandular disorder, possibly aggravated by the strain of the investigation, Manton entered the hospital at the end of February for an operation. Lotsch had learned that an officer from Fort Greene Bank told the government about the $10,000 in cash that was delivered to Lotsch at the courthouse—the bribe money Lotsch used to procure a judgment of acquittal from Judge Thomas in his criminal case. Cahill was looking to serve a subpoena on Lotsch to testify before the grand jury.[18]

Manton had plenty of advice to offer Lotsch. It amounted to a veritable tutorial on obstruction of justice. The matter with Judge Thomas, Manton told Lotsch, "you should carry to your grave." If asked about the $10,000 loan from Fort Greene Bank, Lotsch should lie, and tell the grand jury that it was for legal fees for his attorney, former Judge Millard. "Millard is dead," Manton pointed out, "and no one can testify against him." Better still would be if Lotsch could avoid the grand jury altogether, at least for another few days; the federal statute of limitations on bribery was three years, Manton noted, and Thomas had granted Lotsch's judgment of acquittal on March 9, 1936. Manton suggested that Lotsch "go away for the time being" and visit his daughter in Connecticut, as Lotsch had done during the Dewey investigation. Claiming he could not impose on his daughter again, Lotsch asked for a $500 loan so he could disappear into a hotel in New York. Manton sent Lotsch to John McGrath, the Prudence Company trustee, and Ken Steinreich of Kips Bay Brewery to raise the $500. But with Manton out of power they both refused to lend Lotsch the money.[19]

Meanwhile, the government was having a tough time getting information from Judge Thomas. The government tried to serve Thomas with a grand jury subpoena on February 3, only to discover that he and his wife had set sail that very evening on the SS *Santa Barbara*, bound for a month-long vacation in South America. US Attorney Noonan radioed the ship's captain requesting that Thomas disembark in Sandy Hook,

New Jersey. That message went unanswered for hours until a curt reply was received: "Judge continuing journey."

Alarmed and incensed, Assistant Attorney General Brien McMahon sent an urgent radiogram to Thomas: "Investigation very important to the administration of justice and to you personally. Insist on your immediate return at the first port of call." The first port of call was Cristobal, in the Panama Canal Zone, then still US territory. The government airmailed a subpoena to the US attorney in Cristobal for service upon Thomas when he arrived. In the face of McMahon's edict, Thomas backed down. He cabled US Attorney Noonan that he would return from Cristobal on the first ship available. "No subpoena at Cristobal is necessary," he wrote. The Justice Department promptly leaked the whole story to the press, presumably to pressure Thomas to make good on his promise to return, as well as to show the public that they meant business.[20]

The Justice Department's interest in Thomas extended beyond the Manton investigation. In December 1938, Thomas approved an old-fashioned equity receivership for McKesson-Robbins, Inc., the kind supposedly rendered obsolete by the Federal Bankruptcy Act of 1934, enacted in the wake of Manton's well-publicized IRT receivership scandal. Adding to the oddity, Thomas appointed the mayor of Hartford, one of his close friends, as a receiver, and did so upon an application promoted by several officers of the company without the knowledge of its board of directors. Shortly thereafter, the SEC discovered that McKesson-Robbins had engaged in a massive accounting fraud and that the officers behind the receivership were four brothers masquerading under assumed names, including the company's highly-regarded CEO, "F. Donald Coster," who was in fact a convicted swindler and ex-bootlegger named Philip Musica. Separately, the FBI was investigating rumors that Judge Thomas received a $10,000 bribe from a slot machine manufacturer. Thomas had issued an injunction in favor of the manufacturer preventing Hartford officials from seizing its machines and subsequently testified as a witness for the company in a similar action in the Eastern District of New York.[21]

Thomas did sail back to the United States, as promised. But he then broke an appointment to meet with Cahill and resisted turning over his personal financial records voluntarily, necessitating subpoenas and a court fight. Ultimately, Thomas commenced his grand jury testimony, but before he was finished, he had a mental breakdown. At a party at his house on March 7, after appearing before the grand jury that morning, the judge suddenly "upset the table and threw dishes around." He was admitted to a Hartford sanitarium the next day, suffering from what officials described as a "severe mental disorder." While there, Thomas tried to commit suicide by cutting himself, a few days before he was to reappear before the grand jury. Thomas's doctors pronounced him unable to resume his judicial duties "for an indefinite period," and recommended he resign. Thomas submitted his resignation to President Roosevelt on April 6.[22]

Although Cahill considered indicting Thomas for income tax evasion, no charges were ever filed. Without any corroborating evidence, the government could not have convicted Thomas on the basis of Lotsch's testimony alone. Lotsch had never actually dealt with Thomas, other than in open court; all he knew about Thomas's involvement in the bribery scheme came from Manton. By the end of April the FBI had run down all its investigative leads on Thomas. Unlike Manton, Thomas was left alone to battle his own demons.[23]

* * *

The Manton investigation moved forward with unusual speed. In February, a parade of witnesses was marched before a special grand jury, including Manton himself, who made multiple appearances. Cahill secured Dewey's cooperation in gaining access to the district attorney's corpus of documentary evidence and expanded the probe down new alleys. At one point, according to FBI files, the investigation encompassed twenty-three separate allegations of payoffs to the former senior circuit judge. But Cahill and Murphy were not trying to get to the bottom of each of these allegations or comprehensively untangle all of Manton's sordid affairs. Their goal was to bring Manton to justice swiftly and restore public trust in the integrity of the federal judiciary and the federal government.[24]

On March 2, 1939—barely a month after Manton resigned, and while he was still at St. Vincent's Hospital about to undergo surgery—the US

Attorney's Office announced the first in a series of indictments against the freshly retired jurist. The initial indictment was limited to the Schick razor case and charged Manton, along with the hapless George Spector, with conspiracy. With Manton now under federal indictment, Dewey officially closed down his grand jury, ceding the field to Cahill.[25]

Cahill kept charging ahead and bringing more charges. Two weeks later, the grand jury indicted Manton and Fallon in connection with the Hall Brothers chicken egg incubator case. The next week saw Manton and Lotsch indicted for the $10,000 bribe paid to get rid of Lotsch's criminal case before Judge Thomas. Four days after that, Lotsch pled guilty and agreed to cooperate with the government—the first public acknowledgment of criminality by one of Manton's co-conspirators. A fourth indictment handed up in early April added Forrest W. Davis as a defendant in the Hall scheme. According to FBI files, the grand jury also was "very anxious" to indict George Washington Hill of American Tobacco for the $250,000 loan to Sullivan in 1932, but while prosecutors shared the sentiment, the statute of limitations blocked them from doing so.[26]

The government's investigation also ensnared Fallon's brother, Thomas J. Fallon. In telephone calls in March 1939, Thomas Fallon—echoing Manton's request from a few weeks earlier—urged Alfred Reilly of Evans Case to "bury" incriminating records reflecting his brother's involvement. Fallon then lied in the grand jury about his conversations with Reilly. Fallon did not know that the government, with Reilly's consent, was tape-recording the phone calls. The grand jury indicted Fallon for perjury and obstruction of justice the day after he completed his testimony.[27]

On April 26, 1939, the government filed an "omnibus" superseding indictment, consolidating the charges laid out in the four prior indictments. From the smorgasbord of possibilities, Cahill had chosen six cases in which Manton accepted money from litigants.[28] All but one were patent infringement suits: *Art Metal Works, Inc. v. Abraham & Strauss, Inc.*; *General Motors Corp. v. Preferred Electric and Wire Corp.*; *Electric Autolite Co. v. P. and D. Manufacturing Co.*; *Samuel B. Smith v. A.B. Hall*; and *Schick Industries v. Dictograph Products Co.* The other was *United States v. Lotsch*, the criminal case. Several of the payments in Dewey's letter to Congress were not included (but remained in Cahill's back pocket as possible ammunition for cross-examination if Manton testified in his own defense); on the other hand, Cahill had identified new ones Dewey's investigation had not uncovered.

There were some important differences between the prior indictments and the "omnibus" indictment. The earlier indictments charged Manton in three separate schemes with three different conspiracy counts: conspiracy to obstruct justice, conspiracy to defraud the United States, and conspiracy to solicit and accept bribes. Each of these nine separate conspiracy charges carried a maximum sentence of two years in prison and a fine of $10,000. Stacked together, they added up to a potential prison sentence of 18 years and a fine of $90,000.[29]

The omnibus indictment, however, boiled all these charges down to just a single conspiracy count. That meant a dramatic reduction in the possible punishment: Manton now faced, at worst, a jail sentence of two years and a fine of $10,000. Cahill likely was concerned that if the indictment remained chopped up into multiple different conspiracies, the evidence at trial would have to be slotted into the particular scheme to which it related, complicating the government's trial presentation. Perhaps he also feared a mixed verdict that would allow Manton to claim partial victory. In effect, Cahill traded the possibility of a longer jail term for a greater certainty of conviction.[30]

Notably, the omnibus indictment also dropped the bribery charges. Instead, the remaining conspiracy charge alleged only two objects: to defraud the United States and to obstruct justice. Thus, although in popular imagination Manton was convicted of "bribery," that is not true. The jury was not asked to find, nor did it find, that what Manton did amounted to the crime of bribery under federal law. "The instant case is not a bribe case," the government would later explain in its court filings.[31]

Ironically, Manton had himself to thank for that. According to Milton Gould, who spoke with one of the prosecutors, the government abandoned the bribery charge because of the Second Circuit's rule that a bribe-giver or bribe-taker could not be guilty of conspiracy (based on the theory that bribery inherently involves concerted activity).[32] That rule was set forth in *United States v. Sager*, Manton's 1931 ruling reversing the convictions of Joseph Shalleck, the Mob-connected lawyer, and his confederates.[33] In a way, though, the government probably benefited from that rule; it relieved them of the burden of proving a quid pro quo, i.e., that Manton took money in exchange for favoring the giver's position in cases before him. While there was ample evidence of outright bribery, a bribery charge would have raised the bar for the prosecution and played into Manton's central defense: that none of the loans and payments changed his vote or affected the court's decision, which in all but two instances was unanimous.

Fundamentally, the government's case rested on the legal theory that Manton conspired to defraud the United States of its right to his fair and impartial services as a federal judge. "Fraud" under this statute is a term of art, not confined to schemes to obtain money or property from the federal government. A conspiracy to defraud the United States also means, the Supreme Court held in 1924, "to interfere with or obstruct one of its lawful governmental functions by deceit, craft or trickery, or at least by means that are dishonest."[34] Manton, the omnibus indictment alleged, defrauded the United States of "its right to have the lawful functions of the Judicial Power of the United States exercised and administered free from unlawful impairment and obstruction." By secretly holding a "personal and pecuniary interest in the success of" litigants affected by the outcome of Second Circuit proceedings, he had deprived the United States of "its right to the conscientious, faithful, disinterested, and unbiased judgment and determination of" its judicial officers.[35] In other words, as Cahill explained in his closing argument to the jury, "if Manton took money from a litigant and sat in that case, it doesn't make any difference what the decision he rendered was. . . . The taking of the money was the crime."[36]

According to Gould, Cahill's team "ingeniously came up" with this "novel theory" to overcome the unavailability of a bribery charge.[37] That overstates matters considerably. While no one had ever applied the theory to a federal judge before, federal officials who took money from those doing business with the federal government had for decades been prosecuted for conspiring to defraud the United States of their "impartial" or "honest services."[38] The theory undergirded corruption prosecutions in the 1920s of leading members of the Harding Administration, including former interior secretary Albert B. Fall of Teapot Dome fame.[39] An assistant US attorney in Brooklyn was prosecuted on the same theory for allegedly taking money from a lawyer for a company under indictment.[40]

Indeed, Cahill's prosecutors would have been guided in that direction by reading Manton's own opinions. In 1928, Manton wrote the Second Circuit's decision affirming the conviction of Thomas W. Miller, Harding's alien property custodian, who received money from a Swiss company around the same time he approved releasing back to the company assets seized during World War I. Miller, Manton held, was properly found guilty of conspiracy to defraud the United States by depriving it of "its right to have disinterested and conscientious service."[41] And in *Sager*, the jury convicted one of Shalleck's co-defendants of "conspiring to defraud the United States of the impartial services of a court bailiff." Manton's opinion did not suggest there was any legal infirmity in this charge and strongly intimated that a charge of conspiracy to defraud the United States would lie in circumstances where a bribery conspiracy charge would be invalid.[42] When Manton's lawyers later challenged his indictment, Cahill threw their client's ruling in *Sager* back at them and the judge cited it in rejecting the challenge.[43]

Manton's lawyers also filed a pretrial motion claiming that the "omnibus" indictment impermissibly lumped together different conspiracies that should have been kept separate as originally charged. Cahill successfully refuted that argument by citing a Second Circuit opinion that Manton himself had joined, which rejected a substantially similar argument. Issued on February 6, 1939, the day before Manton's resignation took effect, it was one of the last judicial opinions to bear Manton's name.[44]

It is sometimes said that criminal defendants, by their actions or their admissions, write their own doom. Rarely, however, do they do so by shaping the legal contours of the indictment against them.

* * *

"Hear ye! Hear ye!" cried the clerk in the US Courthouse in Manhattan. For more than two decades, that cry preceded Judge Martin T. Manton's entrance into a courtroom and commanded lawyers, litigants, and spectators to rise in respect as he took the bench. As the clerk's familiar call rang out on a cloudy and chilly morning in March 1939, however, a "pale and haggard" Manton, released from St. Vincent's Hospital only the week before, found himself on the other side of the bar. In the same building he had, until just a few weeks before, reigned as the ranking federal judge in the Second Circuit, Manton now participated in a judicial proceeding as a criminal defendant, facing his arraignment.[45]

To the press Manton appeared "extremely uncomfortable and worried," the strain of his circumstances "written plainly in his bearing," as he sat waiting for his case to be called while District Judge John W. Clancy first dealt with the "dope peddlers, extortionists and still operators" who preceded him. When it was Manton's turn, Judge Clancy looked rather "nervous and ill at ease" himself, nodding ever so slightly in recognition as his former colleague stepped forward. Flanked by his two attorneys, Manton, in a barely audible voice, murmured "not guilty" when Clancy asked how he pleaded.

Anxious to show that Manton would receive no special favors, Cahill sought bail in the amount of $25,000, noting that Manton faced "a very serious series of charges" and that bail had been set at $17,500 for George Spector, Manton's less culpable co-defendant. Manton watched silently as his lawyer, Conboy, ridiculed Cahill's bail request as grossly excessive given who his client was, and Cahill retorted that Manton could not be trusted. "We must approach this matter impersonally," said Cahill, his voice rising. "The defendant Manton is charged with violating his oath as judge in this court. I feel that we must take no cognizance of the statement that the judge won't leave the jurisdiction." Judge Clancy allowed bail at the lower amount requested by Conboy, $10,000.

The "bleak proceeding," as the *New York Times* called it, seemed over, but Manton would have to endure one more indignity. Seeking to avoid reporters on his way out, Manton and his attorneys escaped by using the judges' private elevator. But they, and the government, forgot that Manton was supposed to be fingerprinted first. When the outmaneuvered reporters pointed this out to authorities, they were greeted at first with hemming and hawing, followed by an admission that, in fact, this essential step of the arraignment process had been skipped. After consulting with Cahill, Judge Clancy ordered that Manton return to the courthouse to have his fingers rolled and stained on an ink pad, the same as any accused felon.

Eva Manton refused to accept what was happening to her husband. She always believed in her husband's innocence; "right is on our side," she would later tell reporters.[46] She reached out to the one person in authority she knew who could help: President Roosevelt. In April 1939, Eva handwrote a letter to the president and mailed it to his private White House secretary, Missy LeHand, asking her to present it to FDR. Eva requested an appointment with the president, based "on the strength of the years of friendship between you and Martin, and the admiration and appreciation of him which you expressed to me, only a few months ago," when she and her husband visited. She reminded FDR of his pledge, at the celebration in Basil O'Connor's home after his first election in 1932, that his friends would be able to see him in the White House—"so in the name of friendship," Eva pleaded, "may I see you?"[47]

At the O'Connor dinner in 1932, as Eva's letter recalled, Roosevelt promised a different White House from the "cold" place it had become under Herbert Hoover. Now, after more than six years in office, Roosevelt understood that at times a president needed to give the cold shoulder even to his friends. He forwarded Eva's letter to Attorney General Murphy and asked Murphy if he should see her or not. Murphy drafted Roosevelt's reply, which assured Eva that FDR had read her letter "with the sincere interest that you must know any message of yours will receive" and that he continued to believe the White House doors should be open "at all times when it is possible." Although "I would like to see you," the president claimed, he nevertheless suggested that, as he was dealing with "so many cares and problems, it would be really helpful to me" if Eva met with Attorney General Murphy instead.[48]

Undeterred, perhaps sensing an opening in the warm words wrapped around the president's icy rejection—he closed by expressing "all personal good wishes to you"—Eva persisted. With Manton's trial fast approaching, she scrawled another note to Roosevelt, insisting that her business "is with you alone, and would be futile with anyone else." Therefore, "I am going to ask again for only a few minutes" of his time, either in Washington or New York, where he would be the following Sunday to open the 1939 World's Fair. Eva assured FDR that "I will in no way embarrass you." To that end, she suggested that she could make an appointment "under an assumed name"—a suggestion that one imagines originated with her husband and only confirmed the president's instinct to keep his distance.[49]

This time, after again consulting with Murphy, Roosevelt slammed the door shut. Formally and firmly, Roosevelt replied on May 9, 1939: "I am advised by the Attorney General that because of the case now pending in New York a conference with you at this time would be highly inadvisable. Under the circumstances, I feel obliged to decline your request." He reiterated that Eva should communicate any request to Murphy. "I am sure you will understand," he wrote. No evocations of past camaraderie or expressions of affection sugarcoated this rejection from the president.[50]

Manton and Eva no longer had a friend in the White House. Manton's fate would be left to a jury of his peers.

CHAPTER TWENTY

"A Very Substantial Safe, We Did Have"

Manton on Trial

"THE MOST IMPORTANT LEGAL PROCEEDING IN THE HISTORY OF THE Federal courts," as the *New York Herald Tribune* called it, got underway on Monday, May 22, 1939. Escorted by police and US marshals, a grim-faced, sometimes scowling Manton pushed his way through a milling crowd of almost one thousand persons jammed on the front steps of the Foley Square Courthouse. The threatening thunderstorms may have contributed to his ill-humor. Or he may have been dwelling on a sobering statistic he cited the year before in writing the foreword for a new treatise on federal criminal law: According to FBI Director Hoover, "convictions were secured in 94.67 per cent of the cases investigated by the Bureau during the [most recent] fiscal year which were brought to trial."[1]

Conservatively dressed in a dark gray suit, stiff collar, and subdued striped tie, Manton entered Room 110 on the first floor, the building's largest courtroom and the site of many future famous Southern District trials: the Cold War convictions of Alger Hiss and Julius and Ethel Rosenberg, the post-Watergate acquittals of former Nixon Cabinet officials John Mitchell and Maurice Stans, the marathon IBM antitrust trial that lasted from 1975 to 1982, the white-collar trials of Alfred Taubman and Martha Stewart in this century.[2] Every seat remained filled during the trial and up to 150 people at a time stood in line outside the courtroom waiting for their turn.[3] In a sense Manton, who as senior circuit judge fiercely lobbied for construction of the Foley Square Courthouse, literally set the stage for his own trial.

Manton took his seat at counsel table along with his new legal team. Gone were the former Manhattan US attorneys, Conboy and Adams. In early May, as Eva was making her entreaties of President Roosevelt, Manton hired Poughkeepsie lawyer John E. Mack to lead his defense.[4] Although Mack was a skilled litigator, who previously served as a district attorney and State Supreme Court justice in Dutchess County, his chief qualification for this assignment lay outside the legal realm. Mack, sixty-five, was one of the president's oldest and closest friends, a political mentor when the young FDR first ran for office in Hudson Valley, later given the honor of placing Roosevelt's name in nomination at the 1932 and 1936 Democratic conventions. Mack did not play a significant role in the trial itself. That task fell to two veteran forty-seven-year-old trial lawyers, also curiously from outside New York City: James M. Noonan, of Albany, and Benjamin M. Golder of Philadelphia.

Heavyset and genial, Noonan had handled several high-profile trials and twice persuaded juries not to convict Dutch Schultz on income tax evasion charges. Noonan had argued four appeals before Manton in the Second Circuit (including the appeal in which Manton returned the Liberty bonds posted for Schultz's bail), so Manton had seen Noonan in action and presumably was impressed. Why Manton tapped Golder, a former Republican congressman with no familiarity with the New York legal community, is less clear. Perhaps Manton admired Golder for not allowing his official duties to interfere with his private money-making pursuits. While still serving in Congress, Golder maintained an active law practice. Congressman Golder represented Al Capone when the legendary gangster ran into trouble with Philadelphia law enforcement, and a number of bootleggers as well.[5]

At the other counsel table, closer to the judge, sat Cahill and his assistants. Tall, slim, ramrod straight, with blue eyes and a round face topped by a thin layer of brown, graying hair, Cahill was "filled with restless energy" born of a scrappy upbringing. Raised in Queens, New York, the son of Irish immigrants, Cahill worked during high school, Columbia University, and Harvard Law School as a Wall Street messenger, an

LIRR ticket salesman, a ship steward, and a tutor. In private practice, he accepted special appointments to prosecute gangsters for the Democratic state attorney general and Manhattan district attorney.[6] But unlike Thomas Dewey, Cahill disavowed any political ambitions and seemed to really mean it. He was content after leaving the US Attorney's Office to build a lucrative law practice representing large corporations. The firm that bears his name, Cahill, Gordon & Reindel, remains a Wall Street fixture.

Next to Cahill was Matthias F. Correa, his chief assistant. Just twenty-eight, Correa had been Cahill's favorite junior lawyer in private practice. President Roosevelt named Correa as Cahill's successor in 1941, making him, at age thirty, the youngest appointed US attorney in Manhattan. After World War II Correa rejoined his former boss at Cahill, Gordon & Reindel. Three other young prosecutors in their late twenties rounded out the Manton trial team, including Jerome Doyle, who would also wind up at the Cahill law firm, and the newly appointed Silvio J. Mollo, who would go on to serve the US Attorney's Office for three decades with such distinction that the building that houses its prosecutors is named for him.

For all of Manton's familiarity with the Foley Square Courthouse, when he looked up at the trial judge he saw an unfamiliar face. Because all the sitting Southern District judges were acquainted with Manton to one degree or another, Chief Justice Charles Evans Hughes brought in an outsider to preside over Manton's trial. Consideration was given to a retired Supreme Court justice, either Louis Brandeis or Willis Van Devanter, but ultimately Hughes selected W. Calvin Chesnut, a federal district judge from Baltimore.[7] A native Baltimorean and lifelong Republican appointed to the bench by Herbert Hoover in 1931, the sixty-six-year-old Chesnut was known as a "strict courtroom disciplinarian." He had once served as an assistant state's attorney in Maryland but, as a judge, could be tough on the government in criminal cases. Chesnut earned the unyielding admiration of his New York brethren for undertaking this "most unwelcome duty," as a still-grateful Learned Hand wrote him in 1951.[8]

Jury selection confirmed Chesnut's no-nonsense reputation. To the surprise of veteran court-watchers, it took Chesnut less than two hours to pick a jury from the pool of 250 potential jurors, despite having to individually *voir dire* nearly 150 who asked to be excused. Characteristically for the Southern District, which draws from the Westchester County suburbs along with Manhattan and the Bronx, the twelve jurors selected were a highly educated and professional lot. They included an accountant, a bond trader, a tea importer, two corporate executives, two electrical engineers, three brokers and agents, and two housewives.[9]

* * *

The trial began inauspiciously for Manton. Right after the lunch break, two of Manton's three remaining co-defendants—Forrest W. Davis and William J. Fallon—pled guilty, and indicated they were cooperating with the government. The change of sides by Fallon, Manton's longtime friend and reputed "bagman," hit Manton like a punch in the gut. He "seemed to fall back in his chair in complete amazement" and "the aggressive look in his face vanished momentarily." Even Fallon, his face pale, appeared stunned, consulting uncertainly with his attorney before finally inaudibly mouthing his guilty plea.[10]

Based on press accounts, Manton found it difficult throughout the trial to suppress his emotions. Manton "flushed with anger" and "bit his lip" as Cahill, in his opening statement to the jury, "sketched a sordid picture of bartered justice, solicitation of bribes and legal chicanery almost unheard of in a Federal court." The prosecutor lambasted Manton and his co-conspirators as "merchants of justice" who attempted always "to obtain the most that the traffic would bear."[11]

The first piece of evidence offered by the government was Manton's judicial oath of office. Despite Noonan's offer to stipulate to the contents of the oath, Correa insisted on reading it to the jury to maximize its impact. "I, Martin T. Manton," Correa read, "do solemnly swear that I will administer justice without respect to persons, and do equal right to the poor and to the rich, and that I will faithfully and impartially discharge and perform all the duties incumbent on me as United States Circuit Judge, Second Circuit." A hush fell over the courtroom as Correa paused and then intoned the final phrase, "So help me God." Gimmicky as it may have been, the tactic worked: Manton "bowed his head" and the oath "seemed to impress the jury."[12]

With this opening salvo, Cahill and Correa were off and running with their witnesses, a "rapid fire presentation of sensational accusations" designed to prove beyond a reasonable doubt that Manton had repeatedly and flagrantly violated the oath of office he had sworn.[13] The government crammed forty witnesses, along with more than 125 exhibits, into just seven trial days. Many of the witnesses had bit parts—records custodians, telephone operators, secretaries, and the like—whose testimony took little time and was offered simply to corroborate this detail or that of the government's case. The stars of the show were Reilly, Lotsch, Renkoff, and Hall, who offered first-hand accounts of their corrupt dealings with Manton and Fallon.

Considered in isolation, each of the major witnesses' accounts seemed preposterous, fabricated, unworthy of belief: a senior federal judge could not possibly have done *that*. The *New York Times* called John Lotsch's testimony—which posited that a Second Circuit judge accepted a $10,000 cash bribe in his chambers, and asked a lawyer for one of the parties to draft the opinion for the court—"[a] tale of judicial intrigue which in some of its bizarre elements overshadowed anything ever told in a New York court room." Without corroboration, "Lotsch's recital might have seemed fantastic," the *Times* reporter observed.[14]

Considered collectively, however, the witnesses' stories were mutually reinforcing, synergistically gaining credibility from their strikingly consistent descriptions of Manton and Fallon's modus operandi. The witnesses were completely independent of one another; they came from different states and different socio-economic circles; they had no opportunity to compare notes and collaborate on their stories. Their only common link was that they were, or acted on behalf of, parties to litigation in the Second Circuit that also involved Judge Martin T. Manton. Could *all* of them be lying under oath and telling, in essence, the *same* lie? That possibility ranked as even more far-fetched than their eye-popping tales of judicial skullduggery.

In any event the government offered considerable corroboration for each of the major witnesses' testimony. For example, after Lotsch came off the witness stand, the government called the assistant US attorney in charge of Lotsch's criminal case to authenticate his original trial brief, which Lotsch claimed to have received from Manton, and to testify that he handed it up to Judge Thomas at the beginning of the trial and never got it back. The government also called Theodore Kenyon to corroborate Lotsch's claim that Manton asked him to draft the court's opinion in the General Motors case. And the switchboard operator at Lotsch's law firm identified records showing dozens of calls from Manton and Fallon to Lotsch's office.[15]

The same pattern played out for each of the government's main witnesses. After Reilly's explosive testimony about his February 5, 1939 telephone calls in which Manton asked him to destroy incriminating documents, the government called Evans Case's controller, Nolan, and the bookkeeper who ultimately set the documents afire, both of whom backed Reilly's account. Reilly's wife confirmed that she answered the phone when Manton called Reilly at home that morning. Phone records for the Hotel Madison and the Boston telephone booth confirmed the subsequent calls between Reilly and Manton later in the day.[16]

Similarly, after A.B. Hall's seemingly incredible testimony that Manton had recommended a lawyer to handle the appeal to the Supreme Court from Manton's own ruling, the government brought forth the lawyer, former Third Circuit judge Thomas G. Haight—and for good measure Haight's secretary as well—to confirm that Haight initially met with Hall as a result of a call from Manton's chambers. Hall Brothers' bookkeeper, who accounted for the company's payments to Fallon's Allied Rediscount Corporation, testified that Hall told her the payments were made "to obtain" a favorable decision in the Circuit Court.[17] Even more damning was the copy of the $5,000 note, bearing Manton's indisputably authentic signature, that Hall had secretly retained after surrendering the original to Fallon. Davis, now a government cooperator, corroborated Hall's testimony that the note was made payable to Davis to conceal the connection to Hall.[18]

With Archie Andrews dead, the government had to rely on the irrepressible Morris Renkoff to tell much of the story of how Andrews bribed Manton in the Schick electric razor case. Some documents corroborated Renkoff's testimony; like Hall, Renkoff had hung onto the receipt he got when he took cash from Andrews with which to bribe Manton, "figur[ing] some day maybe I will use it."[19] But the receipt did not have Manton's or even Fallon's name on it, and Renkoff never met or spoke with Manton. Other witnesses called by the government on the Andrews part of the case were no more respectable than Renkoff—such as Renkoff's friends Frank Silinsky, the "betting commissioner" who witnessed Renkoff's interactions with Fallon, and Albert Chaperau, the smooth-talking convicted thief, fraudster, and smuggler who heard Spector boast about having the Schick case overturned on appeal.[20]

The government recognized that the jury might have a hard time taking Renkoff's word. It even tried to bolster Renkoff's claim that he and Andrews bet "two suits of clothes made by the best tailor in New York" on whether their scheme would succeed. "This is the suit," Andrews boasted from the witness stand, holding up a corner of his jacket so the jury could see it. "I didn't have to pay for [it]." On the theory that no amount of corroboration of Renkoff could be too much, the government dragged the tailor, Isaac Rollnick, into court. "Did you at one time make some clothes for Mr. Morris Renkoff?" Cahill asked. Judge Chesnut found the whole effort so odd that he refused to let Rollnick testify.[21]

Yet Renkoff's credibility wound up being inadvertently bolstered in a most unlikely way: through cross-examination by Manton's own counsel, Benjamin Golder. In his direct examination of Renkoff, Correa did not elicit any testimony about Renkoff's own unsuccessful attempt to bribe Manton to overturn Renkoff's criminal conviction; the indictment did not embrace that episode. Apparently unaware and unwarned by his client of the Renkoff bribe attempt, Golder sought on cross-examination to make hay out of the fact that Manton sat on the Second Circuit panel that affirmed Renkoff's conviction.

"You were not able to fix your own case, were you, in Judge Manton's court?" Golder asked with, one imagines, a triumphant air. "Well," Renkoff said, practically goading the unwary lawyer, "you want to know?"

Perhaps feeling he had no choice once Renkoff issued this challenge in front of the jury, Golder took the bait, forgetting the golden rule of cross-examination: Never ask a question to which you do not already know the answer. "I want to know everything, yes," he replied, and shouted, "I can take anything you can give!"[22]

So Renkoff regaled Golder and the jury with his story of how he had, indeed, "tr[ied] to fix my case in Judge Manton's court" by paying $7,500 to Charlie Rich; how Rich assured him the cash was delivered to Manton and would result in a reversal of Renkoff's conviction; and how Rich later refunded the $7,500 to Renkoff after Manton could not persuade the two other judges to go along with him. The genie was out of the bottle now. Judge Chesnut's curiosity was sparked. "Who is this Charlie Rich?" the judge asked Renkoff. "He was the fixer for Judge Manton," Renkoff answered, sending "a gale of laughter" blowing through the courtroom.[23]

Futilely Golder tried to clean up the mess he had made. "He did not fix your case very well, did he?" the lawyer demanded. That just prompted the garrulous Renkoff to relate a conversation after Rich returned the bribe money, when Renkoff "made a big holler about it, that I paid the money for something, and he told me—you want to know what he told me?" Again forgetting the golden rule, Golder said he did want to know. So Renkoff told him: "He says, 'Morris,' he says, 'I will tell you a story how this old man double-crossed my brother.'" At this point, unsure where the witness was going, Judge Chesnut intervened and shut Renkoff down—before Renkoff could tell the jury, and the world, about how an "underworld combination" nearly killed Jack Rich after Manton failed to deliver a promised ruling it had paid $25,000 for.[24]

It was a temporary reprieve. Later Golder probed Renkoff on why he had kept the receipt for the cash bribe rather than destroying it or returning it to Andrews. After Renkoff vaguely replied that he "just felt like" it, Golder insisted: "I want you to tell the jury why you kept this receipt." Renkoff, as if trying to save Golder from his own ineptitude, gave the lawyer one last chance to steer clear of the iceberg: "Do you want it?" True to form, Golder answered: "Why, certainly." Out of Renkoff's mouth poured his tale of Manton's continuing efforts, after Renkoff's appeal failed, first to help procure for Renkoff a suspended sentence from Judge Patterson, and then to engineer a pardon from the Justice Department in Washington. Renkoff explained that he kept the Andrews receipt "as a whip" to pressure Manton to do these things—to interfere with the administration of justice on Renkoff's behalf. If Manton did not do so, Renkoff threatened he "would go to the newspapers and expose the entire proposition."[25]

All this testimony Golder may have been able to dismiss as more tall tales from a professional con man, except for one inconvenient fact: the December 22, 1936 letter Manton wrote on his official letterhead to Justice Department pardon attorney Alexander Holtzoff urging a pardon for Renkoff. When Renkoff mentioned the letter in his long answer to Golder's ill-advised question, Cahill interrupted gleefully to offer to show it to the witness. Introduced into evidence, the letter was passed to Manton, who "got red of face and trembly handed" reading it. Golder could do nothing to dissipate its impact. "The letter speaks for itself," Renkoff and Cahill both said, and so it did: Manton did not dispute that he authored it, and in his own testimony, he simply ignored it, never even attempting to explain it away. Although irrelevant to any of the charges in the indictment, the Holtzoff letter—a defense exhibit—wound up as one of the most devastating documents in the government's case.[26]

Financial records tightened the noose being hung around Manton's neck. Mostly, with exceptions such as the $10,000 in cash that Lotsch delivered to Manton in his chambers, the prosecution's key witnesses had dealt only with Fallon when negotiating the terms of bribes and delivering the bribe money. Logically enough, Manton's defense centered around denying knowledge of Fallon's activities and claiming Fallon acted to enrich himself, a defense that gained some traction by Cahill's decision to forgo calling Fallon as a witness. But the more proof that the money wound up in Manton's coffers, the more implausible Manton's "blame Fallon" defense became.

Mustering that proof in admissible form presented an obstacle for the government. Forensic accounting was still in its infancy, and courts were just getting accustomed to dealing with modern banking records. Banks in New York recently had begun to make photostatic reproductions of checks on "Recordak" machines. FBI agents gathered reams of

"Recordaks" from the banks that housed accounts for Manton, Fallon, and their co-conspirators. But the admissibility of these records in judicial proceedings was an unsettled legal question. No reported federal decision sanctioned the use of Recordaks; three years after Manton's trial, the Supreme Court of Illinois held them inadmissible under the so-called best evidence rule, which generally allows only the original version of a document to be introduced into evidence.[27] In many if not most cases, Cahill's team lacked the original checks.

Cahill's heart must have skipped a beat when he first attempted to introduce Recordaks during Manton's trial. "I am not familiar with these Recordaks," Judge Chesnut said, adding that so far as he knew, they were not admissible in the Fourth Circuit where he normally sat. But Cahill ultimately prevailed, and the Recordaks proved indispensable. Reilly, for instance, was able to identify the Recordak images of checks he had given to Fallon at the Biltmore Hotel and subsequently destroyed. FBI agents trained as accountants spent hours on the stand testifying about their analysis of the Recordaks and other financial records. They traced the flow of bribe funds from, for example, Hall to Fallon's Allied Rediscount Corporation to Manton's Forest Hills Terrace Corporation, and from Andrews to Spector to the Forest Hills Terrace Corporation and to Marie Schmalz, Manton's secretary. It was a maze of numbers and dates and transactions and accounts. But two members of the jury with accounting backgrounds "seemed to be following with ease."[28]

Everything seemed to be falling in place nicely for Cahill, personally as well as professionally. At one point reporters puzzled over the contents of a series of notes that aides passed up to the US attorney, who read them with a serious look. But the mysterious messages cloaked no undisclosed weakness in the prosecution's case. They were progress reports on Cahill's wife, Grace, in labor with the couple's first child. When the trial adjourned for the day, Cahill dashed from the courtroom and leapt into a taxi, racing to Doctors Hospital on the Upper East Side, where he arrived to meet his new daughter, born five minutes earlier.[29]

The moment seemed to speak to a generational truth that the Manton trial symbolized. Superficially, Cahill and Manton shared much in common: Both were born into humble Irish-American families in the outer boroughs of Manhattan, both worked their way through Ivy League law schools, both ascended to the highest strata of the Manhattan legal community, both were Democrats in their politics, both were financially ambitious and achieved great wealth. But they were born a quarter of a century apart, and that made a world of difference. Manton reached professional maturity in a legal culture dominated by Tammany Hall, whose values he imbibed and now embodied. Cahill represented a new generation of lawyers eager to purge New York of the corruption that Tammany and Manton personified. In generational terms, Cahill's slaying of Manton had an Oedipal touch to it.

* * *

For Manton and his lawyers, the trial was one long tribulation. Even when Noonan and Golder's cross-examinations did not end in disaster, as with Renkoff, they did not put much of a dent in the credibility of the Government's witnesses. Noonan's performance was impaired by the untimely reemergence of a painful stomach ulcer. During Lotsch's testimony, the agony drove Noonan to the verge of collapse, his face white and beaded with perspiration, moaning for a brief recess. The lawyer missed two trial days while recuperating.[30]

Noonan and Golder also had to contend with their client, "the chief counsel of his own defense, though there were seven lawyers at his table." Scorn and anger creased Manton's face as the government's witnesses testified. If his lawyers remained silent in the face of a particular question or exhibit their client did not like, Manton prodded them to get on their feet and object.[31] Given that his seat at counsel table abutted the jury box, Manton's visible imperiousness perhaps did not best position him to fall within the 5 percent of FBI-investigated federal trials that ended in acquittal.

Manton's foul mood was on display outside the courthouse as well. Shielding Eva from a gaggle of photographers during a lunch recess, Manton first fled with her toward a subway entrance and then stopped, turned, and shook a fist at the pursuing cameramen. He threatened to have them arrested and advanced toward them menacingly. When one retreating photographer accidently dropped an unused flashbulb, Manton crushed it to pieces underneath his foot, while the other photographers present snapped pictures of him.[32]

After another delay occasioned by Noonan's nettlesome ulcer, Manton's defense case began with a parade of high-profile character witnesses. Five of the witnesses were steeped in Democratic politics and government: former New York governor Al Smith, former US solicitor general John W. Davis, former New York congressman John J. O'Connor, former New York state court judge Alfred J. Talley, and the current head of the New York City Board of Transportation, John H. Delaney (Manton's former business partner). All were on the downslopes of their careers; Smith, Davis, and Delaney ranged in age from sixty-five to sixty-eight, Talley was sixty-one, and O'Connor, though a comparatively youthful fifty-three, had just experienced the end of his political career, a casualty of FDR's purge of disloyal Democrats in the 1938 mid-term elections.[33]

Others whose testimony Manton solicited thought better about publicly vouching for the disgraced jurist. Despite working behind the scenes to thwart Manton's Supreme Court ambitions, C. C. Burlingham remained friends with Manton on the surface, and when the judge resigned Burlingham wrote him a letter expressing sympathy for his situation. But when Marie Schmalz called to ask if the then-eighty-year-old dean of the New York bar would serve as a character witness, Burlingham—who had earlier confided to Frankfurter, "I wouldn't believe Manton under oath"—turned her down. "You can imagine my answer," Burlingham drolly reported to Robert Jackson in a post-trial letter, which also registered Burlingham's amazement that men like John Davis could swear that Manton had a good reputation.[34]

Louis H. Pink, New York's superintendent of insurance, laid bare his conflicting emotions and calculations in a letter seeking Governor Herbert H. Lehman's advice about whether he should appear as a character witness. Pink, who had practiced law in Brooklyn at the same time as Manton, told Lehman he had known Manton "fairly well for a great many years, and never suspected that he was dishonest," adding the caveat that "I have, of course, like everyone else, known that he was fooling around with a great many business deals which it is hardly wise for a Judge to do." Pink believed he possessed sufficient "courage to do an unpopular thing if it is right" and "hate[d] to refuse at a time like this when everyone is turning against him." And "yet," Pink added, "it does seem to me that it would be unwise to do it and would be a disservice to the Department as well as to me personally." Not surprisingly, Pink did not testify.[35]

Manton's other character witnesses included two top businessmen, Emmett McCormick of the Moore-McCormick steamship lines and Raoul E. Desvernines, president of the Crucible Steel Company, along with the Roman Catholic counselor at Columbia University. All the witnesses were asked two questions: What is Judge Manton's reputation for truthfulness and veracity? What is Judge Manton's reputation for integrity and honesty and as a law-abiding citizen? Each answered in the affirmative with varying superlatives, such as "one of the best," "the very best," "excellent," "above reproach," "unquestioned," and Davis's more muted "very good."[36]

Cahill felt, or at least feigned, indifference, asking none of the witnesses a single question on cross-examination. In his closing statement to the jury, Cahill brushed the testimony aside by noting that the witnesses only praised Manton's "reputation" and not his "character." There was a "sharp distinction" between the two, he explained: "reputation is what others think you are—character is what you truly are." Still, the star power of Smith and Davis, two former Democratic presidential nominees, energized the courtroom. Manton grinned with satisfaction and sat back in his chair projecting, for perhaps the first time during the trial, an air of confidence.[37]

Manton's defense case featured another, gloomier procession of witnesses: his former colleagues on the Second Circuit, Learned Hand, Gus Hand, Thomas Swan, and Harrie Chase. None wanted to be there; Learned Hand was so "agitated" that he feared he had failed to show proper courtesy to Judge Chesnut as he left the stand.[38] But none of them had a choice: Manton had subpoenaed them. One by one, the judges testified that during the conferences in the cases in question, they did not observe anything that led them to believe that Manton was conferring and deciding the case other than "according to his oath of office and the dictates of his conscience."[39] Cahill again chose not to cross-examine.

In closing argument, he would call to the jury's attention the fact that, despite the judges' many years of professional association with Manton, "not one of them was asked to give testimony as to his character."[40]

The role Manton's brethren played as defense witnesses—for a man they reviled—left a lasting psychological scar. They "remembered that day as a low point in their lives as well as in the life of the court," according to a later Second Circuit judge, James L. Oakes.[41] Nearly three decades later, at a committee hearing, a senator asked the then–chief judge of the Second Circuit, J. Edward Lumbard, about the "judicial 'esprit de corps'" that prompted Manton's former colleagues to testify "as character witnesses in his behalf." Judge Lumbard immediately corrected this mistaken characterization ("Well, Senator, it is not my recollection that they testified as character witnesses"), explaining he felt duty-bound "to protect and preserve the memory of Learned Hand and Thomas Swan and Augustus Hand to that extent."[42]

Manton also presented testimony, from a deputy clerk in the Southern District's clerk office, that the only judge free to accept a criminal case on March 5, 1936, when Lotsch's trial began, was Judge Thomas and that he was assigned to the Lotsch case by Chief Judge Knox. This attempt to disconnect Manton from Thomas's involvement in the Lotsch case fizzled, however, when Cahill established on cross-examination that the deputy clerk was relying on his minutes from March 5 and that it was possible Thomas had been assigned to the Lotsch case before then by another judge.[43]

Manton's longtime secretary, Marie Schmalz, testified for her boss. Manton was the only boss Schmalz had ever known. She started working for him in 1905, when she was just seventeen, and continued to serve as his secretary after he stepped down from the bench. Her loyalty to him showed, and sapped her credibility. Schmalz admitted routing loans from Spector to Forest Hills Terrace Corporation through her own personal bank account in order to circumvent a court order against the company's assets obtained by a judgment creditor. A puzzled Judge Chesnut asked if she felt free to do that under the terms of the injunction, to which Schmalz replied pragmatically that if she had put the money in a Forest Hills account, the judgment creditor would have attached it. (In his testimony, Manton took the position that the injunction applied only to assets held by Forest Hills when the injunction was issued, and not to subsequently acquired assets. An unpersuaded Judge Chesnut commented, "I do not take that view of the matter.")[44]

Cahill was unsparing in his cross-examination but Schmalz, glaring back underneath her large straw hat, was not intimidated. "Nearly every question developed into an altercation, as Miss Schmalz apparently assumed the attitude that she was being harassed and gave her answers in biting, caustic tones."[45] When Schmalz testified that Manton could not have known she had called Thomas Haight's office to make an appointment for Hall because "Judge Manton wasn't in town at that time," Cahill pressed her if she was saying that she never communicated with Manton when he was out of town. "Why should I?" Schmalz retorted, before finally acknowledging that "certainly" she sometimes did precisely that because, after all, "I was his secretary."[46]

Schmalz testified that it was Fallon, not Manton, who asked her to call Haight's office to make an appointment for Hall. Cahill punctured the plausibility of that testimony by showing that just two weeks earlier, Schmalz told the grand jury that she "certainly did not" know of any connection Haight had to the Hall case. She claimed her recollection had since been refreshed by seeing a letter written to her by Haight following the call. But Haight's letter specifically said that "the Judge had recommended" him to Hall, undermining Schmalz's claim that Manton knew nothing about it.[47]

Schmalz also struggled to defend her claim that of the $22,000 that Spector had "loaned" Forest Hills in early 1937, all but about $4,000 had been repaid. She testified that the repayments were made from her personal account. But as Cahill showed during cross-examination, her account records reflected payments to Spector totaling only $3,950, essentially the mirror opposite of what Schmalz claimed. Moreover, those payments did not begin until October 1938, well after Spector had been contacted by Dewey's investigators. Schmalz then claimed that Manton had made other repayments himself but could cite no proof. "I will refer to that when Judge Manton gets on the stand," Noonan promised Judge Chesnut. But he never did.[48]

According to press reports, Noonan and Golder did not want Manton to take the stand at all. They would have limited the defense case to the character witnesses and the Second Circuit judges and argued to the jury that the government failed to prove Manton's guilt beyond a reasonable doubt.[49] That is a common strategy of defense lawyers, especially when they fear their client will not be liked, or believed, by the jury. But under the law, it is not up to the lawyer to decide whether or not the defendant in a criminal case testifies; the decision belongs to the client. In this case, Noonan and Golder's client decided to trust his own judgment over that of his lawyers.

* * *

On Thursday afternoon, June 1, after Marie Schmalz came down from the witness stand, her boss rose from his seat at counsel table to take her place. The packed courtroom crackled with anticipation, as if the opening bell for a heavyweight prizefight had just rung. Eva, seated in the front row with Manton's two children, offered moral support to her husband. Fans of Cahill were also present. His Georgia-born wife, Grace, had been part of the Pickens Sisters, a popular singing group in the early 1930s. Two of her sisters now added a "bright touch of color" to the courtroom, "rooting in a big way for Cahill, their brother-in-law." As Manton settled into the witness chair, Judge Chesnut turned his own high-backed chair to face the witness and fixed his gaze on the former judge.[50]

Armed with a large black binder stuffed with documents he brought up to the witness stand, Manton assumed a professorial air. Wearing a blue serge suit with polka-dot tie, and peering down through his pince-nez glasses with an expression that some reporters found "benign" and others "ruggedly severe," the former judge testified as if he were "explaining complicated matters to a youthful class." As Noonan led him through each of the six cases in question, Manton issued curt, unequivocal, and indignant denials of any and all wrongdoing. Did Fallon ever attempt to influence him in connection with the Art Metal case? "He certainly did not. . . . He never mentioned [the case] in any manner, shape or form." Did Fallon ever speak to him about the Hall case? "He never spoke to me." Did he know Fallon was getting money from Hall?

"I certainly did not." He also swore he "never" talked to Fallon or Spector about the Schick case and never knew Spector was acquainted with Andrews.[51]

Did he ever receive a draft opinion from Lotsch in the Electric Auto-Lite case? "No, I did not." Had he ever received a draft opinion from a lawyer in any case? "No, I certainly did not." Nothing in Lotsch's testimony about his criminal case before Judge Thomas was true. Manton "never" discussed the case with Lotsch: he "never" had possession of the government's trial brief or gave it to Lotsch; he "would [not]" and "did not" try to communicate with Thomas about Lotsch's case; he "did not" have a ginger ale with Lotsch in Grand Central Station. When asked about Lotsch's claim to have delivered cash to Manton's chambers, Manton felt compelled to add a rhetorical flourish to his forceful denial: "He did not. If he had he would have gone out on the tip of my toe."[52]

Where Manton had no choice but to admit dealings with the government's witnesses, he presented a sanitized version that frequently stretched the bounds of plausibility. For example, Manton admitted knowing Lotsch and that Lotsch helped secure loans for his businesses from Fort Greene Bank. Lotsch arranged one $10,000 loan the month before he argued the appeal in the Electric Auto-Lite case, and another $15,000 loan the month after. Yet Manton testified he had "forgotten" all about Lotsch's involvement in the case. In any event, he assured the jury, the loans "of course" had no influence on his decision-making.[53]

In light of the government's phone records, Manton could not deny calling Reilly on February 5, 1939 from the lobby of the Savoy-Plaza hotel. But he claimed he did so merely to ask what Reilly thought the purpose of the government's investigation was and that it was Reilly, not he, who raised the subject of Fallon's having been on the Art Metal payroll. Manton also admitted that his son David bought chicks from Hall Brothers and that Manton himself had called Hall to ask for help with David's chicken farm, but he claimed that this was all David's idea and he "didn't pay much attention to it."[54]

Noonan ended his direct examination by asking Manton whether, in the six cases that were the subject of the indictment, Manton decided them based solely on the merits and the law and the dictates of his own conscience. "As best I was capable of deciding them," Manton replied. "I certainly was not moved by any other consideration but my conscientious judgment."[55]

* * *

Cahill rose for what would be a donnybrook of a cross-examination. "It was like a tussle between two boxers," the *Daily News* reported. "Manton, the older, wiser, steeled against all attacks; Cahill, younger, more lithe and agile, circling in readiness for a knockout."[56] As a former judge Manton was used to getting his way in a courtroom. Cahill was equally determined to keep him in harness. This would be a head-on collision between two iron wills.

The first words out of Cahill's mouth spewed provocation. "Now, Mr. Witness," Cahill began—a jarring and very much intentional contrast to "Judge Manton," the form of address used by Noonan during direct examination. By the third time Cahill did this, Manton could no longer bear the slight:

Q: Now, let us turn to the question of the indebtedness, Mr. Witness—

A: Mr. Manton.

Cahill again began his question, in the same way, and Manton again interjected: "Mr. Manton." Ignoring him, Cahill continued and completed his question. Cahill did not call Manton "Mr. Witness" again, but neither did he refer to him as "Judge Manton." The tactic tracked one of Lawyer Manton's own cross-examination tips: "If a man is vain, try to destroy that vanity, and he will lose his self-composure."[57]

Like most cross-examiners, Cahill framed his questions to call for a yes or no response. Time and again, instead of answering directly, Manton responded with a speech or explanation of some sort, sometimes before Cahill had even finished putting the question. Or he would prompt Noonan to object ("Any objection?" he asked of Noonan at one point) or offer his own objection (e.g., "I don't see how that helps the jury," or "Is that a question?"). As promptly as he could, Cahill would cut Manton off. "No; if you please, just answer my questions," Cahill instructed. "I will conduct the examination."[58]

As Manton's obstreperousness persisted, Cahill sought help from the only actual judge in the courtroom. Exasperated from sparring with the witness ("Q: That is not what I am asking you. A: That is exactly what you are."), Cahill appealed to Judge Chesnut. "That is not what I am asking him, if your Honor please." Chesnut responded neutrally: "Very well." But when Manton went off on another tangent two questions later, Chesnut intervened:

> The Court: Well, you see, Judge Manton, Mr. Cahill is attempting to ask you—
>
> Mr. Cahill: I would like him to get an instruction on the point, your Honor.
>
> The Court: It is perhaps natural enough that you know about it, but I think you should try not to go beyond the question.
>
> The Witness: I do not see the competency of it all.

Which prompted Cahill to remark: "Now, is the witness sitting as the judge in the court?"[59]

Moments later, another attempt by Manton to reclaim the role of judge—"Now," he scolded Cahill, "will you just contain yourself for a moment and let me finish"—drew another rebuke from Judge Chesnut:

> The Court: Of course, I appreciate, Judge Manton, that this is your personal case and from that you may have some feeling. I am going to ask you—
>
> The Witness: Pardon me.
>
> The Court: I do not think it will be appropriate for you to undertake yourself to admonish the United States Attorney.[60]

Cahill had succeeded in one of the cross-examiner's main missions: getting under the witness's skin. Or as Lawyer Manton put it, in describing the art of cross-examination, "The madder your witness gets the better it is for you." Reporters, and no doubt the jurors, took notice. "Manton was contemptuous of Cahill. That much was obvious." In contrast to the confidence he projected during direct examination, Manton looked "worried" and sounded "bitter" and "derisive" under Cahill's questioning. Manton's face "became wrinkled and his mouth twisted" as he sought "to squirm off the hook of pointed questions."[61]

Substantively, Cahill spent surprisingly little time on the six cases underlying the charges against Manton. He focused instead on trying to destroy Manton's credibility. His chief weapon was Manton's testimony at his deposition by attorneys for the court-appointed examiner for the Bank of the United States. In that deposition, Manton swore that his real estate holdings were all underwater, that his stock interests in National Cellulose and his other businesses had no value, that he had minimal assets overall, and that his liabilities exceeded those assets by more than $500,000 and closer to $750,000. The deposition took place in June 1934. On the basis of Manton's description of his financial condition, the examiner agreed later that month to allow Manton to settle his debt of some $125,000 to the Bank of the United States for $23,500, about twenty cents on the dollar. Yet in May 1935, when he applied for a loan to Fort Greene Bank, Manton provided the bank a letter "certify[ing]" that his net worth was "upwards of $750,000." That amounted to a swing in Manton's net worth of $1.25 million to $1.5 million—the equivalent of more than $25 million in today's dollars—in just eleven months.[62]

In a sense, this meant nothing insofar as the charges against Manton were concerned. None of the funds that flowed to him from the six cases at issue were received between June 1934 and May 1935. Juxtaposed together, however, Manton's testimony at his deposition and his certification to Fort Greene Bank reinforced the government's case in multiple key respects. It showed that Manton had been in dire financial straits, providing the incentive for him to abuse his power; it showed that he engaged in all sorts of financial machinations peculiar for a federal judge;

and, most importantly, it showed that he was a liar, willing to say whatever it took, even under oath, to suit his own interests.

Vainly Manton tried to explain away the wild disparity by pointing to transactions during the eleven-month interval. For example, he had entered into a contract to sell the Alamac Hotel for $400,000 above its mortgage indebtedness. But that only gave Cahill an opportunity to highlight Manton's dishonesty by forcing him to acknowledge that negotiations for the sale of the Alamac at this price were underway at the very same time he testified in his deposition that the stock of the Camala Corporation, which owned the Alamac, was "worthless." Manton likewise only dug himself deeper when he volunteered that his settlement with the Bank of the United States was "approved by the court." His testimony allowed Cahill to show that the judge who provided that approval—New York State Supreme Court justice Kenneth O'Brien— also served as a director of Manton's Alamac Esplanade Corporation.[63]

Cahill's cross-examination also brought to light all kinds of strange and sordid financial dealings that went beyond the six cases in question. On the strength of bank records, Cahill established that Manton had received cash loans totaling roughly $165,000—more than $3 million in today's dollars—over a roughly two-year period in the mid-1930s. This fountain of cash flowed from various sources: $40,000 came from Samuel Ungerleider, the Wall Street broker; the two $25,000 loans from Nat Levy, the Brooklyn brewer; roughly $25,000 from William Backman, connected to a different brewery, Kips Bay; $20,000 from Manton's business partner James Sullivan; $15,000 from Saul and Morrie Weingarten, owners of a shoe store in Brooklyn; $10,000 from Barron Collier, an advertising man who had a contract with the Interborough; $6,000 from Robert Newman, a young man engaged in the theatrical business.[64]

According to Manton, he did not ask for cash. For unknown reasons, the lenders preferred it; it was "a matter of [their] convenience, not mine."[65] In most if not all instances, the cash was delivered to Manton in his chambers and stashed in his safe until he needed to take it out for use in some other transaction.

The vision of a stream of visitors walking into a federal judge's chambers bearing bundles of cash well in excess of the average

American's—and the average federal judge's—annual salary piqued Judge Chesnut's interest:

> The Court: Are you in the habit of keeping large sums of cash like that in your chambers for two or three days?
>
> The Witness: Yes; for two or three days.
>
> The Court: What kind of a safe do you have?
>
> The Witness: A very substantial safe, we did have.[66]

Manton's safe, one press account noted, proved "as provocative to the imagination as the 'wonderful tin box' of ex-Sheriff Tom Farley during the Seabury investigation of 1931."[67]

Thanks to Manton's decision to testify, Cahill also was able to put before the jury other malodorous transactions connected to Manton's official duties, even though they were not part of the charges in the case. Thus Cahill cross-examined Manton about John McGrath's $12,000 loan to Manton when he was the Prudence trustee; Thomas Murray's $22,500 purchase of Forest Hills stock shortly before Manton named him an Interborough receiver; Harry Warner's $50,000 in loans when his company's patent suit was pending before Manton; and, most sensationally of all (if in highly abbreviated form), the $250,000 loan from Lord & Thomas to James Sullivan, the majority of which found its way into companies controlled by Manton.[68]

Interrogating Manton about the Warner loans at the tail end of his cross-examination, Cahill could not resist one last dig at the man with whom he had been locked in verbal combat for hours. The prosecutor sarcastically asked Manton whether, when he went to Warner to ask for a loan, Warner said to him: "You should go out of here on the tip of my boot. You are one of the judges sitting in the case that has been argued involving me and it has not yet been decided?" When Noonan objected, Cahill retorted that he was only using the same expression Manton had used the day before. Judge Chesnut sustained the objection, but Cahill had already made his point.[69]

* * *

Cahill finished carving up Manton late in the day on Friday of the second week of trial. In those days, that did not bring the trial week to a close. The six-day workweek, although it fell increasingly out of vogue during the Depression, still prevailed in much of the workplace, including the federal government. Hence the parties, the jurors, the press, and a horde of spectators found themselves back in Room 110 before Judge Chesnut on Saturday, June 3 for closing arguments.[70]

The packed courtroom included a number of friends and relatives of the main defendant. Eva, who faithfully attended the trial, sometimes over her husband's objections, took a seat in the front row along with their two children, David and Catherine. David had loyally remained at his father's side for the entire trial. Catherine had other demands on her time, having graduated two days before from Marymount College, though she opted to skip the graduation ceremony while her father was in the public spotlight. Manton came and sat beside his family briefly during a recess and then returned to counsel table for Noonan's summation.[71]

Manton looked on hopefully as Noonan, pounding the rail of the jury box for emphasis, attacked Fallon as a "twentieth century Judas" and "vile betrayer" who fraudulently misused Manton's name to line his own pockets. The prosecution, Noonan argued, had not proven that Manton knew what Fallon was up to. "If what the government says is true," he argued, "why didn't they call Fallon to testify?" Cahill repeatedly objected that Noonan was misstating the record. After Chesnut overruled one such objection, applause burst out from Manton's boosters in the audience.[72]

And then, literally in the middle of his summation, Noonan's ulcer intervened yet again. All color drained from the lawyer's fleshy face. He took a sip of water, resumed speaking for a few moments, then fell back from the jury rail, groping for a place to sit down. "I shall have to rest, Your Honor," Noonan muttered as he collapsed into a chair, clutching his stomach. "I can go no further at this time and someone else will have to finish for me." He was taken to a first-aid room in the courthouse.[73]

It fell to an ill-prepared Golder to deliver the second hour of Manton's closing statement, an unenviable task for a lawyer in any case, let alone one on the front pages of newspapers nationwide. Golder understandably "devoted himself more to oratory than the record," continuing the general assault on Fallon and labeling Lotsch, Renkoff, Silinsky, and Chaperau "the Four Horsemen of Viciousness" whose word could not be trusted. The jury "looked a little uncomfortable" when tears crept into Golder's voice as he made his emotional plea for his client.[74]

Now it was Cahill's turn. He began on a mildly tacky note, alluding to two recent submarine accidents that killed more than one hundred American and British sailors gearing up to face the growing menace of Nazism. "It is your duty in this case to protect democracy from the insidiousness of internal corruption," Cahill told the jury, "and in that capacity you are heroes as great as are the naval heroes who are necessary to protect this democracy from external violence." That remark likely would be considered improper prosecutorial summation today, as would Cahill's personal vouching for the credibility of the government witnesses so bitterly attacked in the defense summations. Characterizing the defense arguments as an attempt "to try the prosecutor"—an "old courtroom dodge of lawyers who have no other defense"—Cahill assured the jury that "I will not put on the witness stand co-defendants or convicts whose testimony I have not had an opportunity to scrutinize carefully, and those whose statements cannot be corroborated to the hilt."[75]

Cahill danced around the issue of why he had not called Fallon as a witness. "I don't know whether Fallon pleaded guilty through a genuine desire to help the government or from some other reason," Cahill told the jury. "I, too, fear Greeks bearing gifts. Perhaps Fallon was an attempt to drag a wooden horse into this courtroom."[76] Never-before-revealed FBI interview memos show that Fallon indeed spoke with the government after his guilty plea and directly implicated Manton. He admitted interceding with Manton on behalf of Reilly, Hall, and Renkoff and receiving money from all three for Manton's benefit and with Manton's knowledge—contrary to Manton's sworn testimony. Yet in other respects, Fallon minimized his and Manton's involvement, and his professed recollection of these incidents was weak, highly variable, and often at odds with other evidence. It is not surprising that Cahill did not want to use such a shaky witness.[77]

Cahill did not need to. He had plenty of ammunition to work with, and he was too good of a courtroom marksman to miss his target. The US attorney pilloried Manton for lacking the courage to resist temptation in the wake of the 1929 crash. "Here was a man with a fortune, with honors, a man who had been elevated by his own people to a position above them, a man to whom it was given the right and authority to judge his fellow-men," Cahill said. "And he could not control his greed for money. He could not lay aside his business and devote himself to the judicial duties given him."[78]

The prosecutor blasted the conspiracy to sell justice as "the greatest blackmail scheme ever devised." Litigants were told they had to pay up, and if they declined, the same opportunity would be given the other side to buy a favorable decision. "Blackmail was emanating from the Federal courthouse. There was no more honor among this group than there would be among a group of common thieves."[79]

Cahill repeatedly dramatized the foulness of Manton's deeds by emphasizing they took place inside the courthouse. In this way, the magisterial courthouse itself became a kind of character witness for the prosecution, symbolizing the values of probity and purity and disinterestedness that Manton had besmirched. Thus Cahill invoked the specter of "brokers and brewers and moneylenders lugging cash into the judge's chambers." He railed against Manton's "most monstrous [plot]" flourishing "within the walls of this courthouse." Manton's perfidy had altered the courthouse's very character. "It became, instead of a courthouse, a counting house."[80]

It was now after 5:00 p.m., but Judge Chesnut was not about to send the jury and the parties home. Instead he proceeded over the next hour and a half to deliver his instructions to the jury. At the conclusion of his charge, Judge Chesnut emphasized the historic importance of the jury's task:

The charge of conspiracy to sell justice made against an Appellate Federal Judge is hitherto unprecedented in the 150 years of the federal judiciary. The public rightly expects and demands that all its federal judges shall be independent, impartial, and, above all, scrupulously honest. Our courts are the resort for the peaceable settlement of personal controversies, and it is of vital importance in the functioning of our Government that the confidence of the public in the integrity of its courts be not impaired.[81]

By 7:15 p.m., the charge was finished and the jury retired for its deliberations. Less than four hours later, a rap on the jury room door signaled a verdict had been reached. Yet even that relatively short interval considerably overstates the amount of time the jurors spent considering Manton's guilt. After leaving the courtroom, the jury first ate dinner and did not begin deliberating until about 8:30 p.m. At 9:35 p.m., the jury sent out a note—the only note of its deliberations—focused solely on the Schick razor case and Spector's role. It thus seems likely that the jury took little more than an hour to decide Manton's fate.[82]

Around 11:15 p.m., with all interested persons reassembled in the courtroom, the court clerk asked the foreman, an engineer from the Bronx, for the jury's verdict. In an unsteady voice, the foreman said: "We find the defendant Manton guilty as charged in the indictment." Manton's son David began audibly sobbing. The prosecution team, which had been joined for the occasion by FBI Director Hoover, silently rejoiced. The same verdict of guilty was announced as to Spector. The clerk polled the rest of the jurors to confirm that they agreed. As if to compensate for the foreman's nervousness, a chorus of "We do" rang out strong and clear.[83]

The *New York Times* noted that in most criminal cases, jurors bringing in a guilty verdict avoid eye contact with the defendant, but Manton's jurors did not. As the jurors filed back into the courtroom before announcing their verdict, several of them stared hard at Manton and one flashed him a "hard smile that was half a smirk." Some jurors continued to stare down Manton after the verdict. Even after being discharged by the judge, one juror looked back over his shoulder to cast a final long glance. Manton did not return the jurors' gazes.[84]

After the government agreed to a continuation of bail, Manton stood up, turned, and walked toward the exit, past his son and other well-wishers who reached out with their hands to console him. If he felt their touch he did not show it. Shoulders drooped, he seemed in shock, "like an automaton or a sleep-walker."[85] And then he was gone from the courthouse he once ruled, out on the tip of the jury's toe.

EPILOGUE

"O tempora! O mores!,"[1] a despairing C. C. Burlingham wrote Robert Jackson, now solicitor general of the United States, two days after the verdict. "The purgation was necessary and has been thoroughly done by Cahill; but what a terrible injury Manton has done our beloved Federal Courts!"[2]

The guilty verdict against Manton had "come as a profound shock to the whole country," wrote the *New York Times*. "It is not difficult to understand the reluctance of most citizens to accept his guilt as fact." That was true even for a savvy citizen-lawyer such as Burlingham, who had long distrusted Manton. "For ten years I have never hesitated to say that Manton was devoid of moral sense," Burlingham told Jackson. Nonetheless, "we did not think he had committed crimes, or if he had could be found out," Burlingham admitted, speaking for himself and like-minded New York lawyers.[3]

Like Burlingham, some editorialists rued the damage Manton had wrought. "Nothing could strike a more deadly blow at the foundations of our democracy," said the *Times*. "The very concept of governance by laws and not men," added the *Herald Tribune*, rests upon "the uprightness of the judge," and "if the judge is dishonest, the whole fabric must ultimately fall to pieces." Others saw a silver lining. Manton's conviction was "a reason for feeling renewed confidence in the dependability of the machinery of justice" and a "welcome assurance that exalted judicial office affords no protective covering for corrupt practices," in the words of the *Washington Post*. Praise was heaped on Attorney General Murphy and his "hard-hitting young prosecutor," Cahill, for a "most masterful prosecution."[4]

A few (not many) took note that Manton did not act alone—that "two parties are required to consummate" a bribe, making "the bribe-giver . . . just as guilty as the bribe-taker." There also was criticism of the lawyers who helped buy off Manton and who "doubtless operated on the theory of the gangster-ridden 1920s that it is easier to deal with corruption in power than to attempt exposure and be broken for it."[5]

All agreed on the "villainy" of Manton, a "scoundrel" whose "monstrous" offense was "odious in every detail" and who "degraded" himself "as a man and as a judicial officer" by soiling his judicial robe "in the mud of bribe-taking." Not surprisingly, the *World-Telegram* was particularly scathing. "The verdict calls for no pity. There were no extenuating circumstances." Even the maximum sentence could not "adequately fit the heinous, immeasurable wrong this high judge did to justice." Burt Heath later wrote that Manton "is the only crook to whose downfall I have contributed for whom I have never felt the slightest twinge of pity, in the moment of his misfortune and after he had been emasculated of his potency for evil."[6]

Perhaps the blow that hit the hardest, if Manton read it, was delivered by his hometown paper. Years before, the Sayville-based *Suffolk County News* hailed Manton's appointment to the federal bench as "a source of pride to his townsmen," and later, in 1930, extolled him as "our most distinguished citizen." Now it condemned Manton's judicial conduct as setting "a new low mark in American history" which justified bestowing on him the "dubious distinction" the FBI usually reserved for other types of criminals: "Public Enemy No. 1."[7]

* * *

Public Enemy No. 1, dressed in black, arrived back at the Foley Square Courthouse two weeks later on June 20 for sentencing. First Judge Chesnut had to dispose of the defense's motion to set aside the jury's verdict and order a new trial. James Noonan, his ulcer tamed, created a stir when he announced that he would not be arguing the new trial motion—his client would. Rising to deliver the final oral argument of his career, Manton adjusted his glasses, looked down, and proceeded to read a fifteen-page prepared statement, his mouth "twisted in suppressed bitterness."[8]

Manton began with a personal and emotional plea, proclaiming his "innocence of any legal or moral wrongdoing in connection with this charge." His conviction was "tantamount to a death sentence"; his reputation had been "destroyed by a hostile press"; his life was "shattered." "It matters little what becomes of my poor body during the years I have left in life," he continued, "but it matters what is done here in the name of the law, and how disgrace is visited upon a loyal judiciary in the name of justice." From this paroxysm of self-pity Manton moved on to more lawyerly arguments, portions of which, according to the *Times*, sounded "like a judicial opinion." He allocated all the blame to Fallon, heaped scorn on Lotsch's "preposterous" testimony, and sharply criticized Judge Chesnut's conduct of the trial. With rare exceptions Manton referred to himself in the third person as "Manton" or "Judge Manton" (e.g., "there is no evidence of a conspiracy between Fallon and Manton").[9]

Manton did not shy away from technical legal arguments that in effect assumed his guilt. He contended that the proof at trial showed, at best, six separate conspiracies rather than the one with which he was charged. He also argued that the evidence "shows no action other than giving and accepting bribes" and therefore he should have been charged with "bribery pure and simple" and not with conspiracy. Strangest of all was Manton's assertion that, as a judge, he could not be charged with obstructing justice in a case before him: "A judge can no more be guilty of obstructing justice in his own court than he can be guilty of contempt of his own court."[10]

Judge Chesnut allowed Manton to go on in this manner uninterrupted for some forty minutes. "Like a schoolmaster lecturing a pupil," Manton closed on a condescending note, citing his "twenty-two years of judicial service" that had trained him "to discover errors in the district court." Viewing the record "carefully and impersonally," Manton could assure Chesnut that many such errors took place during Manton's trial. Judge Chesnut was unmoved. "I have not heard this morning any new points that had not heretofore been considered," he said coldly. The motion for a new trial was denied.[11]

Surprising no one, Chesnut then gave Manton the maximum sentence possible: two years in prison and a $10,000 fine. Now it was the district judge's turn to lecture the former circuit judge, delivering a "tongue-lashing" with the significant difference that Chesnut, unlike Manton, spoke with judicial authority. "All public offices are a public trust, but a judicial office is more—it is a sacred trust," said Chesnut, reading from his own prepared remarks, his voice quivering with indignation. Manton betrayed that trust and engaged in conduct "abhorrent to our conception of public justice" that "has shocked the public generally, and particularly the bench and bar of this country." One had to go back more than three hundred years in the history of Anglo-American jurisprudence to find a parallel: the case of Francis Bacon, Lord Chancellor of England, who, after falling into debt, accepted gifts from litigants and was convicted of corruption and removed from office.[12]

Even the maximum sentence, Judge Chesnut noted, "may seem inadequate to some people," echoing editorialists who had called it "a slap on the wrist" and railed that "a corrupt judge belongs more in the category of a traitor."[13] This, however, was the trade-off Cahill had made when he slimmed down the indictment to a single conspiracy count.

It is worth contrasting Manton's two-year sentence with the far harsher penalties under current law. A present-day Manton likely would be charged under a law that did not exist in 1939, the Racketeer Influenced and Corrupt Organizations Act of 1970, more commonly known as "RICO." RICO carries a twenty-year maximum sentence, rather than the two years faced by Manton. Moreover, federal courts today are required to calculate a presumptive sentencing range based on various factors set forth in the US Sentencing Guidelines. Manton would have scored high on many of the factors relevant in a case involving misconduct by a public official, such as the amount of the illicit payments, the importance of the official's position, and the official's role in leading concerted criminal activity. Had Manton committed the same crimes today, his Guidelines calculation likely would have called for imposition of the statutory maximum sentence of twenty years.

* * *

Judge Chesnut also meted out punishment to Manton's co-conspirators. George Spector was sentenced to a year and a day in prison. John Lotsch, weeping bitterly and begging for mercy, received a year, to be served concurrently with his prior bribery sentence. Forrest Davis, described by Cahill as "not overly bright," got probation.[14]

Too ill to appear in court in June, William Fallon was later sentenced to nine months in prison. Chesnut thought Fallon deserved the two-year maximum but relented when Cahill pleaded for leniency based on Fallon's health and the assistance he provided to the government. In the meantime, a jury convicted Fallon's younger brother, Thomas J. Fallon, of perjury for falsely denying to federal investigators that he had discussed destroying incriminating records with Alfred Reilly of Evans Case. Thomas Fallon also was sentenced to nine months.[15]

Three days after Manton's sentencing, Cahill commenced a disciplinary proceeding against Louis Levy and Paul Hahn, seeking to disbar them from practice in the Southern District of New York. After a trial, Judge Knox felt, "upon the whole, that the evidence as to [Hahn] is not so clear and convincing as to warrant disciplinary action." But Knox excoriated Levy. Not only was "Levy, in mind, heart and action, . . . venal and corrupt," the judge found, Levy had engaged in "false swearing and deceit in this proceeding." Separately, Levy was also disbarred by the New York State courts. His legal career was over. The former counselor to corporate titans, director of several large corporations, and trustee of the Guggenheim Foundation died penniless in 1952. His posthumously published memoir looked back on his relationships with famous businessmen, politicians, lawyers, and judges. It did not mention Manton.[16]

The month after Manton's sentencing, former federal judge Edwin Thomas's mental health dramatically improved. He was released from the Neuro-Psychiatric Institute and Hospital in Hartford, where he had been receiving treatment since March.[17] Thomas passed his remaining years in obscurity, untouched by the law.

* * *

Naturally, Manton appealed his conviction. This created another judicial staffing dilemma. Of the six Second Circuit judges, four (Learned Hand,

Gus Hand, Thomas Swan, and Harrie Chase) knew Manton intimately and, indeed, had testified as witnesses at Manton's trial. A fifth, Robert P. Patterson (who had replaced Manton), served as a district judge during Manton's tenure as senior circuit judge. That left only Charles E. Clark, a former dean of Yale Law School who first joined the Court in March 1939, available to hear Manton's appeal.[18]

There was no clear legal path, at the time, to inviting judges from outside the Second Circuit to sit on the panel. One option was for Manton's appeal to be heard directly by the Supreme Court, leapfrogging the Second Circuit altogether. Cahill asked the Solicitor General's Office to draft a petition for certiorari toward that end. Solicitor General Jackson thought this route inadvisable, and told Chief Justice Hughes as much. Ultimately, Hughes decided to constitute a special three-judge tribunal consisting of Judge Clark, Supreme Court justice Harlan Stone (the justice with administrative responsibility for the Second Circuit), and former justice George Sutherland (one of the conservative Four Horsemen, who retired from the Court in 1938).[19]

Manton was having trouble finding appellate counsel. He consulted with Solomon A. Klein, a young Brooklyn appellate specialist. After reviewing the record, Klein came to the conclusion that Manton had "no chance at all on appeal. . . . I could see no legitimate argument that could be made on his behalf." Maintaining his innocence, Manton started ticking off various "neat technical kind of points" he believed could lead to a reversal. Klein empathized with Manton, whom he regarded as an "exceptionally capable lawyer." He felt sorrow that this once giant of the bar had been reduced to such a "pathetic figure." It was nothing short of "heartbreaking." But after scrutinizing Manton's arguments, Klein's professional opinion did not change. He told Manton, " I don't think those points have any merit at all."[20]

Manton wound up retaining William E. Leahy, a Washington, DC, lawyer and experienced Supreme Court advocate, presumably banking on Leahy's familiarity with Justices Stone and Sutherland. Like Manton's trial lawyers, Leahy also had once represented Dutch Schultz and Al Capone. On October 27, 1939, Leahy, Cahill, and a lawyer for Manton's co-defendant George Spector argued the appeal for three hours.

In keeping with Justice Department protocol for appearances before Supreme Court justices, Cahill showed up in full Supreme Court regalia—striped trousers, gray ascot, waistcoat, and a morning coat. Despite his formal attire, Cahill "used the bluntest of shirt-sleeve language" in denouncing Manton. "You've heard of a forgery mill—of a divorce mill—well, this was a mill for the sale of justice," the prosecutor declared, hammering the facts as if he were delivering another jury address.[21]

Manton listened to the argument impassively in the seventeenth-floor Foley Square courtroom over which he had once presided. He got to the courtroom through one final misuse of his former judicial office—by riding the private elevator reserved for Second Circuit judges. Not surprisingly, his former colleagues were "just outraged" by this maneuver; it filled Gus and Learned Hand, in particular, with "indignation."[22]

On December 4, the appeals court unanimously affirmed Manton's conviction (as well as Spector's) in a twenty-five-page ruling by Justice Sutherland. Sutherland "sweat blood" preparing the opinion, he told Stone, "but not enough to require surgical attention." The opinion recounted the trial evidence in detail, leaving no doubt about what the judges believed it showed. "It is enough to say that, if believed by the jury, as we may properly assume it was, it discloses a state of affairs too plainly at variance with the claim of Manton's innocence as to make the verdict of the jury unassailable."[23]

Most memorably, Justice Sutherland shredded Manton's defense that he had decided each of the appeals conscientiously, in accordance with the law, and in agreement with his Second Circuit colleagues. "We may assume for present purposes that all of the cases in which Manton's action is alleged to have been corruptly secured were in fact rightly decided," Sutherland stipulated. That did not matter:

Judicial action, whether just or unjust, is not for sale, and if the rule shall ever be accepted that the correctness of judicial action taken for a price removes the stain of corruption and exonerates the judge, the event will mark the first step toward the abandonment of that imperative requisite of even-handed justice proclaimed by Chief Justice Marshall more than a century ago, that the judge must be "perfectly and completely independent with nothing to influence and control him but God and his conscience."

Manton had one more arrow in his quiver, a petition for certiorari seeking review by the US Supreme Court. But with a former Supreme Court justice having decisively rejected Manton's claims of error in a ruling joined by a current Supreme Court justice, there was little prospect the high court would take the case. On February 26, 1940, the Court turned down Manton's petition, 7–0, with Stone and the Court's newest justice, former attorney general Frank Murphy, not participating.[24]

All the petition accomplished was to rain down upon Manton more derision for advancing yet another self-serving and head-scratching argument. "From a broad viewpoint," Manton's petition argued, "it serves no public policy for a high judicial officer to be convicted of a judicial crime"; to the contrary, "[i]t tends to destroy the confidence of the people in the courts." It was thus imperative "for the honor of the American judiciary" for the Supreme Court to give Manton a last chance at vindication.[25]

In other words, Manton's high office was not an aggravating factor in his crimes; it was grounds for immunity from prosecution. And it was not Manton's corruption that had undermined confidence in the judiciary; it was the fact that he had been caught and convicted. "The moral distortion of such a plea," marveled one editorialist, "ought to have a unique place in records of jurisprudence."[26]

* * *

On March 8, 1940, Manton arrived once again at the Foley Square Courthouse. With tears in his eyes, and no statement for the press, Manton slumped into a blue-green sedan along with US Marshal Leo Lowenthal for a two-hundred-mile drive to the federal prison in Lewisburg, Pennsylvania. There he exchanged his "well-tailored business suit" and his "overcoat with its velvet collar" for "the coarse grey prison uniform." Later he wore blue denim and a farmer's straw hat, working in the prison greenhouse.[27]

Manton suffered a series of mini-strokes in prison and developed a heart ailment. On November 5, 1940, the same day FDR was being re-elected to an unprecedented third term by an overwhelming majority of Americans, Eva wrote the president a letter seeking clemency and an early release for her husband. Through John Mack, David Manton sent his own letter to the president. Roosevelt brusquely dismissed these entreaties, as well as Eva's warning that it was "a matter of life and death," and deferred to the Parole Board, which denied Manton's application.[28]

As Manton approached his official release date in the fall of 1941, Eva implored FDR one last time to intervene in her husband's case. In a handwritten note from "a broken hearted wife and family to your great understanding heart," Eva issued, "[i]n the name of humanity," this appeal: "My plea to you—our friend, for whom we will always have undying affection and admiration, is that you exercise your prerogative and grant Martin a pardon." At Eva's urging, former governor Al Smith also weighed in with his own plea for a pardon "out of sympathy for all involved."[29]

Roosevelt remained an immovable block of ice. He directed his attorney general, Francis Biddle, to prepare replies to Eva and Smith. Biddle advised the president that he construed the pardon request as one to restore Manton's civil rights, and that the administration's policy was to defer consideration of such requests until four years had passed from the defendant's release, absent exceptional circumstances. "I am of the opinion that a waiver of the rule would not be warranted under circumstances of this case," Biddle wrote.[30]

In his reply to Smith, drafted by Biddle, FDR cited this policy, adding that there was nothing "to cast doubt upon Manton's guilt, and the sentence, under the circumstances, does not seem to be excessive." FDR's response to Eva left that part out, but did say "in all candor that your husband's case does not present any considerations which would justify my departing" from the usual procedure. As a result, "I am sorry that I cannot respond favorably to your request."[31]

* * *

With time off for good behavior, Manton served only nineteen months of his two-year sentence. Freed in October 1941, he spent the remainder of his days living with Eva in central New York, in a town called

Fayetteville, near their son David. David continued to run National Cellulose in Syracuse, but his world had been shattered. His engagement to the blueblood Betty Halsey Brown did not survive his father's legal troubles.[32] He also learned that his father and mother were not actually his natural parents—when a reporter accosted him during the scandal and asked, cruelly, "How does it feel to be the adopted son of a crook?"[33]

The news that she had been adopted hit his sister Catherine particularly hard. Angered by Manton's failure to disclose that important biographical fact, and perhaps also by the loss of her previously privileged station in life, Catherine distanced herself from him. She finally summoned enough fortitude to send him well wishes for Father's Day in 1942. Manton, who was afraid he might never hear from her again, replied in a heartfelt note expressing gratitude to his "dear sweet daughter" for her "manifestations of endearment" and praying that she and her husband (one of his former law clerks) would find "all necessary for your comfort and joyful living." It was more of a farewell note than a rekindling of their relationship. Catherine barely ever spoke about Manton with her own children.[34]

Manton emerged from prison "to find his personal finances in a terrible state."[35] The Alamac, the Esplanade, and the Holmes Airport property had all been lost to foreclosure.[36] With them died Manton's dreams of creating dynastic wealth. Gone too was his beloved thirty-eight-acre Fairacres estate in Bayport, sold at a tax sale after Manton failed to pay his 1938 tax bill.[37] Meanwhile, the Bureau of Internal Revenue hit Manton with $259,000 in penalties for fraudulently evading taxes on his unreported cash income.[38]

No longer was Manton invited to deliver commencement addresses or radio talks or after-dinner speeches. Nor was he welcome at Democratic nominating conventions or other political gatherings. His days in the top ranks of the Catholic laity, too, came to an end.

For three decades Manton had been a dominant power in the civic life of the nation's most populous and important city. Now he lived in exile more than 250 miles away from the legal, political, business, and religious circles that once, to no small degree, had revolved around him. For someone who, as Learned Hand once observed, was "by nature an advocate, a man of strong feelings and strong convictions . . . a fighting man," this could not have been easy. Outraged as he was at Manton's deeds, Hand, as he expressed to his law clerk the year Manton resigned, had "an equally strong sense of sympathy for Manton" and an "appreciation of the tragedy of Manton," "a man with good intellectual equipment who had been misled by greed and avarice."[39]

It was Hand who took over Manton's duties as senior circuit judge. Soon the Second Circuit's luster was restored and sparkled even more brightly. Reformer Fiorello La Guardia remained mayor of New York City and Manton's nemesis Thomas Dewey was elected governor of New York State. With the end of World War II came seismic social and economic changes: the population shift to the suburbs, the rise in standards of living and educational levels, the centralization of power in Washington, the ascendance of the welfare state. In time these forces, gradually but inexorably, rendered Tammany Hall, and other urban political machines, obsolete.

Just a half-century earlier, Tammany's George Washington Plunkitt could openly boast about, defend, and even extol "honest graft," Plunkitt's memorable phrase for how city officials routinely exploited their positions of trust for private gain. In his inimitable, unmistakably New York dialect, Plunkitt said he would be proud if his epitaph read: "He Seen His Opportunities, and He Took 'Em." That was the world that a young Martin T. Manton grew up in. It was not the world he left.

On November 17, 1946, Manton's failing heart finally gave out. He died in David's home, at the age of sixty-six. He was buried in Fayetteville, far from the postwar metropolis he had left behind, and that had left behind him.[40]

* * *

Manton went to his grave unapologetic. He never acknowledged any fault or expressed a glimmer of remorse. A lawyer who talked to Manton shortly after his conviction recorded: "It was fascinating to observe. . . . He had no realization whatsoever of having done anything wrong in taking money from litigants." Another lawyer, after conferring with Manton about possibly defending him at trial, was similarly dumbfounded at how Manton "just couldn't understand why he was under fire" and showed "*no* consciousness of guilt." This once-exalted American jurist, the lawyer concluded, must have been "the most amoral man I have ever met."[41]

In a May 26, 1932 speech honoring the late Judge Walter C. Noyes, a former Second Circuit colleague, Manton waxed philosophical about the interplay between and among character, choice, and inclination. "Choice," Manton explained, "determines the act, acts form the habit, and habit makes up the character." As an "act of will," choice "is the answer of liberty to the conflicting claims of inclination." By "inclination" Manton meant

> *the feelings, emotions, the likes and dislikes, the whims and fancies, the prejudices and partialities, the hopes and fears that are forever drifting in and out of the heart, sometimes gathering into dark storms, sometimes falling in a rain of tears, sometimes dissipated into clear bright weather.*

"Good character," he concluded, "is the result of good choice."[42]

This speech was delivered two weeks after Manton received his $250,000 "loan" courtesy of the American Tobacco Company and likely while Manton was composing his rulings, issued two weeks later, in favor of American Tobacco's executives. Had the Noyes ceremony precipitated a rare moment of introspection? Was Manton speaking to himself as much as to his audience, lamenting his inability to tame his "inclinations"—his bribe-induced "partialities," his "fears" of financial ruin, the "dark storms" that sometimes gathered in his heart—and allow "good choice" to guide his conduct? Was he silently doubting his own "character" as a judge while praising that of Judge Noyes?

We can say with confidence that Manton was doing none of these things. In fact, he had simply plagiarized these passages from the writings of Father Francis P. Donnelly, a Jesuit priest and popular moralist.[43] There is every reason to believe that these musings were the result of a last-minute scramble to find something vaguely interesting to say in his speech, and no reason to believe Manton thought deeply about them

342

at all. In the age of the racket, Manton possessed the benumbed moral sensibilities of a racketeer. To paraphrase Father Donnelly, the habits Manton formed during this period of New York history is what made up his character.

"I always thought that [Manton] was one of those men who didn't know the difference between right and wrong," said a ninety-one-year old C. C. Burlingham, looking back a decade after Manton's conviction. "He thought that if a man had done things for him there was no reason why he couldn't do things for them. That's the way it went."[44]

Acknowledgments

When I started down this road some eight years ago, I had no idea how long it would take or how many debts of gratitude I would so happily incur. At every turn, archivists and librarians have amazed me with their dedication to their craft. I am particularly grateful to David Castillo of the National Archives and Records Administration in College Park, Maryland, who uncovered a treasure trove of previously unmined files on the FBI's Manton investigation. Thanks also to Lesley Schoenfeld of Harvard Law School's Historical & Special Collections; Leif Anderson of Stanford's Department of Special Collections; Kevin Thomas of the FDR Library in Hyde Park; Sarah McLuskey of the Bentley Historical Library; Richard Tuske and his colleagues at the Association of the Bar of the City of New York; and Bob Beaumont of the Wallingford (CT) Historical Society.

Three of Martin and Eva Manton's grandchildren—Vicki Kirshner, Jeff Denning, and Peter Denning—were remarkably generous in sharing with me family stories and family photos. Judge P. Kevin Castel and Joe Pecorino of the District Court Executive's Office of the Southern District of New York gave me access to the now-infamous portrait of Judge Manton that the Second Circuit hoped would disappear.

Judge Herbert J. Stern, Roger Newman, Barry Bohrer, David Sternberg, Michelle Stein, and Jeffrey Stein read the manuscript at various points and offered invaluable suggestions (and words of encouragement) which improved the content (and lifted my spirits) immeasurably.

This project never would have come to fruition were it not for the wonderful Rick Wolff of Kevin Anderson & Associates, who has my everlasting gratitude. I also thank Jackie Ashton of Lucinda Literary, and

Rick Rinehart and the team at Rowman & Littlefield for turning *Justice for Sale* into a living, breathing book.

Finally, my biggest thanks go to my wife, Ana Demel—for her unflagging support and encouragement; for accompanying me on research visits; for cheerfully allowing Martin T. Manton to accompany us on countless weekends and vacations; for her (multiple) close reads of the manuscript; and, above all, for a journey of love and laughter.

PROLOGUE

1. "Full Text of Dewey's Speech Outlining His Plans for Racket Inquiry," *New York Times*, July 31, 1935, 6.

2. "Triple War Is Waged Against Racketeers," *New York Times*, January 5, 1936, 10.

3. National Resources Committee, Consumer Incomes in the United States: Their Distribution in 1935–1936 (1938), 19; Seventh Annual Report of the Federal Home Loan Bank Board (1939), 32.

4. "Strike Hits More Buildings; City Declares Emergency," *New York Times*, March 3, 1936, 1.

5. "Manton In Resigning Denies Wrongdoing," *Baltimore Sun*, January 31, 1939, 15.

6. Lotsch's testimony about his dealings with Manton may be found in the Transcript of Record on Appeal in *United States v. Manton*, No. 122, 107 F.2d 834 (2d Cir. 1939) ("Transcript of Record"), 169–81, available at the library of the Association of the Bar of the City of New York.

7. "Judge Manton Is Convicted by Jury of Selling Justice," *New York Times*, June 4, 1939, 1.

CHAPTER ONE

1. Transcript of Record, 860; *New York Post*, June 5, 1939; Milton S. Gould, *The Witness Who Spoke with God and Other Tales from the Courthouse* (New York: Viking Press, 1979), 204.

2. Several book chapters and articles are all that exist. The most informative are *The Corrupt Judge: An Inquiry into Bribery and Other High Crimes and Misdemeanors in the Federal Courts* (New York: Clarkson N. Potter, 1962) by Joseph Borkin, a former Justice Department official, and Professor Allan D. Vestal's "A Study in Perfidy," *Indiana Law Journal*, Vol. 35 (1959), 17–44, both of which hew closely to the trial record. Veteran New York trial lawyer Milton Gould's memoir, *The Witness Who Spoke with God and Other Tales from the Courthouse* (1979), contains an entertaining, if not always reliable, chapter on Manton. Burt Heath, the investigative reporter who "yanked [Manton] down off his bench, stripped the robes from the back of the old thief and kicked him into prison" (Westbrook Pegler, "Fair Enough: Some Background on the Wagner Act," *Washington*

Post, May 10, 1941, 7), takes a victory lap in his contemporary memoir, *Yankee Reporter* (New York: Wilfred Funk, Inc., 1940). An unusual and unconvincing defense of Manton as an innocent victim of an overzealous media and politically motivated prosecutors is presented in Harold W. Sullivan's polemic, *Trial by Newspaper* (Hyannis, MA: Patriot Press, 1961).

3. Benjamin Weiser, "Hang Him Up? The Bad Judge and His Image," *New York Times*, January 27, 2009, A1.

4. Weiser, "Hang Him Up?"; "Special Supplement: Colleagues for Justice: One Hundred Years of the United States Court of Appeals for the Second Circuit," *St. John's Law Review*, Vol. 65 (1991), 949.

5. Julian W. Mack (another Harvard Law School graduate) occasionally served on the Second Circuit during the 1920s. Mack had been appointed to the short-lived Commerce Court in 1911 and remained available as a "floating" federal judge after that court's abolition, choosing to sit mainly as a district or circuit judge in New York. Gerald Gunther, *Learned Hand: The Man and the Judge* (New York: Alfred A. Knopf, 1994), 285.

6. Gunther, *Learned Hand*, 281.

7. "Borrowing Judge," *Time*, February 6, 1939, 9.

8. *United States v. One Book Entitled Ulysses*, 72 F.2d 705, 709 (2d Cir. 1934) (Manton, J., dissenting); Leonard Lyons, "Lyons Den," *Miami Herald*, October 30, 1937, 8.

9. Gunther, *Learned Hand*, 278.

10. *The Remarkable Hands: An Affectionate Portrait*, Marcia Nelson, ed. (New York: Foundation of the Federal Bar Council, 1983), 59; Transcripts of Interviews of W. Graham Claytor Jr., 13, and Charles A. Horsky, 5–6, in Gerald Gunther Papers at Stanford University (Boxes 2–5, 3–33); Transcripts of Interviews of D. Nelson Adams, 12, and Louis Henkin, 8, in Michael Smith and Herbert Packer Research Materials on the United States Court of Appeals for the Second Circuit at Harvard Law School (Box 14–2, 14–32); Oral history of Charles A. Horsky of Covington & Burling, April 23, 1992, 10–11, dcchs.org/CharlesAHorsky/charlesahorsky_complete.pdf.

11. *Remarkable Hands*, 29, 32, 55.

12. Gunther, *Learned Hand*, 507; *Remarkable Hands*, 29, 55, 60; D. Nelson Adams, "Some Recollections of My Year with Judge Learned Hand, 1935–1936," 10, Smith/Packer Research Materials (Box 14–2).

13. Annual Reports of the Attorney General of the United States, 1934 to 1938, Exhibit No. 1 (Cases Handled in the United States Circuit Courts of Appeals and the United States Court of Appeals for the District of Columbia).

14. Federal Judicial Caseload Statistics 2021, Table B. US Courts of Appeals—Appeals Commenced, Terminated, and Pending During the 12-Month Periods Ending March 31, 2020 and 2021, https://www.uscourts.gov/statistics/table/b/federal-judicial-caseload -statistics/2021/03/31. The Second Circuit's caseload is now in the middle of the pack.

15. *Chicago Tribune*, June 22, 1926, 4; *Guardian* (Diocese of Little Rock), October 4, 1930, 5.

16. *Guardian* (Diocese of Little Rock), March 28, 1931, 1; *New York Times*, June 2, 1936, 33; *One Book Entitled Ulysses*, 72 F.2d, 711.

17. "Christian Leaders Sign Hitler Appeal," *Brooklyn Daily Eagle*, March 22, 1933, 1.

18. *Time*, February 6, 1939.

19. Transcript of Interview of Bennett Boskey, 8, Gunther Papers (Box 1–23); Claytor, 14.

20. *Baltimore Sun*, June 21, 1939, 3.

21. Mason B. Williams, *City of Ambition; FDR, LaGuardia, and the Making of Modern New York* (New York: W.W. Norton, 2013), 148–49; Mary M. Stolberg, *Fighting Organized Crime: Politics, Justice, and the Legacy of Thomas E. Dewey* (Boston: Northeastern University Press, 1995), 88.

22. "Goodbye to Judge Manton," *New Republic*, June 14, 1939, 142.

23. Terry Golway, *Machine Made: Tammany Hall and the Creation of Modern American Politics* (New York: Liveright, 2014), 175, 180; Stolberg, *Fighting Organized Crime*, 22.

24. Andrew L. Kaufman, *Cardozo* (Cambridge, MA: Harvard University Press, 1998), 16–19.

25. Stolberg, *Fighting Organized Crime*, 15.

CHAPTER TWO

1. David J. Krajicek, "Judge from Brooklyn Sent to Jail for Bribe Scandal in 1939," *New York Daily News*, January 30, 2016.

2. Estes Kefauver, "Books of the Times," *New York Times*, January 26, 1963, 7.

3. Letter from Augustus Hand to Learned Hand, August 18, 1916, Learned Hand Papers at Harvard Law School (Box 109.11).

4. "Sayville of To-Day," *Suffolk County News*, August 13, 1897, 2.

5. "Gave a $500 Bill for a $50 Bill," *Port Jefferson Echo*, January 27, 1894, 2.

6. *Suffolk County News*, September 3, 1892, 3; November 19, 1892, 3; January 7, 1893, 3; June 3, 1893, 2; July 22, 1893, 3; March 24, 1894, 3; May 19, 1894, 3; August 13, 1897, 2; December 18, 1903, 3.

7. *County News*, March 13, 1914, 1; *Brooklyn Daily Eagle*, May 27, 1918, 7; *Brooklyn Daily Eagle*, July 31, 1942, 2; *Suffolk County News*, November 22, 1946, 3; Church of St. Theresa (Woodside, New York) website, www.saintteresachurch.org/history/history.htm.

8. *Suffolk County News*, February 10, 1894, 3; November 19, 1897, 3; October 29, 1897, 3; December 24, 1897, 3; January 14, 1898, 3; February 4, 1898, 3; December 23, 1898, 3; November 22, 1946, 3.

9. *Suffolk County News*, June 24, 1898, 5.

10. *New York Sun*, January 11, 1897, 7; *New York Sun*, February 9, 1897, 7; *Brooklyn Daily Eagle*, March 19, 1897, 4; *Brooklyn Daily Eagle*, April 1, 1897, 5; *Suffolk County News*, April 2, 1897, 3; *Brooklyn Daily Eagle*, April 2, 1897, 5.

11. "The Law School to Be a Graduate Department," *Columbia Spectator*, January 18, 1899, 1. Of Manton's class of ninety-six graduates, thirty-one had no prior college degree. See Columbia University Commencement Program, 1901, 5–6, http://library.columbia.edu/locations/cuarchives/collection_highlights/yearbooks.html.

12. Record on Appeal, *In re Levy*, 288 N.Y. 489 (1942) ("Levy Record on Appeal"), 358; Transcript of Record, 618; Columbia University in the City of New York, School of Law, Announcement, 1900–1901, 12, 22–26. More than half of Manton's classmates

came from New York City, and about one-quarter had gone to college at Harvard, Yale, or Columbia.

13. *Suffolk County News,* June 14, 1901, 3; *In re Levy,* 30 F. Supp. 317, 319 (S.D.N.Y. 1939); Levy Record on Appeal, 358; Commencement Program.

14. David J. Krajicek, "Judge from Brooklyn"; *Columbia Law Review,* Vol. 1 (1901), 50 (masthead); Levy Record on Appeal, 358.

15. "Lawyer Manton Once a Famous Football Player," *Brooklyn Daily Eagle,* February 7, 1907, 3.

16. *Columbia Spectator,* May 1, 1900, 1; *New York Times,* May 22, 1900, 19; *New York Times,* September 11, 1900, 8; *New York Times,* September 12, 1900, 5; *New York Times,* September 18, 1900, 9; *New York Times,* September 26, 1900, 9; National Football Foundation, Bill Morley, Member Biography, www.footballfoundation.org/Programs/CollegeFootballHallofFame/SearchDetail.aspx?id=7; Bill Morley, Wikipedia entry, https://en.wikipedia.org/wiki/Bill_Morley.

17. Transcript of Record, 619; *Suffolk County News,* December 6, 1901, 3.

18. Transcript of Record, 661; *Suffolk County News,* January 10, 1902, 2; *Komitsch v. De Groot,* 80 A.D. 376 (2d Dep't 1903); "Bank Account Not a Gift," *Brooklyn Daily Eagle,* April 22, 1903, 2; "Left Fortune to Servant," *Brooklyn Daily Eagle,* October 29, 1901, 24; *Chankalian v. Powers,* 89 A.D. 395 (2d Dep't 1903).

19. "Held for Murder," *Brooklyn Daily Eagle,* August 23, 1902, 7; "Toni Torchofski's Trial," *Brooklyn Citizen,* June 18, 1903, 2; "Widow Accused of Crime in Paramour's Confession," *Brooklyn Daily Eagle,* June 22, 1903, 1; "Miles Is Sentenced; Wandell Confesses," *Brooklyn Daily Eagle,* April 23, 1906, 24; "William O. Miles Disbarred," *Brooklyn Daily Eagle,* June 30, 1908, 1.

20. Papers on Appeal, *Kane v. Rose,* 87 A.D. 101 (2d Dep't 1903), 17–25; *Kane v. Rose,* 87 A.D. 101 (2d Dep't 1903); *Kane v. Rose,* 95 A.D. 631 (2d Dep't 1904).

21. *Suffolk County News,* December 18, 1903, 3.

22. "A Fatal Grade Crossing," *Suffolk County News,* December 18, 1903, 3; "Mrs. Michael Manton Killed," *Brooklyn Daily Eagle,* December 18, 1903, 8; "Instantly Killed at Sayville R.R. Crossing," *Brooklyn Daily Times,* December 18, 1903, 10; *New York Sun,* December 19, 1903, 1; "Unavoidable Accident," *Suffolk County News,* December 25, 1903, 5.

23. "Unavoidable Accident."

24. Roger K. Newman, *The Yale Biographical Dictionary of American Law* (New Haven, CT: Yale University Press, 2009), 358.

25. Heath, *Yankee Reporter,* 245; FBI Report, May 22, 1939, 4, Department of Justice Files, Record Group 60, National Archives and Records Administration, College Park, MD; Daniel Danelski, *A Supreme Court Justice Is Appointed* (New York: Random House, 1964), 59.

Chapter Three

1. *Brooklyn Daily Eagle,* November 11, 1904, 8; December 8, 1904, 9; December 8, 1904; December 29, 1904, 2; April 20, 1905, 5; April 23, 1905, 9.

2. *People v. Meringola*, 20 N.Y. Crim. R. 208 (2d Dep't 1906); *Brooklyn Daily Eagle*, June 21, 1904, 8; *County Review*, September 30, 1904, 1; *Brooklyn Daily Eagle*, June 12, 1906, 14; *County News*, June 15, 1906, 1; *Suffolk County News*, June 14, 1907, 1; *Brooklyn Daily Eagle*, June 20, 1907, 20.

3. *County Review*, June 15, 1906, 1.

4. *People v. Hinksman*, 192 N.Y. 421 (1908); *County Review*, December 15, 1905, 5; *County Review*, June 22, 1906, 1; *Brooklyn Daily Eagle*, June 29, 1906, 19; *County Review*, June 29, 1906, 1; *Brooklyn Daily Eagle*, November 17, 1908, 20; *Suffolk County News*, November 20, 1908, 1.

5. *Brooklyn Daily Eagle*, June 29, 1906, 19; *New York Times*, January 27, 1907, 4.

6. *New York Sun*, February 1, 1907, 3; *New York Sun*, February 2, 1907, 4.

7. *Brooklyn Daily Eagle*, January 28, 1907, 1; *New York Sun*, January 31, 1907, 5.

8. *New York Sun*, January 31, 1907, 5; *New York Times*, February 1, 1907, 16; Mike Dash, *Satan's Circus: Murder, Vice, Police Corruption, and New York's Trial of the Century* (London: Granta Books, 2007), 293.

9. *New York Times*, February 1, 1907, 16.

10. *New York Sun*, February 5, 1907, 14.

11. *New York Times*, February 7, 1907, 3; *New York Sun*, February 7, 1907, 5; *New York Sun*, February 8, 1907, 5.

12. Kerriann Flanagan Brosky, *Historic Crimes of Long Island: Misdeeds from the 1600s to the 1950s* (New York: History Press, 2017), Chapter 15; *New York Times*, July 16, 1908; *New York Sun*, October 26, 1908, 1; *New York Sun*, April 27, 1910, 5; *Suffolk County News*, June 17, 1910, 6.

13. *Chicago Tribune*, April 8, 1907, 5; September 21, 1907, 3; September 22, 1907, 1; January 24, 1908, 3.

14. *Chicago Tribune*, May 3, 1903, 26 and July 7, 1907, 28; *Edmond Morier v. Charles Moran*, 58 Ill. App. 235 (1st Dist. 1895); *Chicago Legal News*, July 16, 1892, 377.

15. *Brooklyn Daily Eagle*, July 7, 1907, 9; *County Review*, July 12, 1907, 1.

16. *Brooklyn Life*, November 9, 1907, 4, March 13, 1909, 2, and August 6, 1910, 3; *Brooklyn Daily Eagle*, June 2, 1909, 12; *Suffolk County News*, July 31, 1908, 7.

17. *Long Islander*, January 15, 1909, 3; *Brooklyn Daily Eagle*, January 28, 1909, 8; *Brooklyn Daily Eagle*, May 10, 1909, 18; *Brooklyn Daily Eagle*, May 17, 1909, 1.

18. *Evening World*, February 24, 1909, 2; *Evening World*, February 25, 1909, 2; *New-York Daily Tribune*, February 25, 1909, 2; *New-York Daily Tribune*, February 26, 1909, 5; *New York Sun*, February 26, 1909, 7.

19. *City Record*, February 8, 1907, 1345; *City Record*, May 13, 1908, 5607; *City Record*, August 11, 1908, 8670.

20. "A Talk with Martin T. Manton, the Brooklyn Lawyer Who Is Fighting to Save the Life of Charles Becker," *Brooklyn Daily Eagle*, March 7, 1915, 26.

21. George P. LeBrun, *It's Time To Tell* (New York: William Morrow, 1962), 156; Borkin, *Corrupt Judge*, 29.

22. "B.H. Railroad Mulcted," *Brooklyn Daily Eagle*, February 8, 1909, 2 (Flatbush Avenue pedestrian); *In re P. Sanford Ross, Inc.*, 196 F. 921 (E.D.N.Y. 1912) (dock builder); "Widow Beats Corporation," *Brooklyn Daily Eagle*, March 13, 1913, 4 (same); "Foreman

Censured by Jury," *Brooklyn Daily Eagle*, August 14, 1909, 3 (same); "Gets $12,000 for Loss of Leg," *Brooklyn Daily Times*, May 7, 1910 (dredge worker); "Awarded $12,500 for Husband's Life," *Brooklyn Citizen*, January 6, 1910, 1 (Hudson River accident); "Verdict for $14,000," *Brooklyn Citizen*, October 27, 1907, 3 (LIRR brakeman).

23. Richard A. Posner, "A Theory of Negligence," *Journal of Legal Studies* Vol. 1 (1972), 80.

24. See, e.g., *Peterson v. P. Ballatine & Sons*, 205 N.Y. 29 (1912); *Huscher v. New York & Queens Elec. Light & Power Co.*, 165 A.D. 241 (2d Dep't 1914); *Nosk v. City of New York*, 164 A.D. 582 (2d Dep't 1914); *Griffith v. American Bridge Co. of New York*, 157 A.D. 264 (2d Dep't 1913); *Kiernan v. Gutta Percha & Rubber Mfg. Co.*, 134 A.D. 192 (2d Dep't 1909).

25. "A Talk with Martin T. Manton."

26. *Brooklyn Citizen*, October 21, 1902, 7; *Brooklyn Daily Eagle*, October 22, 1902, 20; *Brooklyn Daily Eagle*, October 23, 1902, 3; *Brooklyn Daily Eagle*, October 24, 1902, 3; *Brooklyn Daily Eagle*, October 25, 1902, 15; *Brooklyn Daily Eagle*, October 31, 1902, 5.

27. "Manton on Roosevelt," *Brooklyn Daily Eagle*, November 1, 1904, 5.

28. *Tammany Times*, April 16, 1904, 5.

29. Furlong is described as "an earnest Democrat in politics" who takes "an active share in party affairs" in Mitchell C. Harrison, *New York States' Prominent and Progressive Men*, Vol. III (New York: New York Tribune, 1902), 123.

30. Golway, *Machine Made*, 181–82.

31. Editorial, *Brooklyn Daily Eagle*, March 3, 1910, 4; "Furlong Convicted; Three More Accused," *New York Times*, March 3, 1910, 4.

32. "Furlong's Attorney Gives Defense Plan," *Brooklyn Daily Eagle*, October 10, 1909, 5.

33. "Furlong to Be Tried February 9," *Brooklyn Daily Eagle*, February 2, 1910, 3; "Cockran Is Ousted from Tammany Posts," *New York Times*, March 14, 1908, 1; James McGurrin, *Bourke Cockran: A Free Lance in American Politics* (New York: Charles Scribner's Sons, 1948).

34. "Furlong, On the Grill; Denies Immoral Past; He Charges Blackmail," *Brooklyn Daily Eagle*, February 27, 1910, 6; "Furlong Case Given to the Jury; Clash Marks End of Trial," *Brooklyn Daily Eagle*, March 2, 1910, 1; "Furlong Is Sentenced; 1 to 2 Years in Prison at Hard Labor Is Term," *Brooklyn Daily Eagle*, March 4, 1910, 1.

35. *People v. Furlong*, 140 A.D. 179, 184, 188 (2d Dep't 1910).

36. "'I'm a Broken Man, But I Will Fight,' Declares Furlong," *Brooklyn Daily Eagle*, November 26, 1912, 1.

CHAPTER FOUR

1. "Must Account for Big Gas Co. Profits," *Brooklyn Daily Eagle*, July 2, 1914, 2; "$750,000 Camera Co. Suit," *Brooklyn Daily Eagle*, July 1, 1914, 2.

2. "$24,896 Award to Laborer," *Bridgeport Evening Farmer*, June 27, 1912, 16; *Griffith v. American Bridge Co. of New York*, 163 A.D. 597 (2d Dep't 1914) ($32,500); "$18,000 for Lost Leg," *Brooklyn Daily Eagle*, June 24, 1915, 18.

3. *Rockland County Times Weekly*, December 30, 1911, 4.

4. J. Edgar Hoover with Courtney Ryley Cooper, "Freeing Our Courts from Peddlers of Corruption," *Cosmopolitan* (November 1939), 84.

5. *Brooklyn Daily Eagle*, December 27, 1915, 3; *Brooklyn Daily Eagle*, March 3, 1916, 18; *Suffolk County News*, March 10, 1916.

6. Andy Logan, *Against the Evidence: The Becker-Rosenthal Affair* (New York: Avon Books, 1972), 19–22.

7. Logan, *Against the Evidence*, 135.

8. Edwin Lawrence Godkin, *The Triumph of Reform: A History of the Great Political Revolution, November 6, 1894* (New York: Souvenir Publishing, 1895), 126.

9. Timothy J. Gilfoyle, *City of Eros: New York City, Prostitution, and the Commercialization of Sex, 1790–1920* (New York: W.W. Norton, 1992), 203.

10. Logan, *Against the Evidence*, 120–25, 130–31.

11. Logan, *Against the Evidence*, 106–7, 149.

12. Logan, *Against the Evidence*, 149; "People Declare War on Protected Crime," *New York Times*, August 15, 1912, 1.

13. *People v. Becker*, 210 N.Y. 274 (1914); "Shay to Withdraw from Becker's Case," *New York Sun*, April 14, 1914, 3.

14. "Shay to Withdraw from Becker's Case," 3.

15. "A Talk with Martin T. Manton"; "Elliott Jurors Find No Verdict; Debate 7 Hours," *Brooklyn Daily Eagle*, February 1, 1913, 16; "Shay to Withdraw from Becker's Case."

16. "Angry at Brother, Shay Quits Becker," *Brooklyn Daily Eagle*, April 14, 1914, 2; "Becker in Court; Manton with Him," *Brooklyn Daily Eagle*, April 15, 1914, 3; Logan, *Against the Evidence*, 286–87; *People v. Becker*, 210 N.Y., 284, 289.

17. "Get Five Jurors for Becker Trial," May 7, 1914, 1; Logan, *Against the Evidence*, 281–85.

18. "Rose Admits Lying in Clash on Stand with Becker Lawyer," *Evening World*, May 13, 1914, 1.

19. "A Talk with Martin T. Manton."

20. *Brooklyn Daily Eagle*, May 13, 1914, 2; "Rose, Unshaken, Is to Be Accused," *New York Times*, May 14, 1914, 4; "Becker Tries to Shift Guilt to Rose," *New York Sun*, May 14, 1914, 5; "Rose Admits Lying in Clash on Stand with Becker Lawyer," *Evening World*, May 13, 1914, 2.

21. "Rose, Unshaken, Is to Be Accused."

22. "Becker Again Found Guilty of Murder, Will Appeal Again; Jury Out Four Hours," *New York Times*, May 23, 1914, 2; "Becker Awaits Jury's Verdict," *Brooklyn Daily Eagle*, May 22, 1914, 1.

23. "A Talk with Martin T. Manton."

24. *People v. Becker*, 215 N.Y. 126 (1915).

25. Logan, *Against the Evidence*, 306–9, 326–27.

26. Logan, *Against the Evidence*, 326–27, 340.

27. "A Talk with Martin T. Manton."

28. Sam Roberts, "100 Years After a Murder, Questions About a Police Officer's Guilt," *New York Times*, July 15, 2012.

29. "Appeal to Hogan Abandoned," *New York Times*, July 30, 1915, 2.

30. "Becker, About to Die, Flays Whitman," *New York Times*, July 30, 1915, 2; Logan, *Against the Evidence*, 349–50.

31. *Brooklyn Daily Eagle*, March 7, 1915, 2; James Huneker, "Mysterious, Beautiful Brooklyn," *New York Times*, July 11, 1915, 21.

32. *Brooklyn Daily Eagle*, May 7, 1918, 18.

33. Sayville Library Postcard Collection, New York Digital Collections (Streets, Homes & Farms—Southeast Sayville); *Brooklyn Daily Eagle*, September 8, 1914, 16; *Brooklyn Daily Eagle*, May 15, 1916, 2; *Suffolk County News*, April 7, 1916, 2.

34. *Municipal Journal and Public Works*, Vol. 30, no. 14 (April 5, 1911), 508 ($88,439; Baltimore); *Municipal Journal and Public Works*, Vol. 30, no. 17 (April 26, 1911), 598 ($18,867; Brooklyn); *Brooklyn Daily Eagle*, May 29, 1912, 3 ($262,000; Passaic Valley Sewer Corp.); *Steam Shovel and Dredge*, Vol. 16, no. 7 (July 1912), 568 (same); *Record and Guide*, April 22, 1911, 756.

35. Transcript of Record, 659.

36. *Brooklyn Standard Union*, July 17, 1908, 3; *Brooklyn Standard Union*, August 9, 1908, 10; *Brooklyn Standard Union*, September 6, 1908, 4; *Brooklyn Standard Union*, September 22, 1908, 11; *Brooklyn Citizen*, September 22, 1908, 10; *Brooklyn Citizen*, October 5, 1908, 1.

37. *Brooklyn Daily Eagle*, October 5, 1910, 7; *Brooklyn Daily Times*, October 5, 1910, 3.

38. *Brooklyn Daily Eagle*, October 28, 1912, 8; *Brooklyn Daily Eagle*, October 31, 1912, 8; *Brooklyn Daily Times*, October 21, 1912, 2.

39. *Brooklyn Daily Eagle*, March 1, 1913, 2.

40. Godfrey Hodgson, *Woodrow Wilson's Right Hand: The Life of Colonel Edward M. House* (New Haven, CT: Yale University Press, 2006), 70.

41. *New York Times*, November 25, 1913, 8; *Brooklyn Daily Eagle*, August 11, 1913, 2; *Brooklyn Daily Eagle*, July 1, 1914, 1; *Brooklyn Daily Eagle*, July 29, 1914, 4; Golway, *Machine Made*, 217–19.

42. "Lathrop Brown, Political Dilettante," *New York Press*, November 10, 1912, reprinted at https://fdrfoundation.org/lathrop-brown-political-dilettante/.

43. See https://www.govtrack.us/congress/members/lathrop_brown/401891.

44. "Drop Manton's Hat in Congress Ring," *Brooklyn Daily Eagle*, July 29, 1914, 4; *South Side Signal*, July 31, 1914, 4.

45. *Brooklyn Daily Eagle*, July 29, 1914, 4; Christopher Oldstone-Moore, "Mustaches and Masculine Codes in Early Twentieth-Century America," *Journal of Social History*, Vol. 45 (2011), no. 1, 48, 50.

46. *County Review*, July 31, 1914, 1 and August 14, 1914, 1.

47. *County Review*, August 21, 1914, 1.

48. *Brooklyn Daily Eagle*, September 16, 1914, 8 and September 17, 1914, 8; *South Side Signal*, September 25, 1914, 4; *County Review*, September 25, 1914, 1; *Long Islander*, September 25, 1914, 3.

49. *Suffolk County News*, January 15, 1915, 1 and February 12, 1915, 1; *County Review*, February 12, 1915, 1, and February 19, 1915, 6.

50. FBI Report, May 22, 1939, 9.

51. *Brooklyn Daily Eagle*, September 1, 1915, 5; March 18, 1916, 12; May 15, 1916, 1.

52. "Manton Is Backed for U.S. Circuit Court of Appeals," *Brooklyn Daily Eagle*, May 15, 1916, 1.

53. "No Tammany Man to Oppose Manton," *Brooklyn Daily Eagle*, May 16, 1916, 2; "Tammanyites Want State Controller," *Brooklyn Standard Union*, August 5, 1916, 2; "The Manton Appointment," *Brooklyn Daily Times*, August 17, 1916, 4.

54. "Plan a New York Bolt to Wilson," *New York Times*, July 1, 1912, 1.

55. *In re Levy*, 30 F. Supp. 317, 319 (S.D.N.Y. 1939); Levy Record on Appeal, 359.

56. Rayman L. Solomon, "The Politics of Appointment and the Federal Courts' Role in Regulating America: U.S. Court of Appeals Judgeships from T.R. to F.D.R.," *American Bar Foundation Research Journal*, Vol. 2 (1984), 316, 322.

57. "M'Cooey Silent on Washington Trip," *Brooklyn Standard Union*, July 27, 1916, 2; "Tammanyites Want State Controller," 2; "Boom B.S. Coler for Governor," *Brooklyn Daily Times*, August 10, 1916, 1; "McCooey's Day's Work," *Brooklyn Daily Times*, August 14, 1916, 4; Levy Record on Appeal, 359.

58. "Brennan for Bench, Carswell, District Attorney, Is Slate," *Brooklyn Daily Eagle*, August 14, 1916, 1; "Carswell Named for Dist. Att'y," *Brooklyn Daily Times*, August 14, 1916, 1; "Brennan and Carswell," *Brooklyn Daily Times*, August 15, 1916, 4; "Carswell Is Selected," *New York Sun*, August 15, 1916, 4.

59. Solomon, "Politics of Appointment," 322; "Wilson Names Hough to Succeed Lacombe," *New York Times*, August 16, 1916, 4.

60. "Manton May Not Accept," *Brooklyn Citizen*, August 16, 1916, 1; "Manton's Place Causes Surprise," August 16, 1916, 2; "Manton Will Accept," August 17, 1916, 1; "Manton Is Confirmed," *Brooklyn Daily Eagle*, August 24, 1916, 1; Letter from Manton to Cockran, August 27, 1916, Cockran Papers at New York Public Library (Box 4, Folder 7).

61. "Two Oppose Manton," *Brooklyn Daily Eagle*, August 23, 1916, 5; Letter from Manton to Cockran, August 24, 1916, Cockran Papers (Box 4, Folder 7).

62. "Manton for Judge," *Suffolk County News*, August 18, 1916, 1; "Judge Martin T. Manton," *Brooklyn Citizen*, August 16, 1916, 6; "Wilson and the Judiciary," *Brooklyn Daily Eagle*, August 16, 1916, 4; *Bench and Bar*, Vol. 11, no. 5 (September 1916), 189; "The Manton Appointment," 4.

63. "Wilson Names Hough to Succeed Lacombe," *New York Times*, August 16, 1916, 4; "Manton Chosen for Federal Bench," *Brooklyn Standard Union*, August 16, 1916, 3; Borkin, *Corrupt Judge*, 29.

64. Westlaw search by author.

65. "Judge Martin T. Manton"; "Wilson and the Judiciary."

CHAPTER FIVE

1. "Judge Manton Is Guest at Dinner," *New York Times*, December 13, 1916, 9.

2. Letter from Augustus Hand to Learned Hand, August 18, 1916 (Learned Hand Papers).

3. "No Tammany Enthusiasm Over Wilson," *Brooklyn Standard Union*, September 3, 1916, 1.

4. See the exchange of letters between Learned Hand and Allston Burr, his fellow member of the Board of Overseers, dated April 10–11, 1934, about "the charges that were made [about Manton] in 1916," available in Learned Hand Papers (Box 50.6).

5. Letter from Manton to Hand, August 21, 1916, Learned Hand Papers (Box 30.5).

6. *New York Times*, January 6, 1917, 20; *Suffolk County News*, January 12, 1917, 2.

7. "Convicts Draft Slacker," *New York Times*, July 31, 1917, 9.

8. "Draft Officers Plead Guilty; Get 2 Years in Prison," *New York Times*, August 21, 1917, 3.

9. John Reed, "About the Second *Masses* Trial," *Liberator*, December 1918, 36–37; David Reid, *The Brazen Age: New York City and the American Empire: Politics, Art and Bohemia* (New York: Pantheon, 2016), 265.

10. John C. Knox, *A Judge Comes of Age* (New York: Charles Scribner's Sons, 1940), 52–53, 132–43.

11. Gunther, *Learned Hand*, 257–59.

12. Gunther, *Learned Hand*, 258; Solomon, "The Politics of Appointment," 322.

13. *Masses Publishing Co. v. Patten*, 244 F. 535 (S.D.N.Y. 1917).

14. *Masses Publishing Co. v. Patten*, 246 F. 24 (2d Cir. 1917).

15. Gunther, *Learned Hand*, 151–61.

16. *Brooklyn Citizen*, May 17, 1917, 2.

17. *Brooklyn Citizen*, March 12, 1918, 1.

18. Letter from Frankfurter to Hand, November 6, 1917 (Learned Hand Papers); Letter from Hand to Lippman, October 3, 1917, in *Reason and Imagination: The Selected Correspondence of Learned Hand*, Constance Jordan, ed. (Oxford: Oxford University Press, 2013), 66; Gunther, *Learned Hand*, 260; Letter from Hand to Frankfurter, January 23, 1918 (Learned Hand Papers).

19. "Manton Named for U.S. Court of Appeals," *Brooklyn Daily Eagle*, March 12, 1918, 20.

20. William Howard Taft, "The Selection and Tenure of Judges," *The Law Student's Helper*, Vol. 21 (October 1913), 9–10.

21. FBI Report, May 22, 1939, 18.

22. Maurice Spitzer, Inc. (*New York Times*, September 19, 1916, 15).

23. Continental Public Works Company (*New York Times*, June 9, 1917, 13); Letter from treasury secretary William G. McAdoo to attorney general Thomas W. Gregory, May 13, 1916 (forwarding Flynn's letter endorsing Manton), in W. G. McAdoo Papers at Library of Congress (Box 491, Pt 1).

24. State Sen. James A. Foley, appointed as receiver for Loretta Corp. (*New York Times*, June 12, 2017, 16); Morris & Pope (*New York Times*, July 3, 1917, 14); William H. Parkerton (*New York Sun*, July 28, 1917, 10); United Dealers' Cooperative Ass'n (*New York Times*, December 19, 1917, 15); Jacob Cohen (*New York Times*, December 23, 1917, 32).

25. State Sen. Edward J. Dowling, appointed as receiver for Profit Sharing Merchandise Co. (*New York Times*, June 22, 1917, 16); Lucien Bilquez (*New York Sun*, December 15, 1917, 14); Catskill & New York Steamboat Co. (*New York Times*, January 6, 1918, 19).

26. I.N. Burdick Inc. (*New York Sun*, September 22, 1916, 6); B&L Auto Lamp Co. (*New York Sun*, June 8, 1917, 20); Intermediate Chemical Corporation (*New York Sun*, June 28, 1917, 11); Pittston Coal Co. (*New York Sun*, August 2, 1917, 8).

27. Mutual McDermott Corp. (*New York Sun*, December 14, 1917, 8); Carl H. Schultz (*The Soda Fountain*, Vol. 20 [March 1921], 81); Isador Krumholz (*New York Herald*, August 12, 1921, 20); L. Druckerman Co. (*New York Times*, June 18, 1922, 30); The J. Dresner Co. Inc. (*New York Times*, September 9, 1922, 18); Manhattan Neckwear Co. (*New York Tribune*, September 10, 1922, 9); Steinhaus & Gumbiner (*New York Tribune*, September 17, 1922, 40); Sinaloa Exploration and Development Co.—but vacated three weeks later when Manton decided a receiver wasn't necessary (*New York Times*, September 15, 1923, 23; *New York Times*, October 5, 1923, 14).

28. Lissman, Needel & Kurtz, Inc. (*New York Tribune*, September 3, 1920, 14); P.A.T. Clothing Co. (*New York Times*, September 10, 1920, 14); G. Ren & Co. (*New York Tribune*, September 16, 1920, 23); Morris Lefkoff (*New York Times*, August 11, 1921, 20); Aaron Schwitzky (*New York Tribune*, September 17, 1920, 16); Colorcraft Corp. (*New York Times*, June 20, 1922, 34); Fishbein Bros. Co. (*New York Times*, September 15, 1922, 35); C&T Furniture Co. (*New York Times*, September 17, 1922, 32); Morris M. Brenner (*New York Times*, September 17, 1922, 32).

29. Elsie Hat (*New York Times*, June 20, 1922, 34); Morganstein & Fenster (*New York Times*, June 20, 1922, 34); Elmer Hat Co. (*New York Times*, September 6, 1922, 27); Bleecker Parts Manufacturing (*New York Times*, September 8, 1922, 31); Harry Fried (*New York Times*, September 8, 1922, 31).

30. "Leader McCooey's Son, Lawyer for a Month, Bankruptcy Receiver," *Brooklyn Daily Eagle*, August 18, 1921, 1; *Brooklyn Citizen*, August 18, 1921, 1; *Brooklyn Standard Union*, August 18, 1921, 1; *Brooklyn Daily Times*, August 18, 1921, 1.

31. Herbert Mitgang, *The Man Who Rode the Tiger: The Life and Times of Judge Samuel Seabury* (New York: Fordham University Press, 1996), 233.

32. Wid Gunning, Inc. (*New York Times*, June 23, 1922, 33); Mayer Bros (*New York Times*, September 13, 1922, 31); Durable Leather Bag Co., Inc. (*New York Times*, September 9, 1922, 18); Elizabeth Chapman (*New York Times*, September 9, 1922, 18).

33. Uhr Schneider (*New York Times*, September 13, 1922, 31); *Brooklyn Daily Eagle*, June 14, 1921.

34. Knox, *Judge Comes of Age*, 135.

35. Seaboard Brass Foundries, Inc. (*New York Sun*, September 13, 1919, 8); National Shipbuilding Co. (*New York Times*, September 6, 1920, 17); Leslie Judge Co. (*New York Times*, February 24, 1921, 27); Louis Kalmanowitz (*New York Times*, August 18, 1921, 25); *G. Ricordi & Co. v. Columbia Gramophone Co.*, 270 F. 822 (2d Cir. 1920).

36. S. Burton Heath, "State to Continue Investigation of Manton Firms' Income Tax," *New York World-Telegram*, January 30, 1939; Letter from Hiram C. Todd (Felder's prosecutor) to the American Bar Association's Committee on Professional Ethics and Grievances, June 23, 1949, reprinted in the Congressional Record (August 2, 1949), A5005–06.

37. Greenwich Hat Works (*New York Times*, March 4, 1917, 80); Joseph Colvin (*New York Times*, March 20, 1917, 12); Emerson Motors Co. (*New York Times*, June 9, 1917, 13; this is vacating Johnston's appointment); Sanger Picture Plays Corp. (*New York Sun*,

August 3, 1917, 10); Ford Tractor Co. (*New York Sun*, December 6, 1917, 3); Pottier & Stimus (*New York Sun*, September 6, 1918, 10); George Graham Rice (*New York Times*, February 5, 1919, 14); Furlong Bros. Inc. (*New York Times*, February 19, 1919, 17); Crystal Film Company (*New York Sun*, June 17, 1919, 15); Goldman Bros. (*New York Times*, September 3, 1920, 21); Arbor Press Inc. (*New York Times*, September 10, 1920, 14); Herrick & Bennett (with Raymond H. Fiero, who later resigned, leaving Johnston as sole receiver) (*Evening World*, February 21, 1921, 1); Diamond Fuel Co. (*New York Times*, March 1, 1921, 19); Dilsizian Brothers (*New York Times*, March 2, 1921, 19); G. Kawahara & Co. (*New York Times*, March 3, 1921, 30); Imbrie & Co., NYSE brokerage house, with Theodore Smith (*New York Times*, March 4, 1921, 31; *Commercial & Financial Chronicle*, March 5, 1921, 890); Peruvian Panama Hat Co. (*New York Herald*, August 9, 1921, 18); Gillette Bros Inc. (w/ Maurice Gillette) (*New York Times*, August 11, 1921, 20); Interstate Coal & Dock Co. (w/ Elias McClellan Paston) (*New York Herald*, August 12, 1921, 15); Mutual Profit Realty Co. and Mupro Realty Corp. (*New York Times*, August 12, 1921, 14); *McClure's* magazine (with Myles Walsh) (*New York Times*, August 18, 1921; *Writer*, Vol. 9 [September 1921], 137); Elder Steel Steamship Co. (*New York Times*, June 20, 1922, 34); A.W. Cowen & Brothers, Inc. (with David Fox) (*New York Times*, September 13, 1922, 31); Gatti-McQuade Co. (*New York Times*, September 16, 1922, 13); Federal Adding Machine Co. (*New York Herald*, September 19, 1922, 17).

38. "Says Manton Gave Ex-Partner Jobs," *Brooklyn Standard Union*, February 22, 1924, 16; "Enough One-Third Judges Here Now Says Livingston," *Brooklyn Daily Eagle*, October 31, 1927, 18.

39. Nathan Brown (*New York Times*, June 22, 1917, 16); American Chair Co. (*New York Sun*, July 25, 1917, 14); Helfgott & Son Inc. (*Sun*, July 28, 1917, 10); Storfer-Spooner Co. (*American Perfumer*, August 1917, 173; *New York Sun*, August 1, 1917, 10); Shaker Abraham (*New York Sun*, August 23, 1917, 10); Greystone Silica Products Co. (*New York Sun*, August 23, 1917, 10); Samuel Botkin (*New York Times*, December 6, 1917, 15); Alfred David of David & David (*New York Times*, December 18, 1917, 20); Sol Jaekel (*New York Times*, January 15, 1918, 16); Julio E. Herrera (*New York Sun*, September 13, 1918, 12); Storm King Paper Co. (*New York Sun*, February 19, 1919, 14); Jaffe & Krakower, Inc. (*New York Times*, June 20, 1922, 34; *Jewelers' Circular*, June 21, 1922, 113); Ratner's Restaurant (*New York Herald*, February 25, 1921, 17; judge not listed but must have been Manton); H.W. Doughten Inc. (*New York Herald*, February 25, 1921, 17; judge not listed but must have been Manton); Sheer, Inc. (*New York Times*, March 1, 1921, 24); B & O Dress Co. (*New York Times*, March 1, 1921, 24); Jacob Blumenthal (*New York Sun*, March 5, 1921, 16); Arrow Dress Co. Inc. (*New York Times*, March 7, 1921, 19); Economy Auto Equipment (*New York Times*, August 9, 1921, 20); Maison Charles (*New York Times*, August 11, 1921, 20); Fishman Brothers, Inc. (*New York Times*, August 14, 1921, 24); Nemo Furriers Supply Co. (*New York Times*, August 20, 1921, 15); Merit Paper Co. (*New York Times*, August 20, 1921, 15); Palace Vegetarian Restaurant (*New York Times*, June 17, 1922, 23); Feingold & Gelb Inc. (*New York Times*, June 18, 1922, 30); George Fox & Co. (*New York Times*, June 24, 1922, 24); Isaac Berger (*New York Times*, June 22, 1922, 34); Ada Gillam Munyon, d/b/a Betsy Ross Coffee Shop (*New York Times*, June 27, 1922, 31); Hollander & Fishman Inc. (*New York Times*, September 8, 1922, 31); Louis Silverstein

(*New York Times*, September 8, 1922, 31); Gordon & Fatowe (*New York Times*, September 9, 1922, 18); M. Winthrop Smith & Co. (*New York Herald*, September 10, 1922, 9).

40. *Chicago Tribune*, June 7, 1913, 14; *Omaha World-Herald*, September 5, 1916, 1.

41. FBI Report, February 24, 1939, 11–12 (DOJ Files).

42. FBI Report, February 24, 1939, 10–11; FBI Report, May 19, 1939, 5–7 (interview of John Johnston).

43. FBI Report, April 24, 1939, 2 (interview of Walter T. Kohn) (DOJ Files); *New York Times*, March 26, 1921, 17.

44. *The Bull*, September 11, 1920, quoted in Martin Mayer, *Emory Buckner* (New York: Harper & Row, 1968), 173.

45. "Court Order Halts Gas Hearings Here," *New York Times*, July 16, 1919, 6; "Lawyers Clash as Court Favors City in Gas Case," *Evening World*, July 25, 1919, 14; "City Asks for Stay in Gas Litigation," *New York Times*, July 26, 1919, 15.

46. Letter from Augustus Hand to Learned Hand, July 29, 1919 (Learned Hand Papers).

47. "Craig Is Sentenced to 60 Days in Jail by Judge Mayer," *New York Times*, February 25, 1921, 1.

48. "Mayer Gives Craig 60 Day Jail Term in Contempt Case," *New York Herald*, February 25, 1921, 1.

49. "Craig Wins Mayer Contempt Appeal," *New York Herald*, April 30, 1921, 18.

50. *Craig v. Hecht*, 263 U.S. 255 (1923); *Ex parte Craig*, 282 F. 138 (2d Cir. 1922).

51. Letter from Taft to Charles D. Hilles, September 17, 1922, in William H. Taft Papers at Library of Congress.

52. William Edward Ross, "People It Pays to Know," *National Magazine* (September 1918), 469 (profile of Malkan); "Armistice Forces Bookshop Failure," *New York Sun*, December 25, 1918, 5; "Henry Malkan in Bankruptcy," *Publishers' Weekly* (December 28, 1918), 2003.

53. Letter from Manton to Hand, March 24, 1919, Learned Hand Papers (Box 30.5).

54. "Harding Expected to Name a Democrat for Supreme Court, Judge Manton Urged," *New York Times*, October 27, 1922, 18.

55. Danelski, *Supreme Court Justice Is Appointed*, 43 n.*.

56. Danelski, *Supreme Court Justice Is Appointed*, 43–47.

57. Danelski, *Supreme Court Justice Is Appointed*, 45, 48, 59; Violet Hurst, "Judge Martin T. Manton's bid for a Supreme Court seat," *Boston Pilot*, September 9, 2022; *New York Daily News*, September 30, 1922, 10; Letter from James H. Ryan of the National Catholic Welfare Council to Will H. Hays, October 6, 1922, in Will H. Hays Collection at the Indiana State Library; Letter from Learned Hand to Felix Frankfurter, December 1922 (Learned Hand Papers).

58. Danelski, *Supreme Court Justice Is Appointed*, 47–48, 73–74; Letter from William H. Taft to Pierce Butler, November 7, 1922 (Taft Papers); Letter from Harding to Hays, November 10, 1922 (Hays Collection); Letter from Learned Hand to Felix Frankfurter, December 1922 (Hand Papers); Louis Pizzitola, *Hearst Over Hollywood* (New York: Columbia University Press, 2002), 198–99.

59. Letter from Learned Hand to Felix Frankfurter, December 1922, and Letter from Felix Frankfurter to Learned Hand, December 11, 1922, both in Learned Hand Papers (Box 104.10); Letter from James Ryan to Will Hays, October 6, 1922 (Hays Collection); Letter from Harry Taft to Chief Justice Taft, October 26, 1922 (Taft Papers).

60. Taft weighed well over three hundred pounds when president but dropped down to about 270 after leaving the White House.

61. "Twelve Greatest Men," *New York Times*, July 23, 1922, 84.

62. Danelski, *Supreme Court Justice Is Appointed*, 45, 47, 51, 59; Letter from Taft to Charles D. Hilles, September 17, 1922 (Taft Papers); Letter from Taft to Pierce Butler, November 7, 1922 (Taft Papers).

63. The opinion was *FTC v. P. Lorillard Co.*, 283 F. Supp. 999 (S.D.N.Y. 1922). Among its convoluted constructions Wickersham may have flagged: "The commerce clause of the Constitution granting power to the Congress to legislate as to the commerce permits only of legislation which has to do with interstate commerce." *Id.*, 1002.

64. Danelski, *Supreme Court Justice Is Appointed*, 47, 63, 74; Letter from Wickersham to Taft, October 10, 1922 (Taft Papers); Letter from Wickersham to Taft, October 11, 1922 (Taft Papers); Letter from Harry Taft to Chief Justice Taft, November 3, 1922 (Taft Papers); Letter from Elihu Root to Taft, November 21, 1922 (Taft Papers); Nicholas Butler, *Across the Busy Years* (New York: Charles Scribner's Sons, 1939), 354–55.

65. Danelski, *Supreme Court Justice Is Appointed*, 42, 45–48, 53; Gunther, *Learned Hand*, 274; Letter from Wickersham to Taft, September 25, 1922 (Taft Papers); Letter from Taft to Harding, December 4, 1922 (Taft Papers); Gay Wickersham Davis, *The Wickersham Family in America* (Bowie, MD: Heritage Books, 2001).

66. Kermit L. Hall, ed., *The Oxford Companion to the Supreme Court of the United States* (New York: Oxford University Press, 1992), 111.

67. Danelski, *Supreme Court Justice Is Appointed*, 49–60; Letter from Taft to Tom Shelton, November 5, 1922 (Taft Papers); Letter from Taft to Butler, November 7, 1922 (Taft Papers).

68. Letter from Taft to Butler, November 7, 1922 (Taft Papers) ("I am for you whether you are a Unitarian, a Catholic, a Presbyterian, an Agnostic or a Mormon, and I resent the suggestion that a man's religion should play any part in the primary reasons for selecting him for our Court").

69. Danelski, *Supreme Court Justice Is Appointed*, 74–75, 87; "Harding Expected to Name a Democrat for Supreme Court, Judge Manton Urged," *New York Times*, October 27, 1922, 18; "Manton Is Likely to Succeed Day," *Brooklyn Daily Times*, October 29, 1922, 4; "Appointment of Manton Urged," *Nashville Banner*, October 30, 1922, 1; Letter from Wynne to W. Bourke Cockran, October 31, 1922, Cockran Papers (Box 6, Folder 3); Letter from Wynne to Taft, November 13, 1922 (Taft Papers).

70. Letter from Burlingham to Taft, December 4, 1922 (Taft Papers); Letter from Learned Hand to Felix Frankfurter, December 1922; Eugene C. Gerhart, *America's Advocate: Robert H. Jackson* (Indianapolis: Bobbs-Merrill, 1958), 171.

71. Danelski, *Supreme Court Justice Is Appointed*, 197.

72. *Oxford Companion to the Supreme Court*, 309.

73. Danelski, *Supreme Court Justice Is Appointed*, 154; Letter from Taft to Harding, October 30, 1922 (Taft Papers); Russell W. Galloway Jr., "The Taft Court (1921–1929)," *Santa Clara Law Review*, Vol. 25 (1985), 2–3.

74. H. L. Mencken, *The Vintage Mencken* (New York: Vintage Books, 1955), 197.

75. Jeff Shesol, *Supreme Power: Franklin Roosevelt vs. the Supreme Court* (New York: W.W. Norton, 2010), 5.

76. Shesol, *Supreme Power*, 193, 219–21; Danelski, *Supreme Court Justice Is Appointed*, 185–86; William E. Leuchtenburg, "Charles Evans Hughes: The Center Holds," *North Carolina Law Review*, Vol. 83 (2005), 1193–94.

CHAPTER SIX

1. Donald L. Miller, *Supreme City: How Jazz Age Manhattan Gave Birth to Modern America* (New York: Simon & Schuster, 2014), 169.

2. Tom Nicholas and Anna Scherbina, "Real Estate Prices During the Roaring Twenties and the Great Depression," *Real Estate Economics*, Vol. 41 (2013), 278–309.

3. Transcript of Record, 658–59; *Brooklyn Daily Eagle*, March 15, 1923, 19; March 27, 1923, 8; January 9, 1924, 44; September 27, 1925, 66.

4. Transcript of Record, 1005–6 (GX 120).

5. Transcript of Record, 659, 679; *In re Levy*, 30 F. Supp. 317 (S.D.N.Y. 1939); Report of John F. Collins, Referee, 29–31, in Levy Record on Appeal.

6. *Brooklyn Daily Eagle*, May 11, 1920, 5; November 12, 1920; 18; January 28, 1921, 16.

7. *New York Times*, February 2, 1921, 17; "Pressman Denied Right to Dictate Terms of Labor," *Brooklyn Daily Eagle*, February 22, 1922, 1; "Arbitration Ends Old Labor Dispute," February 23, 1922, 8; "Positions of Pressmen and Publishers Stated," *Boston Globe*, September 19, 1923, 2.

8. *Brooklyn Daily Eagle*, January 30, 1939, 2.

9. *New York Times*, January 21, 1920, 25; March 4, 1922, 12; October 21, 1923, 67; August 23, 1924, 16; November 13, 1920, 24; December 17, 1920, 32.

10. *New York Times*, April 29, 1922, 28; *New York Herald*, June 15, 1922, 18 *New York Times*, November 7, 1926, 16; *New York Times*, June 13, 1929, 52; *New York Times*, August 10, 1929, 14; *New York Times*, May 17, 1930, 12; Papers on Appeal, *In re Sullivan's Estate*, 255 A.D. 1008 (2d Dep't 1938), 10.

11. *New York Times*, November 15, 1923, 21; *New York Daily News*, November 22, 1923, 6, December 16, 1923, 84; "Spotlight on Winhold Reiss: Art and Design in New York, 1913–1953," www.winoldreiss.org/news/2014-germanconsulate.htm.

12. *Brooklyn Daily Eagle*, June 9, 1925, 17; *Real Estate Record and Builders' Guide*, July 1, 1922, 11; "Esplanade Hotel in $2,500,000 Deal," *New York Herald*, November 19, 1922, 37.

13. Borkin, *Corrupt Judge*, 50.

14. FBI Report, May 26, 1939, 22–23 (interview of Charles Kilby) (DOJ Files); *Chat*, February 14, 1920, 52.

15. *Brooklyn Life and Activities of Long Island Society*, May 14, 1927, 19.

16. S. Burton Heath, "$35,000 Manton Investment Netted Judge $552,082 Over a 14-Year Period," *New York World-Telegram*, January 28, 1939; Frank G. Holmes, "Genius

and Industry of Jacob Mellon Built Great Laundry Organization Here," *Brooklyn Daily Eagle*, September 26, 1933, 1.

17. Levy Record on Appeal, 20; S. Burton Heath, "Partner of Jurist Obtained Money for His Concerns," *New York World-Telegram*, January 27, 1939.

18. FBI Report, April 4, 1939, 59 (showing Manton's ownership of a "hog ranch" in Sayville in 1920) (DOJ Files); *Suffolk County News*, January 9, 1920, 8; May 27, 1921, 10; August 19, 1921, 6; September 9, 1921, 11.

19. FBI Report, April 4, 1939, 59–62 (showing Manton's personal financial statements given to banks on various dates between 1920 and 1931).

20. *New York Evening Post*, April 19, 1924, F15.

21. Miller, *Supreme City*, 171–72, 177–79; Stuart Chase, "Park Avenue," *New Republic*, May 25, 1927, 9–11.

22. Richard Morton, "An Essay on Duplex Apartments in General, and Those at 471 Park Avenue in Particular," in *Apartment Houses of the Metropolis* (New York: G. C. Hesselgren Publishing, 1908), 5–6.

23. "Duplex Apartment Plan Shown to Advantage," *New York Times*, August 16, 1908, 17; *Architects' and Builders' Magazine*, Vol. 41, no. 5 (February 1909), 224.

24. "Federal Judge Rents a Duplex," *New York Times*, October 8, 1927, 30; New York Blue Book—1930, http://bklyn-genealogy-info.stevemorse.org/Directory/Blue/1930.BlueM.html.

25. *Suffolk County News*, September 12, 1924, 2.

26. Author's interview of Jeff Denning (Manton grandson), July 29, 2022; *Brooklyn Daily Eagle*, August 11, 1931, 9 (David); *Brooklyn Times Union*, October 1, 1933, 23 (Catherine).

27. *Suffolk County News*, July 31, 1925, 2; *Motor Boating*, February 1927, 199.

28. Miller, *Supreme City*, 179.

29. "Mantons to Visit Europe," *Brooklyn Daily Times*, July 21, 1922, 3; *Brooklyn Daily Times*, July 30, 1922, 10; USS *America*, Wikipedia entry, https://en.wikipedia.org/wiki/USS_America_(ID-3006).

30. *Brooklyn Life*, July 12, 1924, 14; SS *Leviathan* Passenger List, August 10, 1926https://www.gjenvick.com/Passengers/USL/Leviathan-PassengerList-1926-08-10.html; SS *Leviathan*, Wikipedia entry, https://en.wikipedia.org/wiki/SS_Leviathan.

31. *Brooklyn Daily Eagle*, July 22, 1928, 24; SS *George Washington*, Wikipedia entry, https://en.wikipedia.org/wiki/SS_George_Washington.

32. *New York Evening Post*, October 4, 1927, 11.

33. *New York Times*, February 16, 1927, 15; May 7, 1927, 20; January 3, 1928, 43; October 27, 1930, 23.

34. "Manton and Kelly, Brooklyn Jurists, Knighted by Pope," *Brooklyn Daily Eagle*, July 31, 1924, 4.

35. "St. Gregory Knights Honored by Dinner at N.Y. Catholic Club," *Catholic Advance*, December 13, 1924, 14.

36. "Catholic Throngs Defy Wind and Rain in Pontifical Mass," *Indianapolis Star*, June 22, 1926, 1–2.

37. Letter from Taft to Pierce Butler, November 7, 1922 (Taft Papers).

38. *Brooklyn Citizen*, November 24, 1918, 3; *Brooklyn Daily Eagle*, November 4, 1916, 9.

39. *Brooklyn Daily Eagle*, July 24, 1918, 4; *Brooklyn Daily Eagle*, September 24, 1919, 1; *Charlotte Observer*, January 8, 1920, 1; *Suffolk County News*, July 9, 1920, 2.

40. "Curtin and Manton to Go to the Convention," *Brooklyn Daily Eagle*, February 24, 1928, 15; "Is Judge Manton to Be a Delegate to Houston?," *Brooklyn Standard Union*, February 29, 1928, 2; *New York Times*, March 2, 1928, 12.

41. "Murphy Holds Conference to Solve Puzzle," *New York Sun*, July 5, 1920, 1.

42. Robert K. Murray, *The 103rd Ballot: Democrats and the Disaster in Madison Square Garden* (New York: Harper & Row, 1976), 69; "Ratify on the Leviathan," *New York Times*, July 11, 1924, 2 (Manton and others made speeches aboard the SS *Leviathan* endorsing the Democratic presidential ticket); "Davis Off on 4-Day Speechmaking Trip," *New York Times*, September 25, 1924, 3 (noting that Davis conferred with "several prominent Democrats," including Manton, before setting off on a campaign trip).

43. "Judge Martin T. Manton Questions Coolidge's Sincerity After Letter from President Is Read at Dinner," *Brooklyn Daily Eagle*, October 14, 1924, 4; "Federal Attorney Raps Judge Manton," *New York Times*, October 25, 1924, 25.

44. "Congratulations Pour In on Gov. Smith from All Parts of the Country," *New York Times*, June 30, 1928, 3; Letter from Manton to Raskob, July 23, 1928 (John J. Raskob Papers at Hagley Museum in Delaware); "Manton Return From Europe," *New York Times*, August 18, 1928, 11; "$150,000 Is Pledged to Fight Bigotry," *New York Times*, September 19, 1928, 24.

45. *Brooklyn Standard Union*, August 31, 1922, 2; "Hylan Refuses to Be Shelved in Supreme Ct.," *Brooklyn Daily Eagle*, July 22, 1925, 1; *Brooklyn Citizen*, July 23, 1925, 3; *New York Evening Post*, July 25, 1925, 5.

46. Gunther, *Learned Hand*, 278.

47. *Brooklyn Daily Times*, October 13, 1923, 11; *New York Times*, January 15, 1924, 4.

48. *Brooklyn Daily Times*, June 14, 1923, 10.

49. Daniel Okrent, *Last Call: The Rise and Fall of Prohibition* (New York: Scribner, 2010), 214, 244, 254, 307, 253.

50. H. M. DuBose, D.D., "A Highly Approved Appointment," *Christian Advocate*, March 28, 1918, 347.

51. "Drys Usher in 1922 with Many Raids," *New York Times*, January 1, 1922, 7; "Ignored Dry Law, Café Shut for a Year," *New York Times*, October 12, 1922, 3; "Order Closing Café for Year Sustained," *New York Times*, January 19, 1923, 3.

52. "Invited Minister to Swear He Saw Liquor at Dinner," *Evening World*, May 3, 1922, 8; "Rum and Rowdyism at Riding Class Dinner, Says Preacher; Walked Out, Sent Check Back," *Brooklyn Daily Eagle*, May 3, 1922, 1–2; "Pastor Quit Dinner Because It Was Wet," *New York Times*, May 3, 1922, 34.

53. *Evening World*, May 3, 1922, 8; Lucas G. Rubin, *Brooklyn's Sportsmen's Row: Politics, Society and the Sporting Life on Northern Eighth Avenue* (Charleston, SC: History Press, 2012), 145.

54. "Diners Won't Reply to 'Orgy' Charges," *New York Herald*, May 4, 1922, 3.

55. "Says He Saw Rum Near Judge Manton," *New York Times*, May 8, 1922, 16; "Whisky Bottle Near Judge Manton, Says Pastor, at Banquet," *Brooklyn Daily Eagle*, May 8, 1922, 22.

56. Okrent, *Last Call*, 274.

57. Okrent, *Last Call*, 264.

58. J. Anne Funderberg, *Bootleggers and Beer Barons of the Prohibition Era* (Jefferson, NC: McFarland, 2014), 69–71.

59. *New Republic*, November 15, 1922, 293.

60. Miller, *Supreme City*, 65–67, 85–88.

61. FBI Report, February 17, 1939, 5–6 (interview of Charles Greenhouse [*sic*]) (DOJ Files); *New York Times*, August 17, 1926, 22; August 19, 1926, 4; August 21, 1926, 13; *Dwyer v. United States*, 17 F.2d 696, 698–99 (2d Cir. 1927) (Manton, J., dissenting).

62. Transcript of Record, 618; *Brooklyn Tablet*, June 18, 1921, 8 (Manhattan); *Brooklyn Times Union*, June 8, 1932, 32 (NYU); *Burlington Daily News*, June 19, 1933, 1 (Vermont); *Olean Times Herald*, June 10, 1936, 8 (St. Bonaventure).

63. *New York Times*, June 16, 1926, 19.

CHAPTER SEVEN

1. Brian J. Cudahy, *A Century of Subways: Celebrating 100 Years of New York's Underground Railways* (New York: Fordham University Press, 2003), 49.

2. "Walker Stands on Five-Cent Fare Issue; Hylan Hits Smith," *New York Times*, August 8, 1925, 1; "Smith-Walker Rift on Transit Near," *New York Daily News*, December 16, 1926, 6.

3. Jamison Wilcox, "Autobiography of Thomas L. Chadbourne, Esq.," *DePaul Law Review*, Vol. 35 (1986), 961 (book review); "New Group of Transit Barons, Chadbourne Very Prominent Among Them, Is Disclosed Through Probe Conducted by Untermyer," *Brooklyn Daily Eagle*, May 29, 1927, 15.

4. David Margolick, "Deleted from Book: Gifts to Alfred E. Smith," *New York Times*, May 22, 1985, B2; Wilcox, "Autobiography," 972 and n.45; "New Group of Transit Barons."

5. Margolick, "Deleted from Book," A1.

6. "B.M.T. Is Revealed as a Heavy Owner of Stock in I.R.T.," *New York Times*, May 26, 1927, 1.

7. Clarence Worden, "Traction King Due for Quiz by Untermyer," *New York Daily News*, May 25, 1927, 7; "New Group of Transit Barons."

8. Richard A. Hawkins, "Lynchburg's Swabian Jewish Entrepreneurs in War and Peace," *Southern Jewish History*, Vol. 3 (2000), 60–62.

9. Gil Troy, "Samuel Untermyer: The Superlawyer Who Took on Hitler," *Daily Beast*, November 19, 2017.

10. Clarence Worden, "Traction King Due for Quiz by Untermyer"; "High Transit Chiefs Called for Inquiry," *New York Times*, May 19, 1927, 19.

11. "5-Cent Fare in Serious Danger," *New York Daily News*, June 1, 1927, 14.

12. "Untermyer Tries to Show Control Deal to Control Transit," *Brooklyn Daily Eagle*, May 31, 1927, 1.

13. See, e.g., *Smyth v. Ames*, 171 U.S. 361 (1898).

14. *Consolidated Gas Co. of New York v. Newton*, 267 F. 231 (S.D.N.Y. 1920), modified, 258 U.S. 165 (1922).

15. "5-Cent Fare in Serious Danger," *New York Daily News*, June 1, 1927, 14; "Coming Out in the Wash," *New York Daily News*, June 3, 1927, 17.

16. "Interborough Demands 7-Cent Fare," *New York Times*, February 2, 1928, 1; "I.R.T. Gets a Federal Writ Halting Suits by the City to Block the 7-Cent Fare," *New York Times*, February 18, 1929, 1.

17. "Federal Court Takes Over Jurisdiction in Fare Suit; Bars Rise Pending Ruling," *New York Times*, March 16, 1928, 1.

18. "Federal Court Takes Over Jurisdiction," 1; *Interborough Rapid Transit Co. v. Gilchrist*, 25 F.2d 164 (S.D.N.Y. 1928).

19. "Assails the Critics of Federal Courts," *New York Times*, April 27, 1928, 24.

20. "Interborough Gets 7-Cent Fare Order, But Stay Is Likely on City's Appeal; Walker to Run Again to Keep Up Fight," *New York Times*, May 3, 1928, 1; "I.R.T. Wins 7-Cent Fare," *New York Daily News*, May 3, 1928, 4.

21. *Interborough Rapid Transit Co. v. Gilchrist*, 26 F.2d 912 (S.D.N.Y. 1928).

22. "The Seven-Cent Fare Decision," *Brooklyn Daily Eagle*, May 3, 1928, 8; "I.R.T. Wins 7-Cent Fare," 3; "The Seven-Cent Fare," *New York Times*, May 3, 1928, 19.

23. "The Growing Power of the Federal Courts," *New York Daily News*, May 4, 1928, 31.

24. *Interborough Rapid Transit Co. v. Gilchrist*, 26 F.2d, 925.

25. "Transit Stocks Up Prior to Decision," *New York Times*, May 3, 1928, 1; "B.M.T. May Follow I.R.T. in Fare Fight," *New York Times*, May 3, 1928, 1.

26. This disclosure, which I believe has not heretofore been publicly known, is contained in the unpublished chapter of Chadbourne's autobiography. I thank Charles Goetsch, Esq., one of the editors of the autobiography, for providing me with access to an excerpt of the unpublished chapter pertaining to the subway fare case.

27. *In re Levy*, 30 F. Supp. 317 (S.D.N.Y. 1939); Levy Record on Appeal, 383–85; S. Burton Heath, "Partner of Jurist Obtained Money for His Concerns," *New York World-Telegram*, January 27, 1939.

28. Heath, "Partner of Jurist Obtained Money for His Concerns."

29. *Gilchrist v. Interborough Rapid Transit Co.*, 279 U.S. 159 (1927).

30. *Crescent Mfg. Co. v. Wilson*, 242 F. 462, 463 (2d Cir. 1917) (quoting statute).

31. Referee's Report, Levy Record on Appeal, 26–28, 87–88.

32. "Manton Is Disputed by Witness for Levy," *New York Times*, February 22, 1940, 15; Levy Record on Appeal, 1099–1101.

33. William Woodford, "That Terrible 'Tiger Room' Where Kenny and Al Go Has an Electric Horse!," *Brooklyn Daily Eagle*, May 18, 1928, 3; Testimony of William F. Kenny, Presidential Campaign Expenditures: Hearings Before a Special Committee Investigating Presidential Campaign Expenditures of the United States Senate, 70th Cong., 1st Sess. (May 16, 1928), 310–20.

34. Excerpts of unpublished chapter of Chadbourne autobiography reviewed by the author.

35. Excerpts of unpublished chapter of Chadbourne autobiography reviewed by the author.

36. "Judge Manton and the Supreme Court," *New Republic*, July 19, 1933, 248. The essay was republished in *Felix Frankfurter on the Supreme Court: Extrajudicial Essays on the Court and Constitution*, P. Kurland, ed. (Cambridge, MA: Harvard University Press, 1970).

37. See *City of New York v. Interborough Rapid Transit Co.*, 257 N.Y. 20 (1931), affirming, 232 A.D. 233 (1st Dep't 1931), affirming, 136 Misc. 569 (Sup. Ct. N.Y. Cnty. 1930).

CHAPTER EIGHT

1. Transcript of Record, 1000, 1003 (Manton's testimony in 1934 deposition that the mortgage debt on the Alamac, Esplanade, and Hughes Airport property was $2.49 million, $2.24 million, and $1.85 million, respectively); *Investment Trusts and Investment Companies: Report of the U.S. Securities and Exchange Commission*, Part Three, February 1941, 2710–12; Tom Nicholas & Anna Scherbina, "Real Estate Prices During the Roaring Twenties and the Great Depression," *Real Estate Economics*, Vol. 41 (2013), 278–309.

2. "Inventory of Bank of U.S. Shows Condition the Day Before It Was Closed by State," *New York Times*, February 2, 1931, 10.

3. Mitgang, *Man Who Rode the Tiger*, 166–68; "Bar Asks Vitale Removal on Corruption Charges," *New York Times*, February 16, 1930, 1; "Vitale Says He Made $165,000 in Four Years While on the Bench," *New York Times*, March 13, 1930, 1.

4. Mitgang, *Man Who Rode the Tiger*, 169–70; Stolberg, *Fighting Organized Crime*, 15–16, 21–22; "Thomas Criticizes Chief Magistrate," *New York Times*, January 10, 1930, 15; "Republicans At Odds on Plan for Inquiry into Graft in City," *New York Times*, January 15, 1930, 1.

5. *The Investigation of the Magistrates' Courts in the First Judicial Department and the Magistrates Thereof* (New York: Arno Press, 1974), 31, 47, 125–26.

6. Mitgang, *Man Who Rode the Tiger*, 189–90; *Brooklyn Standard Union*, January 2, 1931, 6; "Goodman, Under Fire, Resigns from Bench; Brodsky Suspended," *Brooklyn Daily Eagle*, January 6, 1931, 1; "Simpson, Facing Probe, 'Ill,'" *New York Daily News*, January 15, 1931, 6; "Miller, Called Court 'Fixer,' Faces New Kresel Grilling After Balking Simpson Quiz," *Brooklyn Daily Times*, January 25, 1931, 1–2.

7. Mitgang, *Man Who Rode the Tiger*, 190–91; "Brodsky Weeps at Quiz," *New York Daily News*, January 28, 1931, 10; "Brodsky Is Cleared of Any Wrongdoing; Five Police Indicted," *New York Times*, January 31, 1931, 1.

8. "Judges Bills Win in Senate by Party Vote," *Brooklyn Standard Union*, March 24, 1931, 1; "Governor Sends Message Urging Curb on Judges," *Brooklyn Daily Times*, April 3, 1931, 3; "Court Reform Bills Beaten at Albany," *New York Times*, April 11, 1931, 10.

9. Mitgang, *Man Who Rode the Tiger*, 216–19, 240–41; "Text of Governor's Findings on Farley," *New York Times*, February 25, 1932, 4.

10. Mitgang, *Man Who Rode the Tiger*, 252–53, 259–60.

11. Mitgang, *Man Who Rode the Tiger*, 247–52.

12. "Roosevelt Orders Walker to Answer Removal Charges," *New York Times*, June 23, 1932, 1.

13. James J. O'Connor, Letter to the Editor, *New York Times*, May 4, 1958, 28–29.

14. Herbert Mitgang, *Once Upon a Time in New York: Jimmy Walker, Franklin Roosevelt, and the Last Great Battle of the Jazz Age* (New York: Free Press, 2000), 183–216.

15. Gladwyn Hill, "Tobacco Executive Center of Stockholders' Fireworks," *Evening Star*, March 30, 1941, E4; Virginia Irwin, "Battle in Giant Tobacco Company," *St. Louis Post-Dispatch*, April 8, 1948, 3D; Neil Hickey, "Cigarette Derby: The Fight for Smokers' Favor Is a Mad (Often Merry) Mélange of Slogans, Symbols and $$$," *San Francisco Examiner*, February 18, 1962 (Sunday magazine), 10.

16. "Easter Sun Finds the Past in Shadow at Modern Parade," *New York Times*, April 1, 1929, 3; Hill, "Tobacco Executive"; Obituary (AP), *Minneapolis Star*, September 13, 1946, 1; Irwin, "Battle in Giant Tobacco Company"; Jean Kilbourne, *Can't Buy Me Love: How Advertising Changes the Way We Think and Feel* (New York: Free Press, 1999), 187; *Big Tobacco in the Big Apple: How New York City Became the Heart of the Tobacco Industry . . . and Anti-Smoking Activism* (Center for the Study of Tobacco and Society, University of Alabama, 2018), 21; "The Personal Reminiscences of Albert Lasker," *American Heritage*, Vol. 6, no. 1 (December 1954).

17. *Rogers v. Hill*, 289 U.S. 582, 585 n.2 (1933).

18. "G.W. Hill's Income Put at $2,200,000," *New York Times*, March 14, 1931, 7; *Rogers v. Guaranty Trust Co.*, 288 U.S. 123, 133–35 (1933) (Stone, J., dissenting); Harwell Wells, "'No Man Can Be Worth $1,000,000 a Year': The Fight Over Executive Compensation in 1930s America," *University of Richmond Law Review*, Vol. 44 (2010), 709–11.

19. Obituary, *New York Times*, November 11, 1949, 26; Obituary, *Lexington Herald*, November 24, 1949, 12; *Indianapolis Star*, February 11, 1912, 44; *Evening Star*, December 18, 1912, 7; *Rogers v. Hill*, 34 F. Supp. 358, 363 (S.D.N.Y. 1940).

20. *Rogers v. Guaranty Trust Co. of New York*, 60 F.2d 106 (S.D.N.Y. 1932).

21. Transcript of Record, *Rogers v. Hill*, 60 F.2d 109 (1932), 211–13.

22. "Court Halts Bonuses," *New York Times*, March 19, 1932, 25.

23. *In re Levy*, 30 F. Supp., 321.

24. Levy Record on Appeal, 374 (testimony of Levy).

25. "Levy Contradicts Manton on Stand," *New York Times*, August 3, 1939, 3; "Ties with Manton Defended By Levy," *New York Times*, August 4, 1939, 3; Referee's Report, Levy Record on Appeal, 29–31; Levy Record on Appeal, 360–63 (testimony of Levy).

26. Referee's Report, 71; *Brooklyn Times Union*, February 9, 1932, 13.

27. Transcript of Record, *Rogers v. Hill*, 108; Transcript of Record, *Rogers v. Guaranty Trust Co.*, 60 F.2d 114 (2d Cir. 1932), 239; *Rogers v. Guaranty Trust Co.*, 60 F.2d, 106 (list of counsel); Referee's Report, 14, 16.

28. Transcript of Record, 774–75; *In re Levy*, 30 F. Supp., 321; "Manton, on Stand, Traces Loan Deal," *New York Times*, July 28, 1939, 7.

29. *In re Levy*, 30 F. Supp., 318; Obituary (Paul Hahn), *New York Times*, August 10, 1963, 17.

30. *In re Levy*, 30 F. Supp., 323.

31. *In re Levy*, 30 F. Supp., 323.

32. *In re Levy*, 30 F. Supp., 322–24.

33. Referee's Report, 33; "Lasker Held Dupe in Loan Deal," *New York Times*, July 25, 1939, 1.

34. *In re Levy*, 30 F. Supp., 322–24.

35. Transcript of Record, 775; *In re Levy*, 30 F. Supp., 323, 329; Referee's Report, 97–99.

36. *In re Levy*, 30 F. Supp., 321; Referee's Report, 21, 42, 61; "Letter Is Offered In Levy-Hahn Case," *New York Times*, July 26, 1939, 3; "Manton, on Stand, Traces Loan Deal," *New York Times*, July 28, 1939, 7.

37. *In re Levy*, 30 F. Supp., 323; "Manton, on Stand, Traces Loan Deal"; Transcript of Record, 782, 785; Referee's Report, 59–64, 98.

38. "Bonus Army Gets Orders to March Past White House," *New York Daily News*, June 6, 1932, 4; "Bonus Army Gathers at Capital, June 17, 1932," *Politico*, June 17, 2017; "Hoover Orders Eviction," *New York Times*, July 29, 1932, 1.

39. *Rogers v. Hill*, 60 F.2d 109 (2d Cir. 1932).

40. *Rogers v. Hill*, 60 F.2d, 113–14 (Swan, J., dissenting).

41. *Rogers v. Guaranty Trust Co.*, 60 F.2d 114 (2d Cir. 1932).

42. *Rogers v. Guaranty Trust Co.*, 60 F.2d, 120–22 (Swan, J., dissenting).

43. Eugene V. Rostow, "Thomas W. Swan, 1877–1975," *Yale Law Journal*, Vol. 85 (1975), 159–63.

44. *Rogers v. Hill*, 60 F.2d, 113; *Rogers v. Guaranty Trust*, 60 F.2d at 117; "Judge Manton and the Supreme Court."

45. *Rogers v. Taylor*, 62 F.2d 1079 (2d Cir. 1933); Note, *Harvard Law Review*, Vol. 46 (1933), 830 n.19.

46. *Rogers v. Guaranty Trust Co.*, 288 U.S. 123 (1933).

47. *Rogers v. Guaranty Trust Co.*, 288 U.S., 133–50 (Stone, J. dissenting); *id.*, 150–51 (Cardozo, J., dissenting).

48. "Tobacco Chiefs Are Assailed by Three High Court Justices," *Chicago Tribune*, January 24, 1933, 6; "Puts Tobacco Suit Up to New Jersey," *New York Times*, January 24, 1933, 27; "Higher Ethics for Corporations," *Asbury Park Press*, February 7, 1933, 8; "Hill Refuses Allotment of Tobacco Shares," *Brooklyn Daily Eagle*, February 11, 1933, 21; "Says Bonus Helps American Tobacco," *New York Times*, February 11, 1933, 23.

49. *Rogers v. Hill*, 289 U.S. 582, 591–92 (1933).

50. "Tobacco Bonuses Must Face Inquiry," *New York Times*, May 30, 1933, 1; "Modest Salaries Replace Big Ones," *Muncie Evening Press*, June 15, 1933, 4; "Attacks Huge Salary Paid Tobacco Company Head," *Baltimore Sun*, September 16, 1933, 1.

51. "American Tobacco Cuts Big Bonuses," *New York Times*, July 14, 1933, 25; *Mathews v. American Tobacco Co.*, 130 N.J. Equity 470, 23 A.2d 101 (Ct. Chancery 1941).

52. "Judge Manton and the Supreme Court."

53. *In re Levy*, 30 F. Supp., 324–25.

54. The Westlaw database shows that Steuer participated in eleven appeals before the Second Circuit from 1926 to 1936. Manton sat in all but one of the cases. On Steuer, see the biography by his son, Aron Steuer, *Max D. Steuer, Trial Lawyer* (New York: Random House, 1950), and the profile in Louis S. Levy's *Yesterdays* (New York: Library Publishers, 1954), 44–57.

55. *In re Levy*, 30 F. Supp., 324–26.

56. *In re Levy*, 30 F. Supp., 326.

57. *In re Levy*, 30 F. Supp., 326–27; John Gunther, *Taken at the Flood: The Story of Albert D. Lasker* (New York: Harper & Brothers, 1960), 251.

58. Gunther, *Taken at the Flood*, 250; *In re Levy*, 30 F. Supp., 327.

CHAPTER NINE

1. "Another Receiver Indicted for Theft," *New York Times*, January 18, 1929, 16; "Say Helfand Told of Court Influence," *New York Times*, March 12, 1929, 27; Knox, *Judge Comes of Age*, 196–205.

2. "Winslow Assailed by U.S. Grand Jury," *New York Daily News*, February 28, 1929, 2; "Judge Winslow Accused in House Move for Inquiry on His Fitness for Bench," *New York Times*, February 13, 1929, 1; "Winslow Impeached Before the House by F.H. LaGuardia," *New York Times*, March 3, 1929, 1.

3. "Judge Moscowitz Now Is Accused," *New York Times*, February 24, 1929, 1; Hearing Before the Special Committee of the House of Representatives Pursuant to H.J. Res. 431 and 434, 70th Cong., Serial 1-Part 1 (April 1929), 1314–28; "House 'Condemns' Judge Moscowitz," *New York Times*, April 9, 1930, 1.

4. "Bank to Be Receiver in All Failures Here," *New York Times*, January 17, 1929, 1.

5. Knox, *Judge Comes of Age*, 199.

6. Knox, *Judge Comes of Age*, 196, 208–9.

7. "Bank's Monopoly as Receiver Scored," *New York Times*, June 15, 1932, 21.

8. "Bank as Receiver Defended by Court," *New York Times*, June 17, 1932, 34.

9. *American Brake Shoe & Foundry Co. v. Interborough Rapid Transit Co.*, 1 F. Supp. 820, 825 (S.D.N.Y. 1932).

10. Letter from Woolsey to Felix Frankfurter, October 31, 1932, in Felix Frankfurter Papers at the Library of Congress (Box 149, Reel 93–94).

11. *American Brake Shoe & Foundry Co.*, 1 F. Supp., 825.

12. *Johnson v. Manhattan Ry. Co.*, 1 F. Supp. 809, 813 (S.D.N.Y. 1932).

13. 28 U.S.C. § 22; 28 U.S.C. § 731 (both since repealed); *American Brake Shoe & Foundry Co.*, 1 F. Supp., 825–27.

14. "Judge Manton Asks Lawyer-Receivers," *New York Times*, July 8, 1932, 3.

15. "Criticizes Irving Trust," *New York Times*, July 9, 1932, 2.

16. *Johnson v. Manhattan Ry. Co.*, 289 U.S. 479, 484 (1933); Hearings Before a Special Committee on Investigation of Bankruptcy and Receivership Proceedings in United States Courts, 73rd Cong., 2d Sess. (June 26, 1934), 1577.

17. *Johnson*, 289 U.S., 484–89; "I.R.T. Ordered into Receivership," *Brooklyn Daily Eagle*, August 26, 1932, 1; "I.R.T. in Receivership; Move Hailed as Aid to Reunification Plan," *New York Times*, August 27, 1932, 1, 8.

18. Letter from Charles C. Burlingham to Felix Frankfurter, September 5, 1932 (Frankfurter Papers).

19. Letter from Burlingham to Frankfurter, September 5, 1932; *see* Michael L. Redmond, "Sir William Schwenk Gilbert and the Illogic of the Law," *Stetson Law Review*, Vol. 39 (2009), 85–118.

20. Letter from Charles C. Burlingham to Felix Frankfurter, September 10, 1932 (Frankfurter Papers).

21. Letter to the Editor, *New York Times*, October 14, 1932, 18.

22. Frankfurter diary entry for September 28, 1932, in Oliver Wendell Holmes Jr. Digital Collection, available through Harvard Law School Library's website.

23. "Holds Manton's Acts Illegal in I.R.T. Case," *New York Times*, September 22, 1932, 1, 3.

24. Letter from Coxe to Frankfurter, September 27, 1932 (Frankfurter Papers).

25. "City Not to Enter in I.R.T. Hearing," *Wall Street Journal*, September 22, 1932, 1; "I.R.T. Receivership Continued by Court," *New York Times*, September 23, 1932, 1.

26. *Johnson v. Manhattan Ry. Co.*, 1 F. Supp., 812, 817.

27. Letter from Woolsey to Frankfurter, October 15, 1932 (Frankfurter Papers).

28. *American Brake Shoe & Foundry Co. v. Interborough Rapid Transit Co.*, 1 F. Supp. 820 (S.D.N.Y. 1932).

29. *Johnson v. Manhattan Ry. Co.*, 61 F.2d 934 (2d Cir. 1932).

30. *Johnson v. Manhattan Ry. Co.*, 289 U.S. 479 (1933).

31. *American Brake Shoe & Foundry Co. v. Interborough Rapid Transit Co.*, 4 F. Supp. 68 (S.D.N.Y. 1933).

32. "Judge Manton and the Supreme Court."

33. "I.R.T. Case Ouster Fought by Manton," *New York Times*, August 3, 1933, 18; "Manton Is Defied on I.R.T. Authority," *New York Times*, August 8, 1933, 9; *American Brake Shoe & Foundry Co. v. Interborough Rapid Transit Co.*, 6 F. Supp. 215 (S.D.N.Y. 1933).

34. "Manton Fight Goes to Supreme Court," *New York Times*, September 18, 1933, 21; Letter from Charles C. Burlingham to Chief Justice Hughes, September 8, 1933 (Frankfurter Papers).

35. "Order in I.R.T. Case Restrains Manton," *New York Times*, September 24, 1933, 1; *American Brake Shoe & Foundry Co. v. Interborough Rapid Transit Co.*, 6 F. Supp. 215, 219–21 (S.D.N.Y. 1933).

36. Letter from Burlingham to Frankfurter, September 10, 1932 (Frankfurter Papers).

37. Gould, *Witness Who Spoke with God*, 194.

38. Transcript of Record, 800–801; FBI Report, April 4, 1939, 11, 17 (DOJ Files); "Not a Pretty Story," *Time*, June 5, 1939, 18; Heath, *Yankee Reporter*, 255–56; Drew Pearson, "The Merry-Go-Round," *Palm Beach Post*, August 21, 1958, 4.

39. "I.R.T. Receivership Continued by Court."

40. Heath, *Yankee Reporter*, 256.

41. Memorandum from FBI Inspector P. E. Foxworth to FBI Director Hoover, March 14, 1939 (DOJ Files); FBI Report, March 11, 1939 (DOJ Files).

42. FBI Report, March 11, 1939, 2, 5 (interview of Alexander Heid), 11 (interview of Philip Farley); FBI Report, March 27, 1939, 7–9 (interview of Kenneth Steinreich) (DOJ Files); FBI Report, April 4, 1939, 35.

43. Foxworth Memorandum, 2.

44. FBI Report, March 11, 1939, 7 (interview of Thomas J. Kennedy), 10 (interview of Ruth McKenna).

45. Heath, *Yankee Reporter*, 260; FBI Report, February 24, 1939, 17.

46. *Chicago Title & Trust Co. v. Fox Theatres Corp.*, 182 F. Supp. 18, 26 (S.D.N.Y. 1960); Transcript of Record, 765–67; FBI Report, September 12, 1939, 1; FBI Report, April 17, 1939, 14–15 (interview of Milton Altmark).

47. Heath, *Yankee Reporter*, 260–61; *Chicago Title & Trust Co.*, 182 F. Supp., 26.

48. "Continues Fox Theatres," *New York Times*, January 12, 1937, 35; "G. P. Skouras Indicted by U.S. in Manton Bribe," *Brooklyn Daily Eagle*, August 30, 1940, 1; "Manton Bribe Laid to Movie Operator," *New York Times*, August 31, 1940, 15; "Fox Theater Firm Here Given Part of N.Y. Building," *St. Louis Star & Times*, May 24, 1944, 4; *Chicago Title & Trust Co.*, 182 F. Supp., 26–27; FBI Report, July 6, 1939, 1; FBI Report, March 20, 1940, 1 (DOJ Files); FBI Memorandum, April 11, 1952 (provided by the FBI pursuant to author's FOIA request).

49. Robert T. Swaine, *The Cravath Firm and Its Predecessors, 1819–1947* (New York: Lawbook Exchange, 2007 reprint), Vol. III, 538 n.1.

50. George Dixon, "Manton Debt Paid by Hines, Records Show," *New York Daily News*, July 7, 1939, 4; "Says Hines Aided Manton 'Because We Needed Him,'" *New York Daily News*, July 8, 1939, 4; Transcript of Record, 767–72; Heath, *Yankee Reporter*, 283–84; FBI Report, February 14, 1939, 28 (statement of Handelsman).

51. *Suffolk County News*, February 8, 1907, 3; *New York Daily News*, May 10, 1924, 3; Transcript of Record, 628.

52. *New York Daily News*, May 9, 1924, 3; May 10, 1924, 3; May 11, 1924, 4; May 12, 1924, 8; *New York Times*, December 15, 1925, 16; *Black Diamond*, January 29, 1921, 16; *Buck Ridge Coal Mining Co. v. Rosoff Eng'g Co.*, 215 A.D. 441 (1st Dep't 1926).

53. Letter from District Attorney Thomas E. Dewey to the Honorable Hatton W. Sumners, Chairman of the House Judiciary Committee, January 29, 1939, reprinted in *New York Times*, Jan. 30, 1939, 1, 3; Heath, *Yankee Reporter*, 257–58; FBI Report, March 16, 1939 (interview of Charles Rogers); FBI Report, February 14, 1939, 33–34 (Rogers letter).

54. *Brooklyn Daily Eagle*, February 1, 1935, 3; Memorandum from Acting US Attorney Gregory F. Noonan, February 2, 1939, 8 (DOJ Files).

55. Transcript of Record, 150–51, 159, 760; S. Burton Heath, "G-Men Study Manton Moves in Prudence Co.," *New York World-Telegram*, June 5, 1939; FBI Report, June 12, 1939, 10 (interview of Herbert Pechman).

56. Letter from District Attorney Dewey to Cong. Sumners, January 29, 1939; Transcript of Record, 760–65.

CHAPTER TEN

1. Larry Clayton, *The Evans Book: Lighters, Compacts, Perfumers, and Handbags* (Atglen, PA: Schiffer Publishing, 1998); Orra L. Stone, *History of Massachusetts Industries* (Boston: S. J. Clarke Publishing, 1930), Vol. I, 286–87; *Women's Wear Daily*, January 24, 1929, 4; *Women's Wear Daily*, March 24, 1932, 2.

2. *The Story of a Life: A Tribute to Louis V. Aronson* (Newark: Colyer Printing, 1929); Robert Wiener, "Newark Inventor Who Set the World on Fire," *New Jersey Jewish News*, April 22, 2015; Obituary (Louis V. Aronson), *New York Times*, November 3, 1940, 59.

3. *Art Metal Works, Inc. v. Abraham Straus, Inc.*, 52 F.2d 951 (E.D.N.Y. 1931).

4. Transcript of Record, *Art Metal Works, Inc. v. Abraham Straus, Inc.*, 70 F.2d 641 (2d Cir. 1934), 103–4.

5. *Art Metal Works, Inc. v. Abraham Straus, Inc.*, 61 F.2d 122 (2d Cir. 1932).

6. *Art Metal Works, Inc. v. Abraham Straus, Inc.*, 70 F.2d 641, 642–44 (2d Cir. 1934); Transcript of Record, *Art Metal v. Abraham Straus*, 1019, 1288–89.

7. Transcript of Record, 100.

8. Transcript of Record, 95.

9. Obituary, *New York Times*, October 7, 1962, 82; Dora Albert, "Modern Millionaire Works Hard," *Brooklyn Eagle*, March 3, 1929, 6.

10. *Coriell v. Morris White, Inc.*, 54 F.2d 255 (2d Cir. 1931). The Supreme Court later overturned Manton's ruling. *National Surety Co. v. Coriell*, 289 U.S. 426 (1933).

11. Transcript of Record, 95–98, 100.

12. Transcript of Record, 48–53; FBI Report, June 2, 1939, 2 (interview of Fallon) (DOJ Files).

13. Rian James, *Dining in New York* (New York: John Day, 1930), 161–63.

14. Transcript of Record, 53–54.

15. Transcript of Record, 54; *H.W. Peters Co. v. MacDonald*, 61 F.2d 1031 (2d Cir. 1932).

16. *Art Metal Works, Inc. v. Abraham Straus, Inc.*, 62 F.2d 79 (2d Cir. 1932); Transcript of Record, 100–101.

17. *Art Metal Works, Inc. v. Abraham Straus, Inc.*, 4 F. Supp. 298, 299 (E.D.N.Y. 1933).

18. *Art Metal Works*, 4 F. Supp., 301.

19. Transcript of Record, 56–61.

20. Transcript of Record, 62–64, 120–24. In early August 1933, Manton did set sail for Europe aboard the RMS *Olympic*. *New York Times*, August 4, 1933, 19. At his trial, Manton denied attending the 1933 World Series and said he had not been to a World Series in two decades. Transcript of Record, 632–33. Fallon told the FBI he may have purchased the box for his own benefit. FBI Report, June 2, 1939, 9.

21. Transcript of Record, 64–66, 123–24.

22. Transcript of Record, 70.

23. Transcript of Record, 70–72, 108, 131, 890–92 (GX 15).

24. FBI Report, February 10, 1939, 18 (interview of Kenneth Neal) (DOJ Files); Transcript of Record, 37–39.

25. Transcript of Record, 77.

26. *Art Metal Works, Inc. v. Abraham Straus, Inc.*, 70 F.2d 641 (2d Cir. 1934); *Art Metal Works, Inc. v. Abraham Straus, Inc.*, 70 F.2d 639 (2d Cir. 1934).

27. Transcript of Record, 77–81.

28. Transcript of Record, 84–85; FBI Report, May 24, 1939, 15–16 (interview of Reilly).

29. "Wage Increase and Bonus Given by Evans Case Co.," *Boston Globe*, February 18, 1937, 14; *Women's Wear Daily*, September 17, 1940, 2; *Women's Wear Daily*, July 11, 1941, 14; "Cigarette Lighter Sales Rise Tenfold in Decade As War Habit Sticks," *Women's Wear Daily*, May 17, 1950, 1.

30. Obituary (Mrs. Louis V. Aronson), *New York Times*, March 17, 1934, 15; "Banker Testifies to Charter Deal," *New York Times*, October 17, 1928, 10; FBI Report, May 24, 1939, 59–62 (interview of Louis Aronson) (DOJ Files); FBI Report, February 10, 1939, 17 (interview of Kenneth Neal).

31. Hoover, "Freeing Our Courts," 84.

32. FBI Report, February 10, 1939, 17–19 (interview of Alexander Harris); FBI Report, February 13, 1939, 29–30 (interview of Joseph Lorenz); FBI Report, May 24, 1939, 57–58 (interview of confidential informant).

33. *Art Metal Works, Inc. v. Abraham Straus, Inc.*, 107 F.2d 940 (2d Cir. 1939); *Art Metal Works, Inc. v. Abraham Straus, Inc.*, 70 F.2d 944 (2d Cir. 1939).

34. Obituary (Louis V. Aronson); Tyler T. Ochoa, "Patent and Copyright Term Extension and the Constitution: A Historical Perspective," *Journal, Copyright Society of the U.S.A.*, Vol. 49 (2002), 72–74.

35. *Art Metal Works*, 70 F.2d, 644.

36. *Art Metal Works*, 70 F.2d, 642, 644.

37. *Art Metal Works*, 70 F.2d, 645 (L. Hand, J., dissenting).

38. *Art Metal Works*, 70 F.2d, 646 (L. Hand, J., dissenting).

39. "Recent Decisions," *Columbia Law Review*, Vol. 34 (1934), 1370–71; "Recent Cases," *George Washington Law Review*, Vol. 3 (1934), 403–5; "Notes," *Yale Law Journal*, Vol. 44 (1934), 353–54.

40. Gunther, *Learned Hand*, 286.

41. "Some Recollections of My Year with Judge Learned Hand," 9; Transcript of Interview of Arthur L. Dougan, 8 and Transcript of Interview of Herman Finkelstein, 28, both in Smith/Packer Research Materials (Box 14–17, 14–21).

42. Transcript of Record, 1011 (GX 120).

CHAPTER ELEVEN

1. *Cinema Patents Co. v. Warner Bros. Pictures*, 55 F.2d 948 (E.D.N.Y. 1932).

2. FBI Report, June 12, 1939, 3 (interview of Harry Warner) (DOJ Files); FBI Report, April 24, 1939, 11–14; Transcript of Record, 788–89.

3. FBI Report, June 12, 1939, 3–4; FBI Report, April 24, 1939, 11–14; Transcript of Record 788–90.

4. *Cinema Patents Co. v. Warner Bros. Pictures*, 66 F.2d 744 (2d Cir. 1933); *Cinema Patents Co. v. Duplex Motion Picture Indus.*, 66 F.2d 748 (2d Cir. 1933).

5. Letter from District Attorney Dewey to Cong. Sumners, January 29, 1939; FBI Report, April 24, 1939, 12; Transcript of Record, 789.

6. "Harry M. Warner Asserts Loan from Personal Funds," *Los Angeles Times*, January 31, 1939, 6.

7. Transcript of Record, 789.

8. Quoted at http://pre-code.com/pre-code-lawyer-man-1932.

9. See, e.g., United States Patent Office: Hearings Held Before the Committee on Patents, House of Representatives, 66th Cong., 1st Sess. (July 24, 1919), 282–90 (Manton's testimony given at the invitation of his friend, Cong. John B. Johnston, before the House Committee on Patents); Court of Patent Appeals: Hearings Before the Committee on

Patents, United States Senate, 75th Cong., 1st Sess. (June 22, 1937), 35 (noting Manton's testimony in 1929 regarding a proposed court of patent appeals).

10. "Not a Pretty Story", *Columbia Law Review*, Vol. 30 (1930), 591–93.

11. Christopher Gray, "Kissing Cousins at 100: Only One Shows Its Age," *New York Times*, September 23, 2007 (calling 940 Ocean Avenue an "elegant Georgian-style house"); *Brooklyn Daily Eagle*, May 10, 1936, 63 (advertisement or public auction listing items that were in the "mansion" at 940 Ocean Avenue and "formerly the property of" Lotsch); *Brooklyn Daily Eagle*, July 5, 1933, 17, and July 8, 1935, 15.

12. *Brooklyn Daily Eagle*, March 4, 1929, 24; March 18, 1929, 24; March 4, 1930, 17.

13. Transcript of Record, 144–46, 203–4. Manton was on the panel that heard Tabenhouse's appeal. *Tabenhouse v. Int'l Oxygen Co.*, 74 F.2d 748 (2d Cir. 1935).

14. Transcript of Record, 145–46; *Electric Auto-Lite Co. v. P & D. Mfg. Co.*, 8 F. Supp. 314 (E.D.N.Y. 1934).

15. Transcript of Record, 229.

16. David L. Lewis and Laurence Goldstein, eds., *The Automobile and American Culture* (Ann Arbor: University of Michigan Press, 1983), 101.

17. "Judge Inch at 82 Is Going Strong," *New York Times*, April 3, 1955, 55.

18. Gunther, *Learned Hand*, 302.

19. *Electric Auto-Lite Co. v. P & D. Mfg. Co.*, 8 F. Supp., 322–23.

20. Transcript of Record, 146–48.

21. Transcript of Record, 148–51.

22. Transcript of Record, 151–55, 911 (GX 24).

23. Obituary (Theodore Kenyon), *New York Times*, April 26, 1978, B4; Obituary (Dorothy Kenyon), *New York Times*, February 14, 1972, 32; Elizabeth A. Collins, *Red-Baiting Public Women: Gender, Loyalty and Red Scare Politics* (Dissertation, 2008), 100–154.

24. Transcript of Record, 155–57, 228–29.

25. *Electric Auto-Lite Co. v. P & D. Mfg. Co.*, 78 F.2d 700, 702–3 (2d Cir. 1935).

26. *American-Marietta Co. v. Krigsman*, 275 F.2d 287, 290 n.3 (2d Cir. 1960) (L. Hand, J.); *American Safety Table Co. v. Schreiber*, 269 F.2d 255, 274 n.11 (2d Cir. 1959); *Callmann on Unfair Competition, Trademarks and Monopolies*, Vol. 6, § 22:44 (4th ed.); *McCarthy on Trademarks and Unfair Competition*, Vol. 4, § 25:51 (4th ed.).

27. *Electric Auto-Lite Co. v. P & D. Mfg. Co.*, 109 F.2d 566, 567 (2d Cir. 1940).

28. Transcript of Record, 156–59, 911–12 (GX 26, GX 27A-E); Memorandum from FBI Director J. Edgar Hoover for the Attorney General, January 10, 1939, 1–2 (DOJ Files).

29. Robert H. Jackson Papers, unpublished autobiography, 1944 (Library of Congress), 194–95; Letter from Manton to Jackson, July 10, 1935, in Papers of Robert Houghwout Jackson in the Library of Congress (Box 84). The letter references a discussion between the two men "on Monday last," which was July 8, 1935, when FDR's calendar shows an 11:00 a.m. meeting with Manton. "Franklin D. Roosevelt Day by Day," www.fdrlibrary.marist.edu/daybyday/daylog/july-8th-1935/.

30. "Brief for Taxpayers Stockholders of the Atlantic Bottle Company" (Jackson Papers, Box 84).

31. Letter from Jackson to Manton, July 15, 1935; Memorandum from J. M. Williamson, Chairman, Assistant General Counsel's Committee, to Jackson, July 19, 1935 (both in Jackson Papers, Box 84); Jackson, unpublished autobiography, 196.

32. Letter from Jackson to Manton, August 29, 1935 (Jackson Papers, Box 84); *Reminiscences of Robert H. Jackson*, Columbia University Oral History Project (1952), 400; Jackson, unpublished autobiography, 196–97.

33. *New York Times*, May 5, 1937, 37; *Investment Trusts and Investment Companies: Report of the U.S. Securities and Exchange Commission*, Part Three, February 1941, 2712; FBI Report, March 1, 1939, 2–3.

34. *General Motors Corp. v. Preferred Elec. & Wire Corp.*, 1935 WL 24947 (E.D.N.Y. June 3, 1935).

35. Transcript of Record, 160–61, 905–9 (GX 23).

36. Transcript of Record, 161–62, 921 (GX 37).

37. Transcript of Record, 162–63.

38. Transcript of Record, 163–67.

39. Transcript of Record, 166.

40. Transcript of Record, 727–44, 916 (GX 31).

41. *General Motors Corp. v. Preferred Elec. & Wire Corp.*, 79 F.2d 621 (2d Cir. 1935).

42. *General Motors Corp. v. Preferred Elec. & Wire Corp.*, 109 F.2d 615 (2d Cir. 1940).

43. Transcript of Record, 167–68, 206–7; Memorandum from FBI Director J. Edgar Hoover for the Attorney General, January 10, 1939, 1–3.

44. "Exuberant City Greets Leap Year with Festive Din," *New York Times*, January 1, 1936, 1.

CHAPTER TWELVE

1. Transcript of Record, 196–98; "John L. Lotsch, Patent Attorney, Arrested in Club," *Brooklyn Times Union*, December 6, 1935, 1; Hoover, "Freeing Our Courts," 82–83.

2. Transcript of Record, 170; Robert A. Caro, *The Power Broker: Robert Moses and the Fall of New York* (New York: Alfred A. Knopf, 1974), 116; "Foley in Politics for the Love of It," *New York Times*, January 16, 1925, 2.

3. Lewis Mumford, *Sidewalk Critic: Lewis Mumford's Writings on New York*, Robert Wojtowicz, ed. (New York: Princeton Architectural Press, 1998), 119–20.

4. *Scraps* (in-house publication of the SDNY US Attorney's Office), Vol. VIII, no. IX, July 23, 1932 (available Heinonline).

5. "New Federal Courthouse in N.Y.," *New York State Bar Association Bulletin*, Vol. 4 (1932), 367; *Scraps*, Vol. VIII, no. IX, July 23, 1932.

6. "First Earth Turned on Court House Site," *New York Times*, July 21, 1932, 19; "Heat Wave Lingers, Rising to 87 Here," *New York Times*, July 21, 1932, 1.

7. Transcript of Record, 171; Obituary (Edwin S. Thomas), *New York Times*, January 22, 1952, 29.

8. Heath, *Yankee Reporter*, 284–85; FBI Report, February 14, 1939, 25 (showing receiver fees) and 28–29 (Handelsman interview); "Receivers Will Share $75,000 in Theaters Case," *Hartford Courant*, November 9, 1933, 2; "Receivership Costs Total $169,578.04," *Hartford Courant*, November 22, 1933, 3.

9. *Annual Report of the Attorney General of the United States for the Fiscal Year 1936*, 165, 181.

10. "Petition of Federal Bar for Additional Judges," *New York State Bar Association Bulletin* (April 1934), 232–35.

11. Transcript of Record, 171–72; *Architecture and Building*, Vol. 51, no. 4 (April 1919), 30–31.

12. "Driggs Found Guilty," *New York Times*, January 8, 1904, 1; "If Driggs Stayed in Jail, His Double Was Elsewhere," *Brooklyn Daily Eagle*, January 13, 1904, 2.

13. Transcript of Record, 172–80.

14. "Manton Tells Lawyers Train to Keep Clients Out of Court," *Brooklyn Daily Eagle*, March 3, 1936, 7.

15. "Judge M. T. Manton Speaks Before Jewish Societies," *Suffolk County News*, January 27, 1933, 2.

16. "Greeley Bust Put in College Shrine," *New York Times*, June 18, 1936, 15.

17. Transcript of Record, 181.

18. Transcript of Record, 181; "Bribery Trial Opens," *New York Times*, March 6, 1936, 16; "Bribery Charge Quashed," *New York Times*, March 10, 1936, 7.

19. Transcript of Record, 181–82.

20. Transcript of Record, 183–84.

21. H. L. Mencken, *Minority Report: H .L. Mencken's Notebooks* (New York: Alfred A. Knopf, 1956), 178.

22. Transcript of Record, 184–85; *United States ex rel. Lotsch v. Kelly*, 86 F.2d 613 (2d Cir. 1936).

23. Transcript of Record, 185; *United States ex rel. Lotsch v. Kelly*, 86 F.2d, 614; "Lawyer Is Cleared in Patent Case Again," *New York Times*, December 1, 1936, 5.

24. "Say Banker Got Part of Loan," *Brooklyn Daily Eagle*, August 5, 1937, 1; *Brooklyn Daily Eagle*, January 30, 1939, 2.

25. "Banker Sobs Jury Plea in Own Behalf," *Brooklyn Daily Eagle*, March 1, 1938, 1–2; "Bank Director Guilty," *New York Times*, March 2, 1938, 6.

26. "Lotsch Draws Year in Bribe," *Brooklyn Daily Eagle*, March 11, 1938, 1; "Former Banker Sentenced," *New York Times*, March 12, 1938, 7.

27. Transcript of Record, 186–87; *United States v. Lotsch*, 102 F.2d 35 (2d Cir. 1939).

28. "Manton's Accuser Admits Blackmail," *New York Times*, May 26, 1939, 24.

29. Transcript of Record, 240, 291.

30. "Let Convict Free for '$403,000' Bribe," *New York Times*, September 21, 1931, 5; "Army Guard a Friend of Prisoner He Freed," *New York Times*, September 22, 1931, 2; "4 Indicted for Escape at Governors Island," *New York Times*, July 28, 1932, 18.

31. "Third Man Arrested in $131,000 Theft," *New York Times*, September 23, 1934, 19; Brief for the United States, *United States v. Renkoff*, 84 F.2d 1018 (2d Cir. 1936), 4–12; "3 Yrs. for Renkoff in Ship Mail Theft," *Brooklyn Daily Eagle*, January 29, 1936, 18.

32. "King of Newsboys Held for Bribery," *Brooklyn Daily Eagle*, March 19, 1913, 10; "Becker Victim of Prison Plot, Reich Testifies," *New York Times*, May 20, 1914, 1, 3; "Merchant's Tip Leads Cops to Stolen Bonds," *Brooklyn Daily Eagle*, April 15, 1939, 1; Transcript of Record, 273; Toney Betts, *Across the Board: Behind the Scenes of Racing Life*

(New York: Citadel Press, 1956), 120–22; FBI Report, June 13, 1939, 128 (interview of court bailiff Peter J. Clark).

33. Transcript of Record, 273; FBI Report, June 13, 1939, 6–10 (statement of Morris Renkoff) (DOJ Files).

34. Transcript of Record, 273–74; *United States v. Renkoff*, 84 F.2d 108 (2d Cir. 1936).

35. "Bucket Shop Fraud Convicts Silinsky," *New York Times*, June 25, 1932, 14; FBI Report, June 13, 1939, 11, 18–19 (Renkoff statement), 107–8 (Abe Silinsky statement).

36. FBI Report, June 13, 1939, 11–12 (Renkoff statement), 106–7 (Abe Silinsky statement).

37. This case is discussed in Chapter Sixteen.

38. Transcript of Record, 277–78; FBI Report, June 13, 1939, 19–20 (Renkoff statement).

39. Transcript of Record, 278; *New York City Guide* (New York: Random House, 1939), 22; "Schultz Exiled, Defies the Mayor," *New York Times*, August 3, 1935, 3; "Racketeers Levy $2,000,000 on Cafes," *New York Times*, September 24, 1935, 48.

40. Transcript of Record, 278.

41. Transcript of Record, 278–79, 285, 949 (GX 46).

42. Hoover, "Freeing Our Courts," 43.

43. FBI Report, March 7, 1939, 3–6 (interview of Leonard Weisman) (DOJ Files).

44. FBI Report, March 7, 1939, 6–21; *United States v. Weisman*, 83 F.2d 470 (2d Cir. 1936).

45. FBI Report, March 7, 1939, 42–48 (interview of Rose B. Weisman); FBI Report, April 17, 1939, 7.

46. FBI Report, April 24, 1939, 5–8 (statement of Albert N. Chaperau); FBI Report, May 18, 1939, 2–4 (statement of David Dubrin) (DOJ Files); *New York Daily News*, December 14, 1938, 60; "Chaperau's Way," *Time*, December 19, 1938, 12.

47. FBI Report, April 24, 1939, 13–14; "Jury Listens to All-Star Cast in Smuggling Quiz," *New York Daily News*, December 16, 1938, 3; "Mrs. Lauer Gets 3 Months as Smuggler," *Brooklyn Daily Eagle*, April 11, 1939, 1.

48. FBI Report, April 24, 1939, 8; FBI Report, June 23, 1939, 8–10 (interview of Jack Katzenberg).

Chapter Thirteen

1. Carl Sifakas, *The Mafia Encyclopedia*, 3rd ed. (New York: Checkmark Books, 2005), 298–99; The Judicial Reform Act, Hearings Before the Subcommittee on Improvements in Judicial Machinery of the Committee of the Judiciary, United States Senate, 90th Cong. 2d Sess. (April 24, 1968), 100; Burton B. Turkus, *Murder, Inc.* (Cambridge, MA: Da Capo Press, 2003), 349.

2. Heath, *Yankee Reporter*, 264; Rich Cohen, *Tough Jews* (New York: Simon and Schuster, 1998), 77–79.

3. Thomas E. Dewey, *Twenty Against the Underworld* (Garden City, NY: Doubleday, 1974), 297–98; Cohen, *Tough Jews*, 116; Stolberg, *Fighting Organized Crime*, 165.

4. "Two Convicted as Fur Racket Terrorists After Federal Jury Deliberates 33 Hours," *New York Times*, November 8, 1936, 1; "Lepke and Gurrah Get 2-Year Terms," *New York Times*, November 13, 1936, 2.

5. Dewey, *Twenty Against the Underworld*, 312–13, 453.

6. *Brooklyn Times Union*, December 4, 1936, 4; *Courier-Post* (Camden, NJ), December 5, 1936, 12.

7. *United States v. Buchalter*, 88 F.2d 625 (2d Cir. 1937); Cohen, *Tough Jews*, 182–88, 204–8.

8. Cohen, *Tough Jews*, 178–81, 195; *New York Sun*, July 28, 1939, 1.

9. George Lardner Jr., "Lawrence Walsh, Taking Pains," *Washington Post*, May 11, 1987, A1.

10. Stolberg, *Fighting Organized Crime*, 95; Dewey, *Twenty Against the Underworld*, 274–78.

11. Stolberg, *Fighting Organized Crime*, 4, 237–38.

12. Stolberg, *Fighting Organized Crime*, 238–39; *People v. Hines*, 284 N.Y. 93 (1940).

13. Stolberg, *Fighting Organized Crime*, 94, 229, 237.

14. Stolberg, *Fighting Organized Crime*, 92; Dewey, *Twenty Against the Underworld*, 100–101; *United States v. Miro*, 60 F.2d 58 (2d Cir. 1932).

15. Stolberg, *Fighting Organized Crime*, 231–32.

16. Dewey, *Twenty Against the Underworld*, 453.

17. "Davis Gets A Year, Schoenhaus Freed," *New York Times*, March 23, 1939, 1; Dewey, *Twenty Against the Underworld*, 453.

18. FBI Report, June 21, 1939, 14–16 (interview of Dixie Davis) (DOJ Files).

19. FBI Report, May 12, 1939, 15 (interview of Dixie Davis) (DOJ Files).

20. FBI Report, May 12, 1939, 15 (Davis interview); *Jacobson v. Hahn*, 88 F.2d 433 (2d Cir. 1937).

21. Heath, *Yankee Reporter*, 258; Craig Thompson and Allen Raymond, *Gang Rule in New York: The Story of a Lawless Era* (New York: Dial Press, 1940), 384; Alan A. Block, *East Side, West Side: Organizing Crime in New York, 1930–1950* (New Brunswick, NJ: Transaction Publishers, 1983), 134–35; FBI Report, June 21, 1939, 29 (interview of Burt Heath) (DOJ Files); FBI Report, May 2, 1939, 2–3 (interview of Herbert L. McCann); "1,800 Kegs of Real Beer Seized in Brooklyn Raid," *New York Daily News*, January 20, 1926, 2; "Charge Links Brewery with Beer Pipe Line," *Brooklyn Daily Eagle*, August 13, 1930, 2; "$50,000 Beer Bribe Links Waxie Gordon to Diamond Attack," *Brooklyn Daily Eagle*, October 16, 1930, 1; "Legal Brewers Get Jump on Racketeer," *New York Daily News*, December 11, 1932, B3; *Sales Management*, September 15, 1933, 255.

22. "Racketeer's 'Ride' Turns to Beating," *New York Daily News*, August 6, 1929, 3; "Two Beaten by Gang in Long Beach Streets," *New York Times*, August 7, 1929, 2.

23. "2 Brewing Concerns Seek to Reorganize," *Brooklyn Times-Union*, July 13, 1934, 12; FBI Report, August 8, 1939, 7–9 (interview of Nat Levy) (DOJ Files); Transcript of Record, 741–43, 757.

24. FBI Report, June 21, 1939, 29 (Heath interview); Journal of Second Extraordinary Session and Proceedings in the Senate on the Charges Preferred against George W. Martin, November 9, 1939, 1254–58.

25. Memorandum from FBI Director J. Edgar Hoover for the Attorney General, January 10, 1939, 5 (DOJ Files); FBI Report, March 7, 1939, 36; "Trap Lawyer in Big Bond Plot," *New York Daily News*, June 12, 1925, 2; "Brinkman Sentenced Again as 'Fence,'" *New York Times*, June 27, 1929, 5; "Disbarred Lawyer Jailed for 5 Yrs.," *New York Daily News*, July 30, 1936, 14; "Ex-Lawyer Sentenced," *New York Times*, January 22, 1942, 23.

26. FBI Report, February 17, 1939, 3; "'Boy Wizard' Guilty of Florida Swindles," *New York Times*, July 31, 1926, 13; "Easterday Guilty in $500,000 Fraud," *New York Times*, March 4, 1931, 4; "Greenhaus Gets 3 Years," *New York Times*, April 10, 1936, 48.

27. FBI Report, June 13, 1939, 21–22 (Renkoff statement).

28. FBI Report, August 8, 1939, 6 (DOJ Files); Turkus, *Murder, Inc.*, 358–61; Dennis Eisenberg et al., *Meyer Lansky: Mogul of the Mob* (New York: Paddington Press, 1979), 167; "U.S. Indicts 14 for Harboring Fugitive Lepke," *Brooklyn Citizen*, April 17, 1941, 1.

29. "Racketeer's 'Ride' Turns to Beating"; "Two Beaten by Gang in Long Beach Streets"; FBI Report, August 8, 1939, 6–7 (interview of Rose Levy), 9–10, 12–13 (Nat Levy interview); FBI Report, June 21, 1939, 14 (Davis interview).

30. FBI Lepke Subject File, 60-1501-4266, The Furdress Case, 46, vault.fbi.gov.

31. Sol Gelb, quoted in Dewey, *Twenty Against the Underworld*, 5–6.

32. Frank G. Holmes, "Genius and Industry of Jacob Mellon Built Great Laundry Organization Here," *Brooklyn Daily Eagle*, September 26, 1933, 1; Frank G. Holmes, "Death of Frankie Uale Made Mellon Czar of Brooklyn Laundry Racket," *Brooklyn Daily Eagle*, September 27, 1933, 1.

33. "Levy Contradicts Manton on Stand," *New York Times*, August 3, 1939, 3; "Manton Plans on Racetrack Told in Court," *Rochester Democrat and Chronicle*, August 3, 1939, 3; "Ghost of Grand Jury in 1915 Haunts Levy," *New York Daily News*, August 4, 1939, 5; Levy Record on Appeal, 364–71; FBI Report, August 8, 1939, 8 (Levy interview).

34. *New York Irish American Advocate*, November 2, 1929, 7.

35. Charles Garrett, *The LaGuardia Years: Machine and Reform Politics in New York City* (New Brunswick, NJ: Rutgers University Press, 1961), 71–72.

36. Quoted in Dewey, *Twenty Against the Underworld*, 5–6.

37. "Profiles," *New Yorker*, August 8, 1936, 22; Thompson and Raymond, *Gang Rule*, 166–68; Graham Nown, *Arkansas Godfather: The Story of Owney Madden and How He Hijacked Middle America* (Little Rock: Butler Center for Arkansas Studies, 2013), 179–80.

38. *United States v. Sager*, 49 F.2d 725 (2d Cir. 1931).

39. *United States v. Sperling*, 560 F.2d 1050, 1055–56 (2d Cir. 1977); *United States v. Center Veal & Beef Co.*, 162 F.2d 766, 770 (2d Cir. 1947); *United States v. Smolin*, 182 F.2d 782, 786 (2d Cir. 1950).

40. *United States v. Wong*, 2000 WL 297163, *1–2 (S.D.N.Y. March 22, 2000).

41. Thompson and Raymond, *Gang Rule*, 173; *Vannata v. United States*, 289 F. 424, 427–28 (2d Cir. 1923); Francis Wharton, *Treatise on Criminal Law*, Vol. 2, 11th ed. § 1602 (San Francisco: Bancroft-Whitney, 1912).

42. FBI Report, February 25, 1939, 25 (interview of Assistant US Attorney John J. Dowling) (DOJ Files).

43. Thompson and Raymond, *Gang Rule*, 188; "Threats Laid to Kantor," *New York Times*, April 19, 1934, 10; "Finds 238 Forgeries in 732 Voters' Names," *New York Times*, April 21, 1934, 11; "Tammany Vote Frauds," *New York Times*, May 12, 1934, 14.

44. "Election Worker Gets 2½ Year Term," *New York Times*, May 22, 1934, 19.

45. *United States v. Kantor*, 78 F.2d 710 (2d Cir. 1935).

46. Charles Barnes, "Recent Criminal Cases," *American Institute of Criminal Law & Criminology*, Vol. 26 (1936), 935.

47. "Leaders of Tammany Admit Close Links to Racketeers as State Opens Crime Study," *New York Times*, November 14, 1952, 1, 13; "Lepke's Link to Solomon Aired at Trial," *New York Sun*, February 15, 1940, 2; "New Figure Bobs Up in Trial of Lepke," *New York Times*, February 15, 1940, 8.

48. *New York Times*, November 14, 1952, 13.

49. Heath, *Yankee Reporter*, 227–31; FBI Report, February 7, 1939, 2–3 (interview of Heath) (DOJ Files); FBI Report, February 14, 1939, 29 (interview of Handelsman); "Says Hines Aided Manton 'Because He Needed Him,'" *New York Daily News*, July 8, 1939, 4.

50. FBI Report, February 7, 1939, 3; FBI Report, February 14, 1939, 30; "Manton Debt Paid by Hines, Records Show," *New York Daily News*, July 7, 1939, 4; "Hines Revealed as Having Gone to Manton's Aid," *New York Sun*, July 6, 1939, 1.

51. Memorandum from Director Hoover for the Attorney General, March 9, 1939, in *FBI Confidential Files: The U.S. Supreme Court and Federal Judges Subject Files* (Alexander Chards, ed., 1991); Memorandum from Edward Tamm to Hoover, March 1, 1939 (DOJ Files); FBI Report, April 12, 1939, 8–9 (interview of Harry Blair) (DOJ Files).

52. FBI Report, April 12, 1939, 9 (interview of William Edwards) (DOJ Files).

53. FBI Report, March 27, 1939, 3–4 (interview of Frank Cohen) (DOJ Files); FBI Reports, March 7, 1939, 36–38 and April 12, 1939, 11–12 (DOJ Files); Memorandum from Director Hoover for the Attorney General, March 24, 1939, 1; "Says Insurance Man Racketeer," *Boston Globe*, May 26, 1937, 1, 5; *American Bankruptcy Institute Law Review*, Vol. 13 (1936), 334; Congressional Record (February 27, 1952), A1233–34.

54. FBI Report, June 13, 1939, 58 (statement of Charles Rich) and 60–61 (statement of Sadie Rich (Jack Rich's wife)) (DOJ Files); FBI Report, May 12, 1939, 4 (interview of Edmund Donald Wilson); Heath, *Yankee Reporter*, 258–59.

55. FBI Report, June 13, 1939, 9 (Renkoff statement).

CHAPTER FOURTEEN

1. Newman, ed., *Yale Biographical Dictionary of American Law*, 358; "Manton and Crane Mentioned for Supreme Court," *Brooklyn Daily Times*, November 6, 1924, 12; Letter from Ullman to Taft, December 24, 1924; Letter from Kelsey to Taft (both in Taft Papers).

2. Letter from Taft to Ullman, December 28, 1924; Letter from Taft to Kelsey, January 2, 1925 (both in Taft Papers); Danelski, *Supreme Court Justice Is Appointed*, 195.

3. Danelski, *Supreme Court Justice Is Appointed*, 195.

4. Testimony of Joseph Borkin, The Judicial Reform Act, Hearings Before the Subcommittee on Improvements in Judicial Machinery of the Committee of the Judiciary, United States Senate, 90th Cong. 2nd Sess., April 24, 1968, 101–2; Borkin, *Corrupt Judge*, 44.

5. Frank Freidel, *Franklin D. Roosevelt: The Triumph* (Boston: Little Brown, 1956), 142 and n.19; Letter from Basil O'Connor to Miss LeHand, January 2, 1931, FDR's Papers as Governor of New York State, 1929–1932 (Container 51), FDR Library, Hyde Park (noting Manton's complaint about being dropped from the guest list in 1931).

6. Letter from Manton to FDR, January 26, 1931; Letter from FDR to Manton, February 5, 1931; Letter from Catherine Eva Manton to FDR, February 11, 1931, all in FDR's Papers as Governor of New York State, 1929–1932 (Container 51), FDR Library.

7. *New York Times*, August 5, 1930, 1, 3; July 26, 1931, 5; August 29, 1932, 1, 8.

8. "Tammany Man from Taunton May Be Floor Leader in Next Congress," *New York Herald*, November 25, 1931 (in John J. O'Connor Scrapbook #1 available through Chapman University Digital Collection).

9. Russell M. Posner, "California's Role in the Nomination of Franklin D. Roosevelt," *California Historical Society Quarterly* (June 1960), 121–39.

10. John J. O'Connor, Letter to the Editor, *New York Times*, October 23, 1949, 45 (Book Review section); John J. O'Connor, Letter to the Editor, *New York Times*, May 4, 1958, 28–29 (Book Review section); Letter from John J. O'Connor to James A. Farley, August 31, 1940, reprinted in the Congressional Record (September 4, 1940), 5418–19; John J. O'Connor article reprinted in the Congressional Record (October 15, 1941), A4666; *Suffolk County News*, July 8, 1932, 2 (noting Manton's attendance at the Chicago convention); Posner, "California's Role," 136–37.

11. O'Connor Letter to the Editor, October 23, 1949; O'Connor article, Congressional Record, A4666.

12. Posner, "California's Role," 137 (quoting Basil O'Connor letter to FDR dated July 8, 1932).

13. Letter from FDR to Manton, August 19, 1932, FDR Library, PPF 5252.

14. "Manton Appoints I.R.T. Case Master," 31.

15. Letter from Eva Manton to President Roosevelt, undated, FDR Library, PPF 5252.

16. *Suffolk County News*, March 10, 1933, 2; "Text of the Inaugural Address," *New York Times*, March 5, 1933, 1–2.

17. Letter from Manton to FDR, February 26, 1934, FDR Library, PPF 5252; FBI Report, May 22, 1939, 14 (DOJ Files). The paper was published in the *United States Law Review*. See Martin T. Manton, "Governmental Defaults in the Payment of Contractual Obligations," *United States Law Review*, Vol. 68 (1934), 131–42.

18. "Judge Manton Is Answered," *Tablet*, May 4, 1935, 2; "Roosevelt Urged to Caution Mexico," *New York Times*, July 9, 1935, 6; George Q. Flynn, *American Catholics and the Roosevelt Presidency, 1932–36* (Lexington: University of Kentucky Press, 1968), 181.

19. FDR's Calendar, July 8, 1935 (showing 11:00 a.m. meeting with Manton); Letter from Assistant Secretary of State to FDR, July 12, 1935, FDR Library, PSF, State Dept., 1935 (Box 69) ("fortunately, the whole matter has fallen through. I do not believe you will hear any more on the subject"); Flynn, *American Catholics*, 189.

20. *Brooklyn Life and Activities of Long Island Society*, July 3, 1926, 29.

21. "Lasting NRA Policy Emphasized to Bar," *New York Times*, September 2, 1933, 1, 5 (speech by Manton before American Bar Association convention). The full text of the

speech was reprinted in Martin T. Manton, "A 'New Deal' for Lawyers," *American Bar Association Journal*, Vol. 19 (1933), 596–600.

22. Gunther, *Learned Hand*, 428–31.

23. "Judge Manton Discusses Our Neutral Stand," *New York Times*, December 1, 1935, E9.

24. Danelski, *Supreme Court Justice Is Appointed*, 196.

25. File memo re Attorney General Cummings, November 20, 1935, in FDR Library, PPF 5252; "Hudson Nominated for World Court," *New York Times*, December 21, 1935, 9.

26. *Panama Refining Co. v. Ryan*, 293 U.S. 388 (1935); Shesol, *Supreme Power*, 43–44, 55–56, 80–83, 90–92, 130–31.

27. Peter H. Irons, *The New Deal Lawyers* (Princeton, NJ: Princeton University Press, 1982), 86–88.

28. *Remarkable Hands*, 35 (quoting Arthur Dougan, Learned Hand's law clerk).

29. *United States v. A.L.A. Schechter Poultry Corp.*, 76 F.2d 617 (2d Cir. 1935).

30. Dougan Interview, 7.

31. Shesol, *Supreme Power*, 134–35; *A.L.A. Schechter Poultry Corp. v. United States*, 295 U.S. 495 (1935).

32. Shesol, *Supreme Power*, 421–22; *Carter v. Carter Coal Co.*, 298 U.S. 238 (1936).

33. *N.L.R.B. v. Associated Press*, 85 F.2d 56 (2d Cir. 1936); Irons, *New Deal Lawyers*, 132–33.

34. *Reminiscences of Robert H. Jackson*, 400; "Electric Bond Suit Waits on Findings," *New York Times*, October 10, 1937, 63.

35. *Elec. Bond & Share Co. v. Secs. & Exch. Comm'n*, 92 F.2d 580 (2d Cir. 1937); William Lasser, *Benjamin V. Cohen: Architect of the New Deal* (New Haven, CT: Yale University Press, 2002), 148; "Bond and Share Test Is Refused Again," *New York Times*, November 9, 1937, 33.

36. *Reminiscences of Robert H. Jackson*, 400; *Elec. Bond & Share Co. v. Secs. & Exch. Comm'n*, 303 U.S. 419 (1938).

37. *Jones v. Secs. & Exch. Comm'n*, 79 F.2d 617 (1935), rev'd, 298 U.S. 1 (1936); *American Tel. & Tel. Co. v. United States*, 14 F. Supp. 121 (S.D.N.Y.), aff'd, 299 U.S. 232 (1936); *United States v. Kay*, 89 F.2d 19 (2d Cir. 1937), vacated on other grounds, 303 U.S. 1 (1938).

38. "Roosevelt Praises All-Faiths' Drive," *New York Times*, February 19, 1936, 21.

39. "Social Teachings of Popes Urged," *New York Times*, May 16, 1936, 8.

40. "Manton Finds Bias in Supreme Court," *New York Times*, March 9, 1936, 8. Manton's full address is reprinted in the Congressional Record (March 11, 1936), 3547–48.

41. FDR Library, OF 4235 (March 6, 1936).

42. See generally Shesol, *Supreme Power*, and especially 2, 298–322.

43. "Flexibility Noted in Constitution," *Buffalo News*, March 15, 1937, 8 (Manton's speech); Jackson, unpublished autobiography, 197; Gerhart, *America's Advocate*, 171; Shesol, *Supreme Power*, 380–81.

44. FDR Library, PPF 5252. Whether Manton was referring to the plan to pack the Supreme Court, which by this point had already been scuttled in the Senate, is not

entirely clear; he may have had in mind Roosevelt's efforts to reform the lower federal courts.

45. Shesol, *Supreme Power*, 429–33, 444–48, 453–56.

46. "Bratton and Reed Mentioned Often for Supreme Court," *Wall Street Journal*, July 30, 1937, 3.

47. Papers of Homer S. Cummings at the University of Virginia Library (Box 126, Folder 201).

48. Letter from President Roosevelt to Archbishop Hayes, January 14, 1938, FDR Library, PPF 5252.

49. File memo re Charles J. McDermott, August 7, 1938, in FDR Library, PPF 5252; Letter from M. H. McIntyre to Judge William Harman Black, December 28, 1938, in FDR Library, OF 4235.

50. FBI Report, May 26, 1939, 3–20.

51. *Reminiscences of Robert H. Jackson*, 400–401; Jackson, unpublished autobiography, 195; Gerhart, *America's Advocate*, 171.

52. "Seek U.S. Loan for Huge Home Plan in Queens," *Brooklyn Daily Eagle*, July 16, 1933, 1; "$45,000,000 Asked for L.I. Housing Plan," *Brooklyn Daily Eagle*, July 18, 1933, 1; S. Burton Heath, "$35,000 Manton Investment Netted Judge $552,082 Over a 14-Year Period," *New York World-Telegram*, January 28, 1939.

53. Memorandum for the Secretary of the Treasury from Peter Grimm, January 25, 1936, in the Diaries of Henry Morgenthau Jr., April 27, 1933–July 27, 1945, Vol. 16, 100 (available digitally through the FDR Library).

54. Grimm January 25, 1936 memorandum; Memorandum from Hoover to Murphy, March 24, 1939 (DOJ Files).

55. *Chicago Daily Tribune*, July 7, 1939, 27.

56. Grimm January 25, 1936 memorandum; Memo to Mr. McIntyre, January 11, 1936, in FDR Library, OF 4235.

57. Memorandum for the Secretary of the Treasury from Peter Grimm, January 28, 1936, in Henry Morgenthau Diaries, Vol. 16, 98, attaching a separate Memorandum for the Secretary of the Treasury from Peter Grimm, January 28, 1936, 101.

58. Memorandum from Secretary Morgenthau to Mr. Grimm, January 29, 1936, in Henry Morgenthau Diaries, Vol. 16, 97.

59. Memorandum from Secretary Morgenthau to Mr. Gibbons, January 29, 1936, in Henry Morgenthau Diaries, Vol. 16, 102.

60. Transcript of telephone call between Secretary Morgenthau and Stewart McDonald, January 30, 1936, in Henry Morgenthau Diaries, Vol. 16, 146A–146B.

61. Stephen Birmingham, *Life at the Dakota: New York's Most Unusual Address* (Open Road Media, 1996), 93; "Peter Grimm Joins Wm. A. White & Sons," *New York Times*, January 27, 1939, 77.

62. Transcript of telephone call between Secretary Morgenthau and Stewart McDonald, February 10, 1936, in Henry Morgenthau Diaries, Vol. 17, 186A–186C.

63. Letter from Manton to FDR, March 7, 1938, in FDR Library, PPF 5252; Letter from FDR to Manton, March 9, 1938, in FDR Library, PPF 5252.

Chapter Fifteen

1. *Who's Who In New England,* Vol. 3 (Chicago: A.N. Marquis, 1938), 574; Donald W. Smith, "62,000 Day-Old Chicks Leave Wallingford for Points South While Railway Express Agency Furnishes Male Nursemaids," *Hartford Courant,* March 17, 1935, D1.

2. Andrew Lawler, *Why Did the Chicken Cross the World? The Epic Saga of the Bird That Powers Civilization* (New York: Atria Books, 2016), 201–5.

3. The Republicans' complete slogan was a "chicken in every pot" and "a car in every backyard, to boot." "'Chicken-In-Every-Pot' Slogan Used by Republican Committee," *New York Times,* October 30, 1932, 12.

4. Margaret Elsinor Derry, *Art and Science in Breeding: Creating Better Chickens* (Toronto: University of Toronto Press, 2012), 131; Joe Cebe Sr., *The History of Cebe Farms,* July 31, 2013, http://blog.cebefarms.com/?p=40.

5. *Everybody's Poultry Magazine,* Vol. 38 (April 1933), 164; *Everybody's Poultry Magazine,* Vol. 39 (January 1934), 18; Transcript of Record, 471.

6. Transcript of Record, 472, 475.

7. *Smith v. Snow,* 294 U.S. 1 (1935); *Waxham v. Smith,* 294 U.S. 20 (1935).

8. "Poultry Raisers Lose Incubator Patent Suit," *Hartford Courant,* July 19, 1935, 14.

9. Transcript of Record, 472–73.

10. Transcript of Record, 473–74, 526.

11. Transcript of Record, 474–77, 526.

12. Transcript of Record, 477, 526–27; FBI Report, May 18, 1939, 11–12 (interview of A.B. Hall) (DOJ files).

13. Transcript of Record, 477–79, 527.

14. Transcript of Record, 479–81, 987 (GX 94); "Two Companies Sued," *New York Times,* August 8, 1939, 3.

15. Transcript of Record, 481–85, 527–28, 533, 987 (GX 95), 996 (GX 117E, 117F).

16. FBI Report, May 18, 1939, 14 (Hall interview) and 51 (Davis interview) (DOJ Files); FBI Report, May 25 1939, 11–12 (statements of Fallon and Hall).

17. Transcript of Record, 485–86.

18. "Unnamed 12 Rule Rackets in City, Dewey Jury Finds, Urging a Two-Year Inquiry," *New York Times,* December 27, 1935, 1–2.

19. Transcript of Record, 486–88; FBI Report, May 18, 1939, 8–9 (notes of Arthur E. Paige).

20. Transcript of Record, 494, 508–9, 511–14, 517, 532.

21. Transcript of Record, 494–95.

22. Transcript of Record, 485, 496.

23. *Smith v. Hall,* 83 F.2d 217 (2d Cir. 1936).

24. *The King v. Smith Incubator Co.,* 1937 S.C.R. 238 (1937).

25. *Smith v. Hall,* 301 U.S. 216, 234 (1937).

26. "Supreme Court Patent Decisions, 1936–37 Term," *Journal of the Patent Office Society,* Vol. 19 (1937), 618–19.

27. Transcript of Record, 496, 988 (GX 96); FBI Report, May 18, 1939, 14 (Hall interview) and 51 (Davis interview).

28. Transcript of Record, 496–501, 529.

29. Transcript of Record, 501–3, 530; *American Bar Association Journal*, October 1920, 116.

30. Transcript of Record, 522–25, 534.

31. Transcript of Record, 519; Heath, *Yankee Reporter*, 262–63. Heath claimed that Manton negotiated the price directly with A.B. Hall when Hall came to see him in Bayport about the appeal. But Hall said he negotiated the deal with Fallon and did not meet Manton until January 1939. FBI Report, May 18, 1939, 15 (Hall interview); Transcript of Record, 508, 510, 518–19.

CHAPTER SIXTEEN

1. "Election Crowd in a Merry Mood," *New York Times*, November 4, 1936, 5.

2. "Democratic Who's Who at Huge Rally," *Brooklyn Daily Eagle*, October 31, 1936, 6.

3. Transcript of Record, 241–42; FBI Report, June 13, 1939, 12–13 (Renkoff statement).

4. "Court Weighs Writ in Andrews Deals," *New York Times*, October 3, 1936, 23.

5. Transcript of Record, 268.

6. Transcript of Record, 272.

7. Gary Dean Best, *The Nickel and Dime Decade: American Popular Culture in the 1930s* (Westport, CT: Praeger, 1993), 37.

8. *Schick Dry Shaver, Inc. v. Dictograph Products Co.*, 16 F. Supp. 936 (E.D.N.Y. 1936).

9. "Dry-Shave War," *Time*, November 16, 1936, 104, 106; Obituary (Archie Andrews), *Greenwich Press*, available at www.archieandrews.com.

10. *Hartford Daily-Courant*, January 17, 1936, 24; "Schick Dry Shaver Sues," *Wall Street Journal*, February 20, 1936, 5; Transcript of Record, 240.

11. *Schick Dry Shaver*, 16 F. Supp., 939.

12. Tax Evasion and Avoidance, Hearings Before the Joint Committee on Tax Evasion and Avoidance, 75th Cong., 1st Sess. (June 17, 1937), 3, 54–58; "7 Named as Using Devices to Reduce Big Income Taxes," *New York Times*, June 19, 1937, 1; "Dry-Shave War."

13. "From Drygoods Box to Mansion: The Story of a Horatio Alger Hero," *New York Tribune*, April 11, 1920, 4; "Archie M. Andrews," *Silent Partner* (April 1921), 798; Obituary, *New York Times*, June 18, 1938, 15.

14. *New York Sun*, August 8, 1920; www.archiemandrews.com (website dedicated to collecting information about Andrews); John Dawson Howe, "Elanor [*sic*] and Archie Take Us for a Trip Through the West Indies on Their Palatial Yacht 'Sialia,'" www.archiemandrews.com/sialia/page1.htm.

15. "The Big Bet," www.archiemandrews.com; "Wins $25,000 at Golf," *Evening Star*, March 23, 1926, 29; *American Mercury* (1932), 234.

16. "Buys Frazee Home in Greenwich," *New York Times*, June 22, 1928, 40.

17. "This Man Accumulates Fortune at Rate of Five Tons of Pennies a Day," *St. Louis Star & Times*, July 15, 1929, 2.

18. *T.W. Warner Co. v. Andrews*, 15 F. Supp. 564 (S.D.N.Y. 1936); "Bedell Wins Suit Against Manufacturer," *Ithaca Journal*, July 31, 1936, 3; *Strickland v. Washington Bldg. Corp.*, 287 Ill. App. 240, 4 N.E.2d 973 (1936).

19. "This Man Accumulates Fortune."

20. Transcript of Record, 242–43, 272.

21. Transcript of Record, 313–15; FBI Report, June 13, 1939, 105 (statement of Abe Silinsky).

22. Transcript of Record, 244–46, 315–16.

23. Transcript of Record, 246–49.

24. Transcript of Record, 297–301.

25. Transcript of Record, 249–53.

26. Transcript of Record, 253–54, 316, 319–20.

27. Transcript of Record, 254.

28. Paul Freedman, *Ten Restaurants That Changed America* (New York: Liveright Publishing, 2016), 91, 95, 116–17.

29. Freedman, *Ten Restaurants*, 94; Jan Whitaker, "Men Only," February 6, 2010, Restaurant-ing through History blog, https://restaurant-ingthroughhistory.com/tag/schraffts/.

30. Transcript of Record, 254.

31. Transcript of Record, 255–56.

32. Transcript of Record, 257–58, 303–4.

33. Transcript of Record, 304–8; FBI Report, February 27, 1939, 13 (statement of Abraham Tulin) (DOJ Files); FBI Report, June 13, 1939, 101–3 (interview of Isaac Rollnick).

34. Transcript of Record, 258–65; FBI Report, June 13, 1939, 37–39 (Renkoff statement).

35. FBI Report, June 13, 1939, 17–18 (Renkoff statement), 57 (Rich statement); FBI Report, May 22, 1939 (Fallon interview), 2.

36. Transcript of Record, 343–47, 363.

37. Transcript of Record, 348–63, 384–402; Papers on Appeal, *Spector v. National Cellulose Corp.*, 267 A.D. 870 (1st Dep't 1944), 81–83, 106–14.

38. Transcript of Record, 590–92.

39. Transcript of Record, 330, 368–77.

40. Transcript of Record, 340–41, 402–53, 608–10.

41. Transcript of Record, 457–60; *New York Sun*, March 3, 1939 (Spector's "penchant for long, fat cigars").

42. Transcript of Record, 292–93, 308–9.

43. Transcript of Record, 309–10; FBI Report, February 27, 1939, 15 (Tulin statement).

44. FBI Report, February 27, 1939, 15–16 (Tulin statement).

45. *Schick Dry Shaver, Inc. v. Dictograph Prods. Co.*, 89 F.2d 643 (2d Cir. 1937).

46. *Schick Dry Shaver, Inc. v. Dictograph Prods. Co.*, 89 F.2d, 647–48 (A. Hand, J., dissenting).

47. *Sales Management*, Vol. 40 (1937), 1001.

48. E.g., *Detroit Free Press*, November 6, 1936, 12; *Baltimore Sun*, November 9, 1936, 21.

49. "Packard Shavers Are Cut 33 to 50%," *New York Times*, August 26, 1938, 28.

50. FBI Report, February 27, 1939, 14, 18–19 (Tulin statement and interview).

51. FBI Report, June 13, 1939, 133 (statement of Moses I. Cohen), 137–38 (interview of Siegfried Fischer).

52. FBI Report, February 27, 1939, 28–39 (interview of Joseph Greenberg); FBI Report, May 8, 1939, 7–14 (contemporaneous notes of Tulin); FBI Report, June 2, 1939, 14 (interview of Fallon).

53. FBI Report, May 8, 1939, 10.

54. *Schick Dry Shaver, Inc. v. Motoshaver, Inc.*, 21 F. Supp. 722, 725 (S.D. Cal. 1937); "Dry Shaver Suit," *Tipton Daily Tribune*, September 27, 1939, 3; "Schick Shaver Patents Upheld in Court Cases," *Hartford Courant*, November 22, 1939, 7.

CHAPTER SEVENTEEN

1. "Goodbye to Judge Manton," *New Republic*, June 14, 1939, 142.

2. Gould, *Witness Who Spoke with God*, 186–87.

3. *In re Prudence Co.*, 88 F.2d 420 (2d Cir. 1937); *In re Prudence Co.*, 88 F.2d 628 (2d Cir. 1937).

4. Memorandum for the Attorney General from FBI Director Hoover, February 1, 1939, 1–2.

5. Darby was so described by the FBI agent who interviewed him. FBI Report, March 15, 1939 (interview of Darby) (DOJ Files).

6. FBI Report, March 15, 1939 (Darby interview); Memorandum for the Attorney General from FBI Director Hoover, March 15, 1939, 1–2; *Lektro-Shave Corp. v. General Shaver Corp.*, 92 F.2d 435 (2d Cir. 1937).

7. FBI Report, March 15, 1939; Obituary (S. E. Darby), *New York Times*, December 7, 1947, 76.

8. Obituary, *New York Times*.

9. Transcript of Record, 231.

10. Transcript of Record, 156–57.

11. Transcript of Record, 229.

12. Transcript of Record, 230–32. Kenyon also testified that, other than the result, "there was no similarity" between Manton's final opinion and the one that Kenyon drafted. Transcript of Record, 230. There is no way of verifying the accuracy of Kenyon's recollection, since he said he could not find his copy of his draft.

13. Transcript of Record, 644.

14. Transcript of Record, 228–29.

15. FBI Report, May 18, 1939, 5–7 (notes of Arthur E. Paige) (DOJ Files).

16. FBI Report, February 10, 1939, 16–19 (Neal interview); FBI Report, February 13, 1939, 29–30 (Lorenz interview).

17. FBI Report, March 3, 1939, 7 (statement of Herbert A. Huebner).

18. Heath, *Yankee Reporter*, 247.

19. FBI Report, June 19, 1939, 2–3 (interview of Somers) (DOJ Files); LaGuardia Records, NYC Department of Records & Information Services, Series 2: Box 11.216 Folder 10 (Investigations: Manton, Martin Thomas, Judge 1932); David L. Porter, *Congress and the Waning of the New Deal* (Port Washington, NY: Kennikat Press, 1980), 7.

20. FBI Report, June 19, 1939, 3–4. Somers said he telephoned Manton's chambers two or three times but never succeeded in speaking with him about Handelsman.

21. The Judicial Reform Act, Hearings Before the Subcommittee on Improvements in Judicial Machinery of the Committee on the Judiciary of the United States Senate, 90th Cong., 2nd Sess. (April 24, 1968), 101–2 (testimony of Joseph Borkin).

22. Transcript of Interview of Joseph Borkin, Gunther Papers (Box 4–7).

23. Heath, *Yankee Reporter*, 247; *Remarkable Hands*, 59.

24. Jackson, unpublished autobiography, 194; Letter from Eva Manton to Judge and Mrs. Hand, July 19, 1936, Learned Hand Papers, Box 57.22; author interview of Pierre N. Leval, a former law clerk to Judge Friendly and now himself a Second Circuit judge, August 14, 2020.

25. Letter from Allston Burr to Learned Hand, April 10, 1934; Letter from Learned Hand to Allston Burr, April 11, 1934, both available in Learned Hand's papers.

26. Gunther, *Learned Hand*, 509 and n.21 (citing bench memo dated October 24, 1939).

27. Gunther, *Learned Hand*, 509.

28. Transcript of Record, 793–94.

29. Claytor Interview, 13; Horsky Interview, 6; Transcript of Interview of Sidney H. Willner Interview, Gunther Papers, 30; Transcripts of Interviews of Milton R. Friedman, 13; Orrin G. Judd, 10; John T. Sapienza, 4, all in Smith/Packer Research Materials (Box 14–25, 14–35, 14–50).

30. Preliminary Report of Interview of Lloyd Cutler, 1, Smith/Packer Research Materials (Box 14–13); Boskey Interview, 6–8.

31. Transcript of Interview of Mr. and Mrs. Lawrence Ebb, 30–31, Smith/Packer Research Materials (Box 14–19).

32. Gunther, *Learned Hand*, 509–10; Finkelstein Interview, 18–20.

33. Borkin Interview, 18.

34. *New York Times*, May 5, 1937, 37; *New York Herald Tribune*, May 5, 1937, 35; John T. Flynn, "Other People's Money," *New Republic*, May 19, 1937, 45.

35. Ray Tucker, "National Whirligig," *Brooklyn Daily Eagle*, February 22, 1939, 8.

36. FBI Report, May 24, 1939, 6–43.

37. Francis Russell, "The Four Mysteries of Warren Harding," *American Heritage* (April 1963), 608; "Walker's Income Tax Under Inquiry," *New York Times*, May 24, 1932, 1. Manton was not even the only federal appellate judge Ungerleider did financial favors for without getting repaid. He extended similar beneficence to J. Warren Davis, a judge on the Court of Appeals for the Third Circuit. *Root Refining Co. v. Universal Oil Prods. Co.*, 169 F.2d 514 (3d Cir. 1948).

38. FBI Report, May 24, 1939, 36; Memorandum for the Director from P. E. Foxworth, April 24, 1939, in *FBI Confidential Files*.

39. Memorandum for the Attorney General from FBI Director Hoover, January 10, 1939, 1–3 (DOJ Files).

40. Hoover Memorandum, January 10, 1939, 5.

41. Hoover Memorandum, January 10, 1939, 3, 5.

42. "Bill Considered to Keep Judges Out of Business," *St. Louis Post-Dispatch*, February 16, 1939, 1; Nomination of Lamar Hardy: Hearings Before a Subcommittee of the Committee of the Judiciary, United States Senate, 74th Cong., 2d Sess. (March 9, 1936),

53 (letter from Ungerleider to Hardy); SS *Manhattan* Passenger List, 29 July 1936, in Gjenvick-Gjonvik Archives (gjenvick.com); Memorandum for the Director from P. E. Foxworth, April 24, 1939, in *FBI Confidential Files*.

43. Peter Irons, "Politics and Principle: An Assessment of the Roosevelt Record on Civil Rights and Liberties," *Washington Law Review*, Vol. 59 (1984), 697; Ray Tucker, "National Whirligig," *Brooklyn Daily Eagle*, June 5, 1939, 10.

44. Hoover, "Freeing Our Courts," 84; FBI Report, March 7, 1939, 38 (FBI agent noting that "[n]o investigation had been conducted" based on Brinkman's information about the Lepke/Gurrah payoff).

45. Drew Pearson, "Merry-Go-Round," *Tampa Tribune*, July 23, 1949, 4.

CHAPTER EIGHTEEN

1. Heath, *Yankee Reporter*, 6–8.

2. Heath, *Yankee Reporter*, 3–5, 64–66, 95–96, 131.

3. Heath, *Yankee Reporter*, 182, 191–92; "Fiorello H. LaGuardia Attacks Tammany Hall, 1933," YouTube clip, https://www.youtube.com/watch?v=SaHflVDIzZo.

4. Dewey, *Twenty Against the Underworld*, 20–24; Rupert Hughes, *Attorney for the People: The Story of Thomas E. Dewey* (Boston, Houghton Mifflin, 1944), 16.

5. Dewey, *Twenty Against the Underworld*, 58, 60, 63–65.

6. Dewey, *Twenty Against the Underworld*, 82–93, 98–101, 103–5, 109–10, 117–38.

7. Heath, *Yankee Reporter*, 215–16; Dewey, *Twenty Against the Underworld*, 143–44.

8. Heath, *Yankee Reporter*, 216–18; Dewey, *Twenty Against the Underworld*, 144.

9. Dewey, *Twenty Against the Underworld*, 144.

10. Heath, "Muckraker: Model 1939," in *American Mercury* (April 1939), 423; Heath, *Yankee Reporter*, 214.

11. Heath, *American Mercury*, 424–26; Heath, *Yankee Reporter*, 227–28.

12. Heath, *Yankee Reporter*, 228–29.

13. Heath, *Yankee Reporter*, 229–32.

14. Heath, *Yankee Reporter*, 264–67.

15. Heath, *Yankee Reporter*, 267–68.

16. Affidavit of John J. Cunneen, July 18, 1942, 11, 19, 20, in Record on Appeal, *In re Sullivan's Estate*, 294 N.Y. 947 (1945); Affidavit of Mary C. Sullivan, May 13, 1938, 18, in Papers on Appeal from Order, *In re Sullivan's Estate*, 255 A.D. 1008 (2d Dep't 1938).

17. Heath, *American Mercury*, 425–26.

18. Record on Order of Certiorari, *Spector v. Allen*, 256 A.D. 902 (1st Dep't 1939), 143–213, 277.

19. Transcript of Record, 187–88.

20. Joseph Borkin, *Robert R. Young: The Populist of Wall Street* (1969), 47–51 and n.16; Affidavit of William M. Kilcullen, July 18, 1942, 106–10, in Record on Appeal, *In re Sullivan's Estate*; Levy Record on Appeal, 1153–55; *Allegheny Corp. v. Guaranty Trust Co.*, 23 F. Supp. 203 (S.D.N.Y. 1938).

21. Borkin, *Robert R. Young*, 50–51 and n.16.

22. *New York Times*, August 25, 1938, 13; *New York Times*, November 11, 1938, 25; Heath, *Yankee Reporter*, 269; George Martin, *CCB: The Life and Century of Charles C. Burlingham* (New York: Hill and Wang, 2005), 404.

23. *New York Times*, July 13, 1938, 39.

24. FBI Report, May 27, 1939, 4–5 (interview of Speiser); FBI Report, April 19, 1939, 3–11 (interview of attorney Joseph Nemerov); FBI Report, April 17, 1939, 11–12 (interview of attorney John Kadel); FBI Report, May 24, 1939, 46–49 (interview of Gallo).

25. FBI Report, June 13, 1939, 53–55 (Rich statement); Transcript of Interview of Robert J. Fitzwilliam, 24, Smith/Packer Research Materials (Box 14–22).

26. *Columbia Alumni News*, Vol. 30 (January 27, 1939), 18.

27. *Patchogue Advance*, June 5, 1935, 2; *Suffolk County News*, September 4, 1936, 7; *Suffolk County News*, July 23, 1937, 2; *Suffolk County News*, September 10, 1937, 2; *Suffolk County News*, September 2, 1938, 10.

28. *New York Times*, January 3, 1936, 22; Susannah Broyles, "The Central Park Casino," Museum of the City of New York blog, September 10, 2013, https://blog.mcny.org/2013/09/10/the-central-park-casino/.ers.

29. Roger Birtwell, "334 Off to Berlin to Beat the World," *New York Daily News*, July 16, 1936, 32; Henry McLemore, "S.S. Manhattan Is All Filled Up for Athletes with the Bar Only Hangout for Writers and Such," *Brooklyn Citizen*, July 15, 1936, 6; Letter from Eva Manton to Judge and Mrs. Hand, July 19, 1936 (Learned Hand Papers).

30. Exactly when Manton moved into the Madison is unclear, but he was there by at least April 1938.

31. Miller, *Supreme City*, 172–73; Scudder Middleton, *Dining, Wining and Dancing in New York* (New York: Dodge Publishing, 1938), 118; Museum of the City of New York, Collections (photographs of the Red Bar and Green Bar).

32. *New York Times*, December 25, 1938, 20; *New York Herald Tribune*, December 25, 1938, A8; *New York Sun*, December 31, 1938.

33. Gunther, *Learned Hand*, 505.

34. Heath, *Yankee Reporter*, 264, 268–69; Dewey, *Twenty Against the Underworld*, 454.

35. Heath, *Yankee Reporter*, 263–64, 269–70; Dewey, *Twenty Against the Underworld*, 454.

36. Memorandum from Hoover for the Attorney General, January 10, 1939 (DOJ Files); Memorandum from Keenan for the Attorney General, January 12, 1939, in Frank Murphy Papers at the Bentley Historical Library (Roll 114).

37. Sidney Fine, *Frank Murphy: The Washington Years* (Ann Arbor: University of Michigan Press, 1984), 35; *New York Times*, January 31, 1939, 8; *New York Daily News*, January 31, 1939, 16; *New York Herald Tribune*, February 13, 1939, 5.

38. Heath, *Yankee Reporter*, 263–64; *St. Louis Star & Times*, February 1, 1939, 4.

39. Heath, *Yankee Reporter*, 270–73; Heath, *American Mercury*, 427; "$228,000 of Loan Is Traced to Judge Manton's Properties," *New York World-Telegram*, January 27, 1939.

40. *New York World-Telegram*, January 28, 1939.

41. *New York Times*, January 29, 1939, 1; *Brooklyn Daily Eagle*, January 29, 1939, 1; *St. Louis Post-Dispatch*, January 28, 1939, 1.

42. "Manton Defers Any Comment," *New York World-Telegram*, January 28, 1939.

43. Dewey, *Twenty Against the Underworld*, 455–60. Dewey's letter is reprinted in the *New York Times*, January 30, 1939, 1, 3.

44. Letter from District Attorney Dewey to Cong. Sumners, January 29, 1939.

45. Dewey, *Twenty Against the Underworld*, 455; "Dewey Lays $500,000 Graft to U.S. Judge," *St. Louis Globe-Herald*, January 30, 1939, 1 (photo of Dewey with reporters at Sunday press conference).

46. "Dewey Says Judge Manton Got $400,000 From Litigants; Sends Charges to Congress," *New York Times*, January 30, 1939, 1; "Dewey Letter on Manton," *New York Times*, January 30, 1939, 1, 3.

CHAPTER NINETEEN

1. *Brooklyn Citizen*, June 8, 1917, 3.

2. *New York Times*, January 31, 1939, 1; *New York Sun*, January 31, 1939; *New York Daily News*, January 31, 1939, 1, 16; *Post-Star* (Glen Falls, New York), January 31, 1939, 1.

3. *New York Times*, January 31, 1939, 8; Borkin, *Corrupt Judge*, 28.

4. *New York Times*, January 31, 1939, 8; *New York Times*, February 1, 1939, 1; *Indianapolis Star*, February 14, 1939, 9 (Winchell column).

5. *New York Times*, January 31, 1939, 8; *New York Times*, January 31, 1939, 9.

6. *World-Telegram*, February 2, 1939.

7. Press Conference #522, Executive Offices of the White House, January 31, 1939, 4:05 p.m., 13, available as part of the FDR Library's Digital Collection; *New York Times*, February 1, 1939, 1; *New York Times*, February 1, 1939, 1; FDR's handwritten comments on draft letter, FDR Library, PPF 5252.

8. *New York Times*, February 2, 1939, 1.

9. *New Republic*, February 15, 1939, 46; *New York Sun*, February 8, 1939; "Political Glamor Boys: Dewey and Murphy Compete for Crime-Busting Honors," *Life*, July 31, 1939, 18–19.

10. John T. Noonan Jr., *Bribes: The Intellectual History of a Moral Idea* (New York: Macmillan, 1984), 568.

11. *New York Daily News*, February 3, 1939, 5; *New York Times*, February 3, 1939, 1; *New York Daily News*, February 14, 1939, 6; Memorandum for Edward Tamm from J. Edgar Hoover, February 19, 1939, and Memorandum for the Special Agent in Charge, March 23, 1939, both in *FBI Confidential Files*.

12. *Brooklyn Daily Eagle*, February 11, 1939, 1–2.

13. *New York Times*, February 10, 1939, 14; *Poughkeepsie Eagle-News*, February 18, 1939, 2.

14. Transcript of Record, 85, 140, 630.

15. Transcript of Record, 86–90.

16. Transcript of Record, 90–93.

17. Transcript of Record, 188, 919 (GX 36A-B).

18. Transcript of Record, 189.

19. Transcript of Record, 189–92.

20. *New York Times*, February 5, 1939, 1; *Brooklyn Daily Eagle*, February 5, 1939, 1.

21. *New York Times*, February 5, 1939, 3; *Brooklyn Daily Eagle*, February 15, 1939, 2; SEC Report on Investigation, *In the Matter of McKesson & Robbins, Inc.*, December 1940, 13–20; Memorandum for the Director, February 15, 1939, in *FBI Confidential Files*.

22. Memorandum for the Attorney General from J. Edgar Hoover, March 11, 1939; Memorandum for the Director from E. A. Tamm, March 26, 1939; and Memorandum for the Attorney General from J. Edgar Hoover, April 1, 1939, in *FBI Confidential Files*; *Yankee Reporter*, 287; *New York Daily News*, February 19, 1939, 4C; *Brooklyn Daily Eagle*, February 20, 1939, 1; *Brooklyn Daily Eagle*, March 27, 1939, 2; *New York Times*, April 13, 1939, 1.

23. Memorandum for the File, April 3, 1939, and Memorandum to the Director from E. A. Tamm, April 29, 1939, in *FBI Confidential Files*.

24. *Brooklyn Daily Eagle*, February 16, 1939, 1; *New York Times*, February 25, 1939, 5; Memorandum to the Director from E. A. Tamm, March 13, 1939, in *FBI Confidential Files*.

25. *New York Times*, March 3, 1939, 1; *New York Herald Tribune*, March 3, 1939; *New York Sun*, March 3, 1939.

26. *New York Times*, March 18, 1939, 7; *New York Times*, March 25, 1939, 3; *New York Times*, March 29, 1939, 1; *New York Times*, April 11, 1939, 10; Memorandum to E. A. Tamm from L. R. Pennington, April 15, 1939, in *FBI Confidential Files*.

27. *New York Times*, April 1, 1939, 8; *New York Times*, January 21, 1940, 3.

28. *New York Times*, April 27, 1939, 32; Transcript of Record, 8–27.

29. *New York Daily News*, April 27, 1939, 17.

30. The dramatic reduction in Manton's potential punishment appears to have caught FBI Director Hoover by surprise. See Memorandum for the Director from E. A. Tamm, April 27, 1939, in *FBI Confidential Files* (confirming news report about reduction).

31. Brief for the United States, *United States v. Manton* (2d Cir. 1939), 26.

32. Gould, *Witness Who Spoke with God*, 205.

33. *United States v. Sager*, 49 F.2d 725 (2d Cir. 1931). The Sager decision is discussed in Chapter Thirteen.

34. *Hammerschmidt v. United States*, 265 U.S. 182, 188 (1924).

35. Transcript of Record, 9.

36. *New York Times*, June 4, 1939, 2.

37. Gould, *Witness Who Spoke with God*, 205.

38. See, e.g., *Haas v. Henkel*, 166 F. 621 (S.D.N.Y. 1909); *Crawford v. United States*, 30 App.D.C. 1 (D.C. Ct. App. 1907); *United States v. Greene*, 146 F. 766 (S.D. Ga. 1906).

39. Marcus Eli Ravage, *The Story of Teapot Dome* (New York: Republic Publishing, 1924), 174 (noting that Fall was indicted for conspiracy to defraud the United States by depriving it of his "honest, unbiased, impartial and unprejudiced service" when he received money from Edward L. Doheny who later obtained lucrative government contracts).

40. *New York Daily News*, August 24, 1934, 19.

41. *Miller v. United States*, 24 F.2d 353, 359 (2d Cir. 1928).

42. *United States v. Sager*, 49 F.2d, 726, 728.

43. *Brooklyn Daily Eagle*, June 20, 1939, 6; *New York Times*, June 21, 1939, 2.

44. *United States v. Twentieth Century Bus Operators*, 101 F.2d 700 (2d Cir. 1939); *New York Times*, May 18, 1939, 18.

45. On Manton's arraignment, see *Brooklyn Daily Eagle*, March 23, 1939, 1; *New York Times*, March 23, 1939, 17; *New York Herald Tribune*, March 23, 1939; *Rochester Democrat & Chronicle*, March 23, 1939, 4.

46. *New York Sun*, May 23, 1939; author interview of Peter Denning (Manton grandson), April 10, 2018.

47. Letter from Eva Manton to Marguerite LeHand, and Letter from Eva Manton to FDR, both undated, FDR Library, PPF 5252.

48. Letter from FDR to Eva Manton, April 26, 1939, FDR Library, PPF 5252.

49. Letter from Eva Manton to FDR, undated, FDR Library, PPF 5252.

50. Letter from FDR to Eva Manton, May 9, 1939, FDR Library, PPF 5252.

CHAPTER TWENTY

1. *New York Herald Tribune*, May 20, 1939; *Brooklyn Daily Eagle*, May 22, 1939, 4; Hon Martin T. Manton, Foreword, in Theodore W. Housel and Guy O. Walser, *Defending and Prosecuting Federal Criminal Cases* (Buffalo, NY: Dennis & Co., 1938), iv.

2. Federal Bar Council, *Courthouses of the Second Circuit: Their Architecture, History, and Stories* (New York: Acanthus Press, 2015), 66; "Historic IBM Case Begins," *Rochester Democrat & Chronicle*, May 20, 1975, 10D.

3. *Brooklyn Daily Eagle*, May 22, 1939, 4; *New York Herald Tribune*, May 25, 1939, 14.

4. *New York Daily News*, May 9, 1939, 40.

5. *New York Times*, May 18, 1939, 18; *Philadelphia Inquirer*, August 25, 1928, 1, 4. For the Noonan appeals, see *Quandt Brewing Co. v. United States*, 47 F.2d 199 (2d Cir. 1931); *Stone v. United States*, 47 F.2d 202 (2d Cir. 1931); *Jacobson v. Hahn*, 88 F.2d 433 (2d Cir. 1937); *Ballston-Stillwater Knitting Co. v. NLRB*, 98 F.2d 758 (2d Cir. 1938).

6. *Pittsburgh Sun Telegraph*, May 28, 1939, 13; *New York World-Telegram*, June 5, 1939.

7. Memorandum for the Attorney General from J. Edgar Hoover, March 18, 1939, in *FBI Confidential Files*; Gunther, *Learned Hand*, 505.

8. *New York Sun*, May 20, 1939; *Brooklyn Daily Eagle*, May 26, 1939, 12; Gunther, *Learned Hand*, 510.

9. *New York Sun*, May 22, 1939.

10. *New York Daily News*, May 23, 1939, 2; *New York Sun*, May 22, 1939.

11. *New York Sun*, May 22, 1939; *New York Times*, May 23, 1939, 4.

12. *New York Sun*, May 23, 1939; *New York Daily News*, May 24, 1939, 6; Transcript of Record, 31–32, 874 (GX 1).

13. *Brooklyn Daily Eagle*, May 27, 1939, 2.

14. *New York Times*, May 25, 1939, 1.

15. Transcript of Record, 225–26, 228–29, 235–39, 920–21 (GX 37).

16. Transcript of Record, 118–29, 137–39, 140, 141–43, 897 (GX 21–22).

17. Transcript of Record, 522–23, 534–36.

18. Transcript of Record, 527–28, 533, 988 (GX 96).

19. Transcript of Record, 251–53, 276–77, 941 (GX 39).

20. Transcript of Record, 457, 468–70.

21. Transcript of Record, 256, 323; *New York Herald Tribune*, May 26, 1939, 44.

22. Transcript of Record, 273; *New York Times*, May 26, 1939, 1, 24.

23. Transcript of Record, 273–74; *New York Daily News*, May 26, 1939, 2.

24. Transcript of Record, 274–75; see Chapter Thirteen above.

25. Transcript of Record, 277–79, 284.

26. Transcript of Record, 278–79, 949 (GX 46), 1021 (DX C); *New York Times*, May 26, 1939, 24.

27. *People v. Wells*, 380 Ill. 347, 44 N.E.2d 32 (1942).

28. Transcript of Record, 79, 92–93; *Brooklyn Daily Eagle*, May 29, 1939, 3.

29. *New York Times*, May 28, 1939, 15; *New York Daily News*, May 28, 1939, 53.

30. *New York Times*, May 25, 1939, 1.

31. *New York Daily News*, June 2, 1939, 6; *New York Herald Tribune*, May 24, 1939, 12.

32. *New York Herald Tribune*, May 24, 1939, 12.

33. Susan Dunn, *Roosevelt's Purge: How FDR Fought to Change the Democratic Party* (Cambridge, MA: Belknap Press, 2012), 202–12.

34. George Martin, *CCB*, 404–5; Letter from Charles C. Burlingham to Robert Jackson, June 5, 1939, Jackson Papers (Box 84). It is unclear whether Burlingham's sympathetic note to Manton was actually sent.

35. Letter from Superintendent of Insurance Louis H. Pink to Governor Herbert H. Lehman, May 24, 1939, https://dlc.library.columbia.edu/catalog/ldpd:211811.

36. Transcript of Record, 570–73.

37. *New York Herald Tribune*, June 1, 1939, 12; *New York Herald Tribune*, June 4, 1939, 18.

38. Letter from Judge Hand to Judge Chesnut, June 8, 1939, Learned Hand Papers (Box 149.15).

39. Transcript of Record, 791–94.

40. *New York Herald Tribune*, June 4, 1939, 18.

41. James L. Oakes, "The Centennial Celebration of the Second Circuit Court of Appeals," *St. John's Law Review*, Vol. 65 (1991), 649–50.

42. The Judicial Reform Act, Hearings Before the Subcommittee on Improvements in Judicial Machinery of the Committee of the Judiciary, United States Senate, 90th Cong. 2nd Sess. (June 6, 1968), 264.

43. Transcript of Record, 578–81. It may also be, as the government argued, that Thomas was the only possible choice because the regular Southern District judges, familiar with Lotsch from his many appearances before them as a lawyer, were conflicted. Brief for the United States, *United States v. Manton* (2d Cir. 1939), 22.

44. Transcript of Record, 581, 587–89, 754–56.

45. *Brooklyn Daily Eagle*, June 1, 1939, 6.

46. Transcript of Record, 599.

47. Transcript of Record, 586–87, 598–99, 994 (GX 113).

48. Transcript of Record, 594, 609–17.

49. *Brooklyn Daily Eagle*, May 31, 1939, 1, 10.

50. *Brooklyn Daily Eagle*, June 2, 1939, 6; *New York Sun*, June 1, 1939.

51. *New York World-Telegram*, June 3, 1939; *Washington Post*, June 2, 1939, 7; Transcript of Record, 628–29, 636, 656–58.

52. Transcript of Record, 644, 647–49.

53. Transcript of Record, 643–46.

54. Transcript of Record, 630–31, 641–42.

55. Transcript of Record, 660.

56. *New York Daily News*, June 3, 1939, 14.

57. Transcript of Record, 660, 662, 667; "A Talk With Martin T. Manton."

58. Transcript of Record, 662, 780, 785, 789.

59. Transcript of Record, 675–76.

60. Transcript of Record, 679.

61. *New York Daily News*, June 3, 1939, 14; *New York World-Telegram*, June 3, 1939; "A Talk With Martin T. Manton."

62. Transcript of Record, 668–88.

63. Transcript of Record, 705–8, 713.

64. Transcript of Record, 701–4, 734, 741–42, 748, 750–51, 757.

65. Transcript of Record, 701, 751.

66. Transcript of Record, 744.

67. *New York Daily News*, June 3, 1939, 2.

68. Transcript of Record, 760–65, 773–86, 787–91, 800–801.

69. Transcript of Record, 789.

70. Philip Sopher, "Where the Five-Day Workweek Came From," *Atlantic*, August 21, 2014.

71. *New York Daily News*, May 24, 1939, 6; *Brooklyn Daily Eagle*, June 3, 1939, 3 and June 4, 1939, 1; Obituary (Catherine Denning), *Darien Times*, November 23, 2015; *Brooklyn Daily Eagle*, June 2, 1939, 2; author interview of Jeff Denning, July 29, 2022.

72. *New York Sun*, June 3, 1939; *Brooklyn Daily Eagle*, June 4, 1939, 15.

73. *New York Times*, June 4, 1939, 2; *New York Sun*, June 3, 1939; *New York Daily News*, June 4, 1939, 2.

74. *New York Herald Tribune*, June 4, 1939, 18; *New York Sun*, June 3, 1939.

75. *New York Times*, June 4, 1939, 2.

76. *New York Times*, June 4, 1939, 2.

77. FBI Report, June 2, 1939 (interviews of Fallon on May 22, 23 and 25, 1939) (DOJ Files).

78. *New York Times*, June 4, 1939, 2.

79. *New York Times*, June 4, 1939, 2.

80. *New York Times*, June 4, 1939, 2.

81. Transcript of Record, 860–61.

82. Transcript of Record, 870–71; *New York Daily News*, June 4, 1939, 3; *New York Times*, June 4, 1939, 2.

83. *New York Times*, June 4, 1939, 2.

84. *New York Times*, June 4, 1939, 1, 2.

85. *New York Times*, June 4, 1939, 2; *New York Herald Tribune*, June 4, 1939, 1.

EPILOGUE

1. "Oh the times! Oh the customs!" The phrase originates with a speech by Cicero lamenting the corruption of the Roman Republic.

2. Letter from Charles C. Burlingham to Robert Jackson, June 5, 1939, Jackson Papers (Box 84).

3. "Justice for Sale," *New York Times*, June 5, 1939, 16; Burlingham to Jackson, June 5, 1939.

4. "Justice for Sale"; "Two Judges Are Tried," *New York Herald Tribune*, June 5, 1939; *Washington Post*, June 5, 1939; "The Mighty Fall," *New York Post*, June 5, 1939.

5. "The Shocking Case of Judge Manton," *Tampa Times*, June 5, 1939, 6; "Judge Manton," *Baltimore Sun*, June 5, 1939, 17.

6. "A Corrupt Judge Convicted," *New York Sun*, June 5, 1939; "Judge Manton's Conviction," June 5, 1939, 6; "Manton Guilty," *New York World-Telegram*, June 5, 1939; Heath, *Yankee Reporter*, 243.

7. "Manton for Judge," *Suffolk County News*, August 18, 1916, 1; "Honor Worthily Bestowed," *Suffolk County News*, March 14, 1930, 4; "Public Enemy No. 1," *Suffolk County News*, June 9, 1939, 4.

8. "Manton Given Maximum Term of Two Years," *Baltimore Sun*, June 21, 1939, 3 (AP story).

9. "Manton Sentenced to Two-Year Term After Futile Plea," *New York Times*, June 21, 1939, 1; "Manton Gets the Limit, 2 Years and $10,000 Fine," *New York Herald Tribune*, June 21, 1939, 1.

10. *New York Herald Tribune*, June 21, 1939; *New York Times*, June 21, 1939, 2.

11. "2 Yrs., $10,000 Fine for Manton; Branded Traitor," *New York Daily News*, June 21, 1939, 16; "The Manton Sentence," *New York World-Telegram*, June 21, 1939.

12. *New York Daily News*, June 21, 1939, 3.

13. "Justice Corrupted," *Pittsburgh Press*, June 5, 1939.

14. *New York Times*, June 21, 1939, 1.

15. "Fallon Sentenced to 9-Month Term," *New York Times*, January 26, 1940, 15; "T.J. Fallon Guilty in Perjury Trial," *New York Times*, January 21, 1940, 3; "Brother of Fallon, Manton Aide, Jailed," *New York Times*, January 23, 1940, 23.

16. *In re Levy*, 30 F. Supp. 317, 329–30 (S.D.N.Y. 1939); "Louis S. Levy Dead; Former Lawyer, 74," *New York Times*, August 5, 1952, 19; "Disbarred Lawyer Who Had Millions Died Broke," *New York Daily News*, March 31, 1954, 8; Levy, *Yesterdays*.

17. "Judge Thomas Returns to Home in Columbia," *Hartford Courant*, July 19, 1939, 3.

18. Memorandum for the Chief Justice from Solicitor General Robert Jackson, September 14, 1939, Jackson Papers (Box 84).

19. Ira Brad Matetsky, "Chief Justice Hughes and Martin Manton's Appeal," *Journal of Law*, Vol. 10 (2020), 321–33; Letter from Jackson to Hughes, September 14, 1939, and Letter from Hughes to Jackson, September 18, 1939, Jackson Papers (Box 84); "High Judges to Sit in Manton Appeal," *New York Times*, October 5, 1939, 22. The draft petition for certiorari may be found in Jackson's papers.

20. *Reminiscences of Solomon A. Klein*, Columbia University Oral History Collection (1962), 51–A.52, 56.

21. "Manton Appeal Heard in Court He Once Ruled," *New York Herald Tribune*, October 27, 1939; "3-Hour Argument on Manton Heard," *New York Times*, October 28, 1939, 17; "Manton Denounced in Special Appeal Court," *New York Daily News*, October 28, 1939, 8.

22. Bennett Boskey, "Seymour J. Rubin: Some of the Origins," *American University Journal of International Law and Policy*, Vol. 10 (1995), 1247–48 n.2; Boskey Interview, 5–6. Boskey was Learned Hand's law clerk at the time.

23. *United States v. Manton*, 107 F.2d 834 (2d Cir. 1939); Letter from George Sutherland to Harlan Stone, November 22, 1939, Papers of Harlan F. Stone, Library of Congress, Case File—*U.S. v. Manton*.

24. *Manton v. United States*, 309 U.S. 664 (1940).

25. "Manton in Appeal to Supreme Court," *New York Sun*, January 15, 1940.

26. "Manton's Final Casuistry," *St. Louis Globe-Democrat*, February 28, 1940, 2B.

27. "Manton, Tearful, Lodged in Prison," *New York Times*, March 8, 1940, 10; "Former Jurist Passes Natal Day in Prison," *Shamokin News-Dispatch*, August 6, 1940, 3 (UP story).

28. Letter from Eva Manton to FDR, November 5, 1940; Letters from FDR to Eva Manton and John Mack, November 27, 1940; Letter from Evan Manton to Missy LeHand, with enclosed letter to FDR dated December 1, 1940, all in FDR Library, PPF 5252; "Manton Stricken in Penitentiary," *New York Daily News*, May 11, 1940, 1; "Manton Denied Federal Parole," *New York Daily News*, November 29, 1940, 33.

29. Letter from Evan Manton to FDR, September 22, 1941; Letter from Alfred Smith to FDR, September 26, 1941, both in FDR Library, OF 4235.

30. Letter from Attorney General Francis Biddle to FDR, October 2, 1941, FDR Library, OF 4235.

31. Letters from FDR to Eva Manton and to Gov. Smith, both October 4, 1941, FDR Library, OF 4235.

32. Betty Brown married Clinton Stuart Lowndes Ramsay in 1941. *New York Times*, December 23, 1941, 24.

33. Author interview of Vicki Kirshner (David's daughter), July 29, 2022.

34. Author interview of Jeff Denning (Catherine's son), July 29, 2022; Letter from Manton to his daughter Catherine, June 21, 1942 (provided by Jeff Denning).

35. *Poughkeepsie Eagle-News*, October 18, 1941, 8.

36. *New York World-Telegram*, January 28, 1939 (Holmes Airport property).

37. *Suffolk County News*, November 24, 1939, 1; *New York Sun*, January 3, 1940, 39.

38. After Manton's death, the Tax Court affirmed the penalties. *Manton v. Commissioner*, 7 T.C.M. 937 (1948).

39. Letter from Learned Hand to Allston Burr, April 11, 1934 (Learned Hand Papers); Gunther Summary of Willner Interview, 4.

40. *Eagle-Bulletin* (Fayetteville), May 24, 1946, 4; "Ex-Judge Manton of U.S. Bench Here," *New York Times*, November 18, 1946, 21; "Rites Wednesday for MT Manton Retired U.S. Judge," *Eagle-Bulletin* (Fayetteville), November 22, 1946, 1.

41. Martin, *CCB*, 405; Gerald Gunther Interview of John Lord O'Brian, 11, Smith/Packer Research Materials (Box 14–41).

42. "Address of Judge Manton Accepting a Portrait of the Late Judge Walter C. Noyes," *Scraps*, Vol. VIII, no. VII, June 4, 1932; "Judge Noyes Portrait Accepted at Ceremonies," *Boston Globe*, May 27, 1932, 10.

43. Francis P. Donnelly, S.J., *Chaff and Wheat: A Few Gentle Flailings* (New York: P.J. Kennedy & Sons, 1915), 195–98; "Father Francis Donnelly," *Irish Monthly*, Vol. 50, no. 585 (1922), 109–16.

44. *The Reminiscences of Charles Culp Burlingham*, Columbia University Oral History Project (1961), 42. The interview of Burlingham was conducted in 1949.

Index